2

Thomas Riplinger

An American Vision of the Church

The Church in American Protestant Theology
1937–1967

Peter Lang Frankfurt/M.
Herbert Lang Bern
1976

ISBN 3 261 02093 8

©

Peter Lang GmbH, Frankfurt/M. (BRD)
Herbert Lang & Cie AG, Bern (Schweiz)
1976. Alle Rechte vorbehalten.

Druck: fotokop wilhelm weihert KG, Darmstadt

TABLE OF CONTENTS

v

ABBREVIATIONS AND TERMINOLOGY

The length and similarity of so many of the commission and organization names referred to in this study has made a system of abbreviations necessary in order to provide for easy identification. The following list follows wherever possible the usage of the World Council of Churches.

ATC	American Theological Committee on the Nature of the Church
BDMS	The Chicago Study Group on the "Biblical Doctrine of Man in Society"
CCULW	Commission on the Church's Unity in Life and Worship
CEDG	Chicago Ecumenical Discussion Group on the Ethical Reality and Function of the Church
COCU	Consultation on Church Union
F.&O.	Faith and Order
MSC	Missionary Structures of the Congregation Study
NAWG	North American Working Group of the Missionary Structures of the Congregation Study Project
SCI	Study Commission on Institutionalism
STEUSC	Study of Theological Education in the United States and Canada
TCCCNA	Theological Commission on Christ and the Church, North American Section
TCTTNA	Theological Commission on Tradition and the Traditions, North American Section
TCWNA	Theological Commission on Worship, North American Section
WCC	World Council of Churches

For a description of the character and work of these commissions see chapter two.

For the same reasons it proved necessary to adopt a series of abbreviations to refer to the literature produced by the commissions. These abbreviations will be found alphabetized along with the other authors and titles in the bibliography at the end of the book.

In the literature there is no fully consistent usage with regard to the capitalization of the words "church," "catholic," and "protestant." The present study observes the following usage (no attempt being made to change the usage of quotations):

1. The word "church" is capitalized: (a) when it is used as part of the proper name of a particular denomination or communion, e.g. "the Roman Catholic Church," the "Orthodox Church"; (b) when it is used to refer to the People of God as a whole abstracting from denominational divisions. In all other cases, the word is written in lower case, thus, "the Church is not identical with the churches."

2. The words "catholic" and "protestant" are capitalized: (a) when
   they appear as a part of or as a substitute for the official
   title of a particular denomination or communion, e.g. "the Roman
   Catholic Church; (b) when they are used to designate a particular historical tradition embracing a number of distinct churches
   or denominations, e.g. "the Protestant churches," the "Catholic
   Churches," i.e. those claiming episcopate in apostolic succession,
   namely, Roman Catholics, Old Catholics, Orthodox, and high-church
   Anglicans.

CHAPTER I

THE CHURCH IN MID-CENTURY AMERICAN PROTESTANTISM

Outline

I. The American Experience of the Church and its theological
    Articulation
II. The Church in Twentieth Century American Protestant Thought
    A. Ecclesiological Renaissance between the Social and the
       Secular Gospels
    B. Pathways of American Ecclesiology
      1. An Historical Sketch
      2. The Dimensions of American Ecclesiology
        a. The Chronological Dimensions
        b. The Experiential and Traditional Dimensions
        c. The Methodological Dimensions
        d. The Stylistic Dimensions
III. A Program of Inquiry
    A. The Systematic Approach
    B. The Sampling Approach
    C. The Non-judgmental Approach

I. THE AMERICAN EXPERIENCE OF THE CHURCH AND ITS THEOLOGICAL ARTICULATION

For the theologian interested in the Church the North American experience offers a most interesting and valuable field of investigation. Thanks to the historical conditions of its settlement the North American territories from the beginning proved a fruitful soil for ecclesial experiment.

In contrast to the regions colonized by the Spanish and Portuguese, the American territories conquered by the English served from the start as a haven for religious dissenters fleeing the oppression of state-church. In the virgin lands of the New World, freed of the restraints imposed by established institutions, these groups dreamed of restoring the true Church of Christ. Each came with its own vision of the shape of this Church. Some dreamed of a theocratic commonwealth linking church and state more intimately than the circumstances of the homeland permitted; others dreamed of a confessionally neutral state granting all believers the freedom to practice religion according to their conscience. Some dreamed of a purified episcopacy, others of a radical congregationalism, still others of a rigorous presbyterianism. Some were high church, others low church; some were Calvinist, others Arminian, still others Lutherans or Moravians, and others yet were adherents of one or another of the many streams of Anabaptism.

Besides the dissenters who came to America with a specific ecclesiastical program, there were vast numbers of traditional Christians who came to America out of motives which had little or nothing to do with religion and who took the organization of the established churches of their homelands unreflectively as something given, a quasi-natural element of human life, something as self-evident as the village elders, the landlords and the royal agents. For them, the transfer to the New World brought a sudden sharpening of their ecclesiastical consciousness. No stately cathedrals or tidy parish church awaited them in the new land; no bishop or pastor preceded them; no paternalistic establishment provided for the upkeep of churches and schools or paid the salaries of clergymen and teachers; no public laws imposed doctrinal uniformity or religious observance. If they wanted churches and schools, they had to build them and maintain them themselves; if they wanted pastors and teachers, they had to fetch them from abroad or create among them-

selves the presuppositions for their selection, training and ordination; if they wanted discipline, they had to obtain the establishment of an appropriate ecclesiastical organization from the authorities of the church they left behind in Europe or create such an
organization by their own efforts.

In the churches established by the immigrants in the new land,
old-world ideals often clashed with new-world realities. The conditions of the frontier, of representative federalist government, of
capitalistic business organization, of racial and ethnic discrimination profoundly modified the shape of the churches transplanted to,
or initiated on the American soil--and this even as their members
proclaimed unchanged loyalty to their hallowed traditions. The
dynamics of this situation created a unique ecclesiastical climate
marked by alternating seasons of denominational rivalry and ecumenical rapprochment.

Not surprisingly, the singular experience of the reality of the
Church in America has profoundly affected the character of American
theological reflection on the Church. This holds true particularly
for what might be termed the American Protestant mainstream represented by the churches which have been most active in the American
ecumenical movement during this century, among these are the Protestant Episcopal Church, the two major Presbyterian Churches, the
Methodist Churches, the Congregational, Reformed, and Evangelical
Churches (which since 1957 have been merged into the United Church
of Christ), the Disciples of Christ, the Northern Baptists, and the
more liberal Lutheran churches. Among the theologians within this
mainstream it is possible to discern certain common patterns of
thought which, even in the face of sharply diverging opinions on
particular issues, justifies speaking of a typically American
Protestant theology of the Church.

This book is a study of this theology; its objectives, however,
are sharply limited. It makes no pretensions to survey the whole
historical sweep of American Protestant ecclesiology; rather it
concentrates on one particular phase of its development, namely
the ecclesiological renaissance of the mid-twentieth century, from the
mid-thirties to the mid-sixties. Within this period it concentrates
on the work of a succession of ecumenically constituted commissions
and discussion groups, which by reason of their composition, methodology and achievements may be taken as typical of the basic trends

of the period. To illustrate these trends it concentrates on two issues which, by reason of their special involvement in the American church experience, served as focal-points for the work of the Commissions. These issues are (1) the relationship between the theoretical idea of the Church and its empirical reality and (2) the relationship between the divine Spirit and the human forms. The investigation ends with an attempt to evaluate the American ecclesiastical achievement as a model for a more universal ecumenical ecclesiology.

These objectives determine the structure of the investigation. This first chapter is devoted to introducing the problematic and explaining the method. The next chapter goes on to survey the work of the individual commissions, giving their history, summarizing of their reports, and calling attention to special features of their methodology and conclusions. Chapter three deals with the efforts of the American theologians to define the church in such a way as to do justice to both ideal and empirical aspects. This leads to the efforts of the Americans to formulate the relationships between the divine and the human, particularly the institutional factors in the Church's life; this is the material of chapter four. Chapter five concludes the study with its evaluation of the American methods as models for a future ecumenical ecclesiology.

II. THE CHURCH IN TWENTIETH CENTURY AMERICAN PROTESTANT THOUGHT

A. Ecclesiological Renaissance between the Social and the Secular
   Gospels

Looking back from our present vantage-point at the threshold of
the seventies, it is hard, even for those of us who lived through the
epoch, to realize that only ten years ago enthusiasm for the Church
in America was at a peak. Thanks to the ecumenical movement then at
the height of its popularity, even the layman could feel the attrac-
tion to things ecclesiastical. No one questioned the importance of
the Church for Christianity; on the contrary, the restoration of
unity and the inner renewal of the Church seemed the principal task
of the day. How different the mood was at the end of the sixties!
Far from presupposing the churchly character of Christianity, laymen
and theologians alike were earnestly debating whether there be any
place at all for the "Church" in authentic Christianity. Official
ecumenism has brought the denominations closer together, but it has
failed to achieve real union. Instead new divisions have occurred
within congregations, clergy, denominational hierarchy and assemblies, as the process of reform and renewal polarized churchmen and
church members into conservatives and progressives, reactionaries
and radicals. So deep are the new cleavages and so unrelated to
traditional denominational divisions, that many wonder whether the
classical ecumenical goal of denominational union still is relevant
to the present state of the Church, to say nothing about the question
of its feasibility. Indeed, many frustrated former ecumenists are
openly wondering whether the union of churches wouldn't lead simply
to greater bureaucracy and leaderlessness, whether ecumenism itself
isn't an excuse for escaping Christian responsibility for the world,
or a subtle attempt to disguise the irrelevance of existing ecclesiastical institutions and to restore the power of crumbling ecclesiastical establishments. Advocates of a Secular Gospel elaborate a
notion of Christian community which bears little apparent relationship to traditional ecclesiology; indeed is an avowed repudiation of
many a notion of classical ecumenism.

The crisis into which the Church has fallen in America marks the
end of an era in American theology. That era began roughly forty
years ago, when--after decades of neglect or open hostility--American
Protestant thinking enthusiastically rediscovered the Church as a
central theme of theological reflection. During the first third of

the century, the Church had been the ugly step-daughter of American theology. As an empirical reality to be reckoned with, no one of course could ignore her. The treatment she received, however was seldom favorable. All too frequently one hears the complaint that the Church in the concrete form of her comfortable Sunday congregation and glutted denominational bureaucracies constitutes the chief obstacle to the realization of true Christianity.[1] The mood of the time is clearly expressed in the form taken by ecumenism. The primary consideration was practical, not theological: denominational division wastes efforts and divides forces which might better be turned to bringing about God's Kingdom. Not introverted self-reflection, but out-going engagement in the burning social issues of the time is the true vocation of the Church.

The very foundations for a theological consideration of the Church were in doubt. Quite generally the conviction prevailed that any elaborate theology of the Church would be futile, since critical exegesis had shown that all the different denominational traditions and polities could with equal right claim New Testament warrant.[2] Far from contributing to the practical unification of Christianity, ecclesiological considerations could lead only to a hardening of denominational divisions and a bolstering of institutional rigidity. Moreover, the very fact that, according to the results of liberal Bible criticism, the Church is not the product of a divine institution but rather an all too human response of the first disciples to the disappointment of their millenial expectations, meant that the study of the Church is more a matter for religious sociology than for theology.

The consequences of such a conception for ecumenism are obvious. If there are no theological norms by which to judge the various ecclesiological traditions, then there is no point to further discussion of denominational differences; it is enough to recognize the relativity of all confessional claims and thus to acknowledge all the denominations as equal partners in a common enterprise, which is the pursuit of the Kingdom of God in the life and structures of modern society. Far from seeking to level the divergent traditions and polities, one can regard them as legitimate and valuable expressions of Christian freedom; only the rivalry and mutual intolerance with which they have traditionally been associated must be abolished. Not one monolithic church with a single

confession and polity, but a federation of different churches, coop-
erating toward common goals, was the aim of much early twentieth-
century ecumenism.[3]

With the thirties began a new era in American theology. A
decade of controversy had sapped the strength of the liberal theology. Despite numerous defeats in public controversy, fundamentalism
showed little sign of losing its hold on a major segment of American
Christianity. Moreover, on the left had arisen a new and more dangerous opponent, humanism. Sharing the same anthropology and ethics,
the humanists challenged Christian liberals to show cause, why one
should continue to hang on to the baggage of an obviously irrelevant
and often positively misleading traditional vocabulary. Unwilling
to accept such a radical consequence of their own position, the
liberal theologians were hard pressed to discover an intellectually
respectable answer. At the same time the Social Gospel movement had
lost most of its dynamism. The mass of church-goers remained indif-
ferent to its appeal, and the appeal itself had become hopelessly
blunted in the platitudes of uninspired Sunday preachers. What
remained of a once vibrant manifesto was often nothing more than a
naive optimism with a utopian socialist tinge.

So badly weakened in its inner fabric, the liberal theology was
one of the first victims of the 1929 economic and social collapse.
The optimistic hopes of the liberals were brutally shattered by the
sudden revelation of the rottenness at the core of America's "Christian" society. Not only the economy but rather the whole nation,
its culture and its institutions, its religion, were forced to appear
in bankruptcy court.[4] Their liberal hopes shattered, Christian
theologians were hard pressed to answer the challenge of the new
totalitarian faiths, Fascism and Communism. In this moment of truth,
the formerly optimistic theologians saw themselves suddenly face to
face with the shocking reality of evil, of deep-seated, irradicable
sinfulness in human hearts and in human institutions.[5] The social-
gospeler's dream of successfully combating evil by enlightenment
burst like a child's toy balloon: stripped of its "Christian" mask,
the World suddenly appeared in all its naked evil and opposition to
the Gospel. In contrast, the Church, for all her faults, stood out
as the faithful remnant, as the rock of salvation.[6] Set over against
the World, the principal task of the Church is simply "to be the
Church": "Let the Church be the Church!"--the motto of the 1937 Life

and Work Conference at Oxford, became the battlecry of a new theological movement in America.[7]

Thus it happened that--bracketed between the old Social Gospel
of the Twenties and the new Secular Gospel of the sixties--an unpar-
alleled flowering of ecclesiology developed in American soil. Clear
across the spectrum of American theology, from the most conservative
to the most liberal, the new concern for the Church is everywhere in
evidence.

B. Pathways of American Ecclesiology

1. An Historical Sketch

The rediscovery of the Church, like most movements in the American religious scene, was a genuinely ecumenical phenomenon. No
particular tradition held a monopoly on the experience; no confession or theological line succeeded in putting its exclusive stamp on
the thinking this experience gave rise to. The ecclesiology that
emerged was a rainbow-like spectrum in several dimensions. Diverse
confessional backgrounds, diverse attitudes toward traditional institutions and form, diverse styles, approaches and organizational principles render impossible any attempt to reduce the pulsating life of
the movement to a static conceptual system or to select out a few
typical examples. The ecclesiology of mid-twentieth century American
Protestantism, in contrast to so many theological movements, was no
academic symposium of systematically developed lectures by a few experts, but rather a kind of mass, free-form, enthusiastic, brain-
storming session, in which ideas were tossed up, handed around,
pulled, squeezed, split, combined, dissolved, and resynthesized with
mind-boggling dexterity. Certain figures stand out of course by
reason of the solidity or provocativeness of their contributions to
the discussion, but it would be a serious error to attempt to reduce
the movement to a few star performers. Ecclesiological reflection
in America in mid-century was like a multi-ring circus, whose versa-
tile performers, both major and minor, come and go--now here, now
there--now in one role and costume, now in another--one act following the other with dazzling rapidity. In such cases the whole is
always much more than the mere sum of its individual components, for
the whole is the process, the stream held in motion and carried along
by the vibrant movements of the individual actors and teams.

Strictly speaking, of course, it is impossible to grasp such a
process as a whole. To be a part of it, meant to be carried along

in the process itself, moving from one position to another in the
flow of the conversation. To reflect back on its literary sediment
--aside from the physical impossibility of reading and digesting the
hundreds of books, articles, working papers, discussion summaries,
meeting minutes, etc. that represent the literary production of these
thirty years--is to see only the tracks and traces left behind along
the way, not to grasp the movement itself. And yet, to pursue this
trail is worth the effort, not only because it helps us better to
grasp our present situation by recalling the pathways that brought
us here, but also because the reflection on past experience can suggest clues and techniques for the further course that stands before
us. Fortunately, much of this ecclesiological activity took place
in the context of theological study groups and commissions sponsored
by the World Council of Churches and other ecumenical organizations
and thus found periodic synthesis in the reports issued by these
studies. Such reports offer us a kind of trail journal of the long
march by which American Protestant ecclesiology came into its own.

The first of these study groups was the Commission on the
Church's Unity in Life and Worship, organized in 1935 in preparation
for the second World Conference on Faith and Order, Edinburgh, 1937.[8]
From the Edinburgh Conference came the initiative for the organization of the American Theological Committee on the Nature of the
Church, which met regularly until 1947.[9] Meanwhile a Life and Work
project had called into being the Chicago Ecumenical Study Group on
"the Ethical Reality and Function of the Church," which was active
between 1940 and 1944.[10] After the War, the Interseminary Movement,
an organization for promoting ecumenical education and cooperation
among theological students, organized a symposium of leading American theologians to prepare materials on the Church and its responsi-
bilities for its 1947 national convention.[11] Another Chicago Group
came into being in 1950 in conjunction with the WCC Study Department
project "the Nature of Man in Society"; it reported in 1954.[12] In
the same year, the American Association of Theological Schools began
an intensive study of theological education in America, in which
they undertook a reexamination of the nature of the Church and its
ministry in order to define more clearly the objectives and criteria
of theological education. The results of this survey appeared in
1956-7.[13] Meanwhile the Faith and Order Department of the WCC had
initiated a series of theological studies on the themes "Christ and

the Church," "Tradition and the Traditions," "Worship," and "Institutionalism." The first three of these were organized with separate American subsections which issued separate reports; the fourth was American based, though it included some European members. The American sections, which got organized in 1953-5, had their first opportunity to report in Sept. 1957, at the North American Regional Conference on Faith and Order, held at Oberlin, Ohio. This Conference was a week of intensive study for the official delegates and observers from over forty American and Canadian denominations; the consensus it achieved was published among the papers of the Conference in The Nature of the Unity We Seek in 1957.[14] The four Faith and Order Commissions continued working for another six years, reporting in 1963 to the Montreal Conference.[15] Meanwhile, in response to Eugene Carson Blake's historic San Francisco sermon "A Proposal toward the Reunion of Christ's Church"[16] the foundations were being laid for the formation of the Consultation on Church Union (COCU), to explore the theological and organizational issues raised by the proposed merger of four, later ten of America's major denominations in a church "truly catholic, truly reformed, and truly evangelical." With the documents passed by the COCU assemblies of 1966-7, the theological work of the study commissions achieved completion.[17] The same period saw the completion of the work of The North American Working Group, founded in 1962 as part of the WCC Study Department project "The Missionary Structures of the Congregation." The crisis this group went through in 1963-4, and the Secular Gospel ecclesiology which its final report gave expression to,[18] dramatically bring to a close the ecclesiocentric epoch in American Protestant Theology.

For the history of ecclesiology in America during these middle decades, the above mentioned commissions and study groups are of pivotal importance. Not only do their reports and working papers constitute some of the most significant publications of the epoch, but also their conversations and reports were a powerful stimulus to and influence on the many books and articles on the Church which appeared during this period. The number of such publications is enormous; a complete bibliography would have to list several thousand titles. To write a detailed literary history[19] is out of the question, the literature is too vast, the lines of development too subtly interwoven. And yet, it is only when one has come to appre-

ciate something of the exuberant richness and endless variety contained in this material that one can appreciate the achievement of
these commissions studies. In order therefore to provide at least
a superficial impression of the various tendencies and moods, leit-
motifs and styles that characterize this material it would seem necessary to attempt a typological sketch of some of the dimensions of
the movement. Typologies of course are tricky instruments: difficult to formulate, and even more difficult to apply. Moreover, they
are often misinterpreted as a device for judging and evaluating the
objects, ideas and persons thus classified. Be that as it may,
typological classification has proven itself to be an indispensible
tool dealing with an otherwise unmanageable complex of detail. The
categories used here are my own; they are based on impressions gathered in a broad, though by no means exhaustive reading in the literature of the epoch; many a suggestion of the authors I have read
have contributed to the formation of these categories, but the bor-
ders between reception and personal insight have become too fuzzy to
attempt any sort of detailed documentation. By the same token I
have refrained from classifying individual theologians in one or the
other category: given the fluidity of the discussion and the limitations of the published sources such an endeavor runs too heavy a
risk of error and distortion.

2. The Dimensions of American Ecclesiology
a. The Chronological Dimensions

The thirty years covered by this study span four theological
generations. Among the men who exercised a formative influence on
the first decade of America's ecclesiological renaissance were individuals like William Adams Brown (1865-1943) whose theological roots
reach back before the ecclesiastical alienation of the Social Gospel.
For the most part, however, the men who dominated the first decade
were of the generation that received their theological education or
began their teaching careers in the midst of the ecclesiological
depression prior to the mid-thirties. For these men, the Church was
a genuine object of discovery. Though their theology has been
called "neo-orthodox," the term is really applicable only in a very
loose sense; "realist" is the expression most would have preferred.
The newly acquired respect for traditional themes like sin, grace,
redemption, christology, the Church, mean for the most part a course-
correction, not a complete about-face.[20] In the course of the

fifties, a new generation of men whose theological careers had been
delayed or interrupted by the War increasingly came into prominence.
Meanwhile, like a great river settling down after a wild passage
through a rocky defile, the American theological renaissance was
coming to move in more or less well defined currents and channels.

By the end of the fifties, three main currents with a number of
side currents were clearly distinguishable. Out of the neo-super-
naturalist element in the realistic theology had emerged on the one
hand a more determinate "neo-orthodox" or, as William Hordern termed
it, "neo-reformation" theology,[21] strongly influenced by British and
Continental models. This current, with its concentration on the
doctrinal exposition of God's primacy--though by no means neglecting
the ethical consequences of Christian discipleship--tended to see
theology as a past-oriented reflection on the Word of God embodied
once-and-for-all in the Bible but echoed and interpreted in the historical confessions and theologies of the Church. Though by no means
identical with this neo-reformation theology, many of the attitudes
of the biblical theology movement of the fifties are similar in character.[22] Meanwhile the more typically American tendency to emphasize
the ethical demands of the Gospel led to a re-affirmation of the
liberal tradition enriched and corrected by the recovery of traditional biblical and dogmatic themes.[23] Inclined to focus on the continuing action of God in history through human agencies, this "neo-
liberal" current tended to see Scripture and the historical witnesses
of the Church's past faith as a succession of models of the Church's
on-going effort to recognize and articulate the future-directed thrust
of God's continuing revelation and action in human history--hence
this group's openness to secular philosophical, ethnological, psychological and sociological influences. Paul Tillich's "method of correlation" offered one of the more influential models for neo-liber-
alism.[24] In the meantime, thanks to the efforts of men like Carl
Henry[25] and Edward J. Carnell,[26] an academically respectable version
of fundamentalism had appeared on the scene. These "neo-evangeli-
cals," as they have sometimes been called, re-affirmed philosophical
apologetics, literal inspiration, and traditional supernaturalism,
at the same time they chided their fundamentalist colleagues for
their neglect of ecclesiology and social ethics. Unfortunately, sus-
picions of liberalism and ecclesiasticism in the World Council of
Churches led the conservatives to remain pretty much aloof from the

ecumenical discussion of the Church,[27] with the result that with
the exception of the internal discussions among Southern Baptists[29]
the ecclesiological renaissance in this current remained rudimentary.

Besides these three main currents, a number of minor currents
must also be noted. Already at the end of the thirties, a "neo-
naturalist" movement had begun to separate out of "Christian realism."[30] Tending to shade off into religious psychology and philosophy of religion, this line of thinking did little to develop an
ecclesiology, though its discussion of the social psychology of
religious experience offers some interesting beginnings. Other currents are represented by confessional dogmatics. Conservative in
outlook, though by no means fundamentalist in the classic sense,
anglo-catholic, and orthodox lutheran, calvinist and mennonite theologies tended to keep to themselves or to prefer the dialog with
their European partners. Only towards the end of our epoch did they
begin to emerge from their isolation and to enter into dialog with
mainstream American Protestantism.

The later fifties/early sixties saw the rise of the fourth gen-
eration--younger men, trained often in the neo-reformation spirit,
who, under the influence of the demythologizing debate,[31] the sociological and pastoral critique of American Protestantism,[32] and the
civil-rights/anti-war movement,[33] embarked on a radical critique of
traditional church-centered theology.[34] Meanwhile, the expanding
ecumenical dialog, the movement of seminary theology to the university or the university accreditation of existing seminaries, the
experience of inner-city and other forms of experimental ministry,
etc. were leading to a breakup of the constellations which marked
American theology at the threshold of the sixties.

b. The Experiential and Traditional Dimensions

The ecclesiology which took form in the middle decades was
quite clearly an ecumenical ecclesiology--elaborated in dialog with
the historical traditions of the Church and with the present sociological reality of the churches; but perhaps more important it
flourished in dialog with living theologians of different traditions and backgrounds, men who found themselves teaching together
in united seminaries and university theological departments or working together in study and administrative groups organized by the WCC
and other ecumenical organizations.[35] Leaving aside the theological

exchange with contemporary British, Continental European, and Asian
theology, all of which had a deep influence on the development of
American ecclesiology, it is important to grasp how diverse the
backgrounds of ecclesial experience and ecclesiological tradition
that its protagonists brought with them.

The American ecclesiastical scene is a crazy-quilt medley of
diverse European traditions interacting with American life and culture.[36] Each immigrant group brought its own confessions, ecclesiastical organization, linguistic and cultural particularities:
Laudian and puritan Anglicanism; Iro-Scottish Presbyterianism; sep-
aratist Puritanism; Quakerism; English and Welsh non-episcopal Meth-
odism; German, Danish, Norwegian, Icelandic, Swedish, Finnish Lutheranism in a variety of orthodox and pietist forms; Swiss, Dutch, German, Huguenot, Hungarian, Waldensian, and Moravian Reformed traditions, Prussian and other German Unionistic traditions; Mennonites,
Dunkers, Schwenckfelder, Brüdergemeinde, etc. In America each was
fated to undergo such an evolution in the process of cultural assimilation, that not infrequently subsequent waves of immigration from
the same European church preferred setting up a new ecclesiastical
organization to integrating into the no longer recognizable church
founded by their predecessors. Meanwhile the American soil had
given birth to its own confessional movements: Congregationalist,
Baptist, Universalist--Unitarian, episcopal Methodist, Disciples of
Christ, Holiness, Adventist, and Pentecostal Churches--to say nothing of the semi-christian Mormons, Jehovah's Witnesses, Christian
Scientists, etc. The response to changing American conditions
brought further modification and division of both imported and
native traditions--e.g. the weakness or absence of official organization on the frontier meant that the initiative for the foundation
and organization of local congregations usually came from covenent-
ing laymen cr free-lance ministers--often in only the loosest relationship to their proper ecclesiastical superiors, gave rise to a
spirit of democratic, voluntary congregationalism even in churches
whose official ecclesiology was hierarchical; reinforcing this tendency was the popular political philosophy of democracy and republicanism. In similar fashion, the conditions of the frontier, rein-
forced by revivalism, tended to give an individualistic, low-church
character to the popular worship service of even the liturgical
churches. Issues of language, slavery and race were responsible for

further divisions arose out of the controversies over high- versus
low-church forms and modernist versus fundamentalist theology.

Meanwhile other factors were at work blurring and confusing the
contours of these divisions. The day to day confrontation with religious pluralism and the upward mobility of many a religious group
led to a blurring of the distinction between "church" and "sect" so
evident in European society. Isolated by language, culture, and
theology, many a European "church" had to do a sect-like apprenticeship before it achieved full integration. On the other hand, many
a former sect achieved temporary political, economic or social as-
cendency in a particular community or region, thus endowing it with
church-like qualities of organization and mentality. The result is
the rise of the distinctively American "denomination,"[37] a sociological hybrid of church- and sect-types, characterized by among other
things, professional leadership, bureaucratic administration, and
acceptance of religious and cultural pluralism.[38] Thus it comes
about that denominations with an officially congregational ecclesiology evolved elaborate ecclesiastical administrations modeled on
American business enterprises, with the result that the exercise of
authority in such churches may be less democratic than in others
whose official ecclesiology is hierarchical, but whose actual polity
is republican.[39] The example of capitalistic business organization
goes further; far more important than its influence on church organization has been its contribution to the popular ecclesiological
theory of "denominationalism,"[40] which sees positive value in the
existence of competing ecclesiastical organizations offering a selection of religious wares broad enough to satisfy every individual
taste and pocketbook. As a counterweight to denominational division,
the last hundred years have seen the growth of innumerable cooperative institutions based on private or official initiatives: e.g.
comity agreements, joint mission and publication boards, community
churches, union seminaries, interdenominational theological departments in the university, church federations and councils.[41] For
those active in these ventures, the ecclesial experience was necessarily different from that of men whose whole life centered around
the institutions of their own denomination. In similar fashion the
cross-confessional mergers which gave rise to the United Church of
Canada (1925)[42] and the United Church of Christ, USA (1957)[43] have
conditioned the ecclesiological thinking of those affected by them.

Finally the cultural experience of the American way-of-life with its strong current of this-worldly millenialism, which sees the United States as the harbinger or reality of God's Kingdom and attributes messianic destiny to the American people and their institutions[44] --Sidney Mead speaks of "the nation with the soul of a church"[45]-- has made its impact on the course of ecclesiological discussion.

Thus the individual theologian in America is the heir not of one, but of several ecclesiological traditions, and more often than not the product of several quite distinct ecclesial experiences, e.g. the different congregations of his youth, interdenominational youth organizations in which he participated, the seminary and grad- uate school communities, European and Third World churches during his years of post-graduate study or missionary activity, the Ameri- can urban or rural congregations in which he served his pastoral apprenticeship, the theological and worship community of the semi- aries and universities where he has taught, the denominational and interdenomational boards, commissions, councils in which he has held office. Needless to say, his reaction to any one of these experiences and ecclesiological traditions can range from radical critique and rejection, through reformistic correction and reinter- pretation, to conservative re-affirmation and defense. For some, the reflection on their own historical tradition is a way of tran- scending its particularism; for others this transcendence is only to be achieved by a re-integration of their particular tradition into the universal tradition of the Church as a whole. For some, the particular tradition provides the glasses through which they read and interpret Scripture and church history; for others, Scrip- ture and church history are the keys to interpreting and correcting their particular traditions. Some see in the documents of the past the norm by which the social and institutional integration of the contemporary Church must be measured; others see the experiences of the contemporary Church as the clue to distinguishing between the permanent and the transitory, the essential and the conditional, in the biblical and traditional witnesses of the past. Small wonder then that so much of ecclesiological thinking in America is con- cerned with methodological issues.

c. The Methodological Dimensions

Just as the recovery of interest in the Church transcended the boundaries of confessional and denominational affiliation, so too it

found adherents clear across the spectrum of the theological disciplines. Thanks to this fact, as well as the (for European and
Roman-Catholic observers) astonishing readiness of American theologians to ignore the borderlines of academic specialization, one
finds ecclesiological reflections in publications of the widest conceivable variety. Biblical theologians publish systematic trea-
tises, dogmatic theologians write books on the New Testament doctrine of the Church. Specialists in church history, Christian
ethics, practical theology, ecumenics, etc. have attempted to illuminate the whole or particular parts of ecclesiology from the point
of view of their particular discipline.

Under these circumstances, it is no surprise that the thought-
structures of American reflection on the Church are enormously varied. Depending on the author's interests and orientation, he may
develop his ecclesiology from the point of view of God's revelation
in history, or from the point of view of the incarnation and the
christology-pneumatology implicit therein, or from the point of view
of a trinitarian economy of salvation. Another approach would locate ecclesiology in the context of the believer's response to the
divine action in history. A "modernist" variant of this approach is
to see ecclesiology as the social-psychology of religious experience
and the sociology of its institutionalization. Theologians of a
speculative cast of mind tend to focus their ecclesiology on concepts like the Body of Christ or the People of God; those of a more
practical cast, on the concrete structures of the Church's life and
ministry. Passionate advocates of ecumenism have attempted to sub-
sume all of ecclesiology under the Pauline and Johannine notions of
unity. Since all of these motifs admit of infinite combination,
inversion, conversion, and modification, the variety of starting-
points and logical organization is endless.

Not surprisingly, for any attempt to do ecumenical ecclesiology
in such a tumult of diverse voices and programs, methodological and
procedural issues loom larger in America than in the more orderly
context of European ecclesiology. In a discussion where everyone
appeals to the Bible and church history to lend weight to his particular views, one cannot help raising the question of the relativity
of all historical hermeneutics. In a denominational topsy-turvy in
which sect-type organizations proclaim fidelity to church-type ecclesiologies, and church-type hierarchies hold fast to sect-type

theories of church order, the relation between empirical reality and
ecclesiastical ideology becomes acutely problematical. In a land
whose civil and ecclesiastical institutions are neither the heritage
of hoary antiquity nor the effect of autocratic dictation but rather
the voluntary product of recent, free-will covenents in a spirit of
messianic destiny, it is evident that the tension between the past-
oriented restoration principle and the future-oriented evolutionary
principle should more quickly and sharply become self-conscious than
in lands whose ecclesiastical and political development has been
more continuous and hierarchical.

d. The Stylistic Dimension

Modern hermeneutics has called attention to the importance of
literary genres for the interpretation of intellectual positions.
Thanks to the special circumstances of American theological research, teaching and publication, the productions of American theologians especially in the area of ecclesiology show marked difference in style and format by comparison to European university theology. The open frontiers between the individual theological disciplines is only one aspect of American distinctiveness. More important still are the limitations imposed by commercial publishing.
Whereas a substantial portion of European, particularly German, production consists in heavily documented, densely argued, dissertations, monographs resulting from seminars, or systematic expositions
emerging from university lectures; American theological publications
are more often popular, easy to read, lightly documented presentations of the conclusions of scientific research without revealing
much of the critical process by which these conclusions have been
reached. At best, as in the case of doctoral dissertations, this
process has been recorded in the microfilm version of the original
manuscript before it had been worked over for commercial publication. For the most part, however, what takes place largely in the
mental dialog of the author with his sources and in form-free conversation with colleagues, professors, and students, remains unre-
corded and thus inaccessible to subsequent control. Add to this the
pragmatic principle that an idea is to be judged more by its consequences than by its origins, and the general American tendency to
subordinate theory to action and experience, and you are faced with
a theological genre which is very difficult to get hold of historically and to evaluate critically. American theology is like a mam-

moth iceberg only a small portion of which is visible above the surface.

This is all the more so the case for American ecclesiology. Even the theologians actively engaged in ecclesiological discussion often failed to appreciate the depth and breadth of American contributions. The literature was too extensive, too diffuse, too "popular" to make an impression. Thus many of the theologians I approached at the beginning of my researches in the late sixties were sceptical about the very existence of an American Protestant ecclesiology comparable to the European discussions of the Church. Such a reaction is symptomatic. With the exception of Daniel Day Williams' God's Grace and Man's Hope (1949) and Harvey Cox' The Secular City (1965)--neither one an ecclesiological tract in the traditional sense--none of the many serious contributions from the pen of American authors made theological history. One of the reasons for this is the fact that so many of these contributions took the form not of book-length systematic expositions but rather of relatively short articles in the hundreds of symposia published in conjunction with commission studies, or edited privately either to commemorate some occasion or simply to serve the needs of popular adult education in theology or in ecumenism. The number of such articles, especially when one includes those published in the numerous scholarly and popular journals, was so enormous, the quality so variable, the volumes so inaccessible, that no single theologian could possibly keep abreast of all of them. Largely he was dependent on chance selection based on copies sent for review, recommended by colleagues or reviews, purchased by the librarian, etc. All of this of course seriously complicates the historian's task of trying to trace lines of development and influence.

III. A PROGRAM OF INQUIRY

The foregoing remarks were intended to explain why no attempt has been made here to write a comprehensive history of the American ecclesiology within the thirty years between the Social and the Secular Gospels. Instead the work of the above-mentioned theological commissions and study groups has been selected as the prism through which the spectrum of ecclesiological ideas in America is refracted. Before proceeding to the analysis of the commission's work, however, some additional remarks are in order concerning the aims and methods of this inquiry.

A. The Systematic Approach

For all its interest in the history of American ecclesiology, the present work is essentially an exercise in systematic theology. Its aim is to take a historical phenomenon—the development of an ecumenical Protestant ecclesiology in mid-century America—and analyze it with a view to discovering the lessons it contains for us in our efforts to develop a future ecumenical ecclesiology still more universal in scope. Ultimately it is the Church itself or better the process of discovering and defining the Church, rather than the particular ecclesiological ideas, which is the focus of this study.

This of course does not mean that the canons of historical inquiry can be dispensed with. Only insofar as the analysis succeeds in faithfully presenting the position of the commissions and the trends which underlie the individual positions, will it be possible to use the commission work as an object-lesson in ecumenical methodology. Nevertheless it should be clear that such an investigation can pass over many of the questions of detail which a strict historical account would be forced to deal with. This holds especially for questions about the origins of particular ideas. Again it is not the particular ecclesiologies which are the center of focus; these are almost as many and as varied as the authors who have contributed to the discussion. The reader interested in such details can himself readily consult the reports of the commissions and the writings of their members. The references in the subsequent chapters might serve as an initial guide for such investigation.

B. The Sampling Approach

The use of a systematic rather than a pure historical approach implies a concentration on the typical rather than on the singular,

on the central rather than the peripheral, on the ripened fruit of
theological inquiry rather than on the first buds. To avoid mis-
conceptions, several points should be noted at the outset.

First as to the value of the commission documents. Committee
reports, as everyone knows, tend to reflect a kind of least common
denominator. Compromise replaces creativity; the dull and commonplace takes precedent over the provocative and revolutionary. Often
committee reports are compiled in haste, one or two persons drawing
up a basic draft which is then hurriedly worked over to eliminate
the points of most serious objection by the other committee members.
In the end perhaps no one is really satisfied with the finished document, but in lieu of a practicable alternative the committee proceeds to give the document its stamp of approval. How much individual reservation and discord is often hidden behind the vague but
full-sounding phrases asserting universal consensus.

It would be rash to assert that the American ecumenical commissions entirely avoided such pitfalls in their work. Nevertheless
this danger should not be exaggerated. Most of the committees had
several years of intensive conversations behind them before they
came to preparing their reports. With the exception of the two
Chicago-based groups, who by reason of local proximity could meet
more frequently, most of the committees used the method of annual
or semi-annual intensive sessions of three days to a week, with the
papers to be discussed being circulated in written form beforehand
to encourage study and comment. The use of such intensive methods
thus gives credibility to the assurances by committee members that
in the course of their work together they experienced a real change
of attitude and opinion as they came to appreciate each others
points of view and to seek in common for new solutions for old
points of controversy.

Naturally such documents cannot be taken simply on face value.
Necessarily they represent only brief summaries of much more extensive investigations, they offer little room for extensive documentation or highly nuanced explanations. Fortunately it is possible
often to get behind the text by having recourse to the published
writings of the individual commission members or to the unpublished
papers, discussion summaries and preliminary reports and drafts preserved in the archives of the World Council of Churches. Nevertheless, in making use of such material one must never forget the opin-

ions ventured by individual committee members are not necessarily
shared by all or even most of their colleagues. Furthermore, such
material is generally considerably older than the final report of
the commission, and it is difficult to assess the degree to which
opinions expressed might have been modified in the light of subsequent study and discussion. Again however it is important to recall that this is a work of systematic rather than strict historical
theology; it is concerned with typical ideas rather than singular
ones. Whether or not the whole or even the majority of the commission members would subscribe to peculiar interpretation of the consensus which emerges from the use of such background material is of
secondary interest, provided of course that the interpretation so
developed accurately represents the way at least some of the members
understood their consensus. Obviously every effort will be made
here to focus on the common consensus rather than on particular
interpretations, but given the nature of the resources at hand, no
guarantee can be offered for a strict adherence to the majority interpretation.

A second point with respect to the sampling approach must be
made concerning the way in which the documents are used. The reports of the committees are not all of a piece. They differ not
only in size and presentation but also in intent. Each has its own
center of focus determined by the circumstances and terms of the
committee's formation. As a result, the individual reports are not
immediately comparable one with another. Topics central to one
group's perspective may be peripheral to another's. Some make an
effort to call attention to outstanding differences of opinion,
others concentrate on points of consensus. Some offer detailed documentation and extensive explanations; others confine themselves to
lapidary thesis-style affirmations. This means that their statements are not of equal value as illustrations of characteristic
positions. To prevent misunderstandings, the next chapter therefore
offers a brief survey of the work of the individual commissions with
an outline summary of their final reports. In the subsequent chapters the material quoted or referred to will then be selected on the
basis of its potentiality for illustrating typical patterns of thinking. The aim here, however, is not to put together a synthetic
ecclesiology as though the statements of the individual commissions
were the intended complements of each other. The order of topics

treated in these chapters does indeed spring in large measure from
the historical and logical progression of the American discussions,
but in the last analysis it remains an arbitrary creation of the
present author, useful to the extent that it calls attention to the
intrinsic connection of many of the topics dealt with by the American theologians. The use of the sampling technique also means no
claim is made to call attention to all the statements of all the
commissions relevant to a particular topic. Cross-references and
historical notes have been inserted where they seem appropriate, but
in general the policy has been to concentrate only on the more
fruitful texts. This of course means that certain committees more
frequently have the floor than others, but as long as intentions of
this study are kept in mind there should be no objection to such
selectivity.

C. A Non-Judgmental Approach

Among the most characteristic features of the American ecumenical ecclesiology is an acute awareness of the provisional character
of the consensuses achieved and the union schemes projected. From
the first commission statements of the thirties through to the union
plan drawn up at the end of the sixties there echoes like a refrain
the protestation that the agreements and divergences, the proposals
for merger and coordination, represent nothing more than steps in a
more comprehensive process by which the divided churches come to
discover and to practice more fully their God-given unity in the one
Church of Christ. As we shall see in the subsequent chapters, much
more is involved here than simply ecumenical courtesy and frankness.
Behind the frequent professions of the provisional character of the
ecclesiological proposals of the Americans lay a fundamental theological conviction, namely that a truly ecumenical theological consensus on the nature of the Church requires a simultaneous practical
experience of the Church's unity--in short, that there is a reciprocal relationship between ecclesiological theory and practice: as
long as the churches in practice remain divided and incomplete, even
the most visionary ecumenical ecclesiology necessarily will remain
broken and unfinished.

Given this self-understanding on the part of the American commissions, it would be neither fair nor particularly useful to attempt to pass judgment on their individual ideas and expressions.
Desirable and useful as a Roman Catholic response to the individual

commission reports would have been immediately following their publication, the time for such direct confrontation has long passed.
With the exception of the COCU Plan of Union (1970), the documents
here under study belong to an epoch in ecumenical relations which
has largely been superceded by the important developments in the
theological disciplines and ecumenical dialog of the past decade.
Particularly in the area of biblical studies, a Catholic-Protestant
consensus on the New Testament teaching on the Church has taken
increasingly concrete form in the course of the last six/seven years.
Likewise in church history a consensus over wide areas of interpretation is increasingly evident. Agreement of this type was not yet
available to the Americans in the epoch here under consideration,
and it would be unfair to criticize their individual statements
about New Testament teaching or points of Church history on the
basis of a vantage-point which was not yet possible to them. Furthermore such a critique would now be of little use, for the ecumenical dialog has also gone on for the Americans, and they have in the
meantime contributed to and today they participate in these new consensuses.

Instead, therefore, of attempting to pass judgment on the individual theses and positions put forward by the Americans, the more
fruitful approach would seem to lie in trying to analyze the inner
dynamic of the American discussion, concentrating more on the methodological principles and options involved than on the particular
solutions offered to particular questions. In this way we come
closest to the fundamental intention of the Americans; precisely
because of their acute awareness of the gradual and provisional nature of every attempt to construct an ecumenical ecclesiology, they
tended to see their own contribution more along the lines of sharpening the focus of the questioning and refining the methods of ap-
proaching the solution of questions than in offering the final solutions themselves. Obviously they too attempted to formulate answers
to the fundamental ecclesiological questions, but it is not to be
overlooked that in the American reports methodological expositions
and excursuses play a much larger role than in the documents prepared
by their sister commissions in Europe and Asia. One might almost go
so far as to say that the concrete answers offered by the American
documents are more valuable as illustrations of the methodological
principles involved than as specific solutions to specific problems.

They are, of course, specific solutions as well, but in view of
their self-consciously provisional character and their rootedness
in the concrete theoretical and practical experience of the individual commissions, they are not capable of standing fully by themselves. They are meant to elicit a creative, critical response, not
simply passive assent.

Given the distance separating our present vantage-point in ecumenical ecclesiology from that of the Americans eight to thirty-
eight years ago, the likelihood is that we are more apt to profit
from the methodological reflections and experiments of the Americans
than from their individual ideas and expressions. Their method,
which in the last chapter of this study is summarized under the
three heads, catholicity, functionalism, and provisionalism, represents a real challenge to contemporary Roman Catholic ecclesiology,
as is evidenced by the inner-Roman-Catholic controversies over the
ecclesiological projects of Hans Küng and other critics of traditional Catholic positions. Perhaps a look at the American experience with the methods adopted by Küng and his allies could provide
the necessary distance for a cooler, more reasoned evaluation of
these methods than the present controversies admit.

In the chapters which follow, therefore, little attempt will be
made to evaluate the individual substantial answers of the American
commissions. At best a certain degree of immanent critique will be
exercised in the chapters dealing with the definition of the Church
(Chapter 3) and with the divine-human interaction in the Church
(Chapter 4), the purpose being to show the extent to which the Americans remained faithful to their own methodological principles and
to evaluate the fruitfulness of these principles in relation to the
questions proposed. Only in the last chapter, devoted as it is to
the methodology of the American ecclesiology, will an attempt be
made to confront the American Protestant positions with Roman Catholic ones. The aim here will be to show the extent to which these
methods can be adopted by Roman Catholic theologians and what consequences such an adoption would entail. Necessarily, a critique of
this sort will remain quite generic and abstract. The ultimate critique of any method can only be had in the concrete practice; hence
the evaluation offered in the last chapter is not so much a sitting
in judgment as an invitation to experiment. Only when Roman Catholic theologians enter seriously into dialog making use of these

principles can their ultimate worth be judged. At the end of this study, therefore, stands not a judgment but a vision, the vision of the One Church of Christ from an American perspective. Whether or not this vision will be verified lies hidden in the future course of ecumenical dialog and practice.

CHAPTER II

STAGES ON THE ROAD TO AN AMERICAN ECCLESIOLOGY

Outline

I. The Commission on the Church's Unity in Life and Worship
      (CCULW)
II. The American Theological Committee on the Church (ATC)
III. The Chicago Ecumenical Discussion Group (CEDG)
IV. The Interseminary Series
V. The Biblical Doctrine of Man in Society Study (BDMS)
VI. The Survey of Theological Education in the United States
      and Canada (STEUSC)
VII. The Oberlin Conference
VIII. The post-Lund Faith and Order Studies (TCCCNA, TCTTNA,
      TCWNA, & SCI)
IX. The Consultation on Church Unity (COCU)
X. The North American Study Group on "Missionary Structures
      of the Congregation" (NAWG)

As a first step in a sampling survey of American ecclesiology
it is necessary to take a closer look at the materials which will
serve as our sources. Because of their diverse character, the documents of the various commissions can hardly be compared directly with
one another. Each has its own specific orientation and thematic.
None is as such an attempt to offer a complete systematic ecclesiology. Each is conditioned not only by the constellation of theologians who drafted or contributed to it but also by the circumstances of its composition. The groups themselves range from ad hoc
study groups to highly organized commissions with subcommittees and
consultants. Each had its specific objectives, sometimes more,
sometimes less inclusive. For some, the Church itself was directly
the object of focus; for others the Church is rather the background
against which a more particular object--social ethics, training for
ministry, etc.--was studied. The orientations are at one time more
theoretical, at another more practical, now more historical, again
more empirical. As a prelude to the use of these documents therefore it is necessary to put them in their theological and social
context, to describe briefly their origin and content, and to lay
the groundwork for their comparison. That is the work of this
chapter.

I. Commission on the Church's Unity in Life and Worship (CCULW)

The first major expression of the new ecclesiological interest in America came in the preparations for the Edinburgh Faith and Order Conference in 1937. At the insistence of the American delegation, the Faith and Order Central Committee set up a special study commission to deal with the topic of paramount interest to American ecumenists: namely the practical pursuit of unity among Christians and their churches.[1] Chairman of the commission was the respected Church historian Dean Willard Sperry of the Harvard Divinity School. The membership of the commission was overwhelmingly American; moreover the five Europeans appointed to it were prevented by practical considerations from taking part in the meetings, though they were able to offer written suggestions and criticisms. The American[2] membership was as follows:

Dean Willard Sperry (Congr.)
Prof. Angus Dun (Episc.)
Dr. Robert W. Ashworth (Bapt.)
Prof. William Adams Brown (Presby.)
Principal Richard Davidson (Canadian Presby.)
Pres. Austen K. de Blois (Bapt.)
Dr. H. Paul Douglass (Congr.)
Prof. Frank Gavin (Episc.)
Prof. Hornell Hart (Quaker)
Pres. Charles M. Jacobs (Luth.)
Dean A. C. Knudson (Meth.)
Prof. H. F. Rall (Meth.)
Pres. George W. Richards (Ev. & Ref.)
Prof. Gaius J. Slosser (Presby.)
Prof. A. R. Wentz (Luth.)

One of the first acts of the commission was to change the original title established by the Central Committee, "The Empirical Approach to Unity," to "The Church's Unity in Life and Worship." This new title, they insisted, better reflected the American concern, which was not to set up an "empirical" approach as an alternative to the "theological" approach so insisted on by the European members of Faith and Order, but rather to stress the need for dealing theologically with the day-to-day practical realities of Christian unity and division. What the Americans understood by "empirical approach" was a specifically theological method which attempted to take account of three factors governing the ecumenical situation: (1) all theological but especially all ecclesiological theories are socio-culturally conditioned; (2) at least under existing conditions of church division it is impossible to achieve agreement on a normative pattern

for the Church in the traditions of the past; and (3) the experience of unity is a necessary presupposition to the institutionalization of unity.[3]

Though it did not fit directly into their program, the Commission also assumed responsibility for the topic, the communion of
saints, which at Orthodox insistence had been incorporated into the
Edinburgh agenda.

To facilitate its work, the commission divided into five sub-
committees, each assigned to investigate a specific problem area.
The sub-committees, aided by various consultors[4] proceeded through a
series of meetings to develop a position paper on their assigned
topics. These papers were drafted by the theologian whose name they
bear, but in view of the critical discussions of the drafts in the
various sections, the reports can be regarded as being more than
simply the personal opinion of their drafters.[5] After a year of
work, the sub-committees submitted their reports to the commission
meeting in plenary session in March, 1936. Here further revision
was undertaken. Practical reasons, in addition to the inherent
value of the individual texts themselves, led the commission to decide to issue all five reports individually instead of attempting to
combine them into one single document as other commissions had done;
in fact, however, the fifth report, Next Steps on the Road to a
United Church, comes very close to offering such a synthesis. After
a final revision, the five documents of the commission were published
in the spring of 1937.

A. The Meanings of Unity
Already at the first meeting of the commission the need for a semantic clarification of terms became evident. They observed that
"unity is a symbol which awakens feeling, but it is not a self-evident idea. As applied to the churches it suggests different things
to different individuals and groups."[6] A committee composed of
Angus Dun, Robert Ashworth, William Adams Brown, Richard Davidson,
H. Paul Douglass, Hornell Hart, A. C. Knudson, A. S. Monahan, Otto
Piper, George W. Richards, Gaius J. Slosser, and Willard Sperry,[7]
undertook to clarify this issue by cataloging the various meanings
which constantly reappeared in discussion and attempting to develop
a neutral terminology to suggest them. The results of this work are
expressed in the document drafted by Angus Dun.

The first part of this document expounds the semantic classification developed by the committee. It distinguishes in the first
place between "Christian unity" (pp. 1-4), the sort of fellowship
experienced by individual members coming out of their separated
churches, and "church unity" (pp. 5ff), marked by the involvement in
one form or other of ecclesiastical institutions. Among the latter
it distinguishes four types:
1. unity of similarity (pp. 5-17),
2. unity of mutual recognition (pp. 17-26),
3. unity of cooperative action (pp. 26-35),
4. corporate unity (pp. 35-44).
In discussing the last of these, the committee made a noteworthy
attempt to disengage the term corporate unity from controversies
over specific organizational forms by showing that the essence of
the corporate unity of particular churches lies less in their polity
--which may in fact be rudimentary or non-existent--as in the sense
of belonging and identity giving rise to integrated behavioral patterns expressed in common agencies and symbols.

The second part attempts to classify some of the underlying differences in theological viewpoint which so often obscure ecumenical
discussion:
1. the corporate versus the individualistic view of the Church
   (pp. 46-7),
2. church-type versus sect-type thinking (p. 47),
3. institutional versus spiritual approaches (p. 48),
4. transcendent versus immanent conceptions of God's relationship to
   creation (pp. 49-50).

B. The Communion of the Saints

Richard Davidson, A. C. Knudson, A. R. Wentz, Frederick C. Grant,
and Gaius Jackson Slosser composed the committee which undertook the
investigation of the topic: the communion of the saints, which at
Orthodox insistence had been incorporated into the Edinburgh program.
As background for their work, they obtained contributions from twelve
scholars of various denominational traditions.[8] Slosser drafted the
report, which takes the form of a systematic comparison of historical
and contemporary views. Nevertheless, despite this general imitation
of a more typically European approach to a topic; the more typically
American concern for levels of practical agreement underlying confessional differences finds expression in the treatment of the role of
the notion in the Church's worship.

The document consists of four parts:
I. Definition of the terms and of the credal article: a historical
   study of the scriptural roots and historical development of the
   expression with particular attention to its role as an article of
   the Creed (pp. 1-12),
II. Some present-day interpretations: A comparative study of contemporary dogmatic teaching and theological opinion (pp. 13-4),
III. The communion of saints in hymnody and liturgy (pp. 42-3),
IV. Disagreements, agreements, tensions (pp. 44-5): a drawing of the

balance, noteworthy for its attempt to trace the epistemological
roots of the divergent ecclesiological conceptions.

C. The Non-theological Factors in the Making of the Church

The experience of denominationalism forced American ecumenists to
focus attention 6n the role played by a variety of sociological factors in making or breaking church unity. To investigate this problem was the task of a committee composed of Willard L. Sperry, W. E.
Garrison, W. W. Harrison, Hornell Hart, Leonard Hodgson, Eliza H.
Kenrick, K. S. Latourette, H. S. Leiper, H. F. Swartz, Lewis Wallis,
Herbert L. Willett and Gerhard May.[9] It was Sperry who drafted the
report. Far from minimizing the role of theological considerations
in matters of confession and organization, the report sought to
trace the way cultural factors interacted with biblical and dogmatic
considerations in the achievement of dissolution of theological
agreement.

The document consists of six parts:
I. The centrality of theological factors (p. 1),
II. The interaction of Church and culture (pp. 1-2),
> These two sections deal generally with the relationship between
> properly theological and more sociological factors in the life
> of the Church, noting that cultural factors are not extraneous
> to the Church's life but rather have a distinct religious value
> which is an integral part of the divine structure of the
> Church,
III. Christian Unity and Church Union,
IV. The sources of the demand for Church Union (pp. 3-9)
> Building on the distinctions laid down in the Dun report,
> Sperry's document here investigates the socio-economic fac-
> tors that have been influential in promoting various forms of
> Church union,
V. The Non-theological factors in Christian theology,
VI. The Non-theological factors in the making and breaking of Church
union (pp. 10-29),
> These two sections draw attention to the disparity between
> broad theological agreement on the one hand and manifold
> ecclesiological disagreement on the other. As a possible
> account for the latter, the document catalogues eleven socio-
> cultural elements which have conditioned the diverse histori-
> cal experiences of ecclesiastical fellowship and organization,
> underlying the variant interpretations of the New Testament
> norm.

D. A Decade of Progress in Church Unity

Most directly empirical, the church sociologist H. Paul Douglass conducted a survey of the various projects proposed or undertaken since
the Lausanne Faith and Order Conference in 1927. The Douglass sur-

vey gives flesh and blood detail to the naked classificatory skele-
ton established by the Dun committee; it describes the intentions of
the various union projects then current and evaluates their degree
of progress or lack thereof.[10]

The Douglass report, in the form of a small book consists of
two parts: The first, (pp. 1-121) the detailed survey itself,
treats the various projects according to the stage of progress they
had realized to date. In all, sixty-two proposals are studied, of
which twenty-three were local to the United States. Left out of consideration were proposals for mere cooperation or federation,[11] since
these were of less interest to the Faith and Order movement. The
second part, (pp. 122-40) composed of two summary chapters, evaluates
the data of the survey in terms of denominational participation, geo-
graphic distribution, and achievement.

E. Next Steps on the Road to a United Church

The drafting of the principal report of the Commission was entrusted
to the dean of American systematic theologians, William Adams Brown
of Union Theological Seminary, a man who had for decades been in the
forefront of the ecumenical movement in America and who, in contrast
to most of his liberal colleagues in theology, had never lost sight
of the place of ecclesiology in an integral theology. Among Brown's
collaborators were Robert A. Ashworth, Yngve T. Brilioth, John R.
Fleming, Frederick C. Grant, William P. Merrill, H. C. Robbins,
Malcolm Spencer, George Craig Stewart.[12] The aim of the Brown document was to propose a course of future ecumenical action, following
the principle that progress in theory and practice must go hand in
hand. These suggestions were part of the inspiration for the formation of the World Council of Churches, which was voted into existence
at the 1937 Faith and Order and Life and Work meetings.

The composition of the document is as follows:
I. Where we start (pp. 1-5): a description of the origins, goals,
    and point of departure of the ecumenical movement. As else-
    where, the distinctively American concern for the interaction
    of historical tradition and present experience characterizes
    the handling of the topic.
II. Types of unity for which we ought to work and pray (pp. 6-14):
    Aim of this section is to elaborate the theoretical foundations
    for a program of Church union; thus it constitutes as it were,
    a miniatute ecclesiology. Of central concern is the relation-
    ship between the sociological and the theological dimensions of
    the Church's life. Thus the definition of the Church which is
    developed in pp. 9-12 is both empirical--in terms of function--
    and ontological--in terms of the Church's divine animating prin-
    ciple.
    From these theoretical considerations Brown derives three
    questions which serve as the focal point for the next three
    chapters.

III. What are the ways in which the existing unity can find more
effective outward expression, in witness, worship, service,
order and polity? (pp. 15-25).
IV. What can be done to achieve such unity in regions where it is
incomplete or lacking altogether? (pp. 26-35): a survey of
existing obstacles and suggestions for overcoming them.
V. What consequences follow for the existing ecclesiastical organizations, denominational, national or international? (pp. 35-
45). It is here that Brown develops the blueprint for the
future World Council of Churches (pp. 42-5).

These then are the documents of the first major ecumenical study
of the Church undertaken in America. Despite their extensiveness
they represent only a beginning, a tentative probing of those problem areas which, with the exception of the Communion of saints topic
will continue to occupy American interest during the next three
decades.

II. The American Theological Committee on the Church (ATC)

The Oxford and Edinburgh meetings in 1937 approved the merger
of the Faith and Order and the Life and Work movements into a World
Council of Churches. As a part of the reorganication, a theological
commission was established under the chairmanship of R. Newton Flew.
At the invitation of the Central Committee, the Americans were invited to form a theological commission of their own, which would
function as a subsidiary of the principal, essentially European commission. The outbreak of World War II, however, prevented the central commission from organizing, and so, since the Americans were
anxious to go ahead on their own with a study of the nature of the
Church, they secured authorization in 1939 to proceed independently.[13]

Chairman of the American Committee was G. W. Richards, who had
already played a significant role in the Edinburgh commission. The
membership was deliberately opened to represent not only the various
denominational traditions--from Anglican to Quaker--but also the
various theological disciplines--biblical, historical, systematic,
practical.[14] Extremists of fundamentalist or liberal tendency were
significantly absent, nevertheless the selection did represent a
cross-section of the mainstream of American theology, ranging from
tradition-minded Neo-orthodox like Richards to Quaker liberal like
Cadbury. Contacts with the Chicago Ecumenical Group through H. P.

Van Dusen secured the voice of the social-gospel tradition. Thus
the membership consisted of:[15]

William D. Barclay (Can. Presby.)
T. Stannage Boyle (Can. Anglican)
B. Harvie Branscomb (Meth.)
Henry J. Cadbury (Quaker)
W. Owen Carver (So. Bapt.)
Clarence T. Craig (Meth.)
Richard Davidson (United Church of Canada)
Burton Scott Easton (Episc.)
Winfred E. Garrison (Disc. of Christ)
Walter M. Horton (Congr.)
Kenneth S. Latourette (No. Bapt.)
Liecester C. Lewis (Episc.)
Frederick W. Loetscher (Presby.)
Harris F. Rall (Meth.)
George W. Richards (Ev. & Ref.)
William C. Robinson (Presby.)
Warren W. Slabaugh (Breth.)
Theodore G. Tappert (United Luth.)
H. P. Van Dusen (Presby.)
Eric H. Wahlstrom (Luth.)
Royden K. Yerkes (Episc.)

From June 1939 til June 1945, the American Theological Commitee
met twice yearly in three day sessions to discuss papers prepared by
the members or by outside consultants. After 1945, age and illness
prevented the group from maintaining its former level of activity.
A reorganization in 1949 under Clarence T. Craig was frustrated by
the adjournment of the European partner commission, which, having resumed
work after the War, terminated its official mandate and financial
support. In 1951 the reorganized commission was reconvened in temporary special session to discuss the matter of non-theological factors, which under the impetus of C. H. Dodd[16] had been put on the
agenda of the 1952 Faith and Order meeting at Lund.[17] In the course
of the twelve years of its work, the committee discussed almost a
hundred papers on ecclesiological topics. In addition it conducted
a survey of denominational ecclesiologies, inviting representative
theologians from the different churches to submit short statements
of their positions; these contributions were then utilized by committee members in preparing the denominational statements which
accompany the committee's report.[18] That report was drafted and
revised early in the course of the committee's work, 1943-4. Thus
topics of later discussions remain untouched by the committee
report.

The published report consists of three major parts: the first
part, "Report on the Study of the Church" (pp. 7-26) is a synthetic

presentation of the state of the question as it emerged in the first
years of discussions. Drawn up by Prof. Clarence T. Craig on the
basis of the discussions through late 1942, this part of the report
constitutes a most valuable delineation of the major ecclesiological
issues as they emerged in American perspective. As such it will be
the principal object of our concern.

The manner in which the Craig report sketches the problematic was the
direct result of discussions in the committee itself. In fall, 1940,
the committee had drawn up a list of eight topics for discussion:
"1. The origin and nature of the Christian koinonia and its
relation to the institutional forms which developed
historically.
2. The relation of the present day of the Christian koinonia
to the organized Churches.
3. The study of the nature of the Church through a due consideration of its functional activity.
4. The relation of the Church and environment; the effect of
environment upon the life, forms and concepts of the
Church, as illustrated today in typical areas.
5. The concept of the Church as related to such basic doctrines as those of God, revelation, Christ, and redemption.
6. The sense in which the New Testament is normative for the
doctrine of the Church.
7. The Church and the Kingdom of God.
8. The significance of dissent in the life of the Church and
for the doctrine of the Church."[19]
After a year of work, a review committee drew up a summary of the
agreements and disagreements which had emerged in the course of the
discussions. The report distinguished four problem areas: (1) continuity and discontinuity in the Church, (2) the norm of the Church's
life and structure, (3) uniformity and dissent in the history of the
Church, and (4) the functions of the Church.[20] These four topics
form the object of the Craig report.

The report is structured as follows:

Introduction (pp. 7-9)
deals with the problem of identifying the empirical reality which
corresponds to the word "church." Craig distinguishes here six
distinct realities: (a) the people of God in all ages and places,
(b) the local congregation of believers, (c) the organized communion of congregations sharing common doctrine and polity, (d)
the totality of such organized communions and congregations, i.e.
the so-called "church militant," (e) the invisible church of true
disciples within and beyond the organized churches, and (f) the
eschatological communion of the saints beyond death, the so-called
"church triumphant."[21] As in the Edinburgh report on the meanings
of union, the discussions of the ATC had revealed that until topical agreement could be reached, ecumenical discussions of ecclesiological matters was fruitless.[22]

I. The Historical Beginnings of the Church (pp. 9-13)
deals with the question of the origins of the Christian Church,
its precedents in the Jewish notion of Qahal and Kingdom (p. 9),
its basis in the eschatological preaching and mission of Jesus

(pp. 9-11) and the development of the Church out of the still
Jewish religious community of the disciples after the resurrection
(pp. 11-13). The report records general agreement that Jesus did
not "found" a church distinct from the Jewish religious community
during his lifetime,[23] but, on the foundation and character of the
post-resurrection community, opinions remained divided. Three
options emerged in the course of discussion: (a) an organized
institution with authoritative patterns of action and leadership
which derived from specific instructions of the risen Christ or the
providential guidance of the Spirit; (b) an informal fellowship
marked by personalistic relationship to the risen Christ and subjection to the guidance of his Spirit; (c) a tertium quid which is
unexpressible in terms of the traditional categories of institution
or fellowship.[24]

II. The Norm or Standard of Authority for the Church (pp. 13-18)
deals with the question which naturally emerges in any discussion
of the New Testament teaching and the historical development of the
early Church: "To what degree do the results obtained from this
study present a norm or standard? Is there some authoritative pattern which has been laid down or does the Spirit blow where it
will, using varied types of organizational expression? Where is
authority to be found in and for the Church?"[25] Here significant
progress toward topical agreement was made by distinguishing between: (a) the ultimate source and norm of authority, God revealed
in Jesus Christ; (b) the derived authority of teaching and ruling
--the latter proper to ecclesiastical institutions as such; and
finally (c) the channels of authoritative information connecting
derived religious and ecclesiastical authority with its source,
namely the Scriptures, the living Church, and the continuing guidance of the Spirit.[26] How these elements were related one to
another remained unresolved, but the discussion did reveal that the
central issue was whether or not a fixed divine norm for the constitution and practice of the Church could be found anywhere in the
historic tradition. Until this question could be resolved, de
facto agreement about particular matters of doctrine practice and
polity would be of little avail ecumenically.[27]

III. Unity and Diversity in Christian History (pp. 18-23)
deals with the question which had already been broached in the
Edinburgh papers: what is the significance of the continued reap-
pearance of dissent and division in the history of the Church?
After tracing the pattern of such manifestations (pp. 19-22), the
report poses the question whether or not a common unity can be
found underlying the apparent disparity of the many ecclesiastical
traditions (pp. 22-23).

IV. The Function of the Organized Church (pp. 24-26)
begins by setting forth the basic principles governing the relationship between function and institutional organization in the Church
(pp. 24-5). There follows a brief sketch of the functions of the
Church, outwardly in respect to the world in which it is set and
inwardly with respect to its own membership (pp. 25-6). The report
concludes with a functional definition of the Church which is
simultaneously a statement of the relationship of the Church to both
the mission of Christ in the past and the Kingdom of God in the
future (p. 26).

Following Craig's report of the Committee's discussions, Part
II of the published papers consists of a series of "Denominational
Statements" (pp. 27-121): rather brief position papers drawn up by
individual members of the committee as a summary of the official
doctrine and prevailing theological opinions within their respective
denominations concerning the nature of the Church. As such they do
not necessarily reflect the views of their authors; nevertheless
they form a valuable supplement to the Craig report inasmuch as they
were discussed in the sessions of the Committee and contributed to
the panoply of opinions to be reckoned with.

The basis for the denominational statements was a questionaire drawn
up by the committee and sent out to representative churchmen of the
various denominational traditions. The questions to which the re-
spondents had to reply were:
1. In what sense did Christ "found" the Church?
2. How does your Church consider that its present organization is related to New Testament doctrine and practice?
3. What are the characteristics of the Church as a fellowship, and
   what are the conditions of entrance into it as laid down by your
   Church?--included here were the notions of the communion of
   saints, people of God, etc.
4. Has your Church a view of the relationship of the Church and
   Christ on which it lays special stress?--intended here were the
   specifically theological definitions of the Church as "continuation of the incarnation," "fellowship of the Spirit," etc.
5. What does your Church consider most essential in the message and
   mission of the Church?
6. How does your Church conceive of the relation of the Church to the
   World? to the State? to the Kingdom of God?
7. In what way or ways does your Church consider that it is maintaining the continuity of the true Church of Christ?
8. What significant changes do you note in the thought and position
   of your Church in the last hundred years?
9. What do you consider to be the distinctive contribution that your
   Church has to make to the Church universal?[28]

On the basis of these replies as well as their own understanding of
their denomination's tradition, individual members of the committee
drew up the denominational statements which constitute part two of
the Nature of the Church report:
George W. Richards, "The Conception of the Church as held by the
    Evangelical and Reformed Church" (pp. 29-38),
Eric H. Wahlstrom, "The Lutheran Conception of the Church" (pp. 39-
    47),
Walter M. Horton, "The Congregational Christian Conception of the
    Church" (pp. 48-53),
Richard Davidson and William Barclay, "The Conception of the Church
    as held by the Presbyterian and United Churches of Canada" (pp.
    54-7),
Winfred E. Garrison, "The Conception of the Church as held by the
    Disciples of Christ" (pp. 58-62),
William O. Carver, "The Baptist Conception of the Church" (pp. 63-
    72),

Warren W. Slabaugh, "The Conception of the Church as held by the
   Brethren" (pp. 73-6),
Henry J. Cadbury, "A Quaker View of the Church" (pp. 77-83),
Liecester C. Lewis, "The Anglican Conception of the Church" (pp. 84-
   93),
Frederick W. Loetscher, "The Presbyterian Conception of the Church"
   (pp. 94-101),
Harris F. Rall, "The Methodist Conception of the Church" (pp. 102-
   12).

Part III, "Historical Statement" (pp. 115-22) consists of a brief
account of the American Theological Committee's organization and
activities through 1943.[29]

   The close relationship between the work of the ATC and the pre-
Edinburgh CCULW is evident at many places. The approaches and emphases which so marked the earlier work reappear here: concern for empirical verification and application, concern for denominational
union, concern for the intersection of theological immanence and
transcendence in the life of the Church, concern for adaptation
rather than repudiation of tradition, concern for the worldly context of the Church's life and mission, concern for functional institutionalization. The pre-Edinburgh commission had carried out an
initial survey of the terrain; the American Theological Committee
pursued a more detailed survey. Its main contribution was to clarify
the issues; it was able to offer no solutions to the issues it raised.
Nevertheless precisely in its calling attention to the issues underlying ecclesiological division it paved the way for the discussions
which were to follow.

III. The Chicago Ecumenical Discussion Group (CEDG)

   Whereas the ATC was an outgrowth of the Faith and Order movement, the next group we have to consider was a product of the Life
and Work tradition. Here too it had become apparent to pragmatic
ecumenists that the ecclesiological issue could not be ignored.
Thus as a follow-up to the 1937 Oxford Conference, the Life and Work
Study Department initiated an investigation of "The Ethical Reality
and Function of the Church" in 1939.[30] As in the case of the Faith
and Order Study, the outbreak of the War gravely impeded European
activity, but in America interest was high, and various groups were
organized to take up the work. Of these, the most important by far
was the so-called "Chicago Ecumenical Discussion Group" (CEDG)

organized by Prof. Edwin Aubrey of the University of Chicago. In
order to insure close collaboration and serious work, all the members were drawn from the Chicago region. A deliberate effort was
made to secure balanced representation of the various denominational
traditions.[31] The members were:

> James Luther Adams (Unit.)
> Edwin E. Aubrey (Bapt.)
> Conrad Bergendoff (Luth.)
> Georgia Harkness (Meth.)
> Joseph Haroutunian (Presby.)
> Harold R. Heininger (Ev.)
> John Knox (Meth.)
> John T. McNeill (Presby.)
> Percy V. Norwood (Episc.)
> Wilhelm Pauck (Congr.)
> Harris F. Rall (Meth.)
> Ovid O. Sellers (Presby.)
> W. W. Slabaugh (Breth.)

During the winter of 1940, the group met several times to discuss and edit a memorandum on "The Responsibility of the Church for
the International Order." Having completed this project in the
spring of that year, they decided to tackle directly the main topic
of the study. On the basis of a preliminary memorandum drawn up by
John Knox of the University of Chicago[32] and discussed at the spring
1940 meeting, they proceeded to draw up a position paper on "The
Ethical Reality and Function of the Church."[33] This paper was circulated through the Study Department in Geneva to the European participants in the project, calling forth a highly critical response
revealing the sharp cleavage between European and American ecclesiological thinking, particularly regarding the relationship of the
Church to the World.[34] The responce of other American groups on the
contrary was quite positive. Thus at the North American Ecumenical
Conference held in Toronto, June 3-5, 1941,[35] twenty-five American
and twenty-five Canadian theologians met to discuss the position
papers of the Chicago Group and W. A. Visser't Hooft, and in the
wake of this meeting, George F. Thomas published a commentary in the
Winter number of Christendom in which he extolled the merits of the
Chicago conception.[36] In a paper on "Preaching as an Expression of
the Ethical Reality of the Church"[37] the Chicagoans further elaborated their position, particularly in respect to the concrete implications of their ecclesiology for the Church's mission. It was
Harold Heininger who contributed the initial draft, which was developed into final form in the course of 1942. Thereafter the group

turned its attention away from ecclesiological questions to specifically ethical problems, ending its activities in 1944.

The paper "The Ethical Reality and Function of the Church" is struc-
tured as follows:
I. The Ethical Reality of the Church
  A. The Reality of the Church (pp. 1-7)
     The paper begins with an investigation of the relationship between
     those aspects of the Church marking her as "an empirical reality
     with a variety of doctrines and disciplines, a body of actual men
     and women who stand in a particular historical succession" and
     those other aspects according to which the Church is marked by
     "a mystical, invisible, supra-historical character or orienta-
     tion"--in a word, between the visible and invisible Church (pp.
     1-4). In the perspective of the invisible, supra-historical
     character of the Church, the paper then raises the question of the
     Church to the Kingdom and to the World (p. 4). Finally, in place
     of an "essential definition of the Church as idea," the paper
     offers a list of "essential marks," i.e. "those features of the
     actual historical community which have been constant and contin-[38]
     uous and which appear to us to be inseparable and constitutive"[38]
     (pp. 4-7).
  B. The Ethical Reality of the Church (pp. 7-12)
     This section deals with the character of the Church as an "ethi-
     cal fellowship" and "agent of God's saving grace." Its three
     subsections treat respectively: (1) the grounds of the Church's
     ethical nature, (2) its distinctive ethic, and (3) the authority
     upon which this ethic rests.
II. The Ethical Function of the Church
     Here the paper treats the way in which specific activities of the
     Church contribute to fulfill her ethical task: teaching and
     preaching (pp. 12-3), worship (pp. 13-4), social criticism (pp.
     14-5), concrete service to human need (p. 15), individual guid-
     ance, challenge and inspiration (p. 16), and finally the fellow-
     ship itself (p. 17).

     Despite the difference in context, the ideas developed by the
CEDG are very similar to those found in the Faith and Order Studies.
At the head stands the problem of the relationship between the empirical and the ideal. In the thinking of the group, phenomenological
description holds a clear priority over essential definition. They
see the Church as a living organism which, obligated on the one hand
to maintain continuity with the New Testament community is nevertheless free under the active presence of God in its life to adapt to
new social situations and cultures.[39] This way of seeing the Church
helps explain why specific structural questions find such little consideration in the paper: the nature of the authority under which the
Church stands is such, that even in questions of faith and order no
answers can be found except in relation to the concrete situation of
an ecumenical discussion.[40] What is particularly significant about

the work of the CEDG is precisely the fact that it gives expression
to the ecclesiological interests of moral theologians, for it is a
distinctively American phenomenon, rooted in the Social Gospel tradition, to locate the theological consideration of the Church in the
context of Christian ethics.

IV. The Interseminary Series

Despite wartime handicaps, the ecumenical movement was gathering steam in the USA and Canada during the early forties. As early
as 1944, plans were laid for a national conference of the Interseminary Movement with the object of confronting theological students "with the claims of Jesus Christ and his Church in terms of
the ecumenical ideal."[41] In preparation for this meeting a series
of commissions were set up "to examine the ecumenical Church and its
task" from the point of view of the American Churches. Each of the
four commissions was charged with producing a volume of studies on a
particular aspect of this theme. The individual articles were to be
written by individually assigned authors, but then so worked over in
group discussion that "the end result will be the outcome of both the
group process and individual thinking."[42] The commissions were
organized as follows:[43]

I.A. "The Challenge of our Culture," under the chairmanship of
Clarence T. Craig, dealt with the ways in which the contemporary world confronts the Church and its Gospel.

I.B. "The Church and Organized Movements," under the chairmanship of
Randolf Crump Miller, investigated the various organizations
and movements with which the contemporary Church found itself
in alliance or competition.

II. "The Gospel, the Church and the World," under the chairmanship
of Kenneth Scott Latourette, attempted to set forth the theological principles and the sociological conditions of the
Church's nature and task.

III. "Toward World-wide Christianity," under the chairmanship of O.
Frederick Nolde, focused its attention on concrete ecumenical
problems of the Church's life and work.

The work of these four commissions appeared in 1947 as the
first four volumes of The Interseminary Series. The task of drawing
together the diverse strands of the commissions work fell to Robert
Bilheimer, the man who had conceived the idea of the study in the

first place and had seen the project through to completion as secretary and editor.[44] His one hundred twenty-one page essay, What
Must the Church Do?, appeared as the fifth volume of the series.

The structure of Bilheimer's summary essay follows generally the
work of the commissions
1. The Essence of the Challenge (pp. 1-27)
   summarizes the work of commissions I.A and I.B, with the aim
   of setting forth the context in which a functionally oriented,
   ecumenical ecclesiology should be developed.
2. The Function of the Church (pp. 28-63)
   Taking "Church" to mean "not primarily ecclesiastical institutions or the sum total of them" but rather "a more fundamental
   reality which is the spiritual bond formed among all who have
   faith in Christ, namely the universal fellowship of the
   Church,"[45] Bilheimer develops a functional characterization of
   the Church in terms of four fundamental propositions:
   a. "The unique possession of the Church is a Gospel" (pp. 28-
      34)--it is in this context that the essay deals with the
      traditional ecclesiological themes of community, divine-
      human interaction, covenant, Kingdom, etc.;
   b. "The basic function of the Church has been to establish the
      Gospel in the lives of people" (pp. 34-43);
   c. "A result, but only a result, of this basic function of
      evangelism has been the transformation of society" (pp. 43-
      53);
   d. "The primacy of the Gospel means that the Church carries a
      responsibility for all men and not any particular section of
      society" (pp. 53-5).
   From this conception Bilheimer proceeds to develop the consequences for the Church's relationship to the World, Christendom,
   world community, and the churches (pp. 55-62).
3. The Ecumenical Reformation (pp. 63-107)
   summarizes the first five chapters of the fourth volume of the
   series, in which the existing denominational divisions and the
   various attempts to overcome them are evaluated.
4. The Task Ahead (pp. 108-20)
   develops the theme of the last chapter of vol. IV, the imperatives concerning theology, worship, evangelism, social action,
   and ecumenical unity (pp. 108-18) and the practical application
   of these imperatives in the life of the local congregation
   (pp. 118-20).

The Interseminary volumes bring to fruition the first phase of

the American ecclesiological renaissance. Among its contributors

one finds many a name familiar from earlier commissions, and the

statements of the earlier groups echo in its pages. The basic pre-

occupations and approaches remain much the same as those of the pre-

ceding, and yet underneath there are new accents which anticipate

the directions taken by subsequent groups. One notes, for instance,

the call for a greater concern for biblical theology as the founda-

tion of a truly ecumenical ecclesiology.[46] Precisely this was the

object of the next ecumenical study we have to consider.

V. The Biblical Doctrine of Man in Society Study (BDMS)

In 1950 a new American study group was called into being by the World Council of Churches Study Department. As part of a wide-ranging project of biblical theology, G. Ernest Wright of McCormick Theological Seminary, Chicago, was asked to form a group of biblical scholars drawn from the theological schools of the area to prepare a document on "The Biblical Doctrine of Man in Society." Under Wright's chairmanship, fifteen exegetes from widely different denominational traditions met seven times during the course of 1950-1 to clarify the issues and to carry out detailed studies of the various topics to be treated. The members were:

Otto J. Baab (Meth.)
Edward P. Blair (Meth.)
Chalmer E. Faw (Breth.)
Floyd V. Filson (Presby.)
Holt Graham (Episc.)
P. E. Keen (Ev. and Ref.)
Walter C. Klean (Episc.)
Lester J. Kuyper (Ref.)
Julius R. Manthy (No. Bapt.)
J. Coert Rylaarsdam (Ref.)
Don E. Schmucker (Menn.)
Eugene S. Wehrli (Ev. & Ref.)
Amos N. Wilder (Congr.)
C. Umhau Wolf (Luth.)
G. Ernest Wright (Presby.),

to which were added three consultants for the fields of sociology, church history and economics:

James Luther Adams (Unit.)
James H. Nichols (Presby.)
Walter Zuurdeeg.[47]

Wright undertook the task of drawing up the final statement, making use of the papers contributed by the other members and subjecting his original draft to the critique of the others for correction and improvement.[48] The revised paper appeared in 1954 as the second number in the series "Ecumenical Biblical Studies."

Although not directly conceived as a contribution to ecclesiology, the orientation of the study on the biblical teaching concerning the "new man and the new society which God creates" necessarily entails an ecclesiological orientation. For, as the Wright committee's report points out, the Church of the New Testament saw itself precisely as this new community, i.e. "the fellowship of those who have been gathered together as in a flock by the Lord, who acknowledge the special work of God for what it is, who have been led to surrender to the Lordship of the risen Christ, who following him take upon themselves the burden of his world's sin, live in him by the power of his spirit and proclaim to the world God's mighty acts over sin, Satan, and the principalities of darkness."[49] In confining itself to the terms of its commission, the group deliberately left out of consideration the application of its findings to the contemporary situation of the Church.[50] Nevertheless, precisely as an exposition of the biblical presentation of the "People of God," the document represents a useful exposition of representative exegetical thinking on ecclesiological issues.

A synopsis of the "Man in Society" document will help to give an impression of the Wright committee's ecclesiology.
I. Individual and Community in the Bible (pp. 7-24)
   Contrasts the modern view of the relationship between individual and community with that of the Bible as a prelude to the subsequent consideration of the specific societies in which the New Testament community developed. To this end it likewise considers the New Testament view of the world.
II. Man and his Societies in the World (pp. 35-62)
   deals with the sinful character of man and its consequences for those societies which are of human origin.
III. The Redemptive Acts of God: The New Man and the New Society (pp. 63-123)
   outlines a biblical ecclesiology under the following topics:
A. The New Society as God's Creation (pp. 64-76)--treating the historical act of God, the fellowship it gives rise to, and the articulation of this fellowship's historical self-consciousness in worship and kerygma;
B. The Nature of the New Society (pp. 77-88)--treating the way in which the community's self-consciousness articulated itself not in organizational terms but rather as the "People of God" (analysis of New Testament images of the Church, and of the New Testament way of correlating the rule of God through the action of the Spirit in a structural context which is charismatic rather than institutional);
C. Individual and Community (pp. 88-101)
   The biblical view individualizes the new man to an astonishing degree, attributing to him a direct, personal responsibility in his relationships which defies the normal subordination of individual to political and religious organization, but this liberation from false forms of human community is at once incorporation into the new and true community, "the fellowship in a common life, under the leadership of the invisible Lord whose spirit 'tabernacled in' and possessed the whole community."[51]
D. The Common Life of the New Society (pp. 101-11)
   The common life of the people of God is based on the righteousness of God, which "had brought the community into being and bound its members to its Giver with ties of gratitude, trust and devotion."[52] This meant a transformation of the role of law, liberating the members of the community for responsible decision. The context of the ethic governing the life of the community was an eschatological one: the community knew that

it was not the Kingdom and that not its action but that of God
was responsible for bringing it about.
E. The New Society in the New Age (pp. 111-23)
   takes up in detail the individual and corporate eschatological
   expectations of the community.
IV. The People of God in the World (pp. 124-69)
   expounds the twofold attitude of the People of God toward the
   world: on the one hand, responsibility for it, on the other,
   withdrawal from it. This is exemplified with special reference
   to the economic, political, and cultural life of the community.

In keeping with its origin as a project of the World Council
Study Department, the work of the Wright committee shows greatest
affinity to that of the CEDG. This similarity appears most significantly in the tendency of both groups to conceive the Church as a
fellowship of common life and faith rather than as an organization,
the difference between the two documents however is equally striking.
In its sharper division between the Church, the Kingdom and secular
society, the Wright committee reveals its distance from the usual
Social-Gospel conception of the Church as an ethical reality. Certainly it would be mistaken to suppose that the work of the Wright
committee can be taken as the consensus of American exegetes regarding the New Testament picture of the Church; the spectrum of opinion is too broad to be so easily synthesized. Nevertheless precisely
as the product of group whose members come from widely different
traditions and schools, it merits serious consideration as an expression of one line of ecumenical thinking.

VI. The Survey of Theological Education in the United States and
    Canada (STEUSC)

In 1954, the American Association of Theological Schools undertook a study of theological education in America. From the beginning it was clear that a study of minister's education required a
penetrating study of the nature and role of the ministry itself.[53]
The direction of the project was entrusted to H. Richard Niebuhr in
collaboration with Daniel Day Williams and James M. Gustafson.[54]
The study involved extensive sociological research, interviews,
questionaires directed to denominational officials, pastors, students, seminary administrators and faculty, laymen. To study the
ministry's historical origin and development, a special commission
composed of Church historians was set up.[55] Their investigations

resulted in the publication of the symposium The Ministry in Historical Perspectives,[56] a collection of essays expounding the conception and varieties of ministry prevailing in the various epochs of
the Church's history. It fell to the director of the project, H.
Richard Niebuhr, to gather together all the many threads of the investigation into a systematic theoretical statement, which he significantly entitled The Purpose of the Church and its Ministry. Un-
mistakably, this book bears the stamp of Niebuhr's own ecclesiological thinking; none the less it is also an expression of group thinking on the subject, a point which the author himself insists on.[57]

The ecclesiological reflections of the Niebuhr essay emerge
from the realization that "education is so closely connected with
the life of a community that inquiries about the aims of teaching and
learning cannot be answered unless ideas about the character and purpose of the society in which it is carried on are clarified first of
all."[58] At the root of the problem in theological education lie
"the perplexities of the contemporary Protestant community and its
ministry."[59] From this perspective, with full consciousness that
discussion about Church and ministry is by no means at an end,
Niebuhr set out to formulate in a tentative and personal way "some
of the recent agreements about the character of the Church"[60] and
"to describe in sketchy outline" what he sensed to be the "emerging
new conception of the ministry" latent in contemporary pastoral
practice.[61] On the basis of these considerations he proceeds to
formulate the nature and function of the theological school.

The Niebuhr essay is structured according to the three themes
outlines above:

I. The Church and its Purpose (pp. 1-47)
   begins by inquiring about the identity of the community to which
   the theological school is ordered (pp. 5-17). In reality it is
   the familiar question of the empirical identity of the Church
   that is raised here. Three units are considered in turn: the
   denominations or "churches," the national religious community
   with its "church-system," and finally the over-arching ecumenical community, "the One Holy Church" transcending denominational
   and national boundaries.

   Having shown that it is the Church in this universal sense
   that is the real context of ministry and theological education,
   Niebuhr proceeds to define its character (pp. 17-27), using
   what he calls "the method of polar-analysis": since the Church
   is a dynamic social reality, its nature can be grasped only "by
   defining certain poles between which it moves or which it represents."[62] Six such poles emerge in his analysis: (a) sub-
   jective--objective, i.e. Church and Kingdom; (b) community--

48

institution; (c) one--many; (d) local--universal; (e) protestant--catholic, i.e. transcendent and immanent; (f) Church--World.

However, since the Church does not exist for its own sake, the question of its nature cannot be separated from that of its objectives (pp. 27-47). First Niebuhr distinguishes the ultimate, unifying objective of the Church from the multiplicity of proximate goals corresponding to the pluralism of Church life and structure (pp. 27-39). This ultimate goal is "the increase among men of the love of God and neighbor."[63] This is the aim and criterion of all Church organization, activity, preaching, ministry and education. Applying this criterion, Niebuhr concludes his discussion of the Church with a consideration of the four maladies that arise from a confusion of ultimate and proximate goals, namely[64] denominationalism, ecclesiasticism, biblicism and christism (pp. 39-47).

II. The Emerging New Conception of Ministry (pp. 48-94) constitutes an attempt to delineate the special form of professional ministry which empirical analysis shows to be emergent in contemporary practice and experience, namely the "pastoraldirector" type.[65] From the study of Ministry in historical perspectives, Niebuhr distills four constants differentially verified in all earlier types of ministry. Using these notes as a criterion, he attempts to demonstrate that the "pastoraldirector" concept is a legitimate successor to the traditional types of the priest, the pastoral ruler, the preacher, the evangelist, and that it finds its historical precedent in the ancient form of the episcopate as the presidency over a local congregation.

III. The Idea of a Theological School (pp. 95-134) locates the theological school in ecclesiological perspective as "the intellectual center of the Church's life": though not the Church in its wholeness, the theological school represents, according to Niebuhr, a distinct and essential member of the Church.[66] Thus also in this last section one finds important ecclesiological considerations, particularly in regard to the nature and role of theology in the Church.

The interest of the Niebuhr study lies not so much in detail as in the overall conception and methodology. The method of "polar-analysis" hinted at in earlier studies is here for the first time systematically reflected and applied as a method of defining the nature of the Church. In a similar way, the factor-analysis used to determine the essential marks of the professional ministry in its various historical forms anticipates later reflections on the nature and use of the historical tradition of the Church. It offers an especially good example of functionalist method in action.

VII. The Oberlin Conference

Early in September, 1957, a momentous event occurred in North American ecumenical history. Officially commissioned delegates from some forty denominations together with observers from some ten non-participating denominations met at Oberlin, Ohio, to discuss "The Nature of the Unity We Seek."[67] The occasion was the "North American Conference on Faith and Order" held under the auspices of the United States Conference for the World Council of Churches, with the collaboration of the Canadian Council of Churches and the National Council of Churches of Christ in the U.S.A. From the beginning it was conceived as a study conference with the aim of examining the dominant issues characterizing the contemporary situation of the Church in North America.

A two year process of preparation preceded the meeting. First leading Christians from diverse denominations and regions were questioned about "areas of consensus and conflict where the unity of Christ's Church was being conspicuously tested in our day." Out of this survey the arrangements committee distilled a tentative list of fruitful discussion topics. To begin the study representative groups were set up in sixteen selected cities of the U.S.A. and Canada. Strong emphasis was placed from the very beginning on the necessity of engaging lay men and women, active pastors and denominational officials as well as professional theologians. These groups, ranging in size from six to thirteen began work in the winter of 1955-6. In August, 1956, a general meeting reviewed the progress of the work, reduced the list of discussion topics for the Oberlin conference to twelve, and assigned these to the regional study groups to prepare the working papers for the conference sections.[68] As the participating churches named their delegates, these were incorporated as far as possible into the regional study groups or special "conversational groups" to insure solid preparation for the conference when it met in seven-day session September 3-10, 1957.

The work of the conference was organized with equal care. The general theme was divided into three "divisions" dealing with theological foundations, organizational principles, and socio-cultural considerations respectively; each of these in turn was broken down into four sections and assigned to a select committee of conference participants. It was here in the section meeting that the main work of the conference centered, and it is in their reports that one finds the richest resources for reconstructing the ecclesiological thinking of the Oberlin conference. Paul Minear explains their value as follows:

"A total of at least fourteen hours was spent by every section on its assigned topic. It was aided in the preparation of its report by its own drafting committee which worked unnumbered hours, day and night, to keep pace with the demand. The major results of this concentrated work will be found in the section reports below. Readers must be aware, however, that probably no section was wholly content with the written product, and that the fruitfulness of ecumenical study is only partially reflected in such reports. There was no time for the plenary session to receive or to discuss these reports. They come therefore direct from the sections to the churches. They seek to convey to the churches the more important discoveries made by the sections, along with their basic convictions concerning the immediate opportunities for ecumenical action by the churches."[69]

A brief conspectus of the Oberlin section reports reveals the themes handled. In the published proceedings, each report is prefaced by a statement of "Situation and Objectives." These statements were part of the preparatory material distributed to the sections at the beginning of their work.

1. "Imperatives and Motivations" (pp. 176-84) dealing with: (a) the theological foundations for Church unity, both the teaching of the Gospel and the contemporary experience; (b) the obstacles to realizing Church unity; and (c) the principles which must shape the unity to be pursued.
2. "Doctrinal Consensus and Conflict" (pp. 186-94) dealing with: (a) the degree and kind of doctrinal consensus already prevailing among the churches; (b) the use and value of the historic confessions and the principles which should govern the interplay of conformity and diversity in doctrinal matters.
3. "Baptism into Christ" (pp. 195-9) dealing with points of agreement and disagreement in the prevailing teachings on baptism and their diverse ecclesiological foundations.
4. "The Table of the Lord" (pp. 200-5) expressing the agreements reached within the section on the nature of the Lord's Supper sacrament and appealing to the churches to draw the consequences of this agreement.
5. "The Life of the Congregation" (pp. 213-7) treating "the meaning of the unity we seek in the Church of Christ in terms of the unity we both seek and find in the local church,"--distinguished into unity in faith, unity in worship, and unity in concern.
6. "The Work of State and Local Councils" (pp. 218-22) analyzing the development, function and ecclesiological significance of such councils and of the "federated" or interdenominational "community" churches that they have often fostered.
7. "Authority and Freedom in Church Government" (pp. 223-9) sketching a theology of church authority and freedom and analyzing its concrete function in diverse church polities.
8. "The Variations in Denominational Polities" (pp. 230-8) treating "the nature of the visible Church and its organizational struc-

ture which underlie all denominational polities"[71] and outlining certain principles which must govern any plan of church
union in North America.
9. "The Mobility of the Population" (pp. 247-54) dealing with the
impact of American population shifts on the realization of the
Church in America, her ministry to people, her organization.
10. "Government Policies and Programs" (pp. 256-63) examining the
interaction between the churches and society especially the
government in terms of its ecclesiological presuppositions and
consequences.
11. "Forces at Work on the College Campus" (pp. 264-9) treating of
the relationship between Church and University not only in its
theoretical basis but also in terms of concrete campus programs.
12. "Racial and Economic Stratification" (pp. 270-2) outlines the
ecclesiological principles which should govern the Church's
reaction to the divisions arising from racial and economic
stratification of denominations and congregations.

Over and above the section meetings, work was carried on in

plenary and division sessions. The plenary sessions were used to

convey important background information to the participants to the

conference[72] and to discuss, revise and officially approve the draft

statements which had been worked out in the divisional meetings as

well as the official "Message to the Churches" which had been pre-

pared by a special drafting committee. This "Message" together with

the Divisional statements constitute the official acts of the Con-

ference.

The Division Reports
    The fruits of the sectional discussions were brought together
in the meetings of the divisions, each of which was responsible for
producing a draft statement to be submitted to the plenary assembly
for revision and approval.[73]

I. The Nature of the Unity We Seek in Faithfulness to the Eternal
    Gospel (pp. 167-74). Embracing the work of the first four sec-
    tions, this text deals with "certain of the more specifically
    theological approaches to our problem."[74] These include (a)
    the statement of the unity already possessed by the Church in
    the churches; (b) the contributions of "biblical theology"
    toward the achievement of even deeper unity in accord with the
    unifying character of salvific history; (c) a definition of
    Church unity; (d) an analysis of the theological and non-theo-
    logical motives for church union; (e) the principles governing
    ecumenical conversation, especially, what constitute the cri-
    teria of "desirable diversity, creative ... and destructive con-
    flict"; and finally (f) a list of unsolved problems which con-
    stitute a challenge to further theological investigation.
II. The Nature of the Unity We Seek in Terms of Organizational Struc-
    tures (pp. 206-12). Summarizing the discussions in sections 5-
    8, this report outlines first the theoretical foundations for
    church organization, namely "the Nature of Christian Unity"
    (a) in Christ, (b) in mission, (c) in visible structure, (d) in

authority and freedom, (e) in worship. In its second part the
report applies these principles to: (a) the life of the congregation, (b) cooperation in state and local councils, (c) the
balance of freedom and authority in matters of polity, and
(d) the development of church union plans.

III. The Nature of the Unity We Seek in View of Cultural Pressures
(pp. 239-46). Corresponding to sections 9-12, the Division III
report begins by outlining the principles which should govern
the analysis of cultural factors in ecclesiology (pp. 239-42).
Next it states six convictions about the nature of unity in
relation to socio-cultural factors (pp. 242-3). In the third
place it sketches four obstacles to church union which arise
from the working of socio-cultural factors (pp. 243-4) and it
concludes by describing the attitudes which must govern further
ecumenical discussion and cooperation if due regard be had for
the working of such elements in the making and breaking of
church unity (pp. 244-6).

It is evident that the divisional reports are quite brief, representing only a superficial sketch of the rich materials found in
the sectional reports. For this reason, despite their official character they are far less fruitful than the latter for revealing the
trends of ecclesiological thinking that found expression at the
Oberlin meeting. On the other hand, in view of their official character they are a better guide to what the group as a whole could
agree on.

The "Message to the Churches" (pp. 28-30)

The last document produced by the Oberlin conference was the
"Message to the Churches" intended as a profession of the assembly's
faith in the unity of God's Church, a confession of its sins against
that unity, an expression of gratitude for the God-given unity it
experienced and an anticipation of the fuller unity for which it
hoped. This message, so rich in ecclesiological content despite the
brevity of its formulation, was drawn up by a drafting committee
under the chairmanship of Truman B. Douglass. Discussed and revised
during the plenary sessions of Sept. 9th and 10th, it was approved by
majority vote on the morning of the 10th, the Orthodox delegates
having previously signified their will to abstain from voting on a
text they found unacceptably protestant in tone and content.[5] In
the following passage the key ideas of the Oberlin Conference come
to expression:

"As we have known a common joy in the unity we now possess, we
have also felt a common sorrow over the continuing fact of our
separations one from another. ... Yet God gives us hope. We
do not see clearly the path that God has set before us, but we
are sure that he is leading us and that at Oberlin he has given
us new light.
In this light we see that the Church is God's Church and that
the unity is his unity. This unity, we believe, is to be:
-- A unity in Christ who died for us, is risen, regnant, and
will come again to gather together all things in his judgment
and grace;
-- A unity in adoration of God--one offering of wonder, love and
praise;
-- A unity of declared faith, sounding the vast Amen of the
whole Church's believing life through all the centuries;
-- A unity of bearing one another's burdens and sharing one

another's joys;
-- A unity in which every ministry is a ministry of and for all the members, bound together in a worshiping and sacramental community;
-- A unity in mission to the world, originating with, sustained by and offered to the one Christ, and conducted with such transparency of love and faithfulness that the world will believe in him;
-- A unity possessing rich variety in worship, life and organization."[76]

VIII. The Faith and Order Studies between Lund and Montreal
      (TCCCNA, TCTTNA, TCWNA, SCI)

The 1952 Faith and Order Conference held at Lund, Sweden, had marked a turning point in the world-wide ecumenical discussion of the Church. Hitherto the Faith and Order movement on the world-wide scale had largely confined itself to comparative studies of points of agreement and disagreement in the official teachings of the various churches. (In connection with earlier projects we have had occasion to note American dissatisfaction with this comparative method and attempts to go beyond it.) The sharp division between catholic and protestant ecclesiologies at the 1949 First Assembly of the World Council had put a rude end to hopes that further progress could be achieved by the traditional comparative method.[77] To escape this debacle, the Lund Conference attempted a bold leap forward. Abandoning comparison, it proposed to tackle directly the ticklish question of the nature of the Church by a systematic theological projection working out of christology and pneumatology.[78] Furthermore it called for renewed and deeper investigation of the problems of historical tradition and socio-cultural influence in church life and organization.[79] Out of these impulses emerged four study projects, the results of which came to expression in the 1963 Faith and Order Conference in Montreal, Canada. As in previous projects, American participation was independent and impressive.

The "Theological Commission on Christ and the Church" was the first study project to be organized.[80] Already in August 1953 it was officially constituted in a North American and a European section. Members of the American section were:

Robert L. Calhoun (U.C.C.)
G. R. Cragg (United Church of Canada)
Nels S. F. Ferré (U.C.C.)
Floyd V. Filson (Un. Presby.)
Georges Florovsky (Russ. Orth.)

Edmund R. Hardy (Episc.)
Walter Harrelson (Am. Bapt.)
Teito A. Kantonen (Luth.)
John Knox (Episc.)
Paul S. Minear (U.C.C.)
J. Robert Nelson (Meth.)
H. Richard Niebuhr (U.C.C.)
W. N. Pittenger (Episc.)
Claude Welch (Meth.)

Calhoun held the chairmanship until 1961, when for reasons of health
he retired in favor of his vice-chairman Pittenger.[81] During the
ten years of its work, the American section met each summer in three-
day session, its discussions ranging widely over the field of christology, pneumatology and ecclesiology. Three times it met jointly
with the European section, namely in 1954, 1957, and 1958; however
the plan to produce a joint final report proved unfeasible. Thus it
came about that the American section issued a separate final report
in preparation for the Montreal Conference in 1963.[82]

In keeping with the terms of its establishment, the commission
report focuses on christology as the foundation for a new ecclesiological approach. The "common affirmation" which opens the report
gives a good idea of the problem:

"The Church is that community in which Christ manifests his
Lordship by the power of the Holy Spirit, in which he claims
for himself the kingdoms of this world, in which he declares his
judgment and bestows forgiveness, and in which he is worshipped
and adored by those whom he has made members, through the Holy
Spirit, of his mystical body. Hence the Church cannot be understood apart from the Lord Jesus Christ and the Holy Spirit. Yet
the Church must be distinguished from the Lord Jesus Christ, who
in his earthly ministry gathered disciples and fitted them to
take their place in the Church of Pentecost. It must be distinguished also from the Holy Spirit, who enlivens it and em-
powers it to carry on Christ's ministry in and for the world."[83]

It is the problem which has continually plagued ecumenical discussion
between churchmen of the "catholic" and "protestant" frames of mind.
For to "protestant" eyes, the "catholic" way of thinking is inclined
to attribute to the Church qualities which appear proper to Christ
alone; whereas in "catholic" eyes, "protestant" thinking fails to
take seriously the incarnational character of the new humanity conferred by the risen Lord on his people. The famous debacle of the
Amsterdam Assembly had documented the magnitude of this dichotomy.
Along with it, however, and running diagonal to this division of
opinion was a secondary one, namely the relationship of the Church
to the World in the context of the new humanity: it is much easier

to attribute incarnational qualities to the Church, if it is set off against the World, than when the Church is seen as a part of the World which as a whole is to be transformed into the new humanity. These issues, already touched on in the earlier studies we have outlined, were the center of the Montreal commission discussions.

The TCCCNA followed the usual procedure of having individual members present position papers at the annual meetings.[84] These papers were mimeographed and circulated in both European and American sections. In most cases they represented quite extensive studies, and though the original plan to publish them as a symposium proved unfeasible, they provided the basis for a number of books published by individual Commission members.[85]

The TCCCNA had several occasions to articulate the results of its discussions. The first came in 1957 as R. L. Calhoun addressed the Oberlin Conference.[86] Two years later members of the American and European sections met at Tutzing, Germany, to draw up a joint Interim Report.[87] More important, however, as an indicator of the American position is the report of the North American Section delivered by J. R. Nelson to the 1960 F. & O. Commission meeting at St. Andrews, Scotland.[88] The central portion of the Nelson report consists of a series of nine theses with appropriate commentary, which proport to articulate the "areas of concord" which the Americans had come to recognize in the course of their discussions.

Because it proved unfeasible to bring the two sections together again to produce a joint final report in time for the 1963 F. & O. Conference in Montreal, the TCCCNA proceeded at its 1960 meeting to lay plans for a separate statement.[89] On the basis of the plan drawn up at this meeting, the individual portions of the text were farmed out to various members for drafting. The task of combining these drafts into a final draft fell to W. N. Pittenger.

The final report of the TCCCNA falls into two parts:
I. Introduction (pp. 9-15)
   explaining the context of thought in which the committee operated, their approach to the subject--described as "catholicity in method," namely "a reflection upon the work of God as a whole, from beginning to end. It participates in the fullness of God's design to sum up all things in Christ. It deals with the Church as a whole--its membership in heaven and on earth, drawn from all tribes and tongues; its common heritage from all ages; its apostolic mission to all people, its emancipation from slaveries to the provincial and the partial; its stewardship of the truth and holiness which God has bestowed."[90] The affinity of this conception with the "Biblical Theology" movement, in which Filson and Minear were prominent, is evident.
II. Christ and his Church
   A. Jesus Christ
   1. Christ the Lord (pp. 16-7)
      affirms the transcendence of Jesus' reality over all the historical attempts to theologically interpret his character and significance.
   2. Aspects of Christology which have a particular relevance to our understanding of the Church:
      a. unity of divine and human--the presence of God in the human life of Jesus was a unifying not a dividing factor; it is pre-

cisely in the human character of Jesus' actions that the divine
element comes to expression (pp. 17-8).
  b. complete humanity--"Jesus' humanity," with all its autonomy and
     recalcitrance "makes a real response to God in faith and love,
     and we who live in him become part of that response. And our[91]
     life in him includes obedience to Jesus as human teacher,..."
     (p. 18).
  c. the unity of the Godhead in the Word incarnate--the activity
     of the Spirit cannot be separated from the activity of Christ:
     "life in Christ is also life in the Spirit. There is no need
     to make precise distinctions in the meaning of these two
     phrases..."[92] (pp. 18-9).
3. From Christology to Ecclesiology (pp. 19-20)
   The variety of New Testament images of the Church point to the
   corporate and familial character expressed by the notions People of God and Body of Christ. The relationship here is one
   of analogy, involving both similarities and differences in the
   predicates of Christ and of the Church. "The Church is a divine fellowship, and yet in its concrete expression can be studied as a visible institution subject to the stresses and pressures of the world."[93] Describing their conception as a "sacramental and trinitarian view of the Church"[94] the section goes
   on to relate the sacramental ordinances of Baptism and the
   Lord's Supper to their ecclesiology.
B. The Church of Christ
   Under two general headings, the commission draws the implications of its trinitarian approach.
1. The Uniqueness of the Church
   in respect to Israel of the Old Covenant (pp. 21-3) and in respect to the World (pp. 22-5). These considerations reveal the
   tension between the empirical reality of the sinful church and
   the essential reality it ought to be; thus the last section
   treats "the Church as essential and provisional" (pp. 25-6).
2. The Church as Event and Institution
   After showing that event and institution, freedom and form, are
   typical of the pattern of the divine work, (pp. 26-7), the report goes on to investigate the relationship between these two
   aspects in the life of the Church (pp. 27-8). In this perspective it sets forth the principles governing the institutional
   structure of ministry, word and sacrament (pp. 29-30). A brief
   concluding note explains the relationship between the unconven-
   tional approach of the commission report and the old controversies about the marks of the Church, the visible and invisible
   Church, etc. (p. 30).
C. The Church in the World (pp. 30-3)
   The relationship of the Church to the World follows the pattern
   of Jesus' incarnation (pp. 31-2). Thus "the Church is that
   community of faithful people wherein and whereby the everliving
   Christ continues his work of salvation in every generation" and
   "where the redemptive, reconciling self-offering of Jesus Christ
   is continually appropriated by faith within the lives of its
   members and in their relations with all peoples in all the
   world."[95] From the peace-making character of the Church's mission follow the imperatives for unity and mission (p. 32).
   Through the whole-hearted participation of Christian people in
   the Church's three-fold liturgy of preaching the faith, worshipping in unity, and serving the world, the redemption goes for-

ward towards its appointed consummation, when the distinction
between Church and world will have been overcome."[96]

In addition to the Commission on Christ and the Church, three
other commissions were set up in preparation for the Montreal Conference. Though they deal with more specialized topics than the
former, the reports of these commissions represent a valuable supplement to the report of "Christ and the Church," for in one way or
another they all deal with the effect of socio-cultural factors in
Church life and structure.

1) Theological Commission on Tradition and the Traditions, North
American Section (TCTTNA)

Formally constituted in 1954, the objective of this commission
was to investigate the relationship between the separate histories
of the divided churches and the "common history which we have as
Christians."[97] Its North American section, under the chairmanship
of Prof. A. C. Outler pursued from the beginning a course quite different from that of its European counterpart, which pursued a theoretical investigation of the concept of tradition. Corresponding
more to the American penchant for phenomenological methods, the
North American section "was primarily concerned with the elusive
task of observing the traditionary process in its actual operation
in specific 'cases' of 'traditions in transit'."[98] Its members,
drawn from the ranks of Church historians and systematic theologians
with historical specialization were:
Sydney E. Ahlstrom
R. Pierce Beaver
William A. Clebsch
Eugene R. Fairweather
Georges Florovsky
David W. Hay
Donald M. Mathews
Albert C. Outler
Jaroslav Pelikan
Glenn Routt
H. H. Walsh.[99]

In brief survey, the report of the North American Section "The
Renewal of the Christian Tradition"[100] deals with the following
topics of ecclesiological relevance: the nature of "ecumenical historiography" (pp. 14-5); the problem of continuity and unity of the
historical Church underlying the divergent historical traditions of
the churches (pp. 15-8); the problem of the norm of the Church's
faith, life, and structure (pp. 18-20); the enculturation of ecclesiastical tradition (pp. 20-4); and finally, the place of historical
perspectives in future ecumenical theological work (pp. 24-7).

2) Theological Commission on Worship, North American Section (TCWNA)

Likewise constituted in 1954, this commission under the chairmanship of Prof. Joseph Sittler undertook to study one of the central
expressions of ecclesial life. Its effective members were:

Markus Barth
Robert E. Cushman
Fredrick Herzog
Winthrop Hudson
Philip Hyatt
William Kelly
Preston Roberts
J. Coert Rylaarsdam
Massey Shepherd
Joseph Sittler
Leonard Trinterud
Franklin W. Young.[101]

The report of the commission's work is less directly concerned with specific ecclesiological issues than the others, and yet in passing it contains many significant sidelights on the ecclesial context of worship and on the problem of the enculturalization of ecclesial forms. Among these may be noted in particular the discussion of the impact of the American frontier experience on the shape of church life and on the sense of continuity or discontinuity with the historical reality of the People of God (pp. 49-51); the relation between the priestly and the prophetic elements and the implications of this relationship for the conception of the relationship between Kingdom, Church and World (pp. 52-3); the relationship between the worship, the mission and the ethical life of the Church (pp. 54-7); the place of Jesus Christ in the life of the Church (pp. 57-8).

3) Study Commission on Institutionalism (SCI)

Established a year later than the others, this commission conceived its objective as one of helping "the churches become self-critical of the manifold ways in which their institutional structures and procedures, in interaction with one another and with society, may either obstruct or support the quest for unity."[102] The central problem confronting it was the relationship between the "spiritual entity" and the "empirical social reality of the Church," between theological reflection and sociological investigation."[103] Under the chairmanship of Walter G. Mueller of Boston University, the Institutionalism Commission united both European and American members:

Hans Dombois [Germany]
Nils Ehrenström [U.S.A.--formerly Sweden and Geneva]
Charles R. Fielding [Canada]
James M. Gustafson [U.S.A.]
Berndt Gustafsson [Sweden]
Walter G. Mueller [U.S.A.]
William Pickering [Canada]
Franklin E. Rector [U.S.A.]
Heinz-Horst Schrey [Germany]
Frederick A. Shippey [U.S.A.][104]

Papers, moreover, were submitted from England, Japan, and India, as well as from the nations mentioned above.[105] Nevertheless, despite this participation of European and Asian thinking, the problems treated and the methodology used are so thoroughly impressed by the experience of the American participants, that, with reservations, of course, one can and must treat the commission's report as an American product.

The report[106] begins with an account of the awakening of ecumenical interest in the problem of institutionalism and a description of the commission's activities (pp. 1-5). The next three sections, the heart of the report, attempt to develop a theology of the institutional process in the Church:

I. A general sociological theory of institutional dynamics (pp. 5-7)
II. The sociological application of this theory to the ecumenical situation of the Church:
--the institutional character of the churches (pp. 7-10)
--the plurality of ecclesiastical types [discussion of various typologies of ecclesiastical organization and social psychology] (pp. 10-1)
--the role of institutionalizing factors in making, breaking or blocking church unity and union (pp. 11-3)
--the particular problems connected with the institutionalization of ecclesiastical leadership [authority--freedom problematic] pp. 13-5), and of ecclesiastical administration [bureaucracy problematic] (pp. 16-7).
III. The theological elaboration of a specific theory of institutional processes in the Church (pp. 17-22) in terms of
a. the interaction of divine and human factors in the Church's life,
b. the relation between community (koinonia) and institution,
c. the distinction between essential principles of Church order and the contingent forms of Church organization,
d. the relation between ecumenical discussion and ecumenical institutionalization.

On the basis of this theory, the next two sections of the report attempt to formulate an ecumenical strategy. In general (pp. 22-4), this strategy is presented as a rigorous application of a sociologically formulable "test of functional adequacy"[107] as criterion for coordinating apostolic continuity and apostolic flexibility, and thus of maintaining a coherent diversification of ecclesiastical institutions relative to the plurality of church needs. In particular (pp. 24-8), the report offers a list of factors which a sociological-theological analysis of typical union endeavors of the past shows to be important in carrying out church unions. A final section (pp. 28-9) calls attention to two series of questions which require further investigation before a more adequate solution to the problem of ecumenical institutionalization can be developed.

The decade during which the four F. & O. commissions were active saw the ripening of the American ecclesiological renaissance to full maturity. In the commission reports summarizing the researches of that period one finds the outline of an answer to the major problems which had emerged in the discussions prior to 1952. The very titles of the commissions serve as a catch-word summary of these topics. More significant perhaps than the specific answers is the maturing of a methodology of ecumenical ecclesiology capable of transcending the cultural limitations of any individual theological epoch. In this respect, the methodological reflections contained in the report constitute the greatest achievement of the period. In the work of

the last two groups we will consider, this methodology would be put
to critical test.

IX. The Consultation on Church Unity (COCU)

At the beginning of the sixties, the Church and the theology of
the Church enjoyed a peak of popularity and influence. The post-
war religious revival had raised church membership to unprecedented
heights; the seminaries were full of eager young men and women burning to give their lives to the work of Christ in the Church; theology
was in demand, in the parish as well as in the university. Years of
ecumenical conversation and cooperation on all levels, local congregation, denominational headquarters, seminary and university, had
dissolved traditional prejudices and leveled the trenches and fences
that had once been the Maginot line of denominationalism. In America, awakened at last from the torpid slumber of the Eisenhower era,
an optimistic reformism was in the air. The old pioneer spirit was
flexing its muscles again; the old American dream of building the
Kingdom of God was stirring men's hearts. The presidential campaign
of 1960 had brought John F. Kennedy to the fore as leader and symbol
of social and political reform. Under the leadership of Martin
Luther King, the Civil Rights Movement was stirring America's Christian conscience. In John XXII and his announced council, American
Catholics had found a new identity. It was only a matter of time
before the progressive, ecumenically oriented wing of American Protestantism would find its self-articulation.

On Dec. 4, 1960, Eugene Carson Blake, then Stated Clerk of the
United Presbyterian Church, mounted the San Francisco cathedral pul-
pit of Episcopal Bishop Pike to make his famous "Proposal toward the
Reunion of Christ's Church," a ringing call to the major Protestant
denominations of America to abandon their antiquated provincialism
and to come together on solid theological foundations in a united
church "both catholic and reformed."[108] Response was enthusiastic.
In May 1961, on the initiative of numerous presbyteries, the 173rd
General Assembly of the United Presbyterian Church passed a resolution "to invite the Protestant Episcopal Church to join with it in
an invitation to the Methodist Church and the United Church of Christ
to enter into the exploration of the establishment of a united
church."[109] In September of the same year the General Convention of

the Episcopal Church accepted the invitation, and on April 9-10,
1962 representatives of the four churches met in Washington, D.C.,
to begin talks.[110]   Thus was born "the Consultation on Church Union,"
COCU for short. The Washington meeting voted further to invite the
International Convention of Christian Churches (Disciples of Christ),
the Polish National Catholic Church, and the Evangelical United
Brethren Church, to enter into full participation by reason of their
links to the four originating members. In addition it extended an
invitation to all the Churches of North America to send observer-
consultants to the future meetings of the Consultation.[111]   Though
the Polish National Catholic Church declined the invitation to full
membership, the entrance of other denominations brought the number
of full participants to ten by 1967:

> The United Presbyterian Church in the U.S.A., 1962;
> The Protestant Episcopal Church, 1962;
> The Methodist Church, 1962;
> The United Church of Christ, 1962;
> The Christian Churches (Disciples of Christ), 1962
> The Evangelical United Brethren, 1962;
> The African Methodist Episcopal Church, 1965;
> The Presbyterian Church in the U.S., 1966;
> The African Methodist Episcopal Church, Zion, 1966;
> The Christian Methodist Episcopal Church, 1967.

As a mode of procedure, the executive committee of the Consultation set the pattern in 1961 by commissioning three committees of
theologians to explore the problems of (1) "Scripture, Tradition, and
the guardians of Tradition"; (2) "the analysis of the participating
communions"; and (3) "the worship and witness of the Church." The
work of these study commissions was presented at the next session
of the Consultation, at Oberlin, Ohio, March 19-20, 1963, where consensus statements were drafted and approved.[112]   In preparation for
the next general meeting, at Princeton, N. J., April 13-6, 1964, new
theological commissions were set up to deal with the problems of
(1) "one ministry"; (2) "one baptism"; and (3) "one table," as a
first step toward resolving the complex matter of Church order.[113]
The same procedure led to the production of the statements of the
fourth meeting at Lexington, Ky., April 5-8, 1965, on "the Ordained
Ministry in a United Church" and "Ordination in a Church Catholic,
Evangelical, and Reformed."[114]

The consensus achieved in these preliminary explorations was
encouraging. The Oberlin Consultation had seen the solution of the
ancient controversy between catholic and protestant attitudes toward

Scripture and tradition, thanks to the distinction between "Tradition" as "the whole life of the Church, ever guided and nourished by the Holy Spirit and expressed in its worship, witness, way of life, and order," on the one hand, and "the traditions--those individual expressions of the Tradition which more or less characterize particular churches and those customs of the churches which have arisen in various times and places," on the other. Whereas the Scriptures are "included in the Tradition," are "interpreted in the light of the Tradition," and are "the supreme guardian and expression of the Tradition"; the traditions "must ever be brought under the judgment of the Scriptures."[115] Princeton brought consensus on the nature and form of the ministry, thanks to the distinction between the three essential "orders of ministry"--(a) "the corporate ministry of the laity; (b) the ministry of qualified church members designated to perform particular functions in worship and discipline, and (c) the ministry of ordained ministers exercised for the well being of the whole Church"--and the three New Testament functions of the ordained ministry, namely diakonía, episcopé, and presbyteré, on which the historical offices of bishops, presbyters and deacons are founded.[116] With this committment to the episcopal office in the united church, the most important barrier to a union of the Anglican and Methodist episcopal tradition with the Presbyterian, Evangelical, Congregationalist and Campbellite anti-episcopal traditions had been passed. Less dramatic, though hardly less significant was the agreement on the baptism-confirmation issue and on the eucharist, e.g. resolution of issues like the role of the celebrant, the relation between presence and memorial, symbol and effect, sacrificial character.

Stimulated by the unexpectedly rapid progress in resolving these problems, the Lexington consultation took the bold step of establishing a committee to draw up a first tentative draft of a plan of union. After a year of intensive work, this draft was presented to the fifth general meeting of the Consultation, Dallas, Tex., May 2-5, 1966.[117]

The "Outline of a Possible Plan of Union" consisted of:
--a preamble stating the principles which guide the proposed union;
--a chapter on faith, dealing with the questions of membership, magisterium, the authority of Scripture, Tradition and confessions, the witness to faith in liturgy and mission;
--a chapter on worship, dealing with the nature, patterns and compo-

nents of the church's worship as well as the matter of a liturgical year;
--a chapter on sacraments: Baptism together with confirmation, and
the Lord's Supper;
--a chapter on ministry: the distinction between general and "representative" (=ordained) ministries, the nature of ordinations,
the offices of bishops, presbyters (=elders), and deacons;
--a chapter on church structure: local, district, regional and
national;
--a chapter on "stages and steps toward a united church" outlining
procedures and agenda for carrying on the process of unification.

At the Dallas meeting the first major crisis in the history of the
Consultation occurred. Though the assembly approved with some minor
amendments the preamble and first four chapters under the title
"Principles of Church Union"; it set aside the last two as not sufficiently thought out. To rethink the whole matter of church polity,
both permanent and provisional, the assembly established a new, much
enlarged Commission on Structure.[118] Furthermore, it supplemented
the "Principles" with an "Open Letter to the Churches," a kind of
ecclesiological confession, outlining in brief the nature of the
Church, her institutional unity, her mission, the gifts she receives
in Christ through the Spirit, the expression of these gifts in the
two sacraments and the manifold ministries, repentance for the sin of
division, resolution to obey God's command to put aside separation
and to accept the fact and cost of unity, finally, the attitudes
marking the COCU approach to unity.[119]

Instead of offering a new draft of the rejected chapters of the
original plan, the new Commission on Structure presented the sixth
plenary assembly, Cambridge, Mass., Aug. 1-4, 1967, with a document
similar to the consensus statements passed by the first assemblies.

The four-part report of the commission consisted of
1. A description of the work of the commission and an explanation of
the nature of its report,[120]
2. A statement of the basic presuppositions of all church structures,[121]
3. A set of proposed guidelines for structures of a future united
church,[122]
4. A list of open questions about church structure.[123]

The Cambridge assembly officially adopted an amended version of the
third part as "Guidelines for the Structure of the Church."[124] In
addition it passed a revised version of the "Stages and Steps"
paper[125] that had been rejected by the previous assembly.

The actions of the Cambridge assembly bring to a close the exploratory phase of the COCU endeavor: the theological groundwork had been laid; the next step would be to draw up the actual plan of union, liturgical books, etc. corresponding to the principles laid down.[126] More than that, however, the documents produced by the first five assemblies put the capstone on an ecclesiological edifice that thirty years of reflection and discussion had been building. In this sense the COCU consensus statements of 1966-7 symbolically bring to an end the epoch that began with the renaissance of ecumenical ecclesiology expressed in the American contribution to the Edinburgh Faith and Order Conference in 1937. It is well that this epoch should have found such a worthy close, for in fact the end of the classical American Protestant ecumenical theology of the Church was apparent to every sensitive observer. COCU would go on with its work: the eighth plenary assembly, St. Louis, May 9-13, 1970, gave its approval to the first draft of the final plan of union, which is now being discussed in the churches.[127] But the mood of the seventies is light-years away from the enthusiastic spirit that gave rise to the COCU ecclesiology, and already in 1967 the climatic shift was evident.[128] Between 1960 and 1967 events had occurred which threatened to render the whole COCU enterprise irrelevant and to undermine the ecclesiological consensus on which it was built.[129]

X. The North American Study Group on "Missionary Structures of the Congregation" (NAWG)

The optimistic reform movement of the early sixties had many a hard blow to take in its attempt to revivify American society and institutions. The murder of President Kennedy, later Martin Luther King, and Robert Kennedy, the split of the reform movement into liberal and radical factions, the rupture of the Roman-Catholic ghetto, the revolution in the third world churches, the rise of Black Power, the "Counter-Culture" of the youth, etc.--all of these opened up a Pandora's box of new ecclesial impulses, both positive and negative. The battle-hardened solidarity experienced in the demonstrations and riots; the fellowship of underground liturgies; the frustrations encountered at the hands of timid church bureaucrats and hostile, white middle-class congregations; were but a few of the factors working to create an entirely new ecclesial experience for many American theologians. Frustrated in their attempts to

thaw "God's frozen people,"[130] many began to ask themselves whether
traditional ecclesiology had anything to do with the real Church of
Jesus Christ. Is the Church really to be found under the neo-
gothic steeple of the suburban congregation and in the skyscraper
offices of the denominational bureaucrats, or is it rather to be
sought "where the action is"?[131] In the work of the last North
American commission this study deals with, the ecclesial and ecclesiological crisis of the mix-sixties found dramatic expression.

Following a suggestion of D. T. Niles, the New Delhi Assembly
of the WCC had commissioned a world-wide, long-range study of "the
Missionary Structures of the Congregation." The question Niles put
to the assembly was: "Is the present form of church life a major
hindrance to the work of evangelism?" To tackle this issue in the
American context, a group of theologians met in New York City in
June, 1962, constituting the North American Working Group under the
chairmanship of Jitsuo Morikawa.[132] About the same time similar
groups were organizing in Western Europe, The German Democratic
Republic, and South-east Asia. Originally conceived according to
the traditional pattern of WCC study commissions--academic, seminar-
like meetings of experts engaged in theoretical exchange--the American group went through an identity-crisis in 1963-4 that led to
the abandonment of this traditional model in favor of a radically
new, practice-oriented, team organization, which set out to test
experimentally by their own group engagement the thesis that the
Church is not something static definable in terms of concepts and
institutions pertaining to some sacral realm, but rather a dynamic
reality to be sought experimentally "in the world, especially at
the point where attempts are being made to respond to the agenda
of the world."[133] The Group's own account of their evolution
offers a classic example of the new mood.

> "...how should the study begin? There was a title: 'The Mis-
> sionary Structure of the Congregation'; and an initial ques-
> tion: 'Do present structures of the church stand in the way of
> the gospel?' But how do you get into it? Do you start at the
> theological end--with a study of 'church' and 'congregation'
> and 'mission'? Armed with an understanding of what our theo-
> logical starting-point must be when we foray into the world, do
> we then turn to the sociologists (and experimental new-formers)
> to discover how this 'given' mission can now be carved out in
> the social structures of contemporary society?
> To most of the group at the beginning that seemed a reason-
> able assumption, and an essential one. ...

So the early meetings centered on these word studies. But the result of these early meetings can perhaps be best termed 'creative frustration!' There was no lack of live argument; but a complete failure of movement. The conviction grew that somehow the problem was being misstated. Somehow our studies on 'church' and 'mission' were still imprisoned within the traditional formulations; so that even when we then tried to relate these formulations to contemporary situations, something out of the past still blocked the way. For example: we had large debates about 'the marks of the church'; and we had lively discussions about whether some of the new attempts that were being made to develop congregations for mission were producing forms that answered the test of these 'marks.' But the nagging question kept coming back: what if the very way these 'marks' are traditionally defined is itself a reflection of the past which the present missionary situation is calling us to revise?

Finally out of frustration, a decision was made--a decision which a minority (particularly the new forms people) had been pressing from the beginning. Why not start from the other side? Instead of starting from the church, and the problem of 'what is the true church?', why not start our investigation in the world, especially at the points where attempts are being made to respond to the agenda of the world? We might then find that some of our traditional formulations might need recasting for our time; and that real freedom for mission will come only when we break loose from assumptions that we have taken for granted.

At this point we were encouraged by the early papers coming from the Western European Working Group, for they too were beginning to face the same question, and their theoretical formulation of this under the slogan 'God-world-church' helped to encourage us to look for that different starting-point in the world.

The effect of this decision was that we began to listen to those in the Group who were involved in attempts to develop new forms of missionary response to different worldly situations. In particular our investigation turned to the civil rights movement, in which several of our members were deeply involved; and it was in no small measure do to what we began to discern in this case study, that the further decision was made to decentralize activities, and to investigate several such situations."[134]

The pivotal meeting was the one held at Seabury House, Greenwich, Conn., Feb. 4-6, 1964.[135] The reports of those active in the civil rights movement--describing their experience of the reality of the Church in the meetings and actions of the movement, whose "charismatic" leadership at that time came so often from the ranks of evangelistic negro preachers--made a deep impression on their listeners.[136] The result was that the group decided to postpone further theoretical work and to divide up into a series of project groups, who would continue the study by practically involving themselves in some cause. The choice of project was random. Rejecting

all "a priori criteria concerning the types of missionary presence
to be investigated," the task-forces chose their projects mostly on
the basis of existing commitments of their members, the circumstances of geographical location, and the desire for widest possible
freedom for emerging insights.[137] Nine task-forces eventually
emerged:[138]

1. Vermont: a mixed group of laymen and clergy concerned with public
   education and increasingly state politics;
2. New York: a group of denominational executives, which came to concentrate its efforts on "trying to expose the 'myths'
   that control the present organization of the churches,
   and to explore the adequacy of those myths in relation
   to the concept of mission which had emerged in the
   study";[139]
3. New York: a mixed group which after a year of search eventually
   involved itself in the Metropolitan Urban Service Training Facility, a new ecumenical program sponsored by the
   Methodist Church for training clergy and laity for mission in the metropolitan setting;
4. Boston: a highly diverse group composed of men and women, Catholic and Protestant, lay and clerical, student, under
   the chairmanship of Harvey Cox; its project was an
   experimental, action-oriented, theological training
   program;
5. Philadelphia: a group of ministers and professional people involved in an urban renewal organization called the
   Metropolitan Associates of Philadelphia, dedicated to
   developing new forms of Christian involvement in city
   life--in business, in government, in organizations, education, press, etc.;
6. Chicago: a group consisting of the indigenous leadership of a
   black neighborhood renewal organization together with the
   staff and trainees of the Urban Training Center, which
   worked hand in hand with the West Side Organization;
7. Nashville: a group of persons active in a variety of organizations involved in the civil rights movement, e.g. church-
   sponsored Commissions on Religion and Race, the Delta
   Ministry, the Southern Christian Leadership Conference,
   the Student Non-violent Coordinating Committee, the
   Committee of Southern Churchmen--groups with quite different attitudes, constituents, objectives and strategies;
8. Los Angeles: a mixed group of persons involved in a city planning
   project, the Los Angeles Goals Project;
9. San Francisco: a study group which involved itself in three projects:
   "Intersection," a coffee-house based forum for artists;
   "Gateway," a young adult initiative group to deal with
      their own problems of adjusting to urban society;
   and "Scientists and Engineers for Social Action," a
      group of professionals concerned about their public
      responsibilities as agents of the technological
      revolution.

The result of this reorganization was a realignment of participants in the study. A number of the theologians who had originally constituted the working group objected either in principle or
from personal motives to the new procedure and therefore dropped
out of active participation. Their places were taken by involved
ministers and laymen whom the local task-forces had attracted.[140]
In addition new task-forces sprang up modeled after those of the
study; though not officially members of the Working Group, their
experience contributed to the impressions gathered by the group.[141]
Unfortunately the North American Working Group was called upon to
report before sufficient time had elapsed to fully evaluate its new
experiment: whereas most of the task-forces had really only gotten
organized in 1964, the group's report had to be ready in time for
the August 1966 meeting of the WCC Department on Studies in Evangelism: Working Committee. To prepare it therefore, the Steering Committee of the North American Working Group together with the chairman of the task-forces formed an editorial committee composed of:

> Jitsuo Morikawa, Chairman
> Thomas Wieser, Secretary
> Arnold B. Come
> Harvey G. Cox
> Archie Hargraves
> Walter Harrelson
> Johannes C. Hoeckendiik
> William Hollister
> Gerald J. Jud
> Letty Russell
> George W. Webber
> Colin C. Williams.[142]

Under the circumstances, they could do no more than elaborate a preliminary survey of the task-forces' experiences and to offer a tentative outline of "some of the basic themes guiding the work of the
task forces, ... pregnant ideas that have emerged in the course of
a wide range of ecumenical study and discussion, ... themes [that]
might be used for 'divining rods' for God's action, clues to the way
in which God is moving in his work in redemption."[143]

The report of the North American Working Group consists of four
parts. The first and the last parts are primarily historical and
methodological: the one traces the history of the whole group and
explains the evolution of its methodology; the other gives a brief
sketch of each of the nine official task-forces. In contrast, the
two middle sections represent the theological heart of the report.
Sect. II "Discovering Missionary Structures"
      After a brief introduction (pp. 68-9), suggesting the relation-
ship between traditional discussions of the marks of the Church

and the Working Group's proposed "clues for identifying the
Church in mission," the report proceeds to discuss six distinct
themes, explaining the distinct clues they give rise to, and
illustrating the application of each clue with examples drawn
from experiences of the task-forces.

1. Theme: "God--World--Church"; clue: missionary structures are
   not sacred: "the structures which are appropriate for the
   church are shaped by the world in which it lives"[144]
   (pp. 69-71).
2. Theme: "History and Self-understanding"; clue: "the church
   is a part of what is happening; it is itself a happening.
   Its structures must constantly be in a process of 'de-
   structing and restructuring'"[145] (pp. 71-4).
3. Theme: "Participation in God's Mission"; clue: "structures
   which reflect the church's participation in God's mission
   will be ad hoc structures because they must be capable of
   change in the light of new situations which arise... The
   continuity of the church is based not on structures but on
   the continuity of God's mission into which men are
   called"[146] (pp. 75-7).
4. Theme: "Humanization"; clue: "Missionary structures are those
   which demonstrate that they are expendable in the interest
   of humanizing society, and which thereby celebrate the gift
   of humanity which God has offered in Christ"[147] (pp. 77-80).
5. Theme: "Laity -- the Reference Group for Mission"; clue:
   "structures which take seriously the ministry of the laity
   must allow for the opportunity of formation of all members
   of God's people"[148] (pp. 80-3).
6. Theme: "Pluriformity of Structures"; clue: "In a pluralistic
   world the structures of the church must be pluriform...
   Each situation calls for an appropriate structure of ministry, and as each situation changes, the structures should
   grow and change. It can be said that complementary and
   even contradictory structures might appropriately be present at the same time..."[149] (pp. 83-6).

Sect. III "Prospects of Renewal"

This section offers a sketch of the forms of church renewal and
of unity in diversity that fit the pattern of themes and clues
outlined in section II (pp. 87-91). From there it goes on to
reflect on "a new theological style" "in the perspective of mission": an ecclesiology open to the world, a theology involved
in action, and a reflection participating in history (pp. 91-4).

In the thinking of the North American Working Group, of which
Harvey Cox' Secular City (1964) offers an original expression,
ecclesiological reflection in America had come full circle. In the
Secular Gospel echo many a theme familiar from the anti-ecclesiology
of the old Social Gospel. Once more the Kingdom of God takes primacy over the Church of God; the Church is the company of those who
recognize and cooperate in God's bringing the Kingdom of God to
realization. Once more spontaneity takes primacy over institution;
none of the structures of the Church are sacred, unchangeable,
essential. Once more the Church's historicity is seen more as an

openness to the future than as a continuity with the past, and the
Church, as the company of those who recognize and follow the workings of God in the history of mankind, is clearly distinguished from
the particular, often reluctant institutions which have appropriated
the name church. Once more the empirical method gains primacy over
the historical and speculative; theology is conceived above all as
a testing of the spirits at work in the present, whereby, of course,
historical scholarship and speculative analysis clearly have a role
to play, albeit a secondary one.

At first sight, the similarities between the old anti-ecclesiology of the Social Gospel and the new anti-ecclesiastical ecclesiology of the Secular Gospel are so eye-catching that one is tempted
to overlook the important differences. The differences are there,
however. The thirty intervening years of ecclesiological renewal
have definitely left their mark on the thinking of the authors of
the North American Working Group's report. The primary concepts of
the Kingdom and People of God are not simply a reedition of the old
liberal ideas; they have been strongly influenced by the thinking
that had been going on in World Council circles in the preceding
decades, the specifically American aspects of which are the concern
of the present study. Likewise the conception of churchly institutions in the secular ecclesiology is intimately connected with the
WCC studies of institutionalism, in which Americans had played such
an important role. Even the apparently so radical methodology of
the secular ecclesiology has its roots in the methodological reflections of the various commissions we have reviewed. Important as
these differences are, however, the most important difference lies
in the fact that the new secular gospel--at least as articulated by
Cox and the North American Working Group--understands itself as an
ecclesiology, albeit a rather anti-ecclesiastical ecclesiology.

The year 1967 saw the publication of summary reports by both
the COCU and the North American Working Group, reports representing
the two tendencies characteristic of the contemporary situation in
ecclesiology the world over. With these reports an epoch comes to
an end. After 1967 it is really impossible to isolate an American
Protestant ecclesiology from the world-wide, ecumenical discussion
of the nature of the Church and her ministry. In the contemporary
debate the lines of division no longer correspond to the boundaries
of geography, culture and confession. The explosion in the field

of theological publication, the association and integration of theological faculties, the coordination and integration of ministry, the
unrestricted dialog between confessional theologies and secular ide-
ologies, are rapidly creating a situation in which even such profound mentality differences as between Catholic and Protestant, between American and European are rapidly losing their relevance, to
be replaced, unfortunately, by new divisions that at the moment seem
more impossible to bridge than the abyss that once separated Catholic and Protestant, European and American.

CHAPTER III

THE CHURCH OF FAITH AND THE CHURCH OF FACT

Outline

I. TOWARDS A DEFINITION OF THE CHURCH

Under the conditions of American church life, it was inevitable that the tension between ecclesiological theory and ecclesiastical reality should more sharply and more directly attract the theologian's attention than in the more orderly and integrated situation of the European churches. Moreover in America the ground for interest in this phenomenon had been prepared by the concern of liberal and social-gospel theology for questions of religious sociology. In the course of the American ecumenical discussions it very quickly became clear that the problem really had two quite distinct aspects, and that the chief task was to find a manner of approach which would prevent these two aspects from losing contact with one another.

The first aspect of the issue to emerge to distinct consciousness was the question of identifying and evaluating the empirical referent for ecclesiological theory: what social phenomena do we have in mind when we talk about the "Church" and its "unity"? What is the empirical, social structure to which such words refer? What are their sociological characteristics and how are these related to our normative theological definitions? At first sight, the answer to such questions seems evident; the ecumenical encounter in America, however, revealed that it was only "evident" within the context of the particular dogmatic tradition to which the theologian adheres. As soon as representatives of different traditions passed beyond the point simply of comparing positions and began earnestly to seek in common for new, ecumenical answers to the old controversial questions, it became painfully obvious that the same words had quite different sociological associations for the participants. Baptists and Eastern Orthodox might achieve consensus on a common conceptual definition of the Church, but as soon as they proceeded to more detailed applications it became clear that they had two entirely different existential realities in mind. The opposite case also appeared: stubborn verbal disagreements persisted on issues of order and polity, for example episcopacy, where in fact sociological analysis revealed little or no significant variation in ecclesiastical practice.

The newly acquired sensitivity to the sociological referent of ecclesiological theory had the effect of sensitizing the American theologian to the problematical character of the traditional normative theological definitions of ecclesial phenomena. How can one define the Church and its constituent structures in theological categories which really illuminate the empirical reality instead of obscuring it in a cloud of mystical incense? Of what value are such biblical images as "People of God," "Body of Christ," "Communion of the Spirit," for this purpose. Can theological speculation about salvation history or christology shed light on the inner dynamic of the Church's life? Such questions represent the other aspect of the problem as it took form in the American discussions.

At this point, however, the full depth of the matter became apparent. That which makes the task of defining the Church theologically so difficult is the antithesis between the ideal Church of faith and the factual Church of history--on the one side, a community of free, sanctified brothers and sisters linked to one another in bonds of love expressed in charismatic service; on the other side, an organization of rival power-groups, divided by race, socio-economic status and religious dogmatism, chafing under authoritarian and bureaucratic structures of command. In the face of the all too evident "realism" of this factual Church, what reality can possibly be attributed to the Church of faith? What possible connection can exist between two such antithetic realities?

To these three problem complexes the American commissions and study groups had to address themselves in the course of their discussions. Their contributions vary, naturally, according to the composition, objectives and approach of the group. For this reason there is little point in attempting to look for a continuous development proceeding from one commission to the next. The contributions are too disparate; yet the theme is always there, appearing now in one context, again in another, now illuminated from one side, again from another. Each commission sought a solution to the problem in terms of its own particular interests and tendencies. Each had to recognize in the end that its solution was imperfect, representing only a first step, not ultimate achievement. Yet for all this diversity and tentative groping in different directions, certain common trends are clear. These common trends and tendencies constitute the material of this chapter.

II. THE EMPIRICAL REFERENCE OF THE IDEA OF THE CHURCH

A. Multivalent Usage of the Term "Church"

Paul Scherer in his contribution to the Interseminary Symposium put his finger on one of the principal obstacles to developing a realistic theology of the Church.

> "What then is the true nature of the Church? So little have we understood it, that many of us find ourselves unable to define the word itself with any accuracy. In popular usage it may mean no more than an edifice or the group that worships there. It may mean, reaching out, the denomination to which that group adheres, or the sum total of all such groups in the community or in the world. When the sociologist thinks of it, he tries to think of it objectively, in empirical terms, He applies to it norms that often enough have very little to do with religion and less with Christianity. He attempts to differentiate it from other corporate bodies on the basis of certain observable criteria which turn out to be altogether too arbitrary and not one of them decisive. Nor is the theologian in a very much happier case. On Monday, Tuesday, and Wednesday he may well lose both himself and the object of his search in some Platonic realm of invisible ideas, having hardly any contact at all with reality, their locus somewhere in heaven above, nothing but their shadow on earth beneath. On Thursday, Friday and Saturday he is likely to become involved in the complexities of an institution, with its panoply of priest and sacrament, which he forthwith makes the keeper of the keys or absolutizes as the Kingdom of God. Over here the Church is the Body of Christ, Over there is the company of the called. One wishes to recognize it by its ethics. Where there is race prejudice, it has been suggested, there is no Church. Where the Word of God is rightly preached, insisted the Reformers, and the Sacraments are rightly administered, there it is! Perhaps the best that ever can be done is to do as they did: to answer the question by begging it...because the question itself is almost never raised in any form that makes anything else possible. When we ask it we are usually engaged in deciding who 'belongs' and who doesn't: who is really a Christian, and who isn't; with whom we may wholeheartedly cooperate and from how many others we must keep ourselves separate. Leaving aside our consciousness of the family itself, we devote our efforts to tracing out the family tree. We are like people strolling in the zoo. We look at the lion and describe it; but there is no lion-ness (!) in the description."[1]

Here jumbled all together are the various meanings of the word "Church" in different contexts: church edifice, congregation, denomination, the church-system, be it local or world-wide, a platonic idea, a priestly institution, the "Body of Christ," the "company of the Called," etc. How are they all related to one another?

This is precisely the question that the American Theological Committee asked at the opening of its report. Attempting to classify the various meanings that kept recurring in their own discussions,

the Committee distinguished six usages which pointed to six distinct
social realities with quite different characteristics and boundaries:

> "1. The Church is the people of God in all ages who have been
>   called by him into his fellowship; this includes those called
>   under the Old as well as the New Covenant.
> 2. It is the congregation of believers in Christ in a local com-
>   munity; sometimes they are enrolled on the basis of their
>   willingness to receive his benefits. Sometimes it includes
>   only those who have manifested real devotion to him. Akin
>   to this usage is the assembly of these members for worship
>   and the building in which they meet.
> 3. It is an organized communion represented in a group of local
>   parishes, which has a common doctrine and polity; some of
>   these groupings follow strictly national or territorial
>   lines; others are bodies which are international in charac-
>   ter.
> 4. It is the total of such organizations of local, visible com-
>   munities regarded as the Church Militant.
> 5. Since these bodies comprise both members who are worthy and
>   others who give little evidence of either faith or love,
>   many would distinguish within and beyond the entire body of
>   organized Christianity those who are the true disciples. To
>   these, the invisible Church known only to God, they would
>   restrict such descriptions as 'the body of Christ.'
> 6. Finally there is the Church Triumphant, the faithful in all
>   ages who have passed to the eternal world and have entered
>   into the communion of saints."

At first sight such a list seems only to be needlessly repeat-
ing the obvious. The commission's experience, however, showed that
it is precisely the over-familiarity with these different usages that
induces one to slip unconsciously from one to the other in the course
of ecclesiological reflection. Moreover in the different denominational traditions, more weight is attached to some of these meanings
than to others, and some traditions go so far as to deny the theological validity of this or that meaning. Such variations are clearly evident in the presentations of the denominational positions in
the ATC report on the Nature of the Church.

A comparison of these "Denominational Statements" one with
another reveals four distinct types of ecclesiological approach to
the question of the empirical referent. (It must be recalled that
in drafting these statements, the authors were attempting to speak
for their traditions rather than to present their own personal views.)
1. A classical position of evangelical Lutheranism was articulated by George Richards in presenting the position of the Evangelical and Reformed Church. This view would simply deny theological
significance to the Church's organizational structures:

> "The Church is the Body of Christ, the fellowship of the re-
> deemed, created by the eternal Word of God made man in Christ
> and is always vitalized and guarded by the Holy Spirit. It is

not primarily an organization or an institution but an organism and a fellowship, a new mode of God's presence and a new
form of man's life in history. In its visible form it consists
of all those, together with their children, whom God calls out
of the whole human race, through the Word Jesus Christ, into
fellowship with himself and through him with one another, and
who respond by repentance and faith to the divine call, working
in faith, laboring in love with the patience of hope for the
eternal purpose of God revealed in Christ."
Organization is "adiaphoron, not a matter of indifference but of
preference"; the criteria of choice are "pragmatic rather than dogmatic." Nothing stands in the way of different forms existing side
by side with each other even in the same locality. Further examples of this type of ecclesiology can be found in Wahlstrom's presentation of the teaching of the Lutheran Church and Horton's exposition of the Congregationalist attitude.

2. Far more radical is the Baptist position in Carver's presentation. According to him, Baptists admit only three legitimate
usages of the term "Church":
"(1) The whole number of spiritual, regenerate believers, constituting 'the Body of Christ' in this world, expounded particularly in Ephesians. The Church, for Baptists, is not and
cannot be ecclesiastically organized; and it has no local seat
nor any administrative human head or headship. (2) the organized church, the functioning body of Christian believers, which
should always be limited to a community in which convenient as-
sembling and functioning are possible. It is a democratic body
under the recognize authority and headship of its Lord and
Savior. (3) the abstract, generic use of the term, as the
church, the school, the court. etc."
In this view the application of the term "church" to a particular
denomination, e.g. the expression "the Baptist Church" or "the Southern Baptist Church," or to organized Christianity as a whole would
appear "misleading and dangerous" for a true understanding of the
faith. Useful as supra-congregational associations and councils
may be, they have no theological significance; they are mere voluntary associations of individuals and congregations for fellowship
and cooperation, whose character is entirely prudential and practical. Significantly, perhaps, Carver passes over the more transcendental meanings of "Church," e.g. as People of God throughout the
ages or the Church Triumphant, are in this context, though later in
the context of a discussion of the "fellowship of saints" he writes:
"the Church is thus 'a fellowship of saints to which only saints
are admitted,' but this admission is exclusively the function
of the Holy Spirit. It includes all who have had this experience, without any reference to the particular 'communion' with
which they are identified. It does not strictly and actually
include 'all who name Christ's name,' for some of these may be
mistaken about their experience and some may have inadequate
experiences or even impure motives in claiming that name. In
a general way, most Baptists would agree that this Church includes the saints in heaven, which would mean also the saints--
by no means all the people--of the Old Covenant."
In effect, all the non-institutional, supra-congregational references merge here into one.

3. The presentations of Davidson and Barclay representing the Canadian Presbyterian tradition present yet another attitude toward the various meanings of the term "Church." They have no difficulty in according theological recognition to both the congregations and the communions:

"the particular church is the local representative of the Church Catholic, and through participation in the redemption of Christ mystically comprehends the whole, of which it is the local manifestation and expression. The historic groups known as 'churches' are all called to share in the life of the whole Church, of all ages and all lands, entering freely into the full heritage of thought worship and discipline and living together in mutual confidence."[11]

The position of the Anglican tradition in Lewis' presentation is essentially the same,[12] as also, it would seem, Loetscher's presentation of the American Presbyterian position[13] and Rall's presentation of the Methodist teaching.[14]

4. Yet another tack is that taken by Garrison in his presentation of the Disciples' teaching. The separate communions are "genuine though erring and fragmented parts of the one Church," the unity of which the Disciples see as lying essentially in "a unity of spirit and purpose, of devotion to a common Master, of voluntary cooperation in carrying out his work, and of free fellowship among all his disciples."[15] Slabaugh's presentation of the Brethren conception[16] and Cadbury's exposition of Quaker thinking would seem to come very close to this view in practice. Both however indicate that the entire way of posing the question is quite foreign to their way of thinking. Cadbury observes of the Friends:

"If they apply borrowed ecclesiological phrases to their own way, Friends tend to spiritualize or universalize them. ... They tend to define as de facto what others would treat as de regula. The Church and its members and its characteristics are to be described from experience, not from a doctrine or constitution."[17]

Reading such statements, one can hardly avoid the impression that the various traditions despite superficial similarities really are speaking quite different languages and moving in quite different worlds of conception and experience. No wonder that the participants in the American Theological Committee were unable to achieve full agreement. Yet in pointing out some of the semantic difficulties involved, they had made a valuable step forward.

B. Diverse Realizations of the Phenomenon "Church"

In the course of the subsequent discussions, the catalog of social referents of the term "church" was completed and clarified, though no subsequent report presents the sort of synoptic list that we meet in the ATC report. Nevertheless it is easy to draw up such a list, using the former as a guide. Terminology, of course, remains a problem; the expressions proposed by the ATC were not consistently followed by subsequent commissions, and in many cases the later commissions had little reason to reflect explicitly on the semantic problem because, in the particular context of discussion,

the prospect of confusion was minimal. In the last analysis, however, it is not the names but the reality that counts. However
variously one might call the different social entities here distinguished, the important thing is to recognize that distinct social
entities are involved, and that all of them are expressions of the
phenomenon "church." Furthermore it is important to note that the
social realities distinguished here are not all of the same order:
parish/congregation and organized communion/denomination are characterized principally by geographical and organizational criteria--
factors which play no role at all in entities like the invisible-
church-of-the-true-disciples or the communion-of-saints, where moral
and soteriological factors predominate, and so forth. It is possible
to recognize a certain ascending scale of numerical extension, but
the point must not be stressed. A denominational assembly may bring
together more believers than are members of a single parish/congre-
gation, and the number of the true believers utterly escapes human
calculation altogether. Furthermore, what is involved here is not so
much the distinction of individual ecclesial entities as of typical
forms of ecclesial existence, some of which admit of further differentiation. The congregation, for instance can be constituted on the
basis of several different principles, e.g. the territorial, the
voluntaristic, the occupational, etc.; and the organized communion
may be a horizontal association of equals or a pyramidal structure of
district, national, and international member churches subordinated to
one another in an ascending or descending order of competence and
command. So much however for preliminaries.

1. The most evident phenomenological manifestation of the Church
is the c h u r c h   m e e t i n g , the principal form of which is
the liturgical assembly. Worship, as the TCWNA points out, "is the
celebration of this new being in Christ by his body, the Church, ...
the corporate attempt to Christians to remember and embody the shape
of God's deed in order to rehearse and to strengthen the life of the
individual believer."[18] For this reason, the liturgical assembly is
a singularly pregnant expression of the Church's reality. It is not,
however, the only one. Indeed the same report immediately calls attention to the fact that cultus is only one form of the Church's
life; mission and ethical service are equally important manifestations of the life of the Church; indeed, they are themselves forms
of worship.[19] This means that not only the preaching rally of an

evangelistic crusade, but also such apparently mundane meetings as
a conference of experts involved in theological reflection,[20] or a
session of the board of trustees to discuss a church financial campaign,[21] or even the Monday night planning meetings of the American
Negro Civil Rights Movement of the early sixties,[22] must be reckoned
as manifestations of the reality of the Church. Not the outward
form of the assembly, but the recognition of, participation in, and
celebration of God's mission in the world is the mark of the true
presence of the Church.[23] In this respect the liturgical assembly
is no less ambiguous than the mundane forms of the Church. Also in
the liturgical assembly, the World can be present both in its neutral
sense of mankind awaiting salvation--one need only think of the un-
baptized catachumen or proselyte--and in its pejorative sense of mankind rejecting salvation--one need only think of the racially exclusive congregation worshiping a projection of its own unreconciled
particularism.

Here, more than anywhere else, the "event" character of the
Church becomes evident, as well as the fact that "event is never
without form," however flexible this form may be.[24] Here above all
the statement of the NAWG report holds: "The church is a happening
'on the road' from one event to the next. It is in history--a pil-
grim people, following the God of history and trusting his promise
to open up the future. Structures which evince clues from the historical nature of the church will be flexible and not tie the church
down to one particular situation, one moment or era in the history of
God with the world. In other words, the church must be where the
action is and by being there, not merely as a spectator but as a
participant, it will help to expose what is really going on: God
being at work in judgment and promise."[25]

2. The event of the church meeting, however, does not stand
alone. It is supported by, at the same time that it constitutes and
expresses, more enduring forms of fellowship, of which the most evident is the traditional p a r i s h   o r   c o n g r e g a t i o n ,
understood as a (generally) residentially based community of Christians small enough and sufficiently circumscribed territorially to
assemble conveniently. Characteristic of the parish/congregation is
that it undertakes to fulfill all the various functions of the
Church, i.e. to exercise a comprehensive program of worship, mission,
education, service, and fellowship.[26] The traditional authority and

organizational visibility of the congregational structure has, however, all too often blinded the theologian to the ecclesiological
relevance of other less comprehensive, more specialized communities
in the Church, consisting of "ordained ministers, lay people, or
both, separated out of the parish-congregation as specialized ministries, missions or services to the world or the Church."[27] For
these, the NAWG coined the phrase "task group."[28]

3. The recognition of the ecclesial significance of such
t a s k   g r o u p s   represents an important advance for Protestant thinking on the Church. For although such groups have always
existed in one form or another in the Protestant churches, their theologians have been reluctant to accord them ecclesial status. This
reluctance is understandable as a reaction against the dissolution
of the congregational structure in medieval Catholicism as a result
of the isolation of a mobile clerical caste from the local lay congregation and the breakup of the latter as a result of the multiplication of religious orders, confraternities and chantries. Not infrequently, however, the Protestant reaction went so far as to for-
bid the ordination of ministers engaged in special ministries or to
exclude the celebration of the Lord's Supper where the congregational
structure had not yet been established. The issue became acute as a
result of the multiplication of non-congregational experimental ministries particularly in the inner-city during the fifties and early
sixties, and found theological expression in the report of the MSC
study.[29] The NAWG report distinguished four typical forms of such
groups: (a) "family-type structure"--the house-church for example,
which gathers neighbors in an apartment complex or a block of houses
in a more intimate experience of worship and fellowship; (b) "perma-
nent-availability structure"--for example a non-parochial cathedral
or a community service center catering to individuals or families
and groups otherwise unrelated to each other; (c) "permanent community structure"--religious communities like Taizé, for example, or
study centers like the evangelical academies, in which emphasis is
placed not only on the particular pastoral service rendered but also
on the communal life-style of the participants; and finally (d)
"task-force structures"--such as various civil-rights and other reform groups concerned with the realization of specific goals within
existing organizations and communities, or teams catering to mar-
ginal groups within the community.[30]

4. Another manifestation of the Church is represented by the regional, national and international superstructure of the o r - g a n i z e d   c o m m u n i o n   or   d e n o m i n a t i o n .[31] As the CCULW noted, what characterizes this manifestation of the Church is not so much the degree of organizational integration-- this being in many communions minimal--but rather the sense of belonging to a single Church over against other churches and the ability to function as a living whole.[32] The investigation of the organizational aspects of this form of the Church's concretization fell particularly within the scope of the COCU, for one of COCU's principal tasts was to work out an appropriate organizational super-structure for the fellowship of congregations and task groups in an organic communion.[33]

5. Related to but by no means identical with the preceding is what Niebuhr's Purpose of the Church report aptly described as the " c h u r c h - s y s t e m "   by analogy to the gasoline service-station system in the United States, in which a group of distinct corporations in competition with each other nevertheless cooperate to provide a network of service-stations supplying essentially the same product under different brand-names and with different styles of packaging and service to satisfy the needs and preferences to the town, region or nation. So also the totality of Christian organizations, be they congregational, denominational or interdenominational provides a similar network for satisfying the needs of Christians in a particular community, region, nation or in the world as a whole.[34] The church-system may find organizational and symbolic expression in church federation and councils, in interdenominational agencies and comity or community-church arrangements,[35] but this is not essential. Even when the rival denominations or congregations take no official notice of each other and engage in no planned cooperation, the very fact that they exist alongside each other offering similar services establishes a relationship between them which a realistic, empirical ecclesiology must take account of.

6. On quite another plane, and yet hardly less "visible" provided one does not restrict the meaning of the term "visible" to legal titles and building complexes is the historical community P e o p l e   o f   G o d   throughout the ages.[36] How this community is experienced depends of course on the ecclesiological views

of its members. In some traditions the institutional continuity of
the Church plays a central role in the experience, in others it is
peripheral or totally ignored. Likewise variable are the attitudes
towards the inclusion or exclusion of the people of the Old Covenant[37] and non-christians in good faith. Thus the outer fringes of
this community lack clear definition: some would more or less tend
to confine it to the Church of the New Covenant or to the Churches
of both the Old and New Covenants, without of course excluding other
men from the realm of God's salvation; others, in contrast, would
tend to extend the People of God to include the whole world inasmuch
as it is the object of God's saving action--in this latter case it
becomes necessary to distinguish the Church, as that segment of
God's people which consciously recognizes and responds to God's
saving action in Christ, from those other segments of human society
in which this action is equally at work but remains anonymous.[38]
In any case what is common to all these conceptions despite their
variations on the boundary-issue is the experience of belonging to
a community in which God is at work, overcoming the divisions which
are the product of socio-cultural dispersion, ignorance, sin and
death.

7. Both the i n v i s i b l e C h u r c h o f t h e
t r u e d i s c i p l e s and the communion of saints can be
viewed as eschatologically qualified versions of the People of God.
The first notion tends to emphasize the eschatological division
between true and false brethren as applied to the present living
members of the Church and finds its principal field of application
in situations in which the organized fellowship is threatened by
schismatical division or by corruption of faith and morals, particularly when this manifests itself in the Church leadership. Under
such circumstances the hope of belonging to the company of the true
disciples is a source of comfort and strength for the oppressed and
afflicted and may indeed be the principal way in which they experience the fellowship of God's people.

8. The C o m m u n i o n o f S a i n t s , by contrast,
tends rather to emphasize the eschatological triumph over death by
reason of which the members of the earthly Church are united not
only in historical continuity but also in real fellowship in the
present with the saints in heaven. Naturally the manner in which
this fellowship is perceived and expressed varies with the prevail-

ing views of salvific mediation and of the last things. In some
confessional traditions this experience is absolutely central, whereas in others it is quite peripheral and tends to merge with the more
generic experience associated with the notion of the People of God
in history.[39]

C. The Social Reality of the Churches

1. A Morphology of Community Consciousness in the Church

The investigation of the various forms of community designated
by the term "Church" brought to light the fact that ecclesial community can be experienced in a variety of ways. From this point of
view, even those communities which seem purely transcendental may
be said to have an empirical aspect. Not only does the believer lay
claim to a perceptual experience of them, but this experience and
the belief on which it is based profoundly modifies his behavior.
The communion of saints, for instance, is an empirical community inasmuch as believing Christians claim here and now to experience it
in faith.[40] By the same token, what ultimately constitutes and
determines the empirical character of ecclesiastical organizations
like the congregation or the denomination is not the institutional
structure but rather the way in which the members perceive the community which these structures articulate. Even the most thoroughly
institutionalized church is more than the sum of its buildings, assemblies, offices, officials and symbols.[41]

In view of the continual temptation of both high and low church
ecclesiologies to confuse "church" and "ecclesiastical organization"
with each other, the American emphasis on the crucial role played by
community consciousness precisely in relation to the ecclesiastical
institution represents an important breakthrough. As soon as one
realizes that ecclesiastical institutions have no other reality than
that accorded them in the consciousness of the community, (i.e.
whatever metaphysical reality they may have, this does not exist in
separation from the human and therefore sociological expression),
the whole issue of community versus institution appears in an entirely new light.

The achievement of this insight came quite early in the American discussions. One of the first problems to attract the attention
of the CULW Commission was the semantic problem associated with
terms like "Christian unity," "church union," "corporate reunion,"

"organic unity," etc. In an effort to clarify the issue the commission drew up a catalogue of the different types of unity manifested by existing churches and ecumenical fellowships or projected
in union proposals. The attempt to distinguish these forms one from
another revealed startling anomalies. In some cases, church federations, for example, there was often a much higher level of institutional unity than in the participating denominations or communions. Yet the latter were perceived by their members as ecclesial
unities whereas the former were not. Thus it became obvious that
the primary constituent of ecclesial unity was not the degree of
organizational integration but rather the way in which the members
experienced community with one another. What began as an exercise
in semantic clarification resulted, therefore, in the commission's
developing a morphology of ecclesial consciousness, which sheds
further light on the various forms of community identified in the
preceding section.

(1) Christian Unity.
    The first form of unity described by the CULW Commission is not
so much a unity of churches as of individual Christians, hence the
name "c h r i s t i a n   u n i t y ."[42] This least institutionalized form of fellowship consists in "a broad community of thought
and feeling and ethical ideals, common to professing Christians
throughout the world, on the basis of which individuals coming out
of widely separated churches can have fellowship with one another..." It is a "unity of experience," a "community of inner life"
based on common participation in the experience of communion with
God in faith, supported by the use of the same Scripture and similar
devotional forms, and expressed in visible acts of common prayer and
common action.[43] As insubstantial as this sort of unity might appear at first glance, it would be inadequate to describe it as purely inward, spiritual, or invisible. Even those who claim that this
is the only legitimate form of supra-congregational or supra-denom-
inational unity would insist that it find outward, visible expression in common prayer and common action.[44] The distinguishing feature of this type of unity, therefore, is not its lack of institutional visibility but rather the fact that it is primarily a union
of individuals precisely in their individuality. From their ecclesiastical allegiance i.e. from their "church-membership" it ab-
stracts completely.

(2) Church Unity.
    Where this abstraction is no longer made, where the church
organization itself or at least individuals in their capacity as
church members are involved in the union, there, in the terminology
of the Commission, one has to do with " c h u r c h   u n i t y ."
Here too, the individual as well as the organization is involved--
it is important to stress this. For the distinction of the different grades of church unity the juridical organization is far less
important than the feeling of belonging which binds the members one

to another and is the presupposition for the harmonious functioning of the organization.[45]

(2a) Unity of Mutual Recognition.

Essential for church unity would seem to be institutional likeness of one sort or another.[46] Such likeness may be found in a variety of contexts: in faith, for instance, as expressed in the sharing of a common creed or belief in Scripture as the sufficient norm of faith.[47] Or it can manifest itself in the sharing of a common worship tradition[48] and similarity of sacramental celebration;[49] or again in similarity of ministerial order or ecclesiastical polity.[50] Nevertheless likeness alone is only the presupposition, not the sufficient condition of church unity. Unity begins only when the likeness has been consciously appropriated. The simplest form of such appropriation is that of m u t u a l   r e c o g n i - t i o n .   Such recognition may take a variety of forms. It may be complete or partial, formal or informal.[51] It may find expression in willing transfers of membership, in exchange of ministers and ministrations or in sacramental intercommunion.[52] Whatever form it may take however, in one sense it remains similar to simple christian unity, that is, that although mutual recognition is accorded to the churches as such, the actual exchange between the thus united communities remains confined to individuals who come out, so to speak, from the community to which they belong.[53] Thus it does not necessarily follow that the communities act together.

(2b) Unity of Cooperative Action.

By no means coextensive with and yet intimately related to the unity of mutual recognition is the u n i t y   o f   c o o p e r - a t i v e   a c t i o n . Obviously cooperative action in purely humanistic projects can exist in situations in which no form of christian or church unity are involved, as for instance in cooperation with secular humanists, Buddhists or Mohammedans. Only to the extent that mutual recognition of likeness in the areas of faith, worship, sacraments, ministry and polity serves as the foundation for cooperation in specifically christian enterprises such as evangelization or ministry is it meangful to speak of a form of church unity.[54] Where cooperative action is involved a certain organization is usually also present to coordinate it. Typical organizational expressions of the unity of cooperative action are the interdenominational boards and agencies set up to oversee the completion of specific tasks such as the publication of religious education materials, or the support of the foreign missions, etc.[55] Church federations and councils represent a method of organizing across-the-board cooperation between denominations.[56] A rather different way of institutionalizing cooperation is exemplified by comity and community church arrangements, by which distinct churches agree to a division or pooling of labor in a particular pastoral situation.[57]

(2c) Corporate Unity.

The most intimate of all forms of church unity is c o r p o - r a t e   u n i t y . Whereas the unity of mutual recognition and the unity of cooperative action presuppose the existence of separate churches with separate institutions, separate internal operations and separate self-consciousnesses, corporate unity consists essentially in a conviction of belonging together, a "consciousness of kind," in the words of the Commission, based on the perception of a common history and a common destiny. Corporate unity "rests

upon a general assent of the parts to the fact that they belong together and are making history together. It is bound up with common memories of a past that is particularly their past and with common hopes of a future which is particularly their future."[58]   That
corporate unity is compatible with the widest variety of organizational cohesion or lack thereof is evident from the examples the
commission offers of such unity. How different is the organizational expression of the unity existing between congregations and
territorial units in such diverse denominations as the Church of
England, the United Lutheran Church in America, or the Northern
Baptist Churches U.S.A., to say nothing of the corporate unity represented by such realities as the Anglican Communion, the Orthodox
Churches or World-Lutheranism, Presbyterian and Reformed, or Congregationalist fellowships.[59]   The same examples show that although
corporate bodies generally manifest a "high degree of likeness in
standards of faith, general type of worship, sacramental usage,
forms of ministry and polity," nevertheless corporate unity is compatible with a considerable diversity in these matters without en-
dangering mutual recognition. Similarly there is normally a high
degree of cooperative action; nevertheless competitive relationships
between individual congregations or groups in the corporate body are
not uncommon.

(2d) Governmental Unity.

In most cases corporate ecclesiastical bodies articulate their
unity in recognized agencies of common action as well as in organs
for shaping and executing the policies of the body as a whole. Such
common institutions serve not only as instruments of corporate life
but in addition have strong symbolic value as expressions of group
unity.[60]   Where such organizational structures are present in the
corporate body, the commission report would acknowledge a distinct
form of church unity, namely that of g o v e r n m e n t a l
u n i t y .[61]   That this form is not to be confused with corporate
unity becomes evident as soon as one considers groups like the Congregational Union of England and Wales or the Congregational Church
in the United States. Juridically there are here no central organs
with power to compel the individual parts to behave as members of
the whole: on paper there is little that would distinguish them
from the Church federations and councils.[62]   Yet in fact the difference in self-consciousness and actual functioning is enormous. In
effect, the parts of such churches are held together by a complex
network of prevailing customs, traditions, attitudes and assumptions to which the apparently autonomous parts instinctively respond.
Such factors are also, of course, to be found in governmental unities, and are in large measure responsible for the allaying of the
tensions, which would otherwise destroy a unity held together by
authority alone. In the Anglican and Orthodox Communions, for instance, it is principally by means of the prestige attached to their
symbolic and instrumental functions that the central organs exercise their influence over the legally more or less autonomous regional churches.[63]

The principal contribution of the CULW Commission's attempt to
describe the various forms of ecclesial unity was to call attention
to the fact that in the last analysis it is not so much the juridical as the cognitive structure which is constitutive for the social

reality designated by the term "church" in all of its different
meanings. The distinguishing mark of a "church" therefore is not
some normatively established level of institutional likeness as contrasted with diversity, nor is it the substitution of cooperation
for competition; institutional diversity and inner-group rivalries
are indeed very often to be found within those groups which perceive
themselves as constituting a single "church." Even less decisive
is the degree of organizational integration; a "church" may have
little or no governmental unity and yet there can be no question of
its ability to think and act as a unified whole. What is ultimately
constitutive is the consciousness shared by all the members, the
sense of belonging together, which enables them to behave as a body,
to function as a living whole and maintain recognizable identity in
space and time, whatever may be the instruments and symbols of this
consciousness.[64]

Once one grasps this point, it becomes clear in what sense even
such apparently invisible, transcendent fellowships as the communion
of saints or the body of true disciples must be regarded as empirical realities. Both the CULW report on The Communion of Saints[65]
and the CEDG paper on The Ethical Reality and Function of the Church
stress this point. The latter describes the invisible Church as "a
form of association that points beyond itself to a God as the object
of its worship and its commitment,"[66] the basis of which is "love
(agape) manifesting the presence of the Holy Spirit."[67] As such it
is normally a dimension of the organized Christian fellowship, from
which it is only virtually distinguishable. Under certain circumstances however it manifests itself distinctly over against the dis-
turbed visible fellowship. Such is the case, for instance, when
"under persecution or tyranny the true church may be unable to maintain outward and visible form, and may be driven temporarily into
invisibility. In this case the church's invisibility is an abnormal
and undesirable state in which it is preserved and awaits deliver-
ance into visible and ordered life."[68] In such circumstances, the
"invisible Church" manifests itself in the fashion of what the
Meanings of Unity report described as "Christian Unity."

2. Community Consciousness and its Institutional Articulation

The role of experiential perception as an ontological consti-
tuant of the various forms of church fellowship is also stressed.

in the papers and reports of the other commissions. Paul Scherer,[69]
for instance, describes the Church as "a unique fellowship of grace
called into being by a divine act and resting on the foundation of
God's revelation in Christ." This fellowship manifests itself to
the believer in the form of an awareness of "a calling and a deed,
of a bond and a Presence and a redeeming power, which here as nowhere else, comes alive with meaning." This awareness transforms
the believer's perception of the world surrounding him. Faith makes
that world, its joys and sorrows, successes and failures appear as
the workshop of God, the place of manifestation for his endless
mercies and unsearchable judgments. The individual is no longer
simply the agent and patient of an irresponsible destiny; instead
the believers perceive themselves collectively as "co-workers with
that sovereignty which shapes" the events of this world, in short,
as a "colony of heaven." So Scherer.

H. Richard Niebuhr makes a similar point in the report of the
Theological Education Survey. Niebuhr describes the Church as "the
subject that comprehends its Object; that thinks the Other; worships
and depends on It; imitates It perhaps, sometimes reflects It; but
is always distinct from its Object."[70] Sensation, thought, appreciation, worship, are the modes in which the fellowship becomes
reality for the believer.[71] That is to say, in the last analysis
the Church even in such highly "visible" forms as the worshipping
assembly, the congregation or the denomination constitute realities
of faith. As Calhoun's presentation of the TCCCNA's work at the
Oberlin Conference points out, the perception which is involved
here is more than mere intellectual assent, more even than an act of
trust, it is an experience which involves "the very roots of the
believer's existence from which acts of thought and will arise.
Faith in God is reorientation of my whole self. It is this sort of
redirection of personal existence that the existence of the Church
at once presupposes, exemplifies and nurtures."[72] It is "the realization of a covenant relationship," which "has in view man's essential nature as social being, and is itself constitutive, not to
say creative, of social, moral, and personal experience."[73]

To emphasize this side of the Church's reality is by no means
to make of it something purely spiritual or to deny the role of
ecclesiastical institutions.[74] From beginning to end, the central
preoccupation of the American ecumenical discussions was to find a

way to overcome the tendency of both protestant-type and catholic-type ecclesiologies to play off communitarian and institutional conceptions of the Church against each other.[75] It was precisely this concern that led them to call attention to the role of the cogni-tional element in the constitution of ecclesial reality. In doing so they were at once presaging and reflecting the tendency of the contemporary social sciences to interpret all social phenomena-- even such massive organizations as the business corporation or the state--as systems of perceived relationships held together by an internalized group ethos at a level far deeper than that on which the chain of command and the system of external sanctions operate.[76]

Already in the CULW Commission's work we find a description of the Church which is characteristic of the prevailing American attitude throughout the whole period here under consideration. Brown's report states: "By the Church, as we use the term in this study, we mean not only the company of persons bound together in a spiritual fellowship by common loyalty to Christ and committed to his service; not merely the group of institutions in which this common spiritual life finds corporate expression; but the unseen factor which gives this common life and institutional activity significance as the point of contact with the eternal and universal."[77] What is meant of course by this last phrase is the divine element represented by the "idea" of the Church: to this we will return in the next section of this chapter; for the moment what should be noted is the link which Brown establishes on the phenomenological level between the spiritual and the institutional aspects of ecclesial reality. As the ATC report points out, this link is effected by the perception in faith of "the revealing, redeeming act of God in Christ, whose purpose has its consummation in a redeeming people." This conviction gives unity and coherence to those beliefs, symbols, and activities in which the life of the community manifests itself,[79] as well as to the organization and institutions by means of which the functions of the Church in the world are exercised.[80] A similar conception is found in the CEDG paper:

> "Hence, the Church, when thought of as a concrete social entity usually refers to a corporate body of believers who recognize Jesus Christ as their head. They acknowledge him to be the source of a socio-historical institution possessing a definite reality and function, and to be the author and perfection of their faith. This corporate body provides those forms of fellowship that arise out of the common concern for Word and

sacrament, and that are needed for the practice of the Christian way of life. Thus the church as a concrete social entity includes all those forms of organization that provide patterns of experience and behavior for men and women who are committed to a common loyalty to Jesus Christ. These types of organization include those forms of fellowship that are given expression through local congregations and through the organic or corporate groupings of the church referred to as denominations, national and provincial churches and sects. They also include those larger organizations that exist for the purpose of providing means of cooperation between these smaller units, organizations such as the World Council of Churches and the Federal Council of Churches in America."[81]

And the same report protests against an attitude which would exclude certain corporate expressions of "the spirit of the Lord and Master," particularly the informal and unofficial but also the institutional, from the theological consideration of the Church.[82]

Likewise Paul Scherer completes the thought quoted above with the observation that the communion of the believer with God and with the whole redeemed people of God "was mediated to us in time through a community divinely chosen. Whenever and whereever along the course of the centuries God has revealed Himself, there has always resulted some kind of fellowship; and always both the character of that fellowship and its function have been conditioned by, though not dependent upon, the degree and extent to which the revelation was apprehended and expressed."[83] Precisely because the Church idea is a force thrusting to expression in human form it was inevitable that from the beginning it should give rise to diversified outward forms in different human cultures and situations: "From within, by struggle and conflict, working and being wrought, building and being built upon, it has fashioned the structure which is yet more than anything else an accident, not indeed the substance of its being."[84] This last expression must not be misunderstood; the language is that of an aristotelian substance-accident ontology, in which accident does not mean something incidental or foreign to substance but rather its proper though environmentally conditioned effect, its normal and necessary manifestation. Thus the substance is more than the sum of all its accidents together and yet it cannot exist without them, howevermuch they may be environmentally modified. So also in the Church, according to Scherer, the particular group of individuals gathered in fellowship, the particular institutional form taken by their fellowship, these are phenomenological accidents, produced

by and giving expression to the Church's substance under the particular conditions of time and place.[85]

Niebuhr's Purpose of the Church report makes much the same
point though in different conceptual terms. Instead of substance-
accident categories, Niebuhr presents the relationship between community and institution as a dialectical polarity in which the Church
may be thought of as a field of force defined by two distinct
poles.[86] On the one side, there are "organizations and rites"; on
the other, "a spiritual, psychological, intellectual and moral common life." From one point of view, membership in the Church is "a
matter of participation in institutional forms and actions"; from
another, an "engagement in common thought, common devotion and worship, common appreciations."[87] The eternal temptation is to play
one aspect off against the other, to give priority to one side over
the other. Against this temptation Niebuhr insists "no community
can exist without some institutions that give it form boundaries,
discipline, and the possibilities of expression and common action.
On the other hand no institution can long exist without some common
mind and drive that expresses and defines itself in institutions.
The questions whether the Church is primarily institution or primarily community, or whether one of these is prior, are as unanswer-
able as similar questions about thought and language. There is not
thought without language and no language without thought, yet
thought is not language nor language thought."[88]

The most intensive reflection on this problem is to be found
in the papers of the Montreal Commissions. The TCCCNA called attention to the Incarnation as the theological justification of the intimate relationship between spirit and form, community and institution in the Church.

> "As in the incarnation God binds himself to concrete manhood,
> so by the Spirit in the Church he works in and through human
> flesh and blood, words and acts, social and historical struc-
> tures. Any adequate view of the Church must give proper at-
> tention to such social and historical structures... Just as
> the Church is an activity and a life in which nature and mis-
> sion are inseparable, and in which being and act are never to
> be set in opposition, so also the Church is inseparably both
> event and institution. ...by 'institution' we mean the estab-
> lished relationships and patterns of historical and social
> order, stable forms and definite structures."[89]

It is however principally in the papers of the Institutionalism Commission that the fullest treatment of the problem is to be found.

Building on the idea developed in the TCCCNA of the continuity between the Old and New Covenant peoples, the Institutionalism report
declares:

"The reconstituting of the people of God as the Church of Christ
in the day of the Spirit meant not an abolition but a transformation of its institutional life. The New Testament freely
uses institutional language in describing the Church, as, for
instance, when it calls the Church a 'royal priesthood' and a
'holy nation' (I Peter, 2:9)--two fundamental institutions in
the history of Israel, now profoundly altered as they were
lifted up into the New Covenant. The Lord's own life offers
other paradigmatic examples: his baptism in John's baptism,
his announcement of the messianic kingdom, his particular manner of presiding at certain meals which already possessed a
sacred significance of their own, his assembly and training of
disciples after a pattern customary in Judaism. In each case,
and in many more, we find institutions with characteristic
purposes, structure and functions, all subjected to change by
their new life.
    To assert that the Church possesses an institutional char-
acter and is articulated in a variety of institutions, does in
no way imply a derogation of the intensely personal quality of
its koinonia. On the contrary, by the term koinonia we understand the communion into which God in Christ through the spirit
binds the believer to himself and to all fellow believers by
baptism and the ministry of reconciliation (II Cor. 5:17).
Thus in the Church, in the community of the Spirit, the dichotomy of institution and koinonia is overcome. The institutional patterns of the Church provide an ordered structure for the
common life, through which God imparts his gracious love to man
and makes a personal existence in freedom and responsibility
manifest."[30]

The fuller consideration of the Institutionalism Study must be de-
ferred for the time being. We shall be meeting it again in chapter
four, where we will have occasion to consider in detail the implications of the position taken in the passage quoted above. What
concerns us here is the study's fundamental insistence on the
essential coherence between koinonia and institution.

This conviction, which the Montreal commissions so clearly
brought to expression, has been the leitmotif of the COCU studies
and negotiations. The Open Letter to the Churches of 1966 begins
with a confession of faith in the theological oneness of the "community bound together in faith, hope, and love, united to its one
Savior and Lord, and commissioned to serve him in the service of
men" on the one hand and the "visible companies of Christian people"
on the other. For this reason, the letter declares, the disunity
of the latter at any time and place is "a challenge to the truth--
even where the supreme claim of conscience seems to require separa-

tion for the truth's sake--and a rejection of the unity implicit in
the saving love of the one God for our single humanity."[91] And the
preamble to the Outline Plan proclaims the participants' intention:
"In considering the organization needed to give effect to our understanding of the Church's true nature, we, humbly and patiently,
seek to create the conditions for a fuller expression of the faith,
the worship, the ministry, and the mission of the one Church of
Christ."[92] At the same time, however, the Guidelines for Structure
warn against an all too undialectical identification of the Church
with its organizational structures

> "Because the Church is more than any one of the images we use
> to describe it can convey, its true nature will not be expressed
> in its organizational structures. Because it is commissioned by
> its Lord for mission in all the world and wills to be faithful
> to its missionary task, its structures for carrying out the
> mission will be adapted to the changing world in which and to
> which it ministers and thus its structures for mission must be
> open to change. In freedom of obedience to the Gospel under
> the guidance of the Holy Spirit we have the responsibility and
> the opportunity as we look toward a united church to fashion
> structures which will, so far as possible, reflect the nature
> of the Church and equip it with the means which will more ef-
> fectively serve its mission."[93]

The expressions and thinking of this document reveal a strong influence of the Missionary Structures of the Congregation study, in
which the antipathy of many radicals and reformers toward traditional
ecclesiastical institutions which have outlived their functions
found vigorous expression. And yet even here there is no suggestion
of a return to the sort of formless spiritual fellowship which seems
to have been the dream of a certain school of the old liberal theology. Not the fact, but the character, flexibility and continuity
of church structure was the central issue in the MSC study.[94] The
North American groups' experiments were experiments with structures,
and it is not without significance that the six "clues for understanding the common life of society [inasmuch] as they constitute
evidence for the action and presence of God in the world," are also
called "clues for understanding structures."[95]

III. THE THEOLOGICAL IDEA OF THE CHURCH

A. Empirical Reality, Symbolic Universe, Theoretical Model

The preceding section attempted to present a cross-section of the American thinking on the empirical reality of the Church. We saw how the American theologians distinguished various forms or levels of ecclesial community, how they attempted to explain the phenomenological mode of being of these communities and their institutional articulation. We noted that in harmony with contemporary sociology they tended to stress the role of perception as the central component of ecclesial reality. The particular mode of ecclesial perception, we saw, is faith: the social reality of the Church is a product of faith and is empirically graspable only as a phenomenon of faith.[96] That is to say, the experience of the Church as empirical reality is necessarily conditioned by the faith-understanding of the theological idea of the Church.[97]

By itself, of course, this way of thinking is hardly new; every denominational ecclesiology in the Church's history has appealed to this principle as the ultimate explanation of why theological arguments fail to convince those who do not share the same faith. Likewise the older liberal theology, particularly under the influence of Ernst Troeltsch, had repeatedly called attention to the sociological connection between the idea of the Church and the society in which this idea is imbedded. What was new about the American handling of the matter, was their willingness to acknowledge this connection precisely in its application to the development of an ecclesiological theory, instead of sharply dividing ecclesiology and religious sociology as the contemporary thinking in Europe was inclined to do.[98] The best illustration of this difference in attitude is the different reactions in European and American circles to Professor Dodd's 1949 Letter on the influence of "non-theological factors" in ecumenical theology.[99] What broke into European Faith and Order circles like an exploding bombshell was received in America simply as a delayed acknowledgment of what the Americans had been trying to tell their European counterparts back in 1937 at Edinburgh. For the American ecclesiologists confronted on every streetcorner with the phenomenon of denominationalism, the sociocultural conditioning of ecclesiological theory was self-evident; their preoccupation was with finding a way to overcome it. To ap-

preciate their discussions of the theological idea of the Church it
is absolutely essential to keep this perspective constantly in mind.

This caution is very much to the point for a proper understanding of the matter to be considered in this present section. It
would be a gross misunderstanding to assume that the American discussion of the empirical referent were a non-theological endeavor
or that what resulted were not an element of a theological conception of the Church. Certainly no such implications are intended by
the use of the expression "theological idea of the Church" to designate the object of the present considerations. The fact, however,
is that traditional ecclesiology tends to concentrate on a number
of ideas, more or less biblical in origin, which seem at first sight
to have a rather different character than the sort of categories we
have previously been using. Very often in traditional ecclesiology
notions like the "Body of Christ" or "People of God" are contrasted
with ideas drawn from the vocabulary of sociology. The so-called
"theological" idea of the Church is then treated as a more profound
way of viewing the Church. It suggests a sort of ideal or normative
essence. The fact is that from the point of view of a sociological
interpretation of ecclesial community such ideas do exercise a profound influence on the community's self-image. One or another of
these ideas very often functions as the central symbol for a highly
selective perception on the part of the community of its own empirical reality. The ATC Denominational Statements earlier described
offer ample illustration of such selective perception.

The role of such "theological ideas" in ecclesiology can perhaps best be explained with the aid of Peter Berger and Thomas Luckmann's notion of a "symbolic universe." Such "universes," they
explain, "are bodies of theoretical tradition that integrate different provinces of meaning and encompass the institutional order
in a symbolic totality."[100] The emphasis here is on the totality
of such a universe; by means of it,

> "all the sectors of the institutional order are integrated in
> an all-embracing frame of reference, which now constitutes a
> universe in the literal sense of the word, because all human
> experience can now be conceived of as taking place within it.
> The symbolic universe is conceived of as the matrix of all
> socially objectivated and subjectively real meanings; the
> entire historic society and the entire biography of the indi-
> vidual are seen as events taking place within this universe.
> What is particularly important, the marginal situations of the
> life of the individual (marginal, that is, not being included

in the reality of everyday existence in society) are also en-
compassed by the symbolic universe. ...
     On this level of legitimation, the reflective integration of
discrete institutional processes reaches its ultimate fulfillment. A whole world is created. All the lesser legitimating
theories are viewed as special perspectives on phenomena that
are aspects of this world. Institutional roles become modes
of participation in a universe that transcends and includes
the institutional order."[101]

These are all functions which are exercised in the ecclesial

community by such "theological ideas." Nevertheless the application

of the "symbolic universe" notion to such ideas can only be analo-

gous. First of all, except for the professional theologian, church-

man, or theologically engaged layman, the Church rarely is experi-

enced today as the kind of total community which is the correlate

of a symbolic universe. Secondly, the notion of "church-idea" as

used in the present section represents a kind of conceptual distil-

late, not the symbolic universe as a whole, but its conceptual quin-

tessence, an abbreviation, a slogan or watchword, reducing to order

the various elements of the symbolic universe in terms of a least

common denominator.

     Perhaps the relationship between the Church-idea and the sym-

bolic universe of the Church can best be illustrated by a compari-

son drawn from the field of astronomy.[102] The symbolic universe of

a society is rather like the gravitational field of a planetary or

stellar system. In order to grasp such a system conceptually, the

astronomer projects a hypothetical model in order to locate the

gravitational center and calculate the orbits of the components.

His aim is the fullest possible coincidence between astronomical

model and astral reality; at the same time the careful astronomer

recognizes that both his model and the observations on which it is

based are to some extent uncontrollably colored by his vantage-

point in relation to the system, by distorting media, etc. As

"created by God" the Church is represented by a single symbolic uni-

verse, but this system is variously refracted in the ecclesial

experience of the different denominational traditions. Every eccle-

siological system is an attempt to project a model of the divinely

constituted original, due compensation being made for the distor-

tions of the particular refracting medium. In such a model, the

"Church-idea" is the equivalent of the theoretically calculated

focal point or gravitational center in terms of which the "orbit"

of all the associated themes can be calculated.

The components of ecclesiological systems are a more or less constant set of themes, for the most part metaphors or conceptions contained in or suggested by the Bible. In a paper for the TCCCNA, Paul Minear counted more than eighty substantive and adjectival expressions for the Church, leaving aside the--in some ways even more important--verbal and prepositional expressions, and he went on to distinguish twenty categories according to which the individual ideas might be thematically categorized.[103] Theoretically, any one of these categories might function as the leitmotif of a distinct ecclesiological model; in practice, however, a variety of factors tend radically to reduce this number. For one thing, certain categories have been more favored than others by the biblical writers than others,[104] and these preferences have been underlined by the weight given to such texts and ideas in the history of the Church and of ecclesiology. For another, the close affinity of certain themes one for another leads to the formation of larger constellations of ideas. Finally, the interrelationships between the diverse accents and emphases of the different thematic categories reinforces the tendency to constellation building. Minear distinguishes eleven such accents:

1. The christological: as exemplified by the pauline body and the johannine vine images, together with the themes of the new creation in Christ, the new Adam, Christ's Lordship over all principalities and powers as well as over humanity;
2. the historical: stressing the relationship of the Church to the life, history, and expectations of Israel;
3. the theological: accentuating the theocentric and pneumatological character of the Church, the trinitarian economy of salvation;
4. the liturgical-sacramental: evoking the motifs of Christian Worship and sacramental life;
5. the sociological: stressing the similarities and dissimilarities between the Church and other human communities, the communal and institutional structures of the Church etc.;
6. the eschatological: calling attention to the yet to be fulfilled promises to the Church, its provisional, imperfect character, etc.;
7. the soteriological: illustrating the various aspects of the new being which is brought to realization the Church;
8. the ethical: calling attention to the Church's duties to the members of her own community and to the world in which the Church finds itself and to which it is sent;
9. the psychological: illustrating the direct personal relationship of each believer with his Lord, to his Father and to his brother;
10. the pedagogical: accentuating the perfectability of the christian community in its divinely given unity, wholeness, maturity and perfection;
11. the missionary: evoking the thought of men and nations yet to

be included within the Church, communities still unevangelized, brothers not yet born.[105]

In fact this list can be further reduced, for out of the at first rather bewildering welter of ideas three principal types of ecclesiological systems seem to have crystalized; these may be designated by the idea which most prominantly determines the shape of the conceptual field within the system. These three themes are (1) the Communion of Saints, (2) the Body of Christ, and (3) the People of God.[106] Each tends to give rise to an ecclesiological model with certain characteristics common to all the individual variants. Thus the Communion-of-Saints model tends to emphasize particularly the sociological and liturgical aspects of the Church; the Body-of-Christ model, on the contrary more the christological, ethical and sociological; the People-of-God model, finally, the historical, theological and eschatological aspects. Besides the general type, there often exist one or two variant forms distinguished from the principal form by certain characteristic shifts of accent without fundamentally departing from the basic model. Thus the Communion-of-Saints model is found in a strongly sacramental-mystical modification as a typical form of Eastern Orthodox ecclesiology. The Body-of-Christ model exists in a strongly institutional form as a typical model of Roman Catholic ecclesiology, but as we already saw in Carver's presentation of Baptist ecclesiology, there also exists an almost anti-institutional variant.

In the following paragraphs we will consider the American discussions of each of these typical models in turn. Although for the most part New Testament themes are involved, the manner in which these are handled in the American discussions is more in the tradition of systematic theology than of pure historical exegesis.

A Note on American Theological Method

Given the nature of Christianity, it is clear that any treatment of these themes must necessarily give prominant consideration to the New Testament formulations. One commission indeed--the BDMS group--concerned itself directly and principally with New Testament materials. Common to all the commissions, however--this holds true not only of those reports where particular factors associated with the terms of the group's commission or dictates of literary style, but also of many individual studies bearing the words "biblical" or "New Testament" teaching in their titles[107]--is a manner of dealing with the biblical materials which at first sight is apt to strike the reader accustomed to Teutonic historical criticism as being all too superficial and schematic. The border-

lines between historical exegesis and systematic elaboration seem
to have evaporated, and one is not always sure whether what is being
offered under the rubric "New Testament Teaching" is intended to be
an historical critical reconstruction or a scripturally inspired,
speculative-systematic construction.

The reasons for this situation are manifold, and it would take
us too afar afield to analyze them all here. Nevertheless a minimum
of explanation is in order if the American discussions of the theological ideas of the Church are to be justly appreciated.

1. Conditions imposed by the literary genre

With the exception of the Man in Society study (which from the
beginning was conceived as a presentation of the biblical teaching
in abstraction from its concrete applications to modern church
life),[108] all of the studies with which we are here concerned were
compelled by the very terms of their commission to deal with actual
problems of contemporary systematic ecclesiology. Even though professional exegetes constituted a substantial segment of the commission memberships, the terms of their assignment dictated a more or
less systematic approach to the problems.[109] Moreover, as several
reports explicitly complain, the space limitations of the group report precluded the possibility of adequately reflecting detailed
exegetical discussions which may have occurred in the course of the
group's investigations.[110]

2. The "Biblical Theology" movement

Traditionally, American Protestant theology has always been
strongly biblically oriented. In the so-called "Biblical Theology"
of the forties and fifties, however, this traditional connection
between the two disciplines took on a new methodically developed
consistency, inasmuch as its proponents insisted on the unity of the
biblical teaching and on the immediate relevance of this teaching
for the contemporary situation.[111] This position was not uncritical;
the biblical theologians neither ignored nor rejected the results of
the preceding decades of historical criticism, and they repudiated
any naive harmonization of the different tendencies which such criticism had brought to light. In the words of the BDMS report, "...
the unity of the Bible is not a static uniformity of all its parts.
The primary area of unity lies in its historical testimony to, or
proclamation of, God's activity...; but the inferences and applications drawn from the testimony in particular historical situations
may show considerable variation." Thus the exegete is left with the
choice either of presenting the theology of the separate books or
traditions individually one after the other--in which case the unity
of the whole fails to find adequate expression--or of presenting the
whole comprehensively and synthetically, even though this necessarily entails a certain amount of artificial construction and connection.[112] The biblical theologians were convinced that this risk
could be undertaken responsibly.[113]

3. The hermeneutical problem of confessional exegesis

Even the most convinced followers of the biblical theology movement in America never lost sight of the hermeneutical problem posed
by the tendency of both "critical" and "theological" exegetes to
interpret the scriptural texts with a particular denominational or
academic bias. In the commissions it often proved impossible to
achieve directly a consensus regarding the interpretation of those
passages or themes which reflect the ideological tensions between

the particular confessional traditions or schools of thought. This
meant that the American theologians were from the beginning confronted with the problem of Tradition, not so much the speculative
question of the relation between "Scripture" and "Tradition" as two
abstractly contrasted sources of faith, but rather the practical
problem of finding a way to overcome the concrete differences in
interpretation between different exegetical traditions.[114] As long
as this problem remained unresolved, the commissions could do little
more than catalog points of agreement and disagreement and to try to
illuminate the latter by excursions into the history of dogma and
the sociology of ecclesiological viewpoints.[115] The alternative was
to try to wrestle with the hermeneutical problem itself; thus one
finds in almost all the reports extended treatments of fundamental
hermeneutical and methodological questions.[116] One of the solutions
proposed is the search for a new way of posing the questions which
hitherto have eluded a consensus answer. This demands however that
one discover a new conceptual structure in which to pose the question, but to do that is to venture into the realm of systematic-
speculative theology.[117]

B. The Communion-of-Saints Idea

At the request of the Faith and Order Central Committee, the
CULW Commission did a special study of the Communion-of-Saints theme.
Its approach was a modified version of the so-called comparative approach: first a presentation of the New Testament teaching and its
elaboration in the course of the Church's history, then an exposition of the various confessional positions, and finally an essay in
evaluation, with the specifically American twist of calling attention
to the sociological factors underlying the theological agreements and
disagreements.

At the outset of its discussion, the report calls attention to
the differing interpretations of the biblical material as a result
of the confessionally opposed attitudes toward the historical development of the theme, and it notes the difficulty, under these circumstances, of presenting the biblical position "objectively."[118]
The report observes that when the term communio sanctorum first
appeared as an article of the Creed in fifth century Gaul, it had a
polemical thrust directed against Vigilantius' criticism of the mar-
tyr and saint cultus.[119] The combined phrase is nowhere found in
the New Testament, but its individual elements are among the most
frequently used ecclesiological categories. The Church is often
described as a "communion" (koinonia)[120] and the baptized members
as "saints."[121] Moreover the general idea of a "communion" or
"helpful interrelations" between the saints on earth and the saints

in glory is to be found at many points in the Old and New Testaments.[122] Nevertheless, where the term <u>koinonia</u> or its derivatives appear in the New Testament, what is meant is the "communion" between the saints on earth with each other or with God as Father, Son, or Holy Spirit.[123] Thus the report sums up the biblical teaching on the nature of this communion in the following way:

"(1) The Christian community or Church is a s p i r i t - u a l   u n i t y   a n d   s o l i d a r i t y (Matt. 13: 31-33; John 17:20-23; Eph. 4:2-6; I Cor. 12:11-27, 1:10-13; Mark 3:24-25; I Peter 2:5; Matt. 16:15-20, 18:15-20; etc.). It will be seen that this view is generally accepted by all the churches, though with widely different beliefs as to the necessity of visible corporate unity and as to the nature and extent of the interplay of life and service between the living and the dead.

(2) The Christian communion of saints involves m u t u a l s h a r i n g   o f   t e m p o r a l   o r   m a t e r i a l b l e s s i n g s . As we shall see, this is a view specially stressed by the Reformed and Presbyterian Churches, the Methodist or Wesleyan Churches, also the Congregational and Baptist groups as one phase of their general interpretation (sharing in a community of goods, also the active giving and receiving of alms: Acts 2:42; Rom. 12:13, 15:26; II Cor. 8:4, 9:13; Phil. 4:14-16; Heb. 13:16; I Tim. 6:18; etc.; also I Thess. 5:11-14; Gal. 6:10; I John 3:16-18; Acts 11:29-30; II Cor. 8:9).

(3) The communion of saints, according to the Holy Scriptures, involves t h e   m u t u a l   p a r t i c i p a - t i o n   i n   o n e   a n o t h e r ' s   g i f t s   a n d g r a c e s . With most evangelicals this is practically confined to the earthly life. Beyond that, they are hopeful without dogmatic certainty. The Catholics, with definite assurances in well-formulated dogmas, believe and practice this participation as between saints in glory and saints on earth (Mutual participation in spiritual privilege and fellowship; united sharing in a communion belonging to Christ: I Cor. 1:9, 10:16; II Cor. 6:14, 13:14; Phil. 1:5, 2:1, 3:10, 4:14-16; Gal. 2:9; I John 1:3, 6, 7; Rom. 15:27; Acts 2:42; etc.).

(4) Saint Paul's 'communion of saints' seems to have been s y n o n y m o u s   w i t h   t h e   C h u r c h (see St. Paul's interchange of 'saints' and 'church' in the salutation of his Epistles)."[124]

The report's treatment of the subsequent history of the Communion-of-Saints theme gives a good example of the typical handling of Church history in the American discussions. The report notes: "it is generally agreed that in the history of the invisible Church there have arisen certain emphases, interpretations, items of doctrine and dogma and phases of church polity not to be found, except perhaps in bare outline or in mere promise in the New Testament Church. All Christians profess to believe the words of Jesus, while He was here on earth, when He said that He had yet many words to say which the Holy Spirit would later reveal (St. John 16:7, 12-13)." Nevertheless the value attached to such developments from full dogmatic acceptance as the divinely willed unfolding of the New Testament teaching, through a more modest judgment which would see them as useful but fallible expressions of the divine intention, to ultimate rejection as needless and corrupt departures from the simplicity of the gospel."[125]

The critical period in this development was that from the second to the fifth centuries: "During these centuries," the report explains, "we witness the rise of the old catholic Church. This involved: (1) the adoption of a canon of Scripture, (2) the formulation of the Nicaeno-Constantinopolitan Creed together with the Chalcedonian Christological definition and (3) the development of the Cyprianic (c. 250) and Augustinian (c. 430) conceptions of the catholic Church, in which the episcopacy became the very esse. As Protestants, generally, interpret these developments, the New Testament Church which was indeed one, holy, catholic and prophetic, with sacerdotal functions when conceived of as a whole, came, by the time of Augustine, to have sacerdotal functions only as its visible life strictly conformed to very fixed ideas both in doctrine and polity. The prophetic function, and the presbyterial and congregational phases of polity, with all that these features imply, had been suppressed. This conviction of the Protestants does not prevent their having a very sympathetic understanding as to why the old catholic Church arose. The Church was in the midst, then as now, of all sorts of heresies and problems which made the maintenance of unity and orthodoxy exceedingly difficult."[126]

Under these circumstances the notion of the communion of the saints also underwent development. "Sainthood came to be the possession of an esoteric group, intellectually orthodox and ceremonially aloof. ... Inevitably there arose the idea of the higher and lower types of Christian living, the religious and the secular. The ideas of separateness, asceticism, strictness, etc. came to be central to the idea of sainthood. ... Miracles in connection with the saints, living and departed, more and more furnished bases for a saint cultus. ... The Church itself took refuge in the original root idea of holiness or sainthood, and it taught...that the holiness of the Church is given it of God and not by the moral or ethical perfection of its membership or clergy. The Church, the communion of saints here on earth, is holy not as the result of adding together the moral attainments, in character and conduct, of its members, but, it is holy since it is Christ's Body functioning in heaven and on earth. Being of the Holy One, it, and it alone, can make men holy, it alone can produce saints. As over against the puritanic Donatists, for example, it ruled that holiness consists in the Church's maintenance of its catholicity and unity (with the foregoing ideas of holiness) at all costs."[127]

The different confessional traditions are at odds in their evaluation of these developments. "In the estimation of the Protestant Churches, all this, in many ways, constituted a departure from the moral and ethical and the essentially Christian definitions of holiness and sainthood and an adoption of the Old Testament and popular pagan ideas of ceremonial and religious holiness. Evangelicals appreciate the Catholic doctrine of the holiness of the Church as being of God and not of men. But they would insist that in the visible historical Church, the manifestation of God's holiness will inevitably be evidenced in moral correctness, in the realization of all the fruits of the Spirit..., in the actual sharing of holiness, as thus defined, for the realization of the will of God on earth. In the teaching of the Catholic churches, it is conceded that there

are moral and ethical lapses and retrogressions during the years
under survey. But they hold that these are not to be attributed to
the maintenance...of the [old catholic] definitions of the essential
features of the true Church of Christ. The Catholics believe that in
all its essential features the old catholic Church with its sacer-
dotalism, with its conception of the episcopacy, as being the esse
of the true Church, and with new meanings which were, as a result,
written into the ecclesia's essential features, namely, into unity,
holiness, catholicity and apostolicity, came as a result of the
leading of the Holy Spirit revealing the whole counsel, love and
life of God. This conviction influences them in their interpreting
the New Testament ideas of holiness and sainthood in such a way as
not to conflict with the fourth and fifth-century views of holiness
and sainthood."[128]

Summing up, the Slosser report calls attention to the multi-
dimensional character of the Communion-of-Saints theme. It involves
the nature of the Church, "its earthly fellowship and polity, its
heavenly life and activity, its ways for the making and perfecting
of the saints, its liturgy, hymnody, prayers, etc. as vehicles for
intercommunion as between the saints here and the saints yonder, its
teachings and ways for actively sharing saintliness throughout the
whole of society on earth and in heaven. And all these include together fellowship with God the Father, Son and Holy Spirit as the
supreme privilege of all saintly communion."[129] As Minear points out,
the New Testament expressions which belong to the Communion-of-Saints
group tend to evoke more directly "the fabric of human relations
within the Church" and to bring out more clearly than other themes
the connection between faith and ethical responsibility.[130] This is
especially true when one reflects on the apparently sociological expressions used to describe the persons belonging to the communion,
e.g. "saints," "faithful," "friends," "servants," etc. Minear warns,
however, against exaggerating this sociological component. Decisive
for the application of such images in the New Testament was not the
mental picture conjured up by the words alone but rather "the total
tradition of the message and mission of Jesus Christ."[131] Echoing
the conclusion of the Slosser report, Minear cautions: "The[se]
images draw their basic meaning from the central relationship to the
work of Father, Son, and Spirit, and not from their immediate social
components."[132] Furthermore both the Wright and the Calhoun papers
call attention to the fact that koinonia means more than simply
social fellowship; to the writers of the New Testament it was a
mode of ontological participation.[133]

The Slosser report goes on to note some of the principal confessionally influenced variations of the Communion-of-Saints idea.
In general, "the Catholic Churches tend to read more of the ideas
of 'separateness,' 'awe,' 'the devoted,' 'the divine,' while the
Evangelical Churches tend to read more of the ethical, moral and
social, more of the idea of sinlessness, impeccability, puritanism,
into the ideas of holiness and saintliness."[134] The report goes on
to list three principal variants. In the first, as illustrated by
the ecclesiologies of the Eastern Orthodox, the Quakers and all Neo-
Platonic mystics, "the Church invisible is a m y s t i c a l
s p i r i t u a l , s u b s t a n t i a l u n i t y , the
totality practically submerging the identity of the individual members." In the second, as manifested in the Roman Catholic, Calvinist, Lutheran, Methodist, Baptist, Disciples and trinitarian-evan-
gelical Congregationalist traditions, "the Church is a s p i r -
i t u a l u n i t y o f r e g e n e r a t e d i n d i v i d -
u a l s u n i t e d i n C h r i s t , the Son of God, not
partaking of the divine Substance but in moral and spiritual union
with Him." A third, typically modernist position, would see in the
notion of the communion of saints simply a c o n c e p t u a l
e x p r e s s i o n , dangerously weighted by an outmoded metaphysical world view, for the sociological reality of the fellowship
and interaction of the believers on earth. Insofar as these latter
would use the expression at all they would tend to understand it
only in those scriptural senses which refer to the communion of the
living with each other and with God.[135]

A special variant of the koinonia theme, which cannot be identified with any of the above, is its use as an idealogical superstructure for a more communal than institutional ecclesiology. The
ATC report records that one group of theologians who lay particular
stress on the koinonia notion "think of the Church as an informal
fellowship gathered about the person of Jesus, continuing his spirit and gradually evolving such leadership and forms of organization
as served the perpetuation of such fellowship."[136] In this version
it is the informal, face-to-face, charismatic character of the New
Testament fellowship, in contrast to the formal, impersonal, hierarchical character of later ecclesiastical institutions that is
stressed. In his contribution to the Interseminary symposium, H.
Paul Douglass, a Church sociologist, points out the advantages of

such an understanding of the koinonia notion for the elaboration of
an ecumenical ecclesiology. Distinguishing between ecclesia--the
institutional phase of the Church's reality--and koinonia--those
aspects of the organized life of the Church which are more fundamental than the institutional--Douglass calls attention to the
broad zone of basic, sub-institutional social phenomena and organization which represent an intermediary form between a purely spiritual unity without visible expression and a fully ecclesiasticized
institutional unity of the church.[137] "Organized social life...below the institutional level is a perfectly verifiable objective
phase of society. Its ways are definable. They are transmitted by
tradition, propagated by habit, made dependable through loyalty and
powerful through devotion; but they lack the meticulous self-consciousness, the brittleness, the over-precision of the legal enactment and conceptually developed creed, the prescribed code, the
legal incorporation."[138]

Douglass is no opponent of organization; in the same article he
calls attention to the need for more effective organizational expression of the already existing ecumenical koinonia.[139] He does
not reject out of hand the institutionalization of the koinonia,
only the "fallacy of institutional mindedness," which "fails to see
that it is equally possible, and much more important, to devote
effort to the development of social processes profounder than the
institutional ones than it is to seek institutional ends. By the
same token it is possible and indeed of primary importance to seek
and promote church unity at the level of koinonia, to hold and
transmit the common ideology without the imposition of rigid creeds,
to seek common ethical ends without demanding identical regulations,
in short, to live at the profounder level of unity than the institutional."[140] Not against institutions but against what the SCI
called the pejorative meaning of "institutionalism" is Douglass'
protest directed, against the tendency of institutional structures
to develop a disfunctional rigidity, uniformity and bureaucracy.[141]
The advantage of the koinonia-idea as an ecclesiological focal-point
is that it makes clear the instrumental character of all ecclesiastical institutions,[142] and thus it offers a barrier to the ideological rationalization of the negative connotations of institutionalism.

C. The Body-of-Christ Idea

No single commission paper offers quite the sort of systematic survey of the Body-of-Christ idea as the CULW Commission's study of the preceding topic. The profoundest reflections on the body theme are to be found in the TCCCNA's papers, though the general trend of this commission's thinking was rather to subordinate the Body-of-Christ theme to the more universal and trinitarian People-of-God notion.[143] (Indeed, this tendency appears in the work of almost all the American commissions,[144] however much individual members may have been inclined to focus on the body motif.[145]) As a result, it is necessary to turn principally to the preparatory papers of this commission as a source for its reflections on the advantages and disadvantages of the body idea.[146]

Regarding the New Testament foundations for this theme, Minear notes that passages which explicitly connect Church and body are confined to five pauline letters: Romans (12:4), I Corinthians (6:15; 10:16-17; 12:12-27; 15:35-44), II Corinthians (4:10-12), Ephesians (1:15-23; 2:13-22; 4:4, 11-16) and Colossians (1:15-20, 24; 2:9-19; 3:15).[147] To these may be added a variety of cognate ideas involving organic imagery, e.g. in-Christ, the fullness of God, the glory, united to the Lord, living and dying in the Lord, the body of righteousness and life, the one new man, the image of Christ, the new Creation, one Spirit; bridal or maternal imagery, e.g. the bride of Christ, the woman of the Apocalypse; botanical imagery, e.g. God's planting, field, olive tree, the Tree of Life, first fruits, the vine with its branches, or architectural imagery, e.g. the holy city, the temple, God's building or house.[148] All of these, Minear notes, even the notion of the body are used to "serve many different motives and functions" and have "multiple and changing associations and nuances which keep shifting from one passage to another, and even within the same passage." For all of them Minear's warning holds that "the changing configurations of ideas center not in the concept body but in the person of Christ and the work of the Spirit."[149]

The primacy given to Christ and the Spirit in this idea-cluster determines its particular ecclesiological slant. Despite the paranetic thrust of Rom. 12:4, I Cor. 12:12-27, and Col. 3:9-13; the emphasis of most of these images is more on the relationship of the Church as a whole to its divine Head than on the fabric of social relations among the members, on the organic rather than the personal, the metaphysical rather than the sociological.[150] In the words of the Wright Committee, "to speak of the new community as Christ's body is to emphasize the fact that it is a living, unified organism by means of the principle of corporate personality so common in the Semetic World. Christ is the community, and the community is 'in Christ'."[151] And further, "...the new community in Christ is a people knit together, not primarily by human structures of organization, but instead by an inner mutuality of spirit provided by God in Christ."[152]

This emphasis makes a Body-of-Christ ecclesiology particularly attractive to both conservative and liberal opponents of an ecumenism which emphasizes organizational union as its goal. Mackay's contribution to the Interseminary Symposium may be taken as a typical expression of this trend among American ecumenists. After developing the need for the unity of the Body of Christ to find expression in common worship, in an "ecumenical theology," and in "the closest solidarity" in life and activity, he concludes his exposition of the Body-of-Christ theme with the warning:

> "Christian unity is, above all else, a unity in the Spirit. Instead of being a unity of order, it is a unity of faith and love and work. Questions of order and organization in the Christian Church must always be secondary to questions of faith and love and work. Biblical theology, and particularly the New Testament view of the Church, do not sanction in any way, the ideal of a single world organization as being the most expressive visible unity of the Christian Church. A true and effective world Christian community does not necessarily involve a single organizational form."[153]

Within the ecumenical movement, however, the most common emphasis is rather on the implications of the Body-of-Christ theme for the overcoming of denominational divisions and the world-wide organization of the Churches in one form or other. Of this tendency, the following passage from the report of one of the Oberlin sections is typical:

> "An outstanding description of the Church's unity is the figure of the Body of Christ (1 Cor. 12:12-31). It is by one Spirit that men are incorporated into the one body. Within the body there are many members, but all are coordinated by Christ who is the head. There are diversities of gifts and ways of service, but under the guidance of the Spirit these are enhanced by the supreme spiritual gift of love and contribute to the upbuilding of the Body. As a physical body is animated by the spirit, so the Church is a visible community in which the risen

Christ is present in the midst of his people in life-giving and unifying love.

Thus the imperative to manifest our unity concretely and visibly in the world is based on the truth that God has made us one in Christ, Christ's sacrifice, which displays the infinite love and undeserved grace of God, places us under obligation to love one another, even as he has loved us (I John 4:7-21). Any form of disunity that prevents the fullest expression of love in community and which promotes strife, jealousy, or factionalism is a denial of the full meaning of the Gospel."[154]

Mackay calls attention to another dimension of the Body-of-Christ notion which found considerable support among liberal, socially and ethically oriented theologians in America. He writes:

"The figure of the body on the other hand, is the appropriate figure to express the reality of the Church militant between the times, between its founding in the apostolic era and its consummation in a mystical marriage at history's close. The body is the figure which sets forth the reality of the Church as the corporate continuation in history of the incarnation of Jesus Christ, who continues in a very real sense in 'the Church which is his body. ... If the figure of the 'body' has any meaning at all, it means that the Church's supreme task is to be in very truth the Body of Christ, in its conscious, active life, responding utterly to the will of Christ, drawing its strength from Him, and in all its relations fulfilling the new commandment of Christ to 'love one another'."[155]

It was in this sense that the CEDG interpreted the Body-of-Christ theme,[156] and in the same vein the ATC declared: "Both historically and metaphysically the Church's function may be regarded as one of carrying on and extending the work of the earthly life of Jesus."[157] This notion is found also in the papers of the TCCCNA. It too emphasizes the indwelling life of Christ through the Spirit and describes the Church's participation in the work of salvation as "that community of faithful people wherein and whereby the everliving Christ continues his work of salvation in every generation."[158] Yet it avoids the expression "continuing incarnation"[159] and warns against a univocal identification of Christ and the Church.[160] In general, moreover, it insists that the Body-of-Christ thematic can only be properly appreciated when it is set in the more historical and theo-logical perspective offered by the People-of-God/New Creation idea.[161]

Claude Welch calls attention to a further theme implicit in "the dialectic of unity and distinction between the head and the body," namely the Church's dependence upon and subjection to Christ.

"There can be no thought of autonomy in the existence of the Church but only of an existence in relation to, by participation

in, Christ the head. Therefore the Church attributes everything to him, is content to belong to him, to live below him
and to follow after him, to confess that all wisdom, holiness,
power and glory are his. The Church acknowledges that he alone
is good and righteousness, and that the holiness and righteousness of the Church consist in the confession of guilt before
God, by those who know better than others how they continually
become guilty before him and one another. The Church is sustained by his mercy.

That the church is subject to Christ as head means also that
the Church is governed by him through the Spirit, that all decisions, acts and words in the church are subordinated to his
decision, act and word, that he is ever free to dispose as he
will of the ways and forms of the church, that infallibility and
impeccability can never be claimed for them, that the church
must continually listen for his voice and distinguish it from
the voices of other lords.

This means also that the church participates in him and his
work after the pattern of his obedience and servanthood, i.e.
by serving him in obedience and self-denial, and that in no
sense by taking his place but by allowing him to express himself in the Church. As conformed to this pattern of Christ,
the forms of church life (which as such are like other social
forms) can be and are transformed by the working of Christ in
them, becoming forms of service and love."[162]

This paranetic accent is found elsewhere in the American documents,
though never with quite the sharpness of formulation and direct association with the Body-of-Christ thematic found here.[163]

One final aspect of the Body theme may be briefly noted, namely
the sacramental and liturgical connotations. Already in the New
Testament the notion is closely associated with the sacraments of
Baptism and the Lord's Supper. In this way it serves to call attention to the liturgical and sacramental character of the Christian
fellowship and to the divine source of this fellowship.[164] Nevertheless the papers warn against certain dangers latent in this thematic. An all too narrow concentration on the mystical or sacramental aspect can lead to a neglect of the historical and eschata-
logical relativity of the Church[165] and to a separation of internal
spiritual reality from outward visible institutions[166] and thus
pave the way for a univocal transfer in its putative "inner reality,"[167] an error which the TCCCNA described as "ecclesiastical
docetism."[168] A further danger is an all too narrow fixation on
the cultic relationship to Christ to the neglect of the broader perspective of the mundane relationship between God and the world of
which the Church is a believing, worshiping and serving part.[169]

D. The People-of-God Idea

The idea of the People of God as it appears in the American
papers is, even more clearly than the Body-of-Christ idea, a construction of systematic biblical theology. A variety of reasons account for this, some of them inherent in the biblical sources, others in the cognitional interests (Erkenntnisinterressen)[170] of the
theologians engaged in the search for an ecumenical ecclesiology.
Among the former is the fact that although the expression "people of
God" or its equivalent "my people" appears expressis verbis in only
two places in the New Testament,[171] a host of political, pastoral.
and cultic metaphors scattered throughout the whole New Testament
point to and expand the same basic idea.[172] Furthermore, as Minear
points out, "the galaxy of images that oscillate around this conception served in a distinctive way to place the New Testament
church in the setting of the long story of God's dealings with his
chosen people."[173] This means in the first place that the continuity and solidarity of the Church with the history and expectations
of the Old Testament people of God is underlined through the use of
this image. By that very reason however the whole story of God's
dealings with the world, from creation to the eschaton, becomes the
context of the Church's self-understanding. Thus the images which
Minear classifies under the New-Creation theme are also drawn into
the orbit of the People-of-God idea.[174] From here it is but a small
step (already anticipated in the pleroma ecclesiology of Ephesians)
to the assimilation of the Body-of-Christ thematic.[175] On the other
hand, the parallel between the Old and the New People invites the
comparison of the social structure of the two communities and thus
easily draws the fellowship motif into its gravitational field.[176]
A further reason inherent in Scripture itself is the very fact that
although the individual texts in which the People-of-God motif is
most clearly alluded to are relatively brief and undeveloped, they
immediately direct the reader's attention to the whole trinitarian
economy of salvation which is graspable only in a synthetic vision
embracing the whole of Scripture and the historical experience of
the "churches" of both covenants.

Of even greater weight for the practical decision to develop
the theme in the way they did, are the cognitional interests underlying the American discussions. One such interest is brought out
by the ATC report. Ecumenism is not simply a concern with the unity

of the Church now in spatial and geographical terms but also with
the unity of the Church with its past in temporal and historical
terms: "We must think of the Church through the centuries; we must
include also the Roman Catholic branch of Christianity and the Orthodox bodies. Although the latter are but a small minority in the
United States, they have a significant part in any complete union of
the Church. Can formulas be found which include all these...?"[177]
In the face of the evident lack of uniformity in discipline liturgy,
ministry and organization, the ATC takes hope from the essential
agreement achieved by the Edinburgh Conference on the doctrine of
Grace, as the manifestation of God's love for sinful divided mankind
expressed in Jesus Christ, and the fellowship shared at the same
Conference as "an experience of God and dedication to his will." Inspired by this experience the ATC report declares: "paradoxically
as it may seen, a broad and universal agreement lies in the very idea
of the Church itself as the people of God. It has been truly said
that this is the most original aspect of our faith. Most religions
have priests and temples, liturgies and codes, but the idea of the
Church is characteristic of Biblical religion in which all Christian
groups share."[178]

H. Richard Niebuhr suggests two further interests operative in
the discussions of the TCCCNA, when he calls attention to the decisions about purpose and context which have hitherto guided ecumenical efforts to define the Church. The one is "the decision to distinguish ourselves from the world. We seem to have decided implicitly if not explicitly that we must define ourselves as church in
opposition to the world. What we are not, is the world." This decision, Niebuhr notes is the product of a specific historical situation, the German Kirchenkampf, the threat of Communism, the secularization of political, economic and cultural institutions, and it is
not without objective basis in Scripture; it is not arbitrary,
nevertheless it is also not necessary, it represents an option which
must consciously be evaluated as to its continued utility.[179] The
same holds true, he adds, for the decision about the context of prevailing definitions. Obviously connected with the search for unity
is "the tendency of the church to define itself almost exclusively by
reference to Jesus Christ and to interpret the Scriptures in Christocentric fashion." Nevertheless, for all its evident advantages for
this purpose,

"there are certain aspects of the present tendency toward decision that strike one as not necessitated either by anything
objective or by previous decision. Among these are the emphasis on revelation in the work of Christ more than on reconciliation, on the deity of Christ more than on the humanity; on
the doctrine of Christ more than on the historical actuality
of the person; on the incarnation more than on the death and[180]
resurrection; on the first more than on the second coming."

Precisely with the aid of the heilsgeschichtliche perspective impli-

cit in the People-of-God motif the Commission sought to correct the

one-sidedness of both tendencies criticized by Niebuhr. With the

aid of this new point of view it sought to dissolve the confessional

dichotomies which remained frozen in the older ecclesiocentric and

christocentric ecclesiology. This was its "interest" in the People

of God theme.[181]

1. The People of God in Cosmic Perspective

As developed in the American discussions, the conceptual con-

stellation of the People-of-God idea is not a symmetrical elipse

but a pear-shaped figure, whose weightier end represents the uni-

versal cosmic dimensions of salvation history, whereas the lighter

end concentrates the more particular associations of the Church with

Israel. Since we will be considering the American reflections on

the divine and human elements in the Church in the next chapter, it

will be sufficient here simply to illustrate this first part of the

figure with a few typical texts. A characteristic summary of the

way the matter was viewed is offered by the following passage from

the COCU Open Letter:

"God calls into being his own people for obedience to his mission everywhere in the world. In Jesus Christ, he has created
the Church which is forever being empowered and renewed by the
Holy Spirit. He constitutes a community bound together in
faith, hope, and love, united to its one Savior and Lord, and
commissioned to serve him in the service of men.
    The Church is one, made so by the act of God in Christ. Its
life is the one Holy Spirit given through Christ. Because of
this given unity, the disunity of the visible companies of
Christian people is at any time and place a challenge to the
truth--even where the supreme claim of conscience seems to require separation for the truth's sake--and a rejection of the
unity implicit in the saving love of the one God for our single
humanity.
    The Church is summoned to the service of the divine purpose
for all men. We share with all Christian people the charge to
be Christ's witnesses 'to the ends of the earth' (Acts 1:8 RSV).
    We are commanded to declare by deed and word that 'Jesus
Christ is Lord, to the glory of God the Father' (Phil. 2:11
RSV). The church is created to make this Lordship known; its

faith, its ministry, its structures, its worship, and its life
are instruments of this mission.

Our impulse to mission and unity comes from the gospel we
proclaim. Our God is a self-giving God, who comes to us in his
Son Jesus Christ. This Man, who gave himself freely and fully
to us, continually makes accessible to us the grace and peace
of a living and loving God. All his gifts come through his
Spirit, who is doing new things among us through his liberating,
surprising power. By giving himself, the Eternal Father has
called into being a single family in the Son and the Spirit.
He has sealed with us all a single covenant, grounded in the
same ultimate demand and promise. He has made us all stewards
of the mysteries of the gospel and the Scriptures, freely opening to us the inexhaustible treasures of the living Tradition
of his people, in its oneness, its holiness, its catholicity
and its apostolicity. To us all he has addressed his commands,
his promises, his abundant mercies. We believe he has gracious-
ly included even the stories of our separate communions within
the story of his mighty acts, from the first day until now."[182]

The first thing to note here is the strong economic trinitarian-
ism of this passage. God calls into being his people; in Jesus
Christ he creates the Church, which is constantly empowered and renewed by the Spirit. God acts in Christ; Christ gives the Spirit.
The Church is called to serve God's purpose, by proclaiming the
Lordship of Christ, communicated by the gifts of the Spirit. Already in the ATC report this perspective is prominent, though the
role of the Spirit is ignored in the context of presenting the
People-of-God theme.[183] The same holds for the exposition of the
Wright Committee's exposition.[184] The other alternative is found
in Mackay's contribution to the Interseminary Symposium. Here God
and Spirit are closely associated in the People-of-God context,
whereas the relationship of the Church to Christ is reserved for the
exposition of the Body-of-Christ notion.[185] The full integration of
the trinitarian perspective is then finally achieved in the Oberlin
report which declares: "Unity rests primarily on what God has done,
is doing, and will do. By his act of creation he has made us for
unity. By his redemptive action in Jesus Christ, he has made us
one. And by the continual activity of his Spirit he renews our life
in order that we may manifest our unity."[186]

A second motif running through the whole passage is the socie-
tal, i.e. the connection between social fabric and social function
of the Church. The Church is a community bound together by faith,
hope and love; it is a community obedient to a divine mission. The
Church is made one by God; it must manifest its unity to the world.
It is called to the service of men, especially to the proclamation

of the Lordship of Christ; to this end all of its actions and insti-
tutions--its faith, its ministry, its structures, its worship, its
life--are instrumentally subordinated. The divine mission and the
divine gifts are the prerogative of all not of a select few, but
this total gift comes to the Church "through many ministries under
his ordering: apostles, prophets, teachers, nurses, physicians,
housewives, musicians, workmen, farmers, missionaries, trustees and
stewards of every talent."[187] The "channels and tokens of God's
self-giving" are many and various, some evident at first glance,
others hidden and easily overseen: "acts of quiet neighborliness;
the simple integrity and honesty of people in their dealings with
one another; personal and public prayers and praise and interces-
sion; the singing of psalms and hymns; the giving and spending of
money; the celebration of festivals and sacraments; voluntary participation in public affairs; dependability in secular vocations;
courageous efforts to secure justice and peace in national life."[188]
These accents too may be considered typical of the American papers
which explicitly develop the People-of-God theme.[189]

A third motif developed in this passage is the use of the
People-of-God notion to bring together the divided traditions and
divided history of the separated churches in the one tradition and
the one history of God's dealings with mankind. By giving himself,
God has called into being "a single family in the Son and the Spirit." Bound together with the same covenant, sharing alike in the
mysteries of the same gospel and Scriptures, enjoying access to the
inexhaustible treasures of the living Tradition, the separate communions are already united by God, endowed with the gifts of oneness, holiness, catholicity, and apostolicity of the People of
God.[190] This too is an emphasis which, for all its conceptual dependence upon the Montreal discussions of the tradition problem,[191]
represents a line of thinking going back to the beginnings of the
American discussions.[192]

2. The People of God in Historical Perspective

The assertion made earlier, that the American papers tend to
subordinate the Israel thematic to the broader perspective of cosmic
salvation history finds confirmation in the failure of the COCU text
quoted above to make explicit mention of either Israel or the Kingdom. Here we have to do with a complex of ideas clustered around
the second pole of the People-of-God constellation. Minear notes

that in the New Testament context the national-political connotations of the People of God thematic are the central focus.[193] Why
the American papers tend to relegate it to second, though none the
less important place, can be explained, it seems, by a variety of
factors. First of all, even in the New Testament, the overall emphasis is on the transcendence of the nationalistic and political
aspects of the Judaic idea: Jews and Gentiles have become one people
under the lordship of Christ, whose Kingdom is real but still hidden
in the present dispensation. Secondly, the systematic application
of the People of God motif to ecclesiology must necessarily call attention to the distinction of the Church from both Israel and the
eschatological Kingdom. Thirdly, as a methodological consequence
of the two previous reasons, it is easier to treat the relation of
the Church to the Kingdom by way of a special excursus rather than
to interrupt the flow of the heilsgeschichtliche narrative.[194]

A typical expression of American thinking on this problem can
be found in the ATC report, where the question is treated in the
context of a discussion of "the historical beginnings of the Christian Church."

> "Two Jewish conceptions," the paper declares, "were fundamental
> for the development of the Church. The first was that of the
> Qahal, which expressed the religious unity of the Jews as the
> one people of God. Israel's prophets felt that she was of
> God's own choosing. She formed a divine society which had been
> created by God and was preserved and governed by him; its laws
> were his laws. As God was a God of judgment, punishment might
> fall even on his people, for they had sinned in violating his
> law. But in God's mercy and in his steadfast purpose to create
> for himself a holy people, at least a 'remnant' would be saved.
> They were not the 'escaped' but the 'saved.' This Jewish con-
> ception of the people of God was basic for Christian thought;
> even one who like Paul made the work of Christ definitive for
> salvation still referred to the whole Church, Gentile as well
> as Jewish, as the 'Israel of God' and the 'seed of Abraham.'
> Closely allied was the other Jewish conception of the king-
> dom or rule of God. God as creator was king in the world which
> he had made. But because of sin, the perfect rule of God was
> not found on earth. It was confined to the devout who 'took on
> themselves the yoke of the kingdom' by recognizing the sover-
> eignty of God in obedience to his Law. But the time would come
> when the kingdom of evil would be overthrown and replaced by the
> consummate rule of God. The resurrection and the judgment would
> accompany that great day when God would assert his power. In-
> stead of the people of God being under the heel of Gentile dom-
> ination, 'the saints of the Most High' would rule.
> Jesus made the idea of the Kingdom of God central to his mes-
> sage and work. He began his ministry with the announcement,
> 'Repent, for the kingdom of God is at hand.' He sought an inner

renewal in view of the imminent coming of the kingdom with power. ... The impending crisis brought a division among men. Since Israel as a whole did not repent, it meant doom and judgment to those who could not read the signs of the times. ...

Alongside this eschatological teaching in the gospels stand other teachings which indicate belief in a certain presence of the kingdom in the work of Jesus. Especially the demon exorcisms and the other healings are interpreted as evidence that the Messianic prophecies were actually being fulfilled. Jesus was actually gathering the outcasts of Israel and in some way constituting the New Israel before the great day came.

Some modern interpreters understand this to mean that Jesus was launching the Messianic kingdom. ... Others, however, insist that these words about the presence of the Kingdom in no sense eliminate the eschatological orientation of the teaching of Jesus. ...

Despite the differences of opinion at this point, most members of the Committee would agree that Jesus did not intentionally found a new religion. His religious and ethical teaching stood in direct continuity with the best thought of his people. Yet Jesus did come into conflict with the leadership of the contemporary Judaism because he stood so definitely in the prophetic tradition. In many ways he showed an attitude of freedom in dealing with the requirements of the national law. ... This liberal ferment in the teaching of Jesus firmly implanted the spirit of innovation in the Christian movement. Though in Jeremiah the new covenant was an inward renewal of the old covenant with Israel, when the early Christians associated that word with Jesus, it came to be interpreted in terms of radical opposition to the old.

The crucifixion of Jesus did not end the movement which he inaugurated. His disciples were soon proclaiming not simply the message of Jesus but further convictions about him. Thus Jesus was the Anointed or the Christ who would rule in the coming kingdom. God had vindicated him by raising Jesus from the dead; the promised Spirit had been sent, the assurance of final salvation. At first the disciples made no break with Judaism but continued to join in the worship of synagogue and Temple. Only as the main company of the Jews refused to accept these beliefs and roundly opposed them did 'those of the way' ...become a separate body.

As more and more Gentiles accepted the message and were not compelled to become obedient to the whole Jewish Law, the separation of the believers in the Messiahship of Jesus from the main body of Jews became increasingly definitive. ... Christ had broken down the middle wall of partition and made of both Jew and Gentile one new people. They applied to themselves all of the holy names for the 'people of God,' as they found in the Old Testament. ... The organization was now entirely separate from Judaism and one early ascribed to the authority of Christ himself."[195]

In this passage it is possible to identify a series of notions which reappear in the other American discussions of the theme. The first point to notice is that although everywhere great stress is laid upon the continuity of the Church with the Israel of the Old Covenant, the principal theme which is developed is that of the new-

ness and uniqueness of the Church.[196] Generally speaking this is
accomplished in the first place by means of the categories of pro-
mise/expectation and fulfillment. Already in the Old Covenant thanks
to the prophets the all too narrow nationalistic and political expectations of God's people have been transcended by the expectation
of a "supra-national, universal people of God with the mission of
proclaiming and embodying the reconciling work of God..."[197] As
Mackay says: "...Israel was never allowed to believe, either that
its election was based upon special racial virtue or goodness, or
that its unity and prosperity would be contingent upon its own wisdom or might. National unity had its source in God. It could only
be maintained through loyalty to God, whose ultimate purpose was
that the unity of Israel should become a rallying point for the
spiritual unity of mankind."[198]

This is also the sense of the exceedingly dense argumentation
of the Christ and the Church paper.[199] It distinguishes a twofold
newness of the Church with respect to Israel, a "radical newness"
indicated by the term "new humanity" and a chronological novelty indicated by the expression "kairos." The radical newness of the
Church is not a break with but the fulfillment of the original covenant: "The promise and the covenant were given to Israel. The
Church participates in that promise and covenant through the fulfillment of the promises and the new establishment of the covenant
in Jesus Christ." Already in the original covenant the Son and the
Spirit were at work; the "new" was anticipated in Israel in the expectation of the Messiah and the vision of the outpouring of the
Spirit already at work in Israel. The "newness" of the Church, therefore, "is a fulfillment, which also entails correction and transformation, accomplished in the person and work of Christ and the Spirit,
of that which was previously known of the 'new' in Israel." This
radical newness indicated by the term "new humanity" finds a "relative and parabolic expression in the chronological novelty of the
Church. The time of the Church is a chronologically new time." The
Son and the Spirit who were already at work in Israel have become
present as Jesus Christ and his Spirit at a specific moment in history. "Here is kairos; but here also is a given and specific
chronos. The Church is defined by this historically visible expression of the promised newness of life."

A second point to note is the way in which the notion of the
kingdom which was the center of Jesus' preaching as both new reality
and new time tends in the American papers to lose its eschatological
distinctiveness by being reduced to the more generic notion of God's
rule over the world. This development is already anticipated in the
Ethical Reality paper, which states:

> "The kingdom of God is the consummation of the divine purpose in
> the world, uniting all these things by the power of love, and
> fulfilling all righteousness. In so far as love and righteous-
> ness are present within the Christian church the kingdom is
> found in that measure in the church. Inasmuch as the Christian
> fellowship is an imperfect manifestation of that love and
> righteousness, the kingdom cannot be identified with the Church.
> Because God's kingdom is to embrace all creation in an ultimate
> unity, it presents to the Church its greatest moral challenge.
> Because God is already the ultimate ruler, the kingdom of God
> is the basis of whatever validity our moral striving may pos-
> sess, and gives to the church its hope and strength. The com-
> munity of all Christians is thus not an end in itself, but a
> means to, and a part of the redemption of the whole world."[200]

In the Christ and the Church paper, the word "kingdom" disappears
completely· instead the matter is treated under the title "(b) The
Church and the World" immediately following and parallel to the
treatment of "(a) Israel of the New and Old Covenants."[201] This is
not to say that the eschatological dimension disappears completely;
in both papers one finds qualifying side remarks indicating that the
ultimate fulfillment of the divine rule is yet to come and that it
is more than anything that can be achieved by way of a more perfect
realization of the unity or moral mission of the Church.[202] The
reality which is not yet is not lost to view, but the stress is on
the already realized: in the words of the TCCC, "the Lord of the
Church not only is to be the Lord of the whole creation; he already
is this" (original italics).[203] The aim here, however is not to
glorify the Church; on the contrary, the emphasis is on the subordination of the Church as servant of the divine rule; it is one but
not the only instrument by which God works in the world to achieve
his purpose of salvation and reconciliation.[204] Not the Church but
the World is the principal object and partner of God's action.[205]
This way of viewing the relationship of the Church to both Israel and
to the Kingdom enables the American papers to integrate the evident
phenomena of imperfection and sin into their idea of the Church.[206]

In the following chapter we shall have occasion to treat these
themes in detail. For the moment, our aim is only to take note of

the way in which the American papers interpret and use these theological idea-constellations. Before leaving this topic, however, it is well to note a third viewpoint, which though not stressed in the texts we have hitherto cited, nevertheless plays an important role in the ecclesiology of all the commissions. This is the notion that the sociological structure of the People of God is a community constituted by the worshipful recollection of the mighty deeds of its Lord.[207] The following passage out of the Wright Committee paper offers perhaps the best expression of this thought:

> "In both the Old and New Testaments the central affirmation is concerned with God's <u>saving work</u> to the end that he might create a people for himself (e.g. I Pet. 2:9-10). The community thus formed was united in common worship in which the central act was a confessional recital of what had happened, accompanied by expressions of joy, praise and thanksgiving, by interpretive statements or exposition of the meaning of what had been confessed, and by reaffirmation of loyalty to the Lord who was the community's Ruler. In other words, biblical people really believed that they had been saved by God through his historical work. God's salvation had made them into a people and had bound them to himself. And this belief was kept alive as the chief constituting factor of community life because it was kept central in worship."[208]

This thought provides a springboard for the treatment of the Church's institutions, e.g. her sacraments, the confessions, the Bible, the organized leadership in a perspective which stresses their functional relativity with respect to both God's action and the response of the community of believers.[209] The Church is seen more "as a people than as an organization." This consciousness is what distinguished it from the numerous "guilds, clubs and religious societies which were as typical of the Roman world as they are of ours." The same consciousness accounted for "the secondary and ancillary role of organization within the community" of both the old and the New Israel.[210]

IV. ECCLESIOLOGICAL IDEA AND ECCLESIASTICAL REALITY

In the preceding section we saw how the American commissions developed the three principal ideas which traditionally have served as the basis for a theological definition of the Church. In point of fact, however, it must be admitted that the commissions not only refused to play these diverse ideas off against each other, as traditional confessional ecclesiology has so often done, but, in the last analysis, they consistently abstained from offering a single compact definition of the Church. One finds time and again statements of the type: "the Church is ...," but it is impossible to isolate any of these statements from their context as though they represented an attempt in a sentence or two to express the "essence" of the Church. The reasons for this abstinence lie deeper than a mere accidental inability of their members to reach agreement on such a definition. The abstention from such definitions has its roots in the epistemological and ontological principles which came to light in the American discussions. These will be our concern in this last section of our investigation of their reflections on the relationship between the Church of fact and the Church of faith.

A first approach to this topic is offered by the <u>Communion</u> <u>of</u> <u>Saints</u> report. Noting that the manifold opinions about the nature of the Church tend to fall into three general classes, the report suggests that these can be compared to the classic philosophical interpretations of the universal. Thus among ecclesiologists there are:

(1) "The N e o - p l a t o n i c   o r   p l a t o n i c   r e a l - i s t s , for whom the Church invisible is a mystical spiritual substantial unity, the totality practically submerging the reality of the individual members..."
(2) "The A r i s t o t e l i a n   r e a l i s t s , for whom the Church is a spiritual unity of regenerated individuals united in Christ, the Son of God, not partaking of the divine substance but in moral and spiritual union with Him."
(3) "The C o n c e p t u a l i s t s ...who regard the Church as having reality merely in the human concept."[211]

As the history of philosophy suggests and the further explanation which the report offers of the last position hints,[212] there are really two distinct but related questions involved here. On the one hand, there is the <u>epistemological</u> question: in what manner is the nature of the Church knowable? how is this knowledge formulable? On the other hand, there is the ontological question: to what extent and in what manner is that which we identify as the

nature of the Church realized in the factual Church we experience?[213]
The American commissions and study groups addressed themselves to
both questions, or better to both aspects of the one question: how
is the Church of faith realized·in the Church of fact, and the answers they worked out are generally combined answers to the more
general question. However for the sake of clearer presentation and
comparison it seems best to distinguish their answers according to
the two aspects of the one general question.

A. How can the nature of the Church be defined?

So far we have been considering various elements of a definition
of the Church; indeed, insofar as they are treated separately, one
might speak of three distinct imperfect definitions. The identification of the distinct empirical referents of the term "Church" was
in effect an exercise in n o m i n a l definition. In admitting,
however, that all of the various communities designated are diverse
manifestations of one and the same reality, the commission papers
point to the need to define this all-embracing reality which is the
"Church" with a capital "C".[214] In attempting to describe sociologically the kind of community constitutive of the Church in all of
its various manifestations, we advanced to what might be considered
a d e s c r i p t i v e definition of the Church, but, as we saw,
the American commissions were not and could not be content with such
a description, for the very nature of the social community implied a
reference to the theological dimension of the Church's life. Thus
we followed the discussion of the three principal biblical ideas of
the Church. Here however the question arises, whether or not these
ideas serve as anything more than a m e t a p h o r i c a l definition of the Church's theological reality?

This question was treated more explicitly in the discussions
of the TCCCNA. Minear's answer is that the attempt to "distinguish
between figurative and non-figurative words and meanings" among the
New Testament pictures, or between a metaphorical and an ontological
sense of a particular image, is really to put a false question, for
"the criteria for valid answers lie not in the images per se but in
the reality to which they pointed and in the imagination that adopted them as pointers." The metaphorical and the ontological are in-
extricably bound up with one another both in the nature of the

Christian community and in the character of the Christian imagination.

> "We might visualize a church that could be described adequately in literal terms only, with exact denotations that could be relied on to answer all ontological questions. Would that be the body of Christ? I do not think so. Or, if you prefer, visualize a church that could be defined adequately in nothing but figurative terms that carried no literal references and had no ontological Referent. Would that be His body? I do not think so. When we treat any of the New Testament figures for the church as merely literal or as merely metaphorical, we disclose all too clearly either the phantasmagorical or the pedestrian abnormality of our own minds."[215]

The explanation for which the commission opted was to speak of such ideas as "analogical," admitting at the same time that some would prefer the expression "sacramental."[216] In speaking of analogy, as Nelson's interim report explains, the point is "to avoid complete identity or utter discontinuity between them [the terms of the analogy], while maintaining the attributes which are in common and those which are distinct."[217]

These observations of the TCCCNA make clear the intrinsic limitations of all of these ideas by themselves in providing a definition of the Church. Applied to the Church even the notions of people and community are analogies which focus the understanding on specific aspects of the Church's reality only at the risk of obscuring or even distorting others.[218] In the words of the COCU Guidelines: "...the Church is more than any one of the images we use to describe it can convey..."[219] This is the ultimate reason why in fact none of the commissions yielded to the temptation to develop one theme to the exclusion or neglect of the others. If the tendency is to give a certain priority to the People-of-God theme, it is only because this provides the most universal context in terms of which the more specific focuses of the other ideas can best be appreciated. But as we have seen, all of the commissions were equally insistent on the need to interpret the People-of-God idea in the light of the correctives and elaborations supplied by these other analogies.[220] Neither by themselves nor collectively can such ideas be considered an adequate essential definition of the Church.[221] Even the most careful systematic elaboration of a theology of the Church can never dissolve or synthetically overcome the essential polarity of the Church.[222] For its "essence," as we shall see in the following section, exists precisely at the moving socio-temporal meeting point, where God's creating and reconciling action in the Word through the Spirit, incarnate in Jesus Christ and communicated through the Spirit of Christ encounters the world of sinning but believing, divided yet united, fallen yet reunited men.

To this ultimate ontological reason for the inadequacy of any theological conception to capture the full nature of the Church comes a second epistemological reason. As Niebuhr pointed out every human attempt at definition is perspectivist, for it is conditioned by a series of implicit practical decisions about purpose, extension, and context, and this is all the more so true when, as in the case of the Church, the reality to be defined is not only a fact but a task. Such perspectives are necessarily conditioned by the empirical experience of the Church at a given moment in its history.[223] But the reality which the theologian experiences is itself always ambiguous: conditioned, on the one hand, by the socio-cultural milieu in which it necessarily participates; distorted, on the other, by sin, which --though the contrary of the Church's essence--cannot be separated from the real being of the Church.[224] And so the ultimate paradox is that the conceptual elaboration of an ecumenical definition of the Church will not so much be the cause as the effect of the experience of the ecumenical unity of the Church. In the words of the preliminary report of the TCCCNA, "it may be that such agreement as is requisite to unity cannot be found on the conceptual level alone, but rather behind and beyond the conceptual level."[225]

To say this is not to derogate from the value of theological inquiry into the nature of the Church, only to point out its limitations and conditions. From beginning to end the American commissions were engaged in an earnest attempt to cope precisely with the problem of theologically understanding the nature of the Church under the circumstances imposed by these limitations and conditions. They refused to be satisfied with either a conceptless pragmatism[226] or a capitulation before paradox.[227] Their recognition of the futility of any attempt to discover the essential definition, in terms of which all the disputed issues might be resolved deductively, only spurred them on in the more modest yet also more promising attempt to construct an inductive synthesis by way of a succession of approximations.

In the course of their attempt, they identified, elaborated, and applied three methodological principles. The first might best

be called the e c o n o m i c   p r i n c i p l e , using the term
"economy" here in the patristic sense. According to this principle,
the nature of the Church can only be viewed properly when it is
viewed in the context of God's dealings with the World; only in this
perspective can the relationship of Christ and his Spirit to the
Church be properly understood.[228] The second is the p o l a r i t y
p r i n c i p l e . Because the being of the Church is a being-in-
relation, its nature can be grasped only by calling attention to the
various aspects of the constitutive relationships which determine
it.[229] It is important to note that more than one relationship is
involved. It is not simply that the Church stands in relationship
to the triune God on the one side and to the World on the other.
Despite the influence of the Hebraic idea of collective personality
in some of the biblical images, the American papers warn against
hypostatizing the Church as though it were somehow an acting subject distinct from the believing yet sinful men who make it up.
The Church itself, taken as a whole, is a complex network of relations between its members, their activities and their institutions.
Moreover these same persons, activities, and institutions are a part
of the world, which after all is itself a relational and not a substantial being. The final principle is, in a sense, only an application of the preceding; it might be designated as the f u n c -
t i o n a l   p r i n c i p l e . It insists that none of the actions or institutions of the Church are ends in themselves; theologically their being is entirely dependent on the function they have
to fulfill in the divine economy. This means that it is impossible
to separate their theological consideration from the empirical evidence of their concrete fulfillment or non-fulfillment of this function.[230]

On the basis of these principles, it would appear impossible to
formulate a single definition of the Church integrating in a single
formula all the essential aspects of its reality. With this reservation, however, one may take the concluding paragraph of the ATC
report as a useful summary of the American way of conceiving of the
Church. No doubt one commission or the other would have preferred a
somewhat different expression here or there--a more explicit statement of the trinitarian economy, a clearer expression of the Church's
imperfection and sin, a stronger emphasis on the reconciliation of
social divisions, etc.--and all the expressions cry for further

explanation. Nevertheless, it is unlikely that any subsequent commission would have disagreed fundamentally with the conclusion of
the ATC report on the Nature of the Church:

> "What is the Church? It is the sphere of God's salvation in
> the present, and it is prophetic of his ultimate triumph in
> the Kingdom of God. It is constituted by the revelation of his
> grace in Jesus Christ. Its message is the gospel of redemptive
> love. It is marked by the presence of his Holy Spirit with all
> of its evidence of divine power. It is the people who have
> given allegiance to God in response to his gracious call. It
> is a body witnessing to his rule by their trust and obedience.
> This Church is set in the midst of a world where God's will is
> not yet done. The forms of organization exist to maintain its
> life and proclaim the message to the needs of men down the ages.
> They are simply earthly vessels which help to protect the heav-
> enly treasure in the midst of its earthly task. But all of the
> branches must be truly united in order to witness to the rule
> of God in a Church Militant. For they all look forward to the
> Church Triumphant, which is the Kingdom of God."[231]

B. How is the Nature of the Church Realized?

1. The Rejected Models

To admit that the Church really is all of this is to repudiate
in principle any idealist or conceptualist attempt to resolve the
essential polarity of the Church by reducing it to a duality of fact
and ideal. George Welch, followed by the TCCCNA report, compares
these inadequate solutions to the ancient christological errors of
ebionism and docetism.

(a) The e b i o n i t e view of the Church sees only the
sociological; it may admit the existence of an "invisible church,"
a transcendent spiritual fellowship of all men or all true believers
with God and one another, but this ideal fellowship constitutes a
realm apart, having little or nothing to do with the actual church
which is simply "a voluntaristic assocation of individual believers."[232] "Although its purposes may be divine, although it may be
modeled after and look to the creation on earth of an ideal fellowship whose principle and spirit are revealed in Christ, the actual
church is a humanly established and constituted community, formed
out of the assent of its members to certain common beliefs and purposes."[233] Very often this notion of the Church is combined with a
privatization of religion, as though the church be simply a "religious society" catering to the essentially private needs of the
believers, but it is also combinable with a society-oriented view

of the church's role. The error of this view is that it focuses exclusively on the human side of the Church, reducing the polarity simply to a moral tension between the Church as it is and as it should be. The New Testament faith that the Church "not only ought to be, but is, the True Israel and the New Humanity is compromised."[234]

The NAWG report denounced a similar error when it warned against "sociological reductionism."[235] The supposition of this attitude is that neither the Church as the organized community of believers nor theology as the interpretation of the community experience "in any way transcend the flow of history." It argues "that all talk of the theologians about 'continuity' in the church because its life is 'given' by God, and all the talk about the renewability of the institution of the church by the Spirit, is crypto-sociology which seeks to give the past institutional forms of the church an authority to which they have no earthly right." For all of its sympathy with the need for radical reform of the Church's institutional structures, the commission as a whole rejected this tendency of the "revolutionary" minority of its members, noting that it fails "to take seriously the historical character of Christian revelation. Because the Christian faith is historical, the forms of this faith and life are open to change and because God is faithful to his purpose, there is continuity in the midst of that change." Behind such an attitude is the irresponsible and ultimately unrealizable wish of its protagonists to "lift themselves out of the continuities of history by opting out of the battle for the re-formation of the continuing institutional life of the church."

(b) The opposite error is an "ecclesiological d o c e t i s m ," which concentrates its view on the divine character of the Church to the exclusion of its human side, especially the imperfection and sin which are the consequences though not the whole of the human side of the Church. Welch notes that this error takes two forms, one typically "catholic," the other typically "protestant."

"It may take the form (1) of a divinization of the historical faith, forms and structures of the church. Thus the church, whatever may be the failings of its members, is itself beyond the ambiguities, contradiction and imperfections which everywhere else characterize human existence. Its dogmatic pronouncements are infallible, its symbols and structure are irreformable. Human language, acts and patterns have been so elevated (or transformed) by the Holy Spirit that they share in the perfection and absoluteness of God himself. Sin and error cannot be attributed to the church as such, and this precisely in its manifest historical form.

(2) A similar judgment about the church takes the form of an apparently opposite assertion, viz., that the church is a purely 'spiritual community.' Here a radical distinction is drawn between true church and institution, to the depreciation of the latter. Churchly institutions there are, but these are not the divinely established ecclesia; at best they are external means. ... The implication...is that there is a 'true' church, a perfect community, the ecclesia above and beyond (or perhaps within) the historical institutions, and it is to this that we ought to direct our concern. This alone is essential, for here is the true community called by God.

What unites these two seemingly quite divergent descriptions is the common judgment that the church (however one may seek to locate and identify it) does not essentially participate in the fallibility and corruption of our common human nature. Whether these elements are assigned simply to the members of the church ...or to accidental and secondary 'institutions' is not for the moment important. In either case, the church qua church is exempt."[236]

The corresponding error diagnosed by the NAWG report was that of "theological reductionism," i.e. "the feeling that only theologians can talk about 'church' and 'mission,' and that sociologists must be the servants of the queen of the sciences. ...it is assumed that 'church' can first be defined in some theological realm above and outside the sociological."[237] This attitude too, the majority of the group rejected, and their argument was the same as that against sociological reductionism, namely that it overlooks "the historical character of the Christian faith and the fact that all traditional formulations arose in particular historical situations."[238] Thus the Church is enslaved to its past, its possibilities narrowed to the criteria developed in past situations quite different from those confronting it today. Over against such a view the majority of the commission took the position that "we cannot know in advance how much institutional reform or displacement might be required. Resistance to both theological and sociological reductionists should leave us open to test the varied 'hunches' which the rough groupings--reformers, radicals, revolutionaries-- present."[239]

(c) Welch goes on to diagnose three other inadequate explanations. The first is the appeal to the distinction visible/invisible, whether in the form of a church within a church, i.e. "the company of true Christians as distinguished from the wider circle of nominal church members either in the sense of a predestined few, or in the

pietistic sense of the select group who have achieved perfection, or
in the form of "a kind of 'Platonic' essence, of which the visible
churches are partial and defective images." Solutions of this type
tend either to remove the "true" church into a purely transcendent
spiritual realm only loosely connected with the empirical reality,
or the transcendent and the empirical church are simply put in parallel with each other, leaving the relationship unexplained. "To
speak of two churches in this way seems to be quite as unacceptable
as to speak of two Christs."[240] In any case, the inadequacy of such
a view is manifest in its inability to do justice to the way the New
Testament speaks of the oneness and solidarity of the empirical community, at the same time acknowledging its sinfulness and imperfection.

(d) Likewise inadequate is the view which would locate the tension simply in the eye of the beholder: "As the body of Christ and
the work of the Holy Spirit, the church is hidden from the eyes of
the world, but it is visible to the eyes of faith. It is one and
the same church, the church in this world, which appears to the outward eye and to faith, but only faith can see that the disunited and
imperfect body is nevertheless the one and holy people of God."[241]
As far as it goes, Welch notes, this view is correct. "It begins at
the right place, with the confession of faith in response to the act
of God. ...as there is a hiddenness, an incognito in the life of
Christ, so is the regenerate life of man and the life of the church
hidden in God." Only the eyes of faith can penetrate the ambiguity.
Nevertheless, to stop here means either to settle for a kind of dou-
ble truth theory or to abandon the theological quest altogether.
"Granted that we must view with the eyes of faith, we need also to
ask what does faith see? We have to inquire what it is which God
has wrought in the incarnation, in the creation of a new humanity
and a holy people. What are the 'hidden' realities we confess, and
how do they relate to the quite earthly and unholy realities so
plainly evident to all?"[242]

(e) The same objection holds for the "both--and" solutions: as
Christ truly is and not only is to be viewed as God and man, so also
the Church "is both the body of Christ and religious institution,
both holy and sinful," but the "how" of these unities is beyond our
comprehension.[243] Admittedly the mysteries of God's dealing with
man is ultimately beyond our comprehension, nevertheless, as Welch

notes, "we can and must explore them to the fullest possible extent.
Otherwise, we risk falling into the trap of making paradox itself a
theological principle, adopting this as the appropriate test of
Christian affirmation. Or we reduce theology to a simple reitera-
tion of biblical terms. Or we find ourselves using such utterly
vague expressions as 'in some real way' God was in Christ or Christ
is present in the church, which really reveal only that we do not
know exactly what we are want to say. The task of theology is precisely to try to avoid such ambiguities, to say so far as possible
in what ways we refer to the church as sinful society and as people
of God, to Christ as man and as God."[244]

2. The Process Model

In point of fact, none of the American commissions settled for
any of these inadequate solutions. Instead, the overall trend was
to adopt a process model for explaining the relationship. In the
reports of the earlier commissions, the terminology remains unclear,
but the intention is unmistakable. The empirical church is the historical manifestation of an "unseen factor," "people of God," or
"transcendental fellowship," which is distinct but not separate from
the particular temporal form of the empirical church. Perhaps the
best expression for what is intended here is the word "nature" in
its aristotelian sense of an internal principle of being and operation. Brown's report of the CCULW speaks of "the unseen factor which
gives this common life and institutional activity significance as the
point of contact with the eternal and everlasting God."[245] That more
is involved here than simply a conceptual interpretation of the sociological is clear from the context. This factor is the source and
determinant of the communion of saints, the locus of the means by
which the divine life is mediated to men in this communion, and the
principle giving being and significance to the empirical expressions
of the Church's essential functions of witness, worship, teaching,
discipline, nurture and service.[246] For the ATC, it is the trans-
historical community signified by the term "people of God" which
calls the empirical organized Church into being inasmuch as "it is
chiefly through its institutional expressions that the function of
the Church can be realized in the world."[247] Or in the words of the
CEG, it is "a dimension of the church which though not separate from
the visible church is also not identical with it," an "invisible
presence of the Spirit of Christ" whose power and authority give

rise to and yet transcend the particular judgments of men which find expression in the momentary forms of the visible church. It represents the norm by which these must be judged, the ideal to which they must be approximated, but it "is also the church that gives power and validity to our efforts as members of visible bodies of Christians."[248] Precisely because it is the inner principle of the life of the visible church, it is the source of both unity and diversity, of continuity and discontinuity, the judgment upon and the victory over the manifest sin and imperfection of the Church.

Paul Scherer's contribution to the Interseminary study speaks of a reality "which is at the very edge of coming into existence, not yet to be seen, but more real than all the communities which are passing away; an emergent, as mind was an emergent through the long ages. The most powerful thing in the world, though not yet conscious of itself, and in some sense invisible. It is a fellowship moving persistently into the world of events, not to be denied, betrayed at our peril, restoring and being itself restored, never destroying but always being fulfilled, existing not of itself but of the spirit of God." He compares the reality of the Church to "the lights and shadows of a portrait begin[ning] to form in the coating of a film under the acid, or...a figure that keeps materializing through the fog of all our human relationships, into a living image of what this torn world of ours could be in the healing grip of that strange man on the cross." It is at once the goal and the power which is shaping human society into the realization of this goal. "From within, by struggle and conflict, working and being wrought, building and built upon, it has fashioned the structure which is yet more than anything else an accident, not indeed the substance, of its being."[249] And yet this "accident" is not something incidental or unessential. Precisely because the Church is a divinely created force thrusting to expression in human form, the diversified empirical forms of the Church represent a necessary development, the embodiment of the very freedom and spontaneity which the divine force would confer upon the Church.

What Scherer here expresses may be taken as typical for the American solution to the problem of the reality of the Church, namely, that the ontological character of the Church can be understood adequately only when the Church is viewed as the social expression of the meeting of God's creative act and man's collective response;

that the Church is a divinely generated and energized reality emergent as a human community in the dialectic of faith and sin. The manner in which this thesis is conceptually articulated varies of course from paper to paper. The TCCCNA, for instance, prefers the ontological category of sacramental participation to express the matter, making use of the analogy between the relation of the divine and the human in Christ on the one hand and in the individual believer on the other to illuminate the Church's mode of being.[250] The other studies and commissions content themselves simply with the assertion that the being of the Church must be understood as the product of the interaction of the divine and human factors, without explicitly developing an explanation in terms of metaphysical categories.

Thus at the end of this chapter we reach the conclusion that in the American discussions the original dichotomy between idea and reality has been transcended and the discussion thus shifts to a consideration of the dialectic of the divine and human factors in the life of the one Church in the many churches. In the next chapter we will proceed to survey first the various aspects of this dialectic under the title "The Church of God and the Church of Men." Here we will attempt to gather together the various strands of the American discussion of the interaction of the divine and human factors in the life of the Church.

CHAPTER IV

THE CHURCH OF GOD AND THE CHURCH OF MEN

Outline

I. THE DIMENSIONS OF THE PROBLEM

The relationship between the divine and the human aspects of
the Church is <u>the</u> <u>central</u> <u>problem</u> for every ecclesiology.

Like every other human institution and community, the Church
can be studied by the behavioral sciences. For well over a century
now such studies have been in progress, bringing to light the extent
to which many an aspect of Church life or structure hitherto regarded
as theologically unique is in fact only a particular instance of phenomena found in other religious, political, academic, or economic
organizations, in social clubs and special interest groups. Indeed
the very nature of the Church as empirical social entity implies
that no aspect of ecclesial reality can a priori be exempted from
the illuminating and demystifying scrutiny of psychological and
sociological analysis.

For decades now, theologians of all confessions have attempted
with varying degrees of openmindedness to come to terms with the
results of the behavioral-science investigations of the life and
structure of the Church. Of course there are still some who cate-
gorically reject such analysis, at least in respect to this or that
aspect of the Church's life: particularly when the results of such
investigation contradict official dogma or traditional teaching,
not a few will attempt to escape the confrontation by appealing to
a hidden dimension of the problem visible only to the eyes of faith.
At the opposite extreme, other theologians are tempted to escape the
confrontation with the results of empirical studies by surrendering
ecclesiastical institutions and communities entirely into the hands
of the social scientists, as though the divine factor studied by
theology had nothing to do with the communal expressions of Christian belief. As we have seen, the American ecclesiologists explicitly rejected both these extremes, maintaining that the whole structure of the Christian faith forbids operating with such reduction-
istic dichotomies.

In taking the position that the divine and human factors of
Church life cannot be separated from one another--however much it
be necessary to distinguish them--the Americans found themselves
face to face with an epistemological problem with important methodological ramifications. The epistemological corollary of the traditional dichotomous theory of the divine-human relationship is the

doctrine of the literal inspiration and absolute inerrancy of Scripture, to which catholic-type theologies add the doctrine of an infallible tradition and magisterium. Like the doctrine of a sharply definable divine dimension of the Church, these doctrines have been severely shaken by the progress of historical and behavioral-science studies. Moreover, the experience of discussing scriptural texts and traditional dogmas ecumenically quickly convinced the American ecclesiologists that even those who still in theory held to the classical doctrines of biblical inspiration or an authoritative tradition, in practice failed, by and large, to follow out the implications of these doctrines: no one acted as though the entire New Testament or the entire tradition was authoritative; their appeal to such authorities was always selective.[1]

Unable thus to find some archemedean point from which to deal with the divine-human interaction in the Church, the Americans turned instead to a variety of theological analogies in the hope of identifying structures common to all the manifestations of divine-human interrelationship. It was the CCULW which first suggested such an approach. At the close of its report on "The Meanings of Unity," it proposed that:

"the institutional and spiritual conceptions of the Church are related to varying conceptions as to the relation of God to the world and His way with men. The former tends to emphasize the transcendence, the power and the otherness of God. The action of God is conceived as direct action, unconditioned: God speaks, and it is done. What is done is therefore conceived as perfect and final, whether in original creation, in revelation through Scripture, in creeds formulated under the direction of His Spirit or merely reproducing the infallible truth of Scripture, or in the establishment of a Church with definitely prescribed orders and sacraments.
In the other case God's relation is conceived in more immanent fashion. Alike in nature and men there is the thought of a living process which is sustained and shaped by the divine Spirit but is not a merely passive or mechanical resultant. As immanence is not lacking in the first position, so the idea of transcendence and power is not wanting here. But the transcendent God is personal-ethical and he deals with man as a personal-ethical being. There can be no religion without the inclusion of both the transcendent and the immanent, the 'ultimate and intimate,' in the concept of God; but there may be a different emphasis and the emphasis will make a great difference."[2]

Although similar suggestions appear here and there in the documents of the immediately following commissions, it was only with the TCCC and the MSC that a systematic attempt to pursue these analogies could be undertaken.

In the course of these systematic discussions, three themes in particular became the focus of attention. The first was the analogy between Christ and the Church, concentrating on the hypostatic union of God and man in Christ as a possible model for interpreting the interaction of divine and human factors in the life of the Church. The investigation of this "metaphysical" analogy, however, quickly revealed the need to take greater account of the "historical" analogies, first the analogy between Israel and the Church, then that between the Church and the World. Although in the end each of these analogies proved to be quite restricted in its application, there emerged in the course of the discussions a widespread consensus about the manner of the Spirit's presence and activity in the Church. This consensus in turn enabled the Americans to work out concrete, though provisional solutions to the much disputed questions concerning the institutionalization of the Church.

In concentrating on the divine-human interaction problem in the American discussions, the present chapter must necessarily be more selective than heretofore. Both because of its pivotal position in the history of the American ecumenical ecclesiology and because of its explicit and extensive preoccupation with the issues at hand, the documents of the TCCCNA have been selected as the principal source for this chapter. The cross-references to the works of the other commissions are intended more to illustrate the content of the TCCCNA's position than to offer a systematic survey of all possible positions. The reader who is interested in the statements of the individual commissions can readily consult the appropriate documents using the preceding chapters and the footnotes of this chapter as a guide. By the same token, no effort will be made here to detail the practical applications of the TCCCNA's principles to the individual issues of church order and organization which were resolved in the course of the COCU discussions. Here too the reader can himself consult the appropriate documents, and judge for himself the degree to which the COCU agreements represent a consistent application of the generic principles worked out by the TCCCNA.

II. ANALOGICAL APPROACHES TO THE DIVINE-HUMAN INTERACTION

A. The Christological Analogy

In its effort to overcome the Amsterdam debacle, the 1952 Faith
and Order Conference at Lund had recommended that a theological
study commission be set up to investigate the connection between the
doctrine of the Church and the doctrines of Christ and the Holy
Spirit. In its final report the Conference declared:

"From the unity of Christ we seek to understand the unity of the
Church on earth, and from the unity of Christ and his Body we
seek a means of realizing that unity in the actual state of our
divisions on earth. We believe that many of our differences
arise from a false antithesis between the Church's being in
Christ and its mission in the world, and from a failure to
understand the Church in the light of Jesus Christ as God and
man, and in the light of his death and resurrection."[3]

The European and American sections of the Theological Commission on
Christ and the Church were organized in response to the Lund declarations. In some respects, the Lund proposal was foreign to the
general tenor of American ecclesiological reflection. Although one
frequently finds reference to the body-of-Christ image, the general
tendency of the American discussion, as the preceding chapter has
shown, was to emphasize the evangelistic and ethical implications
of this theme. Until the TCCCNA, the metaphysical aspects of the
topic had, as Claude Welch pointed out, been largely ignored by
Protestant thinking,[4] and in the TCCCNA itself there existed a general scepticism about the value of all too exuberant speculation on
the basis of the Chalcedonian dogma.[5]

On the other hand, as we have seen, the problem of the divine-
human relationship in the Church's life had from the beginning attracted the attention of the American theologians, and the idea of
an analogy and inter-connection between this and other Christian
beliefs had been present as early as the 1937 discussions of the
CCULW.[6] In the following passage from the ATC report of 1945 the
notion is explicitly mentioned in connection with the presentation
of the Church's mission, though the suggestion was not further developed.

"Both historically and metaphysically the Church's function may
be regarded as one of carrying on and extending the work of the
earthly life of Jesus. In his spirit his followers have continued to preach and to teach, to fill up what was lacking in
his sufferings, and to exemplify his character. Jesus sent
them forth as he was sent forth. He promised them not only rejection like his, but the doing of greater works than he did,

> and the sharing of his glory. To some extent at least, the
> Church may claim to represent Jesus in revealing God and in
> exercising authority."[7]

This statement can be taken as typical of prevailing American opinion up to the time when the TCCCNA began its work. Noteworthy is
the association of the "historical" and the "metaphysical" perspectives, suggesting a concrete, dynamic viewpoint quite in contrast
to the abstract, static way of thinking implicit in traditional
christology. As already noted, this dynamic ontology was characteristic of the whole American approach to theological problems.

1. The Christology of the TCCCNA

During the first years of the TCCCNA, the discussions ranged
widely over the whole field of christology and pneumatology, probing
deeply into many an intricate historical controversy. To follow all
the details of this discussion would take us too far afield; fortunately J. Robert Nelson had occasion to summarize the essentials of
the Commission's discussions in a report delivered to the 1960 Faith
and Order Commission meeting at St. Andrews, Scotland. The heart of
this report consists of a series of nine theses with appropriate
commentary to indicate "areas of agreement or near agreement discovered in this study."[8]

Nelson's first thesis is that "the subject of 'Christ and the
Church' leads quickly and inevitably to that of the triune Godhead
and the Church."[9] From the beginning, members of the American section had insisted on the impossibility of separating christology and
pneumatology and had warned against any "unitarianism" of the second
or third persons of the Trinity. Thus already in 1956 the TCCCNA
was able to record the consensus: "We should view the Church increasingly as a trinitarian enterprise. Our study of the doctrines
of Christ and the Spirit must at no point ignore the relationship
between the doctrine of God and the unity of the Church since in
both the Old Testament and New Testament it is the unity of God
which ultimately is the ground for the unity of God's people."[10]

Such a statement read from the vantage-point of the theology of
the seventies hardly appears revolutionary. Thanks to the Montreal
Conference and Vatican II, the trinitarian approach to ecclesiology
has become a theological commonplace, which subsequent theological
discussions have rendered more and more questionable. To appreciate
the significance of the Commission's option for the trinitarian ap-

proach, it is necessary to call to mind the earlier "Christomonism" of the Roman-Catholic (and to some extent Anglican) "Mystical-Body" ecclesiology or of the "invisible Church" ecclesiology which flourished in Protestant Neo-orthodoxy.

In calling for a trinitarian point of view, the commission had no intention of inviting uncontrolled metaphysical speculations in either christology or ecclesiology. On the contrary, what it envisaged was a reorientation of christological theory itself, with the aim of bringing the historical character of God's Word and Spirit more clearly into focus. This is the implication of the second and fourth theses in the Nelson report: "Jesus Christ is not known to us solely in relation to the Church of the new covenant but also to the Israel of the old covenant"; "the being of Jesus Christ as the Word of God incarnate is inseparable from his work as Savior."[11] The critical point here is the intimate relationship which the Commission posits between "being" and "work." Nelson's commentary underscores the point:

"A proper Christology must include both the ontological meaning of his person and the soteriological consequences of his obedience, death and resurrection. Even though the far greater emphasis in Christian theological thought and debate has fallen upon the question of his person, it may be argued cogently that the New Testament, while emphasizing both aspects of christology, gives priority to soteriology. 'His presence is presented and interpreted in the context of his redemptive work and his redemptive purpose.'
By the christological analogy, the Church also has both a nature and a task. Christians are tempted to give excessive or exclusive attention either to what the Church is or to what it does, when actually these two aspects of ecclesiology need to be kept together, the one explicating the other."[12]

Thus the line taken by the Commission in christology corresponds fully with what the preceding chapter has shown to be the consistent tendency of American ecclesiological thinking. As we have seen, the Americans were deeply concerned with the ontological question, but they understood the question as one about the t h e c o n c r e t e   o p e r a t i v e   n a t u r e   r a t h e r t h a n   a b o u t   a n   a b s t r a c t   e n t i t a t i v e e s s e n c e . Similarly in christology. Nels F. S. Ferré formulated this position most clearly in the paper he delivered to the 1955 meeting of the Commission. He wrote:

"Our starting point is of importance. We do not start with some supernatural superstructure, as though we knew the reality and the nature of God independent of historic revelation. Nor do

we start with any external authority such as book or church.
Rather we begin with the historic events of Jesus' life and
teaching... Jesus Christ, life and teacher is the original
document of our faith."[13]

Jesus Christ, i.e. the historical Jesus whose life and teaching has
been handed down to us through the gospel tradition, is the original
source for all that we know in faith both about God and about the
new humanity which God has given us through him. For this reason,
the Commission felt obliged to insist on a return to historical considerations in christology in contrast to the metaphysical considerations which have dominated traditional thinking. In particular the
Commission criticized the traditional Western approach for having
overly concerned itself with the distinction of natures at the expense of the unity of the acting person.[14]

Nevertheless, a superficial reading of the TCCCNA report would
most likely leave the impression that the Commission had done everything but what it proposed to do. In the official reports of the
Commission we find no detailed presentation of the historical Jesus;
instead methodological and metaphysical theses and explanations
abound. To understand this apparent anomaly, it is necessary to recall the task assigned the commission: It was set up to deal with a
metaphysical question, namely the ontological relationship between
Christ and the Church--the central issue in the ecclesiological controversy between catholic-type and protestant-type thinkers. Given
this task, the Commission sought to show by means of an immanent
critique that such questions pursued to their term can only bring the
inquirer back to the historical considerations from which he originally departed.

The critique of traditional Western christology in terms of a
reconsideration of post-Chalcedonian Eastern christology offers an
interesting example of how the TCCCNA went about its immanent critique. In its final report, the Commission calls attention to three
ideas from this source which provide clues to how history and meta-
physics must be reintegrated in the interpretation of Jesus Christ.

The first is the principle of enhypostasia. The commission report defines this principle as the assertion "that the fullness of
the humanity of Christ was achieved precisely in and because of his
intimate unity with the divinity."[15] The commission interprets this
to mean that at the level of operation, no distinction can be made
between human acts and divine acts: every action and every passion
or suffering of Jesus Christ, from the most humble and ignominious to
the most exalted and glorious, is both human and divine. The commission thus gives an ontological twist to the traditional doctrine
of the communication of idioms:[16] in the approval given by the Eastern Church to the formula "one of the trinity suffered in the flesh,"

the commission sees a modification of the philosophical presupposition of divine impassibility. Such an interpretation, of course, is unthinkable in terms of the scholastic explanation of the distinction between person and nature. There person is seen exclusively as the principle of substantial incommunicability; here it is seen rather as a center of operation.

Fully consistent with the interpretation given to enhypostasia is the Commission's use of the doctrine of the two wills in Jesus. What interested the commission here was the suggestion that in Jesus there could be "a human will sufficiently autonomous to be able to contemplate recalcitrance to the divine."[17] The ability of Christ to experience real temptation is the guarantee for the reality of a human response of Jesus to God in faith and love, the effect of the divine presence in Jesus is not to reduce or eliminate temptations but rather to triumphantly overcome them. That is to say, the divine and the human active principles do not operate independently of each other; rather their cooperation is marked by a kind of compenetration in which the divine factor perfects and transforms the human at the same time that the human factor renders the divine humanly present and perceptible.[18]

A third complex of ideas derived from eastern patristic sources enabled the commission to establish a more intimate connection between christology and pneumatology than is usual in western theology. "The nature of God the Word is to be God in action, and so it is he who became man," but the Word became man only because he was sent by the Father, and the incarnation itself as well as the whole complex of Christ's life, death and resurrection was accomplished only "in the power of the Spirit."[19] In Jesus Christ, "the gift which made men saints and prophets was present in its fullness, and through him the Spirit comes as a permanent source of grace to his followers, so that life in Christ is also life in the Spirit. There is no need to make precise distinctions in the meaning of these two phrases, or between the Holy Spirit as the Spirit of God and the Spirit of Jesus."[20] In the actions and suffering of Jesus Christ, the presence of the Spirit is "exemplified" in a way at once unique and universal. The identity of the Spirit of Jesus and the Spirit of God enables us to see in the life of Jesus the way in which the spirit of God works.

The peculiar twist which the Commission gives to the ideas borrowed from post-chalcedonian oriental christology makes clear the direction of the Commission's own christology. The focus of Commission attention was, in a phrase from Nelson's text, "the humanity of Jesus Christ, a humanity not merely earthbound but one through which the transcendent glory of God in Christ is revealed."[21] The qualifying phrase here is of critical importance: with it Nelson attempts to set off the Commission's christology over against those of the liberal and dialectical theologies, the first being "preoccupied with the simple historical humanity of Jesus of Nazareth," the second, by way of correction, reasserting "the divine, transcendent nature of Jesus Christ."[22] At the same time, it is important to note that precisely in its emphasis on the <u>humanity</u> of Jesus, the Commission's thinking moves in the very opposite direction of the semi-monophysite tendency of the post-chalcedonian christology.[23]

Here again it is import to recall that the Commission was working with a dynamic rather than a static conception of "nature."[24] In speaking of "humanity" and "divinity" in Christ, the Commission focuses its attention on the "nature" not so much in terms of its being potentially the principle of action but rather as it is actually acting. From this point of view the Commission is fully correct in asserting that the divine and human natures in Christ cannot be viewed as two separate, parallel entities united only in their outward manifestation, namely in the effects they jointly or separately produce. In a paper delivered before the Commission, W. N. Pittenger put the matter this way:

"We must honestly recognize the limitations which the fact of Incarnation imposes. We must not seek for the divinity of Jesus in the 'gaps' of his humanity any more than we seek for God in the 'gaps' of his creation. The humanity of Jesus is truly human; and to historical study, in its strict sense, it yields nothing but humanity. The perfection of our Lord's moral character...is a perfection which is the actualizing of the moral possibilities of men, not an alien importation or intrusion. The works of healing which he performed are the work of a man, of human nature, related to God as intimately as human nature can be related; they are not contradictions of the potentialities of human nature. The knowledge of God, the consciousness of his love and care, the reality of religious experience in Jesus are human. That is to say, the principle of the Incarnation, which means the full mediation of God through and in man, is an agreement with the picture of Jesus which serious scientific study will disclose to us. Jesus is fully and really human. ... It is precisely in and under the conditions of manhood that his diety has been discovered and worshipped. ...the judgment that Jesus is divine is a total evaluation of the significance of his <u>whole</u> life, not a description of certain isolated areas of that <u>life</u> which in some fashion are not really human but in some contra-human sense divine."[25]

The Commission itself formulated the same position more briefly and perhaps more cautiously but none the less clearly:

"The presence of God in human life is a unifying and not a divisive factor, and supremely in the perfect man, in whom the divine Son was made like us in all things, sin only excepted. ... Certainly Christ did things which no other man did; but his diety shines forth not only in the picture of the man who did divine things, but even more in the picture of his doing human things divinely."[26]

The Commission underscores t h e   c o m p l e m e n t a -
r i t y   o f   t h e   t w o   n a t u r e s   i n   b e i n g

and   a c t i o n .   On the **one** hand, "the fullness of the humanity of Christ was achieved precisely in and because of his intimate unity with deity";[27] on the other hand, the fullness of humanity
assumed by the Word brings to fulfilment, so to speak, the nature of
the Word: "the nature of God the Word is to be God in action, and
so it is he who became man."[28] The divine impassibility is thus
overcome, inasmuch as "one of the Trinity suffered in the flesh";[29]
at the same time, "in him humanity makes a real response to God in
faith and love; and we who live in him become part of that response."[30] This means too that "our life in him includes obedience
of Jesus as human teacher... He is certainly teacher as well as
savior and expects his disciples to follow his teaching."[31]

Taken by themselves, such statements are apt to sound abstract
and metaphysical, rather than concrete, historical. The abstract-
ness, however, is a consequence of the literary form of a summary
report, not a quality of the Commission's thinking as such. Behind
these summary formulae lies the concrete figure of the historical
Jesus as reconstructed by modern biblical exegesis. Only when we
make an effort to keep this concrete historical figure before our
eyes, can we grasp the intention of the Commission when it speaks of
the humanity of Jesus as one "not merely earthbound but one through
which the transcendent glory of God in Christ is revealed." Not an
abstract "human nature" but the concrete "human life" is always at
the center of the Commission's thinking.[32] In this it claimed to
rest firmly on New Testament precedents:

> "Whether Jesus is formally called 'God' in the New Testament is
> not really the central question, especially since the first
> century was an age of many theoi (I Cor. 8.5). What mattered
> was, and is, the realization that in this human life God is
> present, 'in Christ reconciling the world to himself' (II Cor.
> 5.19). He is what he is and does what he does because in him
> God's Word is decisively uttered for us and in him is with us
> in the world in the actual flesh of a human life (John 1.14)."[33]

Or, as Nelson's report put it, "the New Testament, while emphasizing
both aspects of christology gives priority to soteriology. 'His
presence is presented and interpreted in the context of his redemptive work and his redemptive purpose'."[34] Not in abstract metaphysical speculations about the divine powers and consciousness of
Christ but rather i n   c o n c r e t e   m e d i a t i o n   o n
t h e   h i s t o r i c a l   f i g u r e   o f   J e s u s   o f
N a z a r e t h ,   w i l l   the   C h u r c h   f i n d   t h e

model   for   its   own   existence.   In brief,
the christology of the Commission can perhaps best be summed up in
a statement of G. Florovsky at the 1958 meeting:

> "God works to save with human means, and divine purpose is ac-
> complished in the life which is perfectly human and in the
> events which are perfectly human. The historical life, death,
> transcendended by the mystery of the resurrection and the glori-
> fication of Jesus Christ..."[55]

2. The Ecclesiological Application

When christology is conceived in this concrete, history-oriented
fashion, the legitimacy as well as the limitations of the christol-
ogy-ecclesiology parallel become evident.

The use of the analogy can be traced back to the New Testament
itself. Nelson's report calls attention to the extensive use of
Christ-oriented analogical terms in the New Testament's references
to the Church; among these he mentions the images of the Body of
Christ, the Vine and the branches, the Bride of Christ, and the New
Humanity, as well as the phrases "in Christ" and "Christ in you."[36]
Although the interpretation of these images differs widely, the Commission could point to a broad agreement on the basic principle of
the Christ-Church analogy: "it is generally acknowledged that the
Church's nature and mission are best understood in the light of
Christ's life in the body and in succession to him as a corporate
community."[37] Furthermore a survey of the history of trends in
christological and ecclesiological thought reveals a de facto paral-
lelism illustrating the oft unconscious working of the analogy:

> "There was a time when a preoccupation with the simple historical
> humanity of Jesus of Nazareth seemed to dictate an almost com-
> pletely sociological view of the Church as a religious associa-
> tion. Corrective teaching in christology which reasserted the
> divine, transcendent nature of Jesus Christ the Lord tended to
> encourage an almost non-historical, 'docetic' view of the
> Church. This in turn has given way to a renewed interest in
> the humanity of Jesus Christ, a humanity not merely earth-bound
> but one through which the transcendent glory of God in Christ
> is revealed."[38]

Given the way the Commission itself conceived the divine-human
unity in Christ, an initial consequence for ecclesiology immediately
springs to mind. Nelson formulated it as follows: "By the christological analogy, the Church also has both a nature and a task.
Christians are tempted to give excessive or exclusive attention to
what the Church is or to what it does, when actually these two

aspects of ecclesiology need to be kept together, the one explicating the other."[39] This first conclusion represents more a matter of methodological principle than concrete explanation. The same holds true for the observation that: "assertions of the transcendent as well as the mundane aspects of the Church's life are reflections of the confessed proposition that both divinity and humanity reside in the one person of Jesus Christ."[40] Nevertheless we should not underestimate the value of these statements. Formalistic though they may be they provide an important confirmation for the ecclesiological standpoint of the American theologians, namely that the divine and human elements in the Church cannot be separated one from another, however much a truly adequate ecclesiology may need to distinguish them; more to the point, t h e   t r a n s c e n d e n t   e l e -
m e n t   i n   t h e   C h u r c h   c a n n o t   b e   s e p a -
r a t e d   f r o m   t h e   h u m a n   a n d   t h e r e f o r e
o f t e n   s i n f u l ,   e m p i r i c a l   r e a l i t y :   we know it only as a dimension of the latter, not as a separate, empirically identifiable institution or action.

In order to achieve more substantial results from its inquiry into the christological analogy, however, the Commission had to achieve greater clarity about the nature of the relationship between Christ and the Church. Here the Commission found itself on difficult ground. The New Testament images clearly point to a certain identity between Christ and the Church. The question, of course, is whether or not more is involved here than mere attribution and metaphor, and if so, how might this relationship be denominated and conceived. The texts propose three terms to designate this relationship: "analogical," "sacramental," and "participation."[41] Unfortunately, the members of the Commission never really succeeded in formulating a clear definition of any of these terms.

To say that the relationship between Christ and the Church is analogical may well be correct, but it is hardly calculated to shed new light on the proper understanding of the analogical relationship between the divine and human factors in Christ on the one hand and in the Church on the other. As a logical category distinguished over against univocal and equivocal predications, the term " a n a l -
o g y " may rightly be used to call attention to important elements for a proper understanding of the relationship between Christ and the Church. In this sense it appears in Nelson's report (Thesis 3):

"Analogy is generally understood to communicate both identity and difference between two entities. The ontological relation between Jesus Christ and the Church cannot be understood univocally, because there would then be no distinction in their being, such as the New Testament teaches. Yet to understand their relationship equivocally would imply only a common interest or a similitude between Christ and the Church. The method of analogy may be used in such a way as to avoid complete identity or utter discontinuity between them, while maintaining the attributes which are in common and those which are distinct.

It is clear that analogical terms are used extensively in the New Testament itself. The image of the Body of Christ comes to mind immediately. ... However its interpretation may vary between metaphor only (the Church is like a body) and ontological reality (the church is really Christ's Body), it is generally acknowledged that the Church's nature and mission are best understood in the light of Christ's life in the body and in succession to him as a corporate community."[42]

Here the ontological question is kept open; instead the question is referred back to the phenomenological manifestation of the ontological relationship, namely to the solidarity and historical continuity uniting the life and mission of Jesus with those of his disciples in the corporate community which is the Church. In the following statement of the final report, however, the term "analogical" has been transformed into an ontological category, which more obscures than illuminates the nature of the relationship involved:

"The great variety of images which the New Testament uses for the Church...suggest the kind of relation which may be called analogical, or as some would prefer to say, sacramental. It is not a relation of simple identity which would allow us to say without qualification that the Church is Christ--though one may venture to say in St. Augustine's phrase, based on Pauline thought, that the whole Christ, totus Christus, includes the human members as well as the divine and human Head."[43]

Inasmuch as no explanation of the positive meaning of the term "analogical" here is offered, it is hard to avoid the suspicion that the term here is used mainly as a verbal cipher to designate an object which had not yet been sufficiently analyzed. In this regard, the Commission's recourse to the terms "sacramental" and "participation" really does not lead too much further.

The term " s a c r a m e n t a l , " proposed by M. Thurian in the discussion of the Nelson report at the St. Andrews meeting,[44] seems to have found only partial sympathy among the American theologians.[45] Moreover the term itself is as much open to divergent interpretation as the term "analogical" when used as an ontological category. Nevertheless, a Commission discussion of Word and Sacra-

ment[46] which Nelson summarized in his ninth thesis does shed some
light on the way the Commission understood the ontological relation
between Christ and the Church. The thesis reads: "The Word and the
Sacraments together, which in various classical definitions are requisite to make the faithful congregation become the Church, refer to
the indwelling of Christ in the Church."[47] Nelson's explanation
calls attention to the fact that the original expressions logos and
musterion "refer essentially to the mystery of God's working in history" and "have taken recognizable institutional forms in history,
through what we know as teaching, preaching and sacraments." Furthermore, he points out, "these are not the prime reality of God's
whole work itself. They point to the ultimate reality, but are
themselves conditioned by history and culture."[48] Applying this
understanding of the term "sacramental" to the Church-Christ relation, it is clear that this usage calls attention to the historical
cultural conditioning of the Church's dwelling in Christ. About the
nature of the relationship itself, however, little is said by the
term.[49]

There remains the term " p a r t i c i p a t i o n . " As we
saw in the preceding chapter, Claude Welch had developed this notion
in the course of the study he did for the Commission,[50] and it found
extensive use in the joint interim report One Lord one Baptism.[51] In
addition, several European participants in the discussion of the
Nelson report at the 1960 meeting at St. Andrews recommended the
term "participation" as an alternative to both "analogical" and
"sacramental."[52] Nevertheless, the TCCCNA remained reserved in its
use of the term, although its description of particular aspects of
the relation between Christ and his Church reveals general agreement
with the notion of "participation" developed by Welch. This for instance is the implication of the final report's statement that "the
whole Christ, totus Christus, includes the human members as well as
the divine and human Head" or that "as members of the Church we are
incorporated into Christ," etc.[53]

Ultimately the principal difficulty which stood in the way of
the Commission's formulating a clear statement of the nature of the
relation between Christ and the Church was t h e   p r o b l e m
o f   s i n   i n   t h e   C h u r c h : "Here, as we know only
too well, the sinfulness of the members contrasts with the perfection of the Head."[54] Historically, as the Commission report points

out, Christians have interpreted this contrast between the sinfulness of the members and the sinlessness of the Head in ways which
tend simply to reproduce the dichotomous understanding of divine-
human interaction. Thus some would admit that the Church itself is
sinful but redeemed; others would insist that the Church itself is
sinless, and that its members, inasmuch as they sin, have ceased to
be true members of the Church. The first view tends to see the
Church primarily in terms of its here and now existence on earth and
thus sharply distinguished from Christ its Lord and Savior; the second view, on the contrary, includes within its purview Christ himself and the saints departed, and therefore separates off the sinful
members.[55] Since both views find their legitimation in the New Testament (the text cites Eph. 5:27 and 4:13), the Commission is unable to
come to a clear resolution of the question; its resolution is little
more than an affirmation of "both...and."

> "As members of the Church we are incorporated into Christ, and
> at the same time continue to live our human lives in the parti-
> cular concrete situations of human existence. The Church is a
> divine fellowship, and yet in its concrete expression can be
> studied as a visible institution subject to the stresses and
> pressures of the world. We have not been called away from the
> common life of man in the world, although in another sense we
> are indeed 'called out of the world'; and yet we believe that
> we are able by the Spirit to acknowledge Jesus as Lord (I Cor.
> 12:3), and that we do in truth live in him and in the Spirit."[56]

Referring to the sacramental ordinances of the Church, the final
report of the TCCCNA attempts at least to shed a little light on the
nature of our incorporation into Christ. Calling attention to Luke
24:35, it declares, "to us, as to the first disciples, Jesus is known
in the breaking of bread... As we receive his sacramental body he
makes us more and more truly members of his mystical body... As we
remember his death we join in his life of sacrifice." This statement, however must not be interpreted narrowly; the Commission declares that it means to include the Quaker notion that the spiritual
reality can be experienced even apart from the external sign, and
that the Lukan phrase suggests not only the celebration of the Eucharist but also the presence of the living Christ in the ordinary
circumstances of our lives now and our future presence at his table
in his coming kingdom.[57] Nevertheless, such statements elucidate
more the mode rather than the nature of the relation between Christ
and the Church.

Thus the problem of the sinfulness of the Church proved an insurmountable barrier to the Commission's drawing further conclusions from the Christ-Church analogy. Unable to define precisely the ontological relationship between Christ and the Church, the Commission could only develop the heuristic-methodological implications of the analogy. In brief, the fact that the divine element in Christ is not to be found separate from the human serves as a proof that in the Church too the divine element should not be sought in separation from the concrete, culturally conditioned human social and institutional forms. This insight may not provide ready answers to the many questions posed by the search for an ecumenical ecclesiology, but it does offer an initial orientation, whose significance is not to be underestimated.

> "As the incarnate Son was truly man, so is the Church wrought out of the stuff of human existence. The Church is shaped in and out of the realities of human historicity and sociality. Therefore the Church is not some 'ideal' community, existing in airy abstraction from the affairs of men. Neither is it 'spiritual' in the sense that it is to be contrasted with the hard and inevitable materialities of that world of history and sociality. To call the Church ideal or spiritual in those senses is to fall into ecclesiological docetism akin to the ancient heresy which denied to our Lord his physical body, his historical actuality, his immersion in the stuff of common life. We protest against every view of the Church which in a mistaken effort to exalt its nature as the body of Christ, succeeds only in making it 'purer' than its Lord."[58]

B. The Israel-Church Analogy
1. The Continuity of God's Work

To penetrate more keeply into the nature of the divine-human interaction in the church, the Commission turned its attention to the analogy between the Church and Israel.

Here too the foundations of the analogy are found in New Testament usage. Images like "God's People," "royal priesthood," "holy nation," "God's elect," "his Temple," the "New Jerusalem," etc. all point to such an analogy.[59] Indeed, even the analogy of Christ and the Church can be traced to Old Testament precedents, as the final report observes: "The ancient people of God were so intimately related to their Lord that Israel can be called his child and his bride as well as his servant. Now transformed, as promised, into a universal fellowship, the Church continues to be the people of God, so closely united to him in Christ that it can be called his body."[60]

Moreover Jesus Christ himself is known to us not only "in relation
to the Church of the new covenant but also to the Israel of the old
covenant."[61]

The history of God's dealings
with Israel has the advantage of
showing us the interaction of divine and human factors in a situation in which sin also finds place.
The Commission's discussion of the working of the Spirit of God in
the Old Testament thus proved particularly fruitful, though literary considerations prevented an explicit development of this inquiry
in the final reports of the commission (the insights acquired in the
course of the 1956-7 discussions are incorporated in the Nelson report and the final report under other topical headings). Welch's
"Extracts" offers a valuable guide to the salient points of this
discussion.

In the paper with which he opened the discussion, W. Harrelson
drew attention to the preparation of the Incarnation in the history
of Israel:

"There is an incarnational movement within the totality of
Israelite history. ... Israel is a holy people, elected from
the nations to be God's people. She is thus the body prepared
by God for the disclosure of the very being of God to all the
nations. This body is intended to include all peoples and
natures. ... It is a living body, then it must have spirit,
breath. But if it is the body of the people of God, then the
human breath bestowed and preserved by God will not suffice.
Divine breath or Spirit is required. ... When God places his
Spirit within Israel (Ezek. 36:26; 37:14), when he pours out
his Spirit upon all flesh (Joel 3:1-2), then what is created
is a true and faithful people of God, in whom God dwells in the
flesh--the flesh of Israel and of the nations which are incorporated within Israel.
    At the same time this leads to no deification of Israel,
since this unity of selfhood created by the body and Spirit is
a unity dependent upon the divine Spirit, never to be confused
with the human."[62]

In the New Testament faith, this understanding of the community is
taken over but with a radical change, inasmuch as what was formerly
attributed to the community as a whole is now realized in a pre-
eminant way in one of its sons:

"Israel becomes faithful Israel in the coming of God Himself in
the person of a son of Israel who is God's own Son. ...the
Spirit of God which rested upon Jesus of Nazareth God's Son
(Luke 4:16ff; Isa. 61:1-3), constitutes the full presence of

God himself among his people, testified to by the perfect obedience, the mighty acts, the sufferings, the death and the resurrection of Jesus."[63]

In the discussion which followed, objection was raised to
Harrelson's sharp dichotomy between human spirit and divine Spirit.
In answer, Harrelson called attention to the p r o v i s i o n a l -
e s c h a t o l o g i c a l   c h a r a c t e r   of the presence of
God's Spirit in Israel: "the identification of God's Spirit with
His people is viewed eschatologically as a condition that will come
in the future when God pours out His Spirit upon all flesh, or in
the past where the primal relationship between God and Israel is defined in the Covenant." The Church, however, as the Nelson report
points out, finds itself in a position similar to Israel's, inasmuch
as it moves between the proleptic realization of the promises at
Pentecost and the full realization which awaits the final coming:

"The Church has its being in movement, not in static establishment. Despite its possession of history and tradition, of settled institutions and abiding forms, the Church is still characterized by its anticipation of the Savior and the final reign
of God. The inherent connection between ontology and eschatology in the Church's life is thus a perennial concern. And
awareness of this connection is derivative from a knowledge of
the place of Jesus Christ in God's redeeming activity in history. The full presence of God's ultimate reign in the person
and life of Jesus Christ, the signs of the new age of man inaugurated in him, the forming of the new being or new humanity
in the new community, the outpouring of the Holy Spirit, the
sending of the apostolic Church on its earthly mission, the
designating of the Church as the Bride whom Christ prepares as
a perfect offering to be presented ultimately to God--all these
are essential indications of the eschatological dimensions of
the Church's essence and existence."[64]

Given the eschatological character of the Church, parallel to
though transcending the eschatological character of the old Israel,
t h e   p h e n o m e n o n   o f   s i n   i n   t h e   C h u r c h
becomes more understandable. In Nelson's words:

"There is much false belief, erroneous teaching, sinful behavior,
division and infidelity in the community of Christians. These
defections do not cancel out the theological claim that the
Church finds its Christ-like life by the inspiration and indwelling of the Spirit. As negative aspects due to sin, they
contrast with and enhance the true life given by the Spirit,
which is the communal life of faithfulness, love and unity.
Thus the participation or communion (Koinonia) in the Spirit
which is the distinctive mark of the Church's life is neither
an easy human achievement nor an unattainable ideal; it is the
fully given gift of the Spirit which may be either appropriated
in faith or rejected in sinful disdain."[65]

As the history of God's dealings with his People shows, the marks of
the Church which have been defaced by sin are neither "lost treasure[s] to be found and furbished" nor "ecclesiastical condition[s]
to be effected by our own ingenuity and effort." Rather they are
eschatological gifts "which by God's grace and according to our fidelity will be partially restored until [they are] perfectly expressed in the Church's glorified life."[66]

The study of the Israel-Church analogy was also able to shed
light on another aspect of the divine-human interaction in the
Church not immediately illuminated by the christological analogy,
namely t h e   p r o b l e m   o f   u n i t y   a n d   d i v e r -
s i t y . The discussion of the work of the Spirit in Israel turned
to the "connection between the Spirit and the unity or disunity of
God's people." Two points raised in this discussion are of special
interest. On the one hand the Commission members noted that the Old
Testament shows the people of Israel not only thinking about the
Spirit in diverse ways but also having to respond in diverse ways.
It is significant that it was the false prophets who "assumed a uniformity in the operations of the Spirit in order to claim an authority for their own work and to weld the people into unilateral obedience to them..." The Christian Church has not escaped this temptation: "The doctrine of one Spirit can thus be made the basis for
false unity, can be the basis of disastrous schism within the people
of God." On the other hand, the true teaching of the Old Testament
concerning the Spirit of God emphasizes its role in "creating re-
ceptivity among the people to the Word of God" and thus to flexible
response according to the situation in which God's people find themselves. Moreover, the unity which the Spirit creates in response to
the Word is not simply a unity between man and God but also between
man and his fellow men in the community. "Thus the Spirit at work
in community is inseparable from the processes by which the community arrives at unity within itself in its relationship to God."
This unity however presupposes real diversity: "Where unity is
found in responsiveness, responsibility and obedient action, an
enormous diversity is encouraged, expected and cultivated at every
point. The freedom of the person to respond, to accept responsibility, and to act is recognized, and divers actions are accepted
as valid expressions of the work of the one Spirit."[67] An echo of

this discussion appears in the following brief but pregnant statement in Nelson's report:

> "A most important characteristic of the Spirit's work in both the
> Old and New Testaments is the building up of human community and
> unity by the very diversity of his gifts. The oft-expressed
> fear of ecclesiastical uniformity as the concomitant of unity is
> denied and should be allayed by the biblical demonstration of
> the inseparability of diversity and true unity. Freedom and
> diversity are not the preconditions but the irreconcilable ene-
> mies of division."[68]

2. The Freedom of God's Work

A final point to emerge out of the discussion of the role of the
Spirit in Israel concerns God's abiding freedom to work outside as
well as within his Church. As the Nelson report concisely put it:
"Finally it must be said of the Spirit that he is not the possession
of the Church only, but is free to dwell and work in whom he
pleases."[69]   In the minutes of the discussion the formulation is
much sharper:

> "The spirit retains its freedom to call those who are not his
> People and to reject those who are his people. At the same
> time the spirit is free to use the Christian Church as the body
> of Christ through whom the message of reconciliation is to be
> brought to all men. Jesus Christ both creates and shatters
> the bond of the Church. He can not easily be naturalized either
> as a Jew or a Christian. He is an enemy both of the exclusive-
> ness of the Jew in the O.T. and of the exclusiveness of the
> Christian in the New Age. The Word of God in the O.T. tore down
> the claims to superiority on the part of the Jews with reference
> to their own communal achievements. So too, the Word of God
> brought by the Spirit tears down the claims of the Christian
> Church that it is superior because it possesses the Spirit."[70]

Despite the polemical sharpness, the Commission members were not
denying here the fact that the Church is the privileged instrument
of the Spirit. On the contrary, it is the very presence of God's
spirit in the Church which "brings judgment upon those who speak of
it and upon those who receive it." The Old Testament prophets,
Jeremiah especially, illustrate the point. The Spirit of God who
comes to the prophet sets him over against his people. At the same
time, the prophet himself is part of the people who is faithless;
indeed his solidarity with the people in their sinfulness is one of
the conditions of his receiving the prophetic Word of judgment. "The
community created by the spirit, therefore, is indispensable, always
inevitable, but it is also always insufficient, inadequate, and sinful, and therefore the reception of the Spirit is a mark of the hu-

mility of the community and its receptiveness to the creative redemption of God."[71]

The point is however, that the history of God's dealing with
Israel makes abundantly clear, that G o d   i s   n o t   b o u n d
t o   t h e   c o m m u n i t y ;   he is its Lord not its slave.
In committing himself to act in and through the community he has not
surrendered his sovereignty, his promises do not constrain him to
act only in and through the community or commit him always to act in
and through the community, when in fact the community is pursuing
its own self-centered interests rather than those of God's reign.
The community has no right to expect his help for its own sinful purposes nor can it afford to ignore his working outside the official
channels established by the covenant.

3. The Ecclesiological Application

Nevertheless, despite its evident utility the Israel-Church
analogy too suffers from a severe limitation. In its application to
ecclesiastical reality it can easily mislead the theologian into
underestimating w h a t   i s   t r u l y   n e w   a b o u t
t h e   N e w   T e s t a m e n t   r e l a t i o n s h i p   b e -
t w e e n   t h e   d i v i n e   a n d   t h e   h u m a n   f a c -
t o r s   i n   t h e   l i f e   o f   G o d ' s   p e o p l e .
In its final report, the TCCCNA attempted therefore to define more
clearly the uniqueness of the Church with respect to Israel and thus
to stake out the limits of the analogy. Rather than drawing up a
simple table of continuity and discontinuity of the sort attempted
in the joint interim report,[72] the Commission called attention to
two distinct "modes or orders of newness," in both of which both
continuity and discontinuity are manifest. The first and most fundamental of these modes is the ontological one signified by the term
"new humanity" the second is the chronological one marked by the
coming of the Messiah. In both of these modes, the Commission found
both continuity and discontinuity between the Church and Israel.[73]

What is ontologically new in the Church is "the presence of
eternity, the effectual reality of the structure of salvation." It
is a new relationship to God established by a new presence of God in
his incarnate Son. Nevertheless this new presence is not entirely
new; already in Israel it was not only expected but also anticipated.
"The redeeming, incarnate Son of God was the Messiah of Israel, sent

to Israel and representing and including in himself Israel as God's people. The Old Testament knows the reality of the Spirit, and Israel's life was shaped by visions of the outpouring of that Spirit in the Last Days." The Church on the other hand also continues to await the full realization of this new relationship. The newness of the Church, therefore, is indeed the fulfilment, entailing both correction and transformation, of the newness already present in Israel,[74] and yet it too, like Israel, remains provisional, awaiting fulfilment.[75]

The chronological novelty of the Church is the correlate of the radically new presence and work of Christ and the Spirit. The coming of the Messiah and the outpouring of the Spirit mark the beginning of a new time, and "the Church is defined by this historically visible expression of the promised newness of life. The Church is thus both the continuation of Israel and its successor. There is genuine novelty here: "God's action in this new time is not simply the same as his action in the old time. Changes are real; the Spirit is present after Christ in a different mode from his presence before Christ (John 7:39). It is the same triune God who is present in a new way, but the way in which he is present is a genuinely new way. ... The old is present in the new but is present in it as surpassed [original italics]." And yet, insofar as the Church itself must still look forward to the Last Days for its own fulfilment, its time is also a continuation of Israel's time; it remains a provisional time.[76]

Here too, therefore, just as in the case of the christological analogy, a fundamental ambiguity opened up, preventing the Commission from drawing clear answers to its questions about the specific nature of the interaction of divine and human factors in the life of the Church. On the one hand, there is the fact of a fuller, more perfect presence of the Spirit in the Church as opposed to Israel; on the other, there remains the fact of the Church's provisional character. The Commission failed to find a way to conceive the relationship between these two aspects so as to define clearly the boundaries of the Israel-Church analogy. Here as at so many other points in the Commission discussions the fundamental divergence of catholic- and protestant-type thinking came out into the open. As the minutes of the 1956 discussion put it:

"The Reformation reminds the Catholic of the sovereignty of God over his tradition. The Catholic reminds the reformer that the sovereignty of God can easily become an abstraction apart from the incarnation of God. ...

Thus though the group agreed that the Holy Spirit was operating in the creation and in the living tradition of the Church,
we could not find agreement as to how the doctrine of the Holy
Spirit could enable us to reconcile the conflict between the
Protestant and Catholic emphases. ... On the one hand there
was a hesitation to identify the work of the Spirit wholly with
the community and with the institutions by which it tries to
express its unity. On the other hand there was hesitation to
underplay the extent to which the Holy Spirit in the life of
the community has produced an institutional embodiment which
itself is the work of the Spirit."[77]

Nevertheless, this was not the Commission's last word on the subject.
The leads given by the Christ-Church and Israel-Church analogies were
confirmed and developed as the Commission turned to the most fundamental of all the analogies.

C. The Church-World Analogy

We have already seen how in dealing with the christological
analogy the Commission drew attention to the work of Christ as the
fulfilment of the Incarnation. In similar fashion, the discussion
of the Israel analogy pointed to the need for a deeper investigation
of the nature of salvation brought by the Incarnate Word. The
adequate object of the divine mis-
sion, the Commission quickly agreed, is not the
Church but the whole world; the unique-
ness and universality of the Church is derived from the uniquely
universal work of God in Christ, a work whose object is the totality
of creation.[78] Only in relation to "the over-all will and purpose of
God for his world" do the full implications of the other analogies
become clear.[79] Thus the TCCCNA moved on from the treatment of the
Christ-Church and Israel-Church relationships to consider the
Church's relation to the world.

The Church-world relationship had from the beginning been a
primary focus of American ecclesiology. A brief review of some of
the earlier approaches to this question will help to put the statements of the TCCCNA and the NAWG in historical perspective.

The Chicago Ecumenical Group was the first ecumenical study commission to deal extensively with the topic. Placing the Church in
the context of God's activity, it declared: "It [the Church] is part
of a redemptive process by which God is bringing the world to himself."[80] The context makes clear that the word "part" is important.
The Church as a "concrete social entity" is by no means the goal of
the redemptive process: it is a part, not the whole; only as a part

of the whole does the church find its raison d'être. The redemptive
process both anticipates the Church and looks beyond it: "This process of redemption antedates the Christian movement, going back to the
great work of God in calling Israel and in giving men the law and the
prophets. This historical community extends back into the creative
activity of God, and his transcendent reality is the basis of the
faith in one holy, universal church."[81] At the other end of history,
the Church looks to the consummation of the redemption in what the
New Testament describes as "the Kingdom of God."

The manner in which the CEDG formulates the relationship between
the Church and the Kingdom of God anticipates a line of thinking which
was more extensively developed by the TCCCNA and which ultimately led
to the ecclesiological revolution proposed by the NAWG. The "Ethical
Reality" paper declares: "Because God is already the ultimate ruler,
the kingdom of God is the basis of whatever validity our moral striv-
ing may possess, and gives to the Church its hope and strength. The
community of all Christians is thus not an end in itself, but a means
to, and a part of the redemption of the whole world. The church is
the servant of the kingdom of God. The kingdom of God is the consummation of the church's common work and fellowship." The Church is
thus not an alternative to the world but a part of the world, in the
whole of which the reign of God is already present. What differen-
tiates the Church from the world is not that the Kingdom of God is
present in the one and absent from the other; the Kingdom "is present
wherever faith, purity, love and obedient service reign," i.e. in the
world as well as in the Church. What characterizes the Church as
distinct from the world, is that the Church recognizes these qualities
as "the love of Christ (agape)" and therefore has the duty "to make
more explicit and effective in human conduct" "the invisible bond of
union among men." Where this ideal is realized, the Kingdom is present in the Church; but its full realization can never be found in the
Church alone: we have in the Church only "an earnest of its coming."[82]

The more extensive "Man in Society" study of the Wright Committee pursued a similar line. Like its predecessor, it set the Church
in the context of an over-arching divine redemptive process which is
directed to the world, not to the Church as its goal: "The most ex-
traordinary thing in history is not simply the evil and the alienation of the world but rather the work of God the Redeemer to reconcile the world to himself." This work both antecedes the Church and
looks beyond it to a fulfilment greater than the Church. Even more
clearly than the CEDG, the Wright Committee stresses the historical
relativity of the Church with respect to the universal activity of
God in the world. "This work has taken place in a certain specified
time and among one people; it began with Abraham but it has been fulfilled, it has culminated in Christ. And the Church is the fellowship of those who have been gathered together as in a flock by the
Lord, who acknowledge the special work of God for what it is, who
have been led to surrender to the Lordship of the risen Christ, who
following him take upon themselves the burden of his world's sin,
live in him by the power of the spirit, and proclaim to the world
God's mighty acts over sin, Satan and the principalities of darkness."[83]

The Wright Committee called attention to the difference between
this New Testament notion of the Church with its concentration on the

activity of God and subsequent ecclesiologies which have tended to
concentrate on the institutions and activities of the Church. Not
that the New Testament view overlooked the human media which God
uses to fulfil his purposes; on the contrary, its conception of a
direct heavenly rule exercised by God "by chosen human media and by
direct communication through his heavenly messengers (angels), his
word (as wisdom), and his Spirit" meant an enormous inflation of the
authority of Church institutions: "This meant that all organization
and government were conceived to be of divine institution and sanction, or else they were useless, unprofitable, even sinful."[84]   At
the same time, however, this very consciousness of the direct rule
of God preserved the New Testament Church from simply identifying
its organization and activities with the work of God. Precisely the
awareness of God's living direction of community life by Word and
Spirit made clear to the Church the provisional character of its own
institutions and functions.[85] On the one hand, the subjection of the
Church's life to the divine rule "meant that any institution which
apparently had received a permanent blessing could find itself in
condemnation and deprived of blessing when it failed to fulfil its
God-given task."[86] On the other hand, it meant that the New Testament Church clearly distinguished its activities from the divine
work in its full depth and breadth. "God was inaugurating his own
Kingdom by his own methods, using to be sure the witness of the
elect; but the ethics of the community had not the purpose of 'building the Kingdom.' It was rather considered as the obedient and normal life of a community that was 'in Christ.' It was simply 'following Christ'; it was a discipleship which God would reward in his own
way, but it was not considered as a necessary step without which the
new age would not arrive. Since God requires it, it is essential;
but its precise efficacy in relation to the Kingdom of God is his
alone to decide."[87]

This type of thinking, echos of which can be found in the documents of most of the other commissions prior to the TCCCNA,[88] is
typical of the ecclesiology which emerged in America after the collapse of the Social Gospel. In the course of the sixties, thanks to
the Montreal Conference and Vatican II and the subsequent general
re-orientation of Protestant and Catholic theology signified by the
debates over the "Secular City," "Honest to God," "God is dead,"
"Political Theology," "Theology of the Revolution," and the other
polarizing slogans of recent years the sort of thinking pioneered
here by the Americans has become a commonplace in both Catholic and
Protestant theological circles. In the forties and fifties, the prevailing mood in European ecumenical circles was quite different, as
George F. Thomas pointed out in an article contrasting the approaches
of the European and American contributions to the "Ethical Reality"
study. In particular he calls attention to the American concern for
the Church as a concrete "empirical" social reality as lying at the
root of the contrast. Where the Church is seen as an empirical entity with a theological inner dynamic, it becomes necessary to consider it within, rather than over against the world. This in turn
entails the recognition that the divine purpose is directed towards
and at work in the world and not simply in the Church. In the European contributions, on the contrary, Thomas noted a close parallel
between the tendency to view the Church primarily in terms of its
mystical, "invisible" form and to view the world likewise mystically
as the theological antagonist of the corpus Christi.[89]

1. The Priority of the World to the Church

From the outset, the TCCCNA committed itself to a fundamental
option with far-reaching consequences: "we cannot speak of the
Church in relation to the world without first speaking of Christ and
his relation to the world..."[90] In other words, the Church itself
cannot be defined in itself or solely in terms of its relation to
Christ; its reality can only be adequately understood when it is
viewed as a part of the historical trinitarian mission to the world.

One of the obstacles to an adequate appreciation of the world
as the object of the divine activity is a conceptual ambiguity which
is rooted in the Scriptures. From one point of view the world appears as the object of the divine creative and redeeming love and
providential rule; from another viewpoint, however, it may be viewed
as the "fallen world of sin and death, under the rule of Satan in
New Testament language." By consistently distinguishing between
these two meanings of the term (to designate the world in its fallen,
sinful aspects, the text uses single quotation-marks, thus 'world'),
the Commission sought to bring out more clearly than heretofore the
positive aspect of the solidarity of the Church with the world.[91]

The central affirmation of the TCCCNA concerning the relationship between God the world and the Church is that "the Lord of the
Church not only is to be the Lord of the whole creation; he already
is this [original italics]." The report then goes on to develop the
meaning of this affirmation in a series of five propositions:

(1) "The universal dominion of God over the world is the dominion
of the same God who was in Jesus Christ, and whose work as the
one triune God is indivisible."

(2) "The event of Jesus Christ established this lordship of God in
a way new to the temporal and historical process."

(3) "The action of God in Jesus Christ, moreover, is directed to all
humanity."

(4) "By his resurrection Christ is declared to be the Lord of all.
Not only are all things to be put under him, but this is already accomplished fact."

(5) "Jesus Christ is the one who is to come as judge and redeemer
of all."[92]

Whereas the first two propositions, in effect, are simply a
recapitulation of the earlier Commission discussion of christology
and of the Israel-Church relationship, the third proposition comes
to grips with the heart of the Commission's soteriological conception. The text expands upon it as follows:

> "The being of Jesus Christ is a sending and a giving for the
> whole world, that it may be saved through him. Christ takes
> to himself the humanity which belongs to all men, and in his
> living and dying he makes the suffering and the need of all
> mankind his own. In him the enemy has been defeated. In the
> decisive struggle in the wilderness, in the work of his minis-
> try, and in the offering of himself on the Cross, the victory
> has been won over the evil world and for the whole world."[93]

At first sight, the assertion that the whole world, humanity, is the
object of Jesus Christ's redeeming action hardly seems astonishing.
What creed or theological system proclaims anything else? What is
important to remember is that the statement here is made not simply
in a soteriological but in a specifically ecclesiological context.
Hence the explanation of the next proposition asserts: "The risen
Christ freely and in sovereign right continues to work in the Church
and in the world."[94] And shortly thereafter the report declares:
"In obedience to Christ and the Spirit, as the event of their presence and as properly patterned after Christ himself, the Church is
necessarily in, as well as with and for the world [original ital-
ics]."[95]

In effect, the TCCCNA is repudiating here all those ecclesiologies which consciously or unconsciously identify the Church with
the new humanity incorporated into Christ as though the two were coextensive. For the TCCCNA, t h e   d i s t i n c t i o n   b e -
t w e e n   C h u r c h   a n d   w o r l d   i s   s e c o n d a r y
t o   t h e i r   r a d i c a l   i d e n t i t y ;   t h e i r
d i s t i n c t i o n   i s   p o s s i b l e   o n l y   b e -
c a u s e   t h e   C h u r c h   i s   s o m e t h i n g   l e s s
t h a n   t h e   f u l l n e s s   o f   r e d e e m e d   h u -
m a n i t y .[96] Repudiated therefore are all those ecclesiological
theories which by idealizing some aspect of the concrete, empirical
Church--be it the "invisible" fellowship of true believers or the
"visible" system of sacraments and hierarchy--in effect identify the
"true" Church and the Body of Christ. Such attempts violate both
incarnational and eschatological principles. Inasmuch as they abstract the Church from the affairs of men and from the "hard and

inevitable materialities" of the world of history and sociality, such attempts, as pointed out earlier, "fall into ecclesiological docetism"; we recall how the Commission protested vigorously against every tendency to make the Church appear "purer than its Lord."[97] By the same token, the Commission points out, such theories, inasmuch as they banish from the Church the 'world' in the sense of sinful mankind, attribute to the Church, here and now, a perfection which the new humanity is destined to possess only after the Parousie. In the words of the Commission,

> "The Church indeed participates in the fulness of victory and life which is in Christ; it is indeed given the 'first-fruits' of the Spirit; it has indeed already begun to live in the new age. But the final 'end' is not yet. The struggle for the right acknowledgment of the sovereignty of Christ is still waged within the Church itself. There is sin within the Church. ... Together with the whole creation it awaits and longs for the final word of God's gracious judgment in Christ. The glory of the Church is nowhere more clearly visible than in the repentance whereby it recognizes that it is not, in empirical fact, the reality which it ought to be, and which eschatologically it already is."[98]

The corollary of the Commission's position is that the Church must reckon with a presence and work of Christ and the Spirit in the world as distinct from the Church: "We must affirm the works of Christ and the Spirit outside the Church, in manifold expressions of mercy and reconciliation, in the various pursuits and discoveries of truth, in human creativity, and in countless other ways."[99] T h e Church is right in claiming all such works for Christ the Lord and his Spirit; indeed she is duty-bound to do so, "for there is no other Lord than Christ, no other Spirit than the Holy Spirit." There is even a sense in which it can be claimed that

> "...the Church is essential to all those other works of Christ and of the Spirit, for only in the Church do men hear the name of him who works true reconciliation and true mercy... Apart from knowledge of the name of Christ, apart from him as the source and norm, and apart from true destiny in Christ, these many works lack their true context. It is in the light of Christ's historical coming, made a continuing event, known in the worship of the Christian community of faith, that all these find their proper ordering, their right proportion, and are given their true name."[100]

One thing, however, the Church may not do; s h e m a y n o t c l a i m t h e w o r k s o f t h e L o r d a n d t h e S p i r i t a s t h o u g h t h e y w e r e h e r o w n . To claim the manifold workings of Christ and his Spirit as her own would be blasphemous. "Neither in its own life nor outside the visible community can limits be set upon that presence and action."[101]

2. The Manner of the Divine Presence and Operation

With these clarifications in mind, we must now return to the original question: what does the analogy between the active presence of Christ and his Spirit in the world as a whole tell us about the special active presence of Christ and his Spirit in the Church?

Going back to the explanation of Nelson's proposition three quoted above (p. 146) we find the Committee asserting a solidarity, an assumption of the renewed world in Christ, but no clear ontological explanation of how such a solidarity is to be understood. The text recalls biblical and patristic expressions, but makes no effort to translate these into the conceptual world of any contemporary ontology. Evidently, this is at least partially the result of an inability of the Commission members to agree on such a translation.[102] It would appear, however, that something more than mere committee-compromise led the TCCCNA to refrain from elaborating an ontological explanation at this critical point. Already back in its 1956 discussion of the workings of the Spirit, a question had been raised about the presuppositions of our contemporary interpretations of the Spirit:

"In the modern period we have become too greatly concerned with the metaphysical problem of how in God and in man there can be a combination of spirit and body. This very concern is Greek rather than Biblical, yet this metaphysical concern frequently determines our reading of the Old Testament, a form of unconscious modernization. We might be closer to the fundamental ways of thinking in the Bible, closer to the basic problem of Biblical men, if we stressed the epistemological problem. How does that which is subjective in man become related to that which is objective in God? How can flesh really hear God's Word in such a way as to respond to it? When God speaks and is heard, what sort of correspondence between the subjective and the objective factors must be presupposed? When the prophet says, 'The Word of the Lord came to me,' is he not interpreting what has happened in such a way as to say indirectly, 'Don't listen to me, I do not have God in me. God is out there in the movements of the army, in the coming of the plagues, in the storms of nature, in the events of history.'? In so far, then, as the people have the Spirit, a condition has been established for their apprehension of God's Word."[103]

In effect, this is the approach we find in the TCCCNA's reports. Instead of offering a metaphysical analysis of the working of Christ and the Spirit in the world, the "Christ and the Church" report offers a description of the ways in which the divine presence finds "subjective" human expression. At this point, however, the limits of the Church-world analogy become painfully evident. The Commission acknowledges that Christ and his Spirit are actively present in the whole world and not simply in the Church; at the same time it has to concede that it is only in and through the Church that this presence can be recognized for what it is, and furthermore that the Church is the principal instrument of the divine action in the world. Does this mean that the Church-world analogy has proven to be a blind alley, incapable of leading to a deeper penetration of the divine-human interaction in the Church?

3. The Ecclesiological Application

The answer need not be so negative. The mere distinction between Church and world (in the sense developed above) has, as we have seen, led to a variety of restrictive conclusions about the divine-human interaction in the Church, e.g. the saving action of God is not confined to the Church; the Church is not separable from the materialities of the world nor from the sinfulness of the 'world.' These conclusions may not be a direct answer to the ontological question about the divine-human interaction in the Church, but they are very valuable clues to answering the "epistemological" questions about this interaction. This becomes evident in the Commission's description of the mission of the Church to the world: "In obedience to Christ and the Spirit, as the event of their presence and as strongly patterned after Christ himself, the Church is necessarily in, as well as with and for the world." The text goes on to distinguish three senses in which the Church is "in and with the world":

> "...as testifying to an act of God's gracious calling, a decision and determination which apply not alone to the members of this community, but to the whole of humanity and to every individual within that whole."

> "...by its taking the world to itself as the object of its love and concern, by identifying itself with the world as Christ identified himself with sinful humanity."

> "...as representing the whole of mankind in its praise, its thanksgiving, its confession, its petition, and also in its penitence and constant seeking for forgiveness."[104]

Far more is involved in these statements than merely a description of the mission of the Church in the world. Implicit is a fundamental epistemological option, whose implications--as we shall see --became the central preoccupation of the Missionary Structures study; implicit is the assertion that the question "what is the Church" presupposes an answer to the more fundamental question "where is the Church," or better, where do we encounter the salvation which God has effected in Jesus Christ through the Spirit. The reference-points defining the Church's true self-identity are more encompassing than their ecclesiastical manifestations: Christ's Lordship is not confined to the boundaries of the Church; neither is the "New Humanity" which his saving work brings into being. The Church is never more in danger of mistaking or losing its true self-identity than when it makes itself the central point of reference, seeing Christ and the New Creation only in their ecclesiastical manifestations.[105]

Thus, although it must ultimately be acknowledged that the Church-world analogy like its predecessors fails to provide clear, unequivocal answers to the ontological questions concerning the divine-human interaction in the Church, it does offer a very fruitful approach to the epistemological question underlying the ontological ones. At the root of the question about the divine-human relationship lies the scandalon of an outrageous discrepancy between the promise of the Church and its reality. It is this discrepancy which has driven so many classical and contemporary ecclesiologies to offer dichotomous answers to the ontological question. By explicitly focusing on the epistemological question, the TCCCNA was able to identify the source of error in such solutions and thus to relativize the whole ontological dimension of the problem. What stands in the way of acknowledging a divine-human interaction in the Church is above all the presence of sin in the Church. The christological analogy can account for the materiality, and historicity of the Church, but it fails when faced with the phenomenon of sin in the Church.[106] The Israel analogy can encompass the phenomenon of sin, but only at the expense of remaining unclear about the specific newness of the Church. The World analogy, on the other hand, puts the Church into a broader context of soteriology and eschatology, in which the sinfulness of the Church loses much of its force as an epistemological obstacle. Without denying or in any way making light of the Church's burden of guilt, the C h u r c h - w o r l d

analogy enables the theologian to
transcend the scandal by delivering
him from a narrow, ecclesiocentric
perspective. The Commission put the matter this way:

> "Whereas the world normally looks first at the Church for evi-
> dence of uniqueness, the Church looks first to its Lord, and
> then at the instrument through which he is working in history.
> When men find a dreadful discrepancy between the two, we of
> the Church must be the first to acknowledge in shame that this
> is indeed the case, while at the same time we insist that in
> all its imperfection and sin the Church which men see is yet
> that Lord's instrument and can only be understood in relation
> to him, his person, his work, his purpose, and his power."[107]

From here it is but a short step to the radical ecclesiological
program theoretically formulated and experimentally practiced by the
American Working Group of the Missionary Structures of the Congregation study. Their report declares:

> "It is the task of theology to learn how to discern what God is
> doing not only in and through the churches but also in those
> impulses and forms of God's presence which the 'old' church
> has not yet learned to incorporate--and more, in those places
> of God's presence which the church is not called to master by
> drawing them to itself but to serve by giving itself to
> them."[108]

For the members of the NAWG this meant going out into the world to
seek the future shapes of the Church, seeking to learn what the
Church is by practicing to be the Church where the Church should
be. Without repudiating or underestimating the value of abstract,
"metaphysical" considerations in ecclesiology, the NAWG came to
believe that the question of the active
divine presence in the Church cannot ultimately be answered on the
abstract level, and that to attempt to do so almost
inevitably leads to an illegitimate fixation upon particular culturally conditioned appearances.

> "...we often speak of 'church' and 'mission' in an abstract way
> --out of relation to the present world. But 'mission' and
> 'church' are not abstract realities; they are about what God
> is doing in his world and how he is drawing us into what he is
> doing. One frequent result of our formal, abstract theology,
> therefore, is that the words are given the content of some
> particular past historical situation--say the sixteenth century,
> or the eighteenth--and tend to limit the freedom of the church
> for its mission in the living moving world where God is at work
> now [original italics]."[109]

III. IMPLICATIONS AND APPLICATIONS

A. The Church as Event and Institution

From the beginning, the American ecumenical discussion of the divine-human interaction had sought to reconcile two opposing ways of thinking. The CCULW had spoken of "the institutional and spiritual conceptions of the Church."[110] At the end of its discussion of the three analogies, the TCCCNA moved to address this issue under the title "the Church as Event and Institution." This section of its report represents an attempt to draw conclusions for an ecumenical understanding of a future united Church.

Far from opposing event and institution, as traditional catholic and protestant ecclesiologies have done, the TCCCNA insists that their interrelationship is a characteristic of God's dealings with his creation: "a common pattern of activity is to be seen in every aspect of the divine work. At every point event and institution are to be found -- whether as freedom and form, or variety and order, or dynamism and structure. When they are found, they are inseparably related one to another, interwoven and complementary."[111] The text goes on to trace this pattern through the history of the world. Already in the order of subhuman creation, the report claims, one finds "the integration of novelty and continuity, fluidity and form," and this on all levels, "from the microscopic to the macroscopic." At the level of human existence, it goes on, this pattern becomes even more evident in the "unending dialectic of freedom and order." And in the drama of salvation, culminating in the supreme event, the coming of God himself in the historical man Jesus Christ, the same pattern reappears; here too there is both structure and event. As event, Jesus Christ "displays the freedom of God in action, that entering of God into the historical process which always has the character of mystery and spontaneity and novelty. As event, Jesus Christ represents and embodies the sovereign freedom of God in his relation to the world which he has created." And yet, this event is also a structure, "for this event like all events has its own particular given form, and no other form. In this instance of manhood God was signally declared; it was this humanity which was 'assumed,' as the ancient Fathers phrased it, and became the vehicle of the divine presence and the instrument of the divine energizing."[112]

What is here identified as the universal pattern of divine activity in the world is also the pattern of divine activity in the Church:

> "A similar dialectic of freedom and form characterizes the work of the Holy Spirit. It would be quite wrong simply to identify the work of the Spirit with spontaneity and freedom. Yet it would be equally wrong simply to identify the work of the Spirit with the established structures of, say, an ecclesiastical order. Both elements are present and must be preserved."[113]

Though event and institution are inseparably linked to one another, there is an order in their relationship: t h e e v e n t i s p r i o r t o t h e s t r u c t u r e ; t h e s t r u c - t u r e e x i s t s o n l y f o r t h e s a k e o f t h e e v e n t . This is the consequence of the order in the relationship between the divine and the human factors: "God in Christ acting through the Spirit" initiates the action; man responds.[114] Obviously this does not mean that the structure is of little or no importance. Without form the event could not exist: the divine action and the Spirit-empowered human response can only come into existence insofar as they take on concrete historical form; without this they remain empty abstractions.[115] Nevertheless, the priority remains, and it concretely affects every aspect of the Church's life:

> "In any sacramental ordinance the event of Christ's act is prior to the ritual form which may be employed. In Scripture and in creed Christ as the living Word is prior to the words and constructions which speak of him. Christ's own ministering is prior to, and is the ground of, all general and all special institutions of ministry in the Church."[116]

B. The Spirit of God and the Institutions of the Church
1. The Point at Issue

Alone the recognition of such an order in the relationship between event and institution yields no immediate solutions. Ultimately the question remains open, to what extent has the divine action bound itself to the institutional structure. This after all was the question which previous commissions had failed to resolve. Although all could agree that God acts through the structures and institutions of the Church, there invariably remained an unbridgeable division between those who held that God had quasi-absolutely committed himself to certain particular structures (e.g. the biblical text, the dogmas canonized by church councils or patristic

tradition, specific liturgical and sacramental rituals, specific offices and means of their transmission) and those who did not recognize such a divine commitment. At issue was always the question,
w h a t   i n   t h e   h i s t o r i c a l   t r a d i t i o n
o f   t h e   C h u r c h   i s   n o r m a t i v e .   Here is how
the ATC described the issue:

"The membership of the Committee and the Churches which they
represent fall into two very distinct groups. Each group is
very diverse in its complexion, but on the issue of norm or
authority the watershed between them is definite.

(a) There is a group which believes that a divinely ordained
norm for the constitution and practice of the Church exists and
that departure from it must therefore be disobedience to the
will of God. Some find it in an episcopal form of organization
which transmits by regular succession the valid teaching and
grace. Some find it in the presbytery which affords the divinely appointed continuity. Some find equally binding sanction for congregational autonomy. All three types of Churches
hold that some form of baptism is a definite condition of membership, but some find believer's baptism by immersion to be
an essential feature of the divinely established order. Still
other definite requirements are laid down as authoritative
standards without which the Church would not properly exist.
Different as these teachings are, their representatives agree
at one crucial point. Somewhere in the historic tradition is
something normative for the constitution and practice of the
Church. To enter into any union which did not make this particular requirement would be a denial of the authority of God
in the channel through which it is recognized.

(b) The second group is also united by a common conviction.
They recognize the authority of God in church organization and
practice, but do not believe that this is expressed in norms
that have been communicated in specific and unchanging patterns. From their study of history, these find no divinely
authorized pattern of the Church. They believe that the appeal
to development as validating any particular form of government
as normative is fallacious because the laws of biological
growth and of institutional change are entirely different.
They recognize the nature of religion as corporate and the need
for church order. They appreciate the presumptive value of
what has been historically tested. But they do not believe
that any given stage in the Church's life may be made a binding
law for the Church of today. They recognize the sacramental
historic rites. In the interest of Church unity, this group
would gladly join with those who hold different opinions in
these various areas. But they would not assent to the position
that there are many devoted followers of Christ who lack something essential for belonging to the body of Christ. To agree
that the particular form of organization adopted, whatever it
might be was necessary for the existence of the Church as such
would mean nothing less than to deny their convictions concerning the will of God."[117]

2. The Freedom of the Spirit

Although the members of the TCCCNA came from more or less the
same confessional traditions as the members of earlier Commissions,
they managed to reach a consensus on this long debated issue. Their
resolution is contained in the section dealing with the working of
the Spirit in the Church.[118] At the head of their statement, they
put the text of II Cor. 3:17, "where the Spirit of the Lord is,
there is freedom." This they assert is God's own answer to "those
who think of structures as absolutized and utterly inflexible and
who find the pattern and presence of Christ and the work of the
Spirit wholly and without remainder given in the institution." The
Spirit of God remains sovereign over his work. T h e   S p i r i t
i n d e e d   g i v e s   g r a c e   a n d   a u t h o r i t y   t o
t h e   C h u r c h ,   b u t   t h e s e   g i f t s   n e v e r
b e c o m e   t h e   C h u r c h ' s   p o s s e s s i o n   t o
t h e   e x t e n t   t h a t   s h e   a c q u i r e s   a b s o -
l u t e   d o m i n i o n   o v e r   t h e m .   "The Church lives
in the Spirit as the Spirit dwells in it, but the Spirit is God's
Spirit and can never become identical with the human spirit or with
the corporate 'spirit' of the empirical Church."[119]

The Spirit comes to the Church in judgment as well as blessing.
The blessing is primary. "The dominant note in the New Testament's
witness to the Spirit is not judgment or even awe, but rather blessing and joy and power. The work of the Spirit is notably marked by
richness and variety."[120] Its gifts are concrete, historical; they
have form. "As in the Incarnation God binds himself to concrete
manhood, so by the Spirit in the Church he works in and through human flesh and blood, words and acts, social and historical structures."[121] Nevertheless, the Commission insists, the Spirit also
comes in judgment, particularly when the individual or group, or even
the Church as a whole in its empirical expression arrogates to itself
the Spirit's authority as an immediate possession or when the Church
takes to serving its own interests in opposition to the divine mission.[122] However, the Commission notes, even when the Spirit exe-
cutes judgment on "distorted, inordinate, pretentious forms" in ecclesiastical life, the element of blessing is not negated; such
judgment is wrought "not by the total destruction of all forms, but
by the creation of new forms more appropriate to God's intention.[123]
This form of "judgment" by the Spirit is the necessary consequence

of the way in which the Spirit of God interacts with the human spirit. The Commission writes:

> "How then does the Spirit work? not by replacing or coercing
> the human spirit, but by releasing and engaging the freedom of
> man's spirit. The guidance of the Spirit is not, so to say,
> additive to man's insight and understanding; it is directive of
> that insight and understanding, by a gentle leading into the
> truth which is in Christ Jesus or by a catastrophic shattering
> of pretensions to knowledge by sinful men. To be 'filled with
> the Holy Spirit' does not mean that freedom is negated or that
> human spontaneity is destroyed; it means rather that one is
> grasped by that obedience to God which leads to true freedom
> and spontaneity."[124]

3. The Authority of the Spirit

The manner in which the Commission justifies these statements
on the Spirit's operation in the Church offers a valuable illustration of the implications of its position. The Commission report itself offers little by way of explicit justification for its statements here. In addition to the sentence quoted from II Cor. 17, only
four other texts are mentioned, namely Eph. 4:28, John 16:8, Gal.
5:22, and I Cor. 12.; instead of explicit texts one finds generic
assertions like: "the Bible makes clear," "the Scriptures constantly
warn us," etc.[125] In large measure, of course this style of argumentation is a consequence of the literary genre: in a brief summary
report, there is no place for the detailed exegetical studies carried
out in the course of years of discussion. For what lies behind such
generic claims about the teaching of Scripture, one must go back to
the individual papers prepared for the Commission meetings and the
discussions to which these papers gave rise. In the present instance, it is to the paper of F. V. Filson on "the Holy Spirit in the
New Testament"[126] which dealt most explicitly with the matter that
one must above all look. Here it becomes clear that the Commission
was more concerned to grasp overall trends in the scriptural witnesses rather than in isolating individual texts.

As an example of the use of Scripture by the Commission but also
for its exposition of the nature of authority in the Church, the Filson paper deserves closer study.

In his study Filson drew attention to certain patterns in the
New Testament texts dealing with Church leadership. As to the Gospels, he asserts "there is no clear statement that Jesus imparted
the Spirit to his disciples during his ministry." Matt. 10:20, Luke
12:12 and Mark 13:20 contain promises "that Jesus is to give the
Spirit, and John 20:22 reports the initial post-resurrection fulfillment of that promise. Nowhere in the Synoptics, not even in Luke

24:33, 49 is this promise limited to special ministers, though it may be argued that such a limitation is intended in the gift of John 20: 22."[127]

Though Acts generally associates the Spirit with the leadership of the community (e.g. Acts 1:2, 5), in Peter's Pentecost sermon it is promised to all who believe (Acts 2:38).[128] More significant, however, is the fact that in the course of Acts the role of the Twelve so prominent at the beginning of the life of the community gradually diminishes. "Nothing is said of successors of Peter or of the others of the Twelve, and as time goes on other leaders are raised up by the Spirit to accept and fulfill the decisive work of the Church. The initiation and promotion of a world mission is sub-stantially in the hands of others than the Twelve."[129] The notion of apostle is wider than that of the Twelve, and both the Twelve and the other believers "recognized that there were other Spirit-filled men who could exercise leadership," e.g. the Seven (among whom Stephen and Philip are singled out as playing "a role which none of the Twelve except Peter surpassed or equaled; though at least in the case of the Samaritan mission their ability to communicate the Spirit was re-stricted), Barnabas, and above all Paul, in whom the work of the Spirit appears to center in the second half of Acts."[130] Signifi-cantly it is the Spirit inspired opening up of the Church to world mission which lets the Twelve fall into the background. "What this means is that the work of the Spirit is not limited to or continuously controlled by the group which Jesus chose; after Acts 1-5 independent and unexpected leadership dominates in the expanding work of the Spirit. ... The conclusion seems to be that while individuals and groups are called by the Spirit to lead the Church, this leadership is not channeled into formal and unalterable patterns which divide the Church into two fixed groups, the ministry and the others. The ministry appears to be a function rather than an unchangeable or-der."[131]

This conclusion is fully consistent with the Pauline "picture of the diversity of ministries of the one Spirit as found in I Cor. 12. Here Paul speaks of the spiritual gifts as given to all members of the Church. All have a gift or gifts all have a ministry; in a real sense there is no laity; there is no fixed order. No doubt there were in Paul's churches, even at Corinth, recognized regular leaders. But they did not define permanently the way by which the Spirit would lead this church or other churches. This functional and inventive pattern of leadership is what Acts pictures; it is what Paul de-scribes. The Spirit remains free and yet is far from justifying anarchy. The ministry belongs to the entire Church but it has no fixed and final form."[132]

Though the later New Testament writings, especially the Pasto-rals, are often adduced to show the Spirit working "in more chan-neled ways in the setting up of church officers," the fact is that the Spirit appears to recede from community consciousness in these writings. Whereas in Acts 20:28 the Ephesian elders are "said to have been made bishops or guardians by the Holy Spirit," no such statement appears in the Pastorals, nor is there any mention of the Spirit among the qualifications of bishop-elders and deacons.[133]

In the discussion which followed the presentation of Filson's paper this position seems to have found general acceptance. The question, however, was raised: "How does the history of the Church and the history of doctrine help us when the New Testament leaves us in the dark as it does on the matter of the order and structure of particular ministries?"[134] To this question the final report of the

Commission gives an unequivocal answer. Church history matters; it
would be pressing the divine freedom too far were we to make of the
Church "a community with no identifying structures possessing historical continuity."[135]   T h e   C h u r c h   m u s t   r e -
s p e c t   i t s   o w n   h i s t o r y -- i t s   t o t a l
h i s t o r y   h o w e v e r ,   n o t   m e r e l y   t h i s
o r   t h a t   p a r t i c u l a r   h i s t o r y .   The conflict
between Scripture and the traditions is not original; it is rather
the product of an absolutizing of particular histories at the expense of the universal and thus a violation of a fundamental principle of the working of the Spirit. Over against such particular traditions, the whole of Scripture read in the light of the whole historical experience of the Church has priority.[136] We shall return
to this point in the next chapter.

This position was not an a priori postulate of the Commission;
rather it represents a deep conviction which emerged gradually in the
course of its efforts to come to grips ecumenically with the historical action of God in its totality. As their discussions increasingly
"moved in the direction of 'catholic' comprehensiveness,"[137] the conviction grew that many of the assumptions and presuppositions inherent in the traditional manner of posing the question "By what
authority" are "incompatible with the kind of authority exercised
over creation by the triune God and with the manifestation of authority in the life of the incarnate Word. His authority was not such
as to demand assent but rather such as to elicit consent [italics
added]."[138] Precisely their respect for the manifold forms of the
Spirit's testimony in both Scripture and the living historical Tradition of the Church forbade their seeking the "locus of authority"
in any particular expression of the Spirit's working. They wrote:

"...we did not use the Bible as a kind of reference book for
settling questions in the fashion of a 'perfect dictionary' or
a verbal court of last appeal. We did use the Bible as sure
witness to him who is the source and norm and goal of truth,
and to his activity among men. In perceiving the illuminating
and empowering centre of the Bible in the living Lord Jesus
Christ, we tried to avoid the all-too-simple ways of conceiving
the relationship between this centre and the whole course of
the biblical record. ... Our concern for the centre did not
allow us to ignore the endless pluralism in the Spirit's activity and in the conscious responses which have been made to
that activity. We have found that openness to the variety-in-
unity of the biblical writings is an essential expression of
faith in the one holy catholic Church and a manifestation of
that 'catholicity' in method which is alone appropriate to our
study. We are convinced that whenever awareness of this 'catholicity' of the whole Bible is deficient, the conception of
catholicity in the Church will be similarly deficient."[139]

Thus the Commission's own experience of trying seriously to
come to grips with the institutionalized forms of the Spirit's work-

ing and the experience of a profound consensus emerging from this
effort served in effect as the ultimate verification of the way in
which the Commission came to explain the Spirit's working. Precisely their respect for the historical, institutional forms of the
Spirit's operation drove them to the conviction that ultimately the
"locus of authority" is to be found nowhere "apart from the living
Lord himself."[140] Not of course that the living Lord can ever be
separated from the Church; its Scriptures, creeds, rituals, and
ministry remain the principal witnesses to the living Lord.
From Jesus Christ, through his
Spirit, these institutions derive
real authority, but it is always a
derived, relative authority, subject like every creature to the
living Lord, open like every creature to error and misuse. The Commission
writes:

> "The 'eventful' nature of the presence of Christ and of the
> Spirit--that is, the freedom and variety to which we have re-
> ferred--forbids the absolutizing of the words of Scripture,
> creeds, or confessions, or of any ritual forms, or of any or-
> dering of ministry as exclusive or even indispensable agencies
> for the Lord's work. These structures cannot be regarded as
> simply perfect and unchangeable embodiments of the event which
> constitutes the Church; God cannot be 'bound' by such words,
> creeds, rites, and ministries."[141]

Against those who would claim for themselves as individuals or for
particular organs and agencies of the Church an exclusive, infallible possession of the Spirit the Commission formulates the stern
warning:

> "...the authority of the Spirit is never simply given over to the
> Church. It must not be taken for granted that in any given in-
> stance the pronouncements of an ecclesiastical dignitary, the
> views of some solemn assembly, the particular views of this or
> that agency, have the divine authority of the Spirit. The
> Spirit does operate within the community, and through the com-
> munity's properly constituted agencies. But the Scriptures
> constantly warn us against the pretension to omniscience or
> absolute authority on the part of any person or group, even the
> Church in its empirical expression. The Scriptures also warn
> us against those who, claiming the Spirit's authority as an
> immediate possession, decry all institutional forms or chan-
> nels."[142]

At the end of his paper, Filson posed the obvious question which
such a conception of the Spirit's workings must give rise to: "If
the Church of the Spirit is under no fixed law or final pattern of

organization, how can we be sure that the Church is really Christian and the Holy Spirit is really the cause of any specific utterance, decision, or action?"[143] The answer given by the Commission is that a n   a b s o l u t e ,   i n f a l l i b l e   m e a s u r e   o f t h e   S p i r i t ' s   a c t i o n   d o e s   n o t   e x i s t : "...no easy boundaries, no neat delimitations, no ultimate disjunctions, can be established between the necessary freedom which marks the Church as 'event' and the necessary ordering which marks the Church as 'institution'."[144] In the last analysis the Church has no other test than the Lord himself and the Spirit he sends; in a word, the Church must live by faith. This, of course, is not meant as an invitation to quietism. F a l l i b l e   t e s t s   t h e r e a r e   i n d e e d ,   [145] and the Church must make use of them, relying on the Spirit of God to correct its human mistakes.

C. The Spirit of God and the Coming Great Church

For the members of the TCCCNA, the years of study and discussion to penetrate the mystery of the divine-human interaction in the Church was far more than a mere exercise in theological reasoning; more than anything else i t   w a s   a   p r o f o u n d   e x p e r i - e n c e   o f   h o w   t h e   S p i r i t   w o r k s   t o b r i n g   b e l i e v e r s   o f   w i d e l y   d i f f e r e n t t r a d i t i o n s   t o   c o n s e n s u s   i n   q u e s - t i o n s   d e e p l y   a f f e c t i n g   c h u r c h u n i t y . Two passages from the final report offer remarkable testimony to this experience:

"We have studied the Scriptures in the context of the living experience of the Church and have believed that the Holy Spirit still takes of the things of Christ and shows them to his people. We thank God that in our years of meeting we have found an unexpected measure of unity. We dare to say that this unity is not of our own making but is a gracious working of the Spirit in sinful men who have sought, however imperfectly, to know the truth as it is in Jesus Christ."[146]

"Thus we have gone about our common task together, loyal to the one holy catholic Church, grateful for the tokens of oneness in Christ which we have glimpsed, humbled by the disclosure of our blindness, thinking together as those who in faithfulness to their own separate traditions would yet apprehend the wholeness and fullness of the one catholic tradition, and finding in the process ample evidence of unity in Christ--a unity which, even while it deepens our ecumenical despair, also heartens us and gives us ecumenical courage."[147]

To dismiss such confessions as mere pious rhetoric would be just as
unfair as to accuse the Commission of a spirit of eclecticism and
inclusivism unconcerned for truth and right. Every page of the
minutes of the Commission meetings testifies to the deep concern and
forthrightness of the debates. That under these circumstances a
consensus emerged which was not already present at the start is a
weighty argument against the all to facile charges raised by Protestant and Catholic fundamentalists against the work of such ecumenical
theological commissions.

What happened here, of course, is no privilege of the TCCCNA.
The history of this Commission is but one example of a process which
can be observed not only in the other American ecumenical groups and
commissions dealt with in this study; the same process can be observed wherever believers from different theological and ecclesiastical traditions undertake to penetrate beyond their separate institutionalized formulations of the faith to the underlying Truth,
which is their source and norm. Can this experience really be dismissed as subjective, irrelevant? Can the churches and individual
theologians who hold fast to the irreformability of their own particular traditions and institutions continue to ignore this experience
or patronizingly dismiss it as an imperfect, propaedeutical working
of the Spirit, valid only insofor as it leads "separated brethren"
to acknowledge one's own particular tradition as the perfect working
of the Spirit? Clearly to pose such questions is not by itself to
answer them. Nevertheless, only those who are prepared to face
these questions honestly have the right to pass judgment on the contributions of such ecumenical theological commissions to the discovery of the true visage of the Church of Christ for our time.

The TCCCNA was honest enough to admit that it had not been able
to solve all the outstanding issues in the debate over church
unity.[148] In general, its consensus took the form of an agreement
on broad general principles; even in the rare instances in which it
addresses specific questions of ecumenical disagreement, as for
example the question of ministry,[149] its pronouncements remain quite
general and abstract. The same holds true for the other pre-Montreal
F. & O. Commissions. Nevertheless, the work of these commissions did
not remain without fruit. The fundamental, though still quite generic solutions to the ecumenical issues worked out by these commissions
were to be taken up and developed in the direction of increasing con-

creteness by the COCU commissions. In one issue after the other--
"Scripture Tradition and the Guardians of Tradition," "Worship and
Witness of the Church," "One Ministry, One Baptism, One Table,"
"The Ordained Ministry in a United Church," "Ordination in a Church
Catholic, Evangelical, Reformed," "Guidelines for the Structure of
the Church," etc.---the COCU commissions were able to achieve theological consensus so concrete and detailed, that in the end they were
able to formulate a concrete plan of union. True to the principles
worked out in years of intensive theological discussion concerning
the divine-human interaction in the Church, the COCU commissions
refused to consider their documents to be the last word on the complicated issues of ecumenical ecclesiology. In humble confession of
their own human fallibility and confident trust in God's power to
use such fallible human instruments to achieve his purpose, the COCU
declared:

> "Measured by his [God's] immense understanding of our nature,
> and his unfailing expectation, we will continue to fall short
> of the glory he wills to reveal to us. Even to use the word
> 'Church'--whether in referring to our own denomination or the
> wider unity we seek--places us under the awesome judgment of
> the one Lord of that one Church. Nonetheless, we must obey
> God who is calling us to a kind of obedience today only pos-
> sible to those who give themselves wholeheartedly to a delib-
> erate relinquishing of every separation, and a resolute will to
> accept the fact and cost of unity.
>   We recognize also that the united body proposed will be far
> from the wholeness of the Body of Christ. To this we say that
> we think of it as a uniting as well as a united church. We
> have imagined its structure as best we could, in such a way as
> to keep it open to all others who with ourselves seek a wider
> unity of catholic and evangelical traditions, alike reformed by
> every true obedience to God. Similarly so have we tried to
> design it so that exponents of greater freedom and of greater
> authority alike must listen to that gospel which alone gives
> true freedom and authority in our service of Christ. We seek
> a form of the Church which, in faithfulness to that gospel,
> will order our Christ-given liberties for the more effective
> discharge of our Christ-given tasks.
>   ...
>   We offer all these hopes and thoughts, and the proposals born
> of them, in the spirit of the Apostle's ascription? 'Now to him
> who by the power at work within us is able to do far more abun-
> dantly than all that we ask or think, to him be glory in the
> church and in Christ Jesus to all generations, for ever and ever.
> Amen.' (Ephesians 3:20-21 RSV)"[150]

Is this perhaps the attitude which the Spirit is fashioning in the
pursuit of the ecumenical goal, the coming great Church of Christ?

CHAPTER V

FROM THE EXPERIENCE OF THE CHURCH TO A VISION

I. THE ONE, HOLY, CATHOLIC, AND APOSTOLIC CHURCH BETWEEN VISION AND
   EXPERIENCE

In the third chapter we saw how the Americans sought to combine
empirical reality and theoretical ideal in their attempts to define
the Church, and in the fourth chapter we saw how they explained the
tension between these two aspects of the Church in terms of the relationships between the divine and human factors in the Church's life.
We must not forget, however, that from their inception, the American
discussions were eminently practical: their aim was not the development of an academic ecclesiology but rather the discovery of paths to
a more fuller realization of the God-given unity of the Church. From
the beginning, as we saw in the presentation of the work of the
CCULW, they sought not only to elaborate a vision of the "coming
great Church" but also to propose and practice practical steps to
achieve and perfect this vision. The corollary of their way of understanding the nature of the Church, and of the divine-human interaction
in it, was an insistence on the interrelationship of theory and practice, between vision and experience.[1]

It was the concern that this aspect found too little attention
among the European members of the Faith and Order Movement that led
to the creation of the first of the American commissions. It was
the Americans who first called attention to the need to take account
of the "non-theological factors" in the making and breaking of Church
unity, who initiated the studies of previous and on-going unity ventures in an attempt to learn from their experience, who insisted both
on the need for daring experiment breaking ground for theological
progress and on the need to institutionalize step by step the advances on the road to unity. Over the decades these concerns have
come to be shared and further developed also in European and Third
World ecumenism. In varying degrees they are even recognized in the
most orthodox circles of high-church Roman Catholicism, Anglicanism
and Orthodoxy. It would be rash to attribute this development exclusively to American influence; the political and cultural events
in European and the Third World during the thirties, forties, and
fifties generated ecclesial experiences in these regions which parallel those which earlier had led the Americans to such a position. On
the other hand the influence of American theologians and churchmen in
international and ecumenical organizations cannot be ignored. In any

case, the American discussions offer a particularly interesting
model on which to study the applications of their own theories.

The major portion of this chapter will be devoted to a consideration of some of the major underlying principles of methodology
practiced and articulated by the American Protestant ecclesiologists
in the course of their discussions. These have been grouped together under the three catchwords "catholicity," "functionalism,"
and "provisionalism." Here an effort will be made to confront these
methods with certain typical objections arising from Roman Catholic
points of view and to offer an answer to these objections which at
the same time further illuminates the principles involved. The chapter ends with a brief sketch of the vision of the Church which
emerged in the American ecumenical Protestant perspective. The vision of the American ecclesiologists is by their own admission an
imperfect one, a hypothesis based on existing ecumenical experience.
With the growth of ecumenical experience, particularly through the
more active participation of the catholic-type churches this vision
is bound to be modified; in part it is already being modified thanks
to the discussions which have taken place since 1967: The 1973 COCU
Plenary voted to put aside for the time being the direct work on a
plan of union. Nevertheless the COCU vision has opened up new perspectives for the ecumenical dialog, perspectives which emerged from
the more fundamental ecclesiological ideas investigated in this
study, coming at the end of this present work, the COCU vision is
meant to suggest some of the implications which remain to be investigated.

II. STRATEGIES OF ECUMENICAL ECCLESIOLOGY

A. Catholicity

The term "catholic method" is a creation of the TCCCNA, but the
practice goes back to the beginnings of American commission work.
Already in the work of the CCULW, the ATC, and the STEUSC, important
elements of the "catholic method" find application and expression.
Ultimately, however, it was the failure of the comparative dogmatics
method at the Lund Faith and Order Conference that stimulated the
American sections of the Christ and the Church (TCCCNA) and the Tradition and Traditions (TCTTNA) Commissions to explicitly elaborate
the method's presuppositions and implications.[2]

1. Catholicity versus Denominational Bias

What stimulated the development of the "catholic method" by the
post-Lund commissions was "the realization that the traditional pattern of denominational bias in the interpretation of the separate
histories of our divided churches has created a real dilemma in the
ecumenical dialogue."[3] Time after time ecumenical discussions revealed that theologians of different confessional backgrounds were
unable to reach agreement in doctrinal matters because each tended to
read the Bible and church history with the blinders of his own dogmatic tradition. This was the shoal on which the original comparative method of the F. & O. conversations had foundered. In the words
of the TCTTNA, "even at its best, it could scarcely do more than
clarify the actual issues in disagreement; at its (normal!) worst,
it allowed for self-justification in moods that varied from smug in-
transigence to pious truculence."[4] For the Americans this was hardly
a new discovery, the proximity of so many confessional and denominational traditions to one another on the American scene, the evident
socio-cultural conditioning of these traditions in the course of
their transplantation to America, the frustration of earlier unity
efforts by theologically mantled ethnic, economic, and cultural
interests had long-since awakened among the American theologians the
awareness of the cultural conditioning of theological responses.[5]
The problem was to find a way out of this dilemma, but already its
mere recognition was an important step forward. Until theologians
were willing to concede the existence of denominational bias in their
interpretation of the sources, the appeal to return to Scripture or

tradition was necessarily doomed to reproduce the melancholy experience with the comparative method.

The first step to overcoming the denominational bias was to uncover its sources. One obvious source is the explicit commitment to
a doctrine of Scripture and tradition, such as is held by many Roman
Catholics, Orthodox and Catholics of non-Roman varieties. Whether
this tradition is regarded as evolving or unchanged over the centuries, the assumption is that this tradition at least in its fulness
is possessed by only one denomination or confession, and that all the
other churches have lost or obscured it as they separated from this
one true church. In this view church history is really identical
with the history of the particular confession or denomination, and
the historical experience of the "separated brethren" are of little
or no relevance to understanding the normative "tradition." Classical Protestantism rejected the twofold source theory, proclaiming
the sufficiency of Scripture alone, but in practice its attitude
differs little from the catholic-type position. Here too the true
church is in effect identified with an individual confession or denomination, and church history is viewed as the process by which one
Christian church maintained or recovered the truth when all others
fell away. Though this classical Protestant position does not directly accord the post-biblical traditions a normative or supple-
mentary character, its own interpretation of Scripture is as much
determined by tradition as in the two-source position, and deviations from the received interpretation are just as quickly denounced
as heretical.[6]

Yet even where doctrinal orthodoxy is less strictly maintained,
a subtle conditioning of interpretation takes place. C. H. Dodd
called attention to this more subtle form in his now famous letter;
his example was the continuing failure of Anglicans and Nonconform-
ists, despite the increasing liberalism with regard to the historic
confessions, to reach agreement. He wrote:

"In England, I believe, the real division between Anglican and
Nonconformist lies not so much in the field of doctrines about
episcopacy, or in matters of dogmatic theology...it rather
perpetuates a diversity of tradition in English life going back
at least to the civil wars of the 17th century...since the 17th
century English life has largely flowed in two separate currents, one of which has been mainly associated with the established church, and the other with the dissenters. On each side
there are standards, ideals, habits, convictions, prejudices,

> which taken together make up a distinctive mentality, largely
> determining our first response at least to any question that
> comes up. This mentality is only partly, perhaps only to a
> slight degree, dependent on distinctive religious convictions
> or traditions, but it is intimately bound up with them, and
> constantly acts upon them. We always need to ask whether our
> tenacity in defending certain positions may be due to something
> other than pure doctrinal logic."[7]

That is to say, even where an explicit dogmatic commitment is not the
decisive factor, each denomination has its own ethos which colors the
thinking of its theologians. As the TCTTNA put it, "the tradition of
a particular denomination is an extremely complex entity, forming a
denominational 'mind' which manifests itself in characteristic ways
of 'seeing' and 'hearing' and speaking. Their political and social
histories interact with their specifically doctrinal emphases to
shape and mold traditional patterns and these are surprisingly tena-
cious, even in the midst of conscious protestations on behalf of
sola Scriptura."[8]

The "catholic method" as proposed by the American commissions
is meant to overcome the ethnocen-
trism which results from such traditioning processes. In sharp contrast to those
dogmatic and historical ecclesiologies which, consciously or unconsciously identify the Church of God with a particular denomination
or tradition, the "catholic method" postulates that God's work must
be seen as a whole, which is larger than any particular church or
family of churches. The TCCCNA put it this way:

> "[By 'catholicity' in method,] we mean that thinking becomes a
> reflection upon the work of God as a whole from beginning to
> end. It participates in the fulness of God's design to sum up
> all things in Christ. It deals with the Church as a whole--its
> membership in heaven and on earth, drawn from all tribes and
> tongues; its common heritage from all ages; its apostolic mis-
> sion to all people; its emancipation from slaveries to the pro-
> vincial and the partial; its stewardship of the truth and holi-
> ness which God has bestowed."[9]

A somewhat more concrete formulation was offered by the TCTTNA:

> "...what we mean by our phrase 'ecumenical historiography' is
> nothing esoteric or recondite. It is neither more nor less than
> a mood and method of historical study which operates on the as-
> sumption that the Christian community is a reality; that this
> community has had some sort of identity and continuity in time
> and space; and that its perimeter is roughly indicated by some
> such radius as the so-called Basis of the WCC. Given such
> presuppositions as these, the ecumenical historian works in

whatever epoch or area he is best qualified, to discover and
communicate significant historical 'insights' to those who mistake their partisan history for that history which Christians
have in common by virtue of the historical existence of the
Church and the life of faith."[10]

In other words, the "catholic method" is diametrically opposed to
every attempt to restrict the ecclesiological perspective to but one
manifestation of the Church, be it (a) the church of the New Covenant
to the exclusion of the ecclesia ab Abel justo and of Israel, (b) an
ecclesiastical organization to the exclusion of the world in which the
Church lives, or (c) to one ecclesiastical tradition to the exclusion
of the others.

This last point is the one of greatest practical import. Concretely the "catholic-method" as elaborated in the American discussions means that papalists would be bound to take account of the
historical experience of non-papal churches, episcopalists of the
experience of presbyterians and congregationalists, free churches of
that of the confessional Volkskirchen, etc. and, of course, always
vice versa. "Taking account" here means naturally something quite
different from the old apologetics technique of concentrating only
on the faults of the opposed tradition, holding them up as scary
specters of the evil consequences of departing from this or that
truth. But it also means going beyond a smug tolerance of contrary
opinions as though these had nothing to say to us.[11] The "catholic
method" is no license for vague inclusivism or indiscriminate eclecticism unconcerned about truth and right.[12] "Taking account" of each
other's traditions means wrestling with them as possible alternatives
or corrections to our own; it also, however, means wrestling with
them as possible temptations and errors. Excluded is not judgment as
such but only the prejudgment about the truth or falsity, justice or
injustice of every position, our own included. The initial suspen-
sion of judgment is not an end in itself. The goal remains a critical judgment touching all the traditions, both one's own and the
alien. This however is only possible when we have first come to
understand the other traditions. The TCTTNA wrote:

"In every case of dogmatic disagreement, an effort must be made,
an effort of historical reason and imagination, to get behind
the tradition of the dogmata in question, seeking out their
activating spirit and recognizing their intention to represent
some sort of identity and continuity within the Christian com-
munity-in-time. Every doctrine has a history and every doctrinal controversy its own Sitz im Leben. It arises in the con-

text of living faith (and unfaith!); it is always influenced ambiguously by the total situation of the human participants. This means that every doctrinal controversy (and all serious ecumenical conversation as well) must be illuminated by competent reference both to its historical origins and also to its subsequent developments. Similarly, the various denominations, whose distinctive patterns and characters have been affected by their respective histories, have to be understood and appreciated in their historical origins and evolutions if their peculiar manifestations in ecumenical conversation are properly to be appraised and appreciated. Doctrines regularly take on something of the idiom and style of the church which authorizes them. Thus, it is necessary for the ecumenical movement to develop what might be called a denominational hermeneutics which can ask the right questions of various Christian groups in conflict or coma--always in the effort to understand and interpret them in their different situations, and not merely to tolerate them in the spirit of ecumenical 'good manners' [original italics]."[13]

In the course of the last fifteen years, cross-denominational studies of the type envisaged by the TCTTNA have become almost a commonplace. Roman Catholic theologians have rediscovered Luther, Calvin and the other classical reformers as well as some of the later movements in Protestantism like Pentecostalism and the Ecumenical Movement. Protestants are increasingly studying the works of contemporary Roman- Catholic authors and revising their judgments about once anathematized Roman dogmas. Hardly any serious theologian today questions the need to judge historical controversies in context and to assume basic good faith on the part of all contestants until the contrary is proven. Thus we easily forget how revolutionary the TCTTNA proposals were back at the threshold of the sixties. Though pioneering work along these lines already existed then, this attitude was by no means yet general. Be that as it may, however, the American proposal of a "catholic method" went well beyond the demand for more objective cross-denominational study; in its call for a recognition of "a corollary in church history to the principle of historical relativism in general historiography,"[14] the TCTTNA took a step which, even today, by no means finds general acceptance. This step, therefore, requires more careful assessment.

2. The Unity of the Tradition in the Variety of Traditions

A "catholic" view of the Church in its historical fulness reveals a multitude of differing traditions. This variety can be traced back to a common matrix of origin, but not necessarily to a single source. The multiplicity is already there in the New Testa-

ment, and there is no direct one-to-one correlation between the
later strands of tradition from this or that New Testament tradition.[15] Other factors have come into play in subsequent epochs,
factors cultural, social, economic and political as well as theological, to initiate and transform the traditions which lead to the
whelter of present day denominations.[16] This being the case, the
TCTTNA declares, "the deepest and most urgent question is whether or
not one can affirm the reality of an integral, essential tradition
present, in however varying degree, in the multiple traditions which
are the visible data in any historical view of Christianity?"[17]

The answer to this question worked out by the Commission is a
complex one, which could easily be misinterpreted. The first part
of the Commission's response is a categorical negation: "Historical
inquiry," it declares, "cannot be used to locate or establish any
single historical tradition as the Christian Tradition [original
italics]"; at best, "if it is sufficiently objective it [historical
inquiry] exercises a useful veto power over anti-ecumenical absolut-
isms of various sorts--biblicist, ecclesiastical, ideological."[18]

Alone from the manner of expression, one might be tempted to
see in these statements nothing more than a resurgence of the historical relativism characteristic of liberal Protestantism. Taken
in context, however, it is clear that such is not the case. What is
intended by the Commission is a statement of fact not an arbitrary
postulate. De facto, what historical inquiry has hitherto brought to
light, is primarily the variety and not the unity of the Christian
tradition. Though numerous denominationally conditioned historians
have attempted to establish the existence of a single normative tradition; de facto none of these attempts has succeeded in winning
broad acceptance outside the particular tradition in which it originated; to the outsider the biased selection and interpretation of
the evidence by such attempts is all too evident. Nor is there any
indication that an exclusive reliance on critical historiography is
going to improve this de facto situation in the future; on the contrary, the more objective the historian's approach the more variety
he discovers in the history of the Church. Anyone requiring verification of this assertion need only review the development of historical study among Roman Catholics over the last hundred years.

It is this experience of the de facto inability of historical
study to discover a single normative pattern of faith that prompted

the Commission to call for an "historical relativism" in dealing
with the variety of traditions. That is to say, the Commission calls
upon the theologian as historian to adopt an attitude which, on principle, is prepared to "regard each tradition as a phenomenon in its
own right, each with its own system of convictions which are more or
less 'natural' to the 'true believer' and more or less peculiar to
the 'outsider,' i.e., a true believer in a different tradition."[19]
Conceived in this way, the historical inquiry may not be able to discover any single normative tradition, but it can help to clarify the
reciprocal interaction of the various traditions in the historical
course of the Christian community.

At this point, however, the other half of the Commission's answer must be considered. At the same time that the Commission demands an attitude of historical relativism of the theologian qua
historian, it acknowledges that

> "as a Christian, he is committed to a belief in one God, one Lord
> Jesus Christ, one Spirit, one holy, catholic and apostolic
> Church. As historian, he may judge that the unity of the Church
> is nowhere fully manifest on earth, or, for that matter, that it
> has never been fully manifested. But, as believer, he can
> scarcely avoid the theological judgment that it should be, and
> that, in the intention and providence of God, it shall be. He
> may, therefore, rejoice in the rich variety of Christian life;
> or, grieve over the differences of divided Christians; or, sad-
> ly conclude that some developments in the traditionary process
> have been so aberrant that he must deny them the name of Chris-
> tian. But in all this, he will go on believing that the mani-
> fold traditions embody and conceal an essential unity."[20]

That is to say, according to the Commission, there is indeed a n
e s s e n t i a l   T r a d i t i o n   u n d e r l y i n g   t h e
m a n y   t r a d i t i o n s .   This Tradition, however, is not
one particular tradition alongside other, deficient traditions; it
is neither the simple sum of all the individual traditions, nor their
least common denominator.[21] In fact it is something of an entirely
different order; in the words of the Commission, it is "the self-
givenness of God in the self-giving of Jesus Christ, 'for us men and
for our salvation'," or, put in another way, it is the "divine origination, maintenance and prolepsis of the people of God in their
historical existence."[22]

At this point, a somewhat fuller explanation of the TCTTNA's
handling of the tradition question might prove useful. Terminolog-
ically the Commission distinguished three phenomena, which it designated with varient forms of the word "tradition."

(1) "tradition" (lower case, singular) is used as "the general category which includes both the process of transmission from person to person, region to region, generation to generation, and also the substantive contents of whatever is transmitted."⁻² Where it becomes necessary to distinguish these two elements, the documents use the word "traditum" to designate the substantive content. It is perhaps important to note that the "traditum" is the whole object transmitted, and not simply some putatively isolatable, unchanging kernel unaffected by its variable forms of expression. The whole thrust of the Commission's argumentation is opposed to any facile distinction between an unchanging "substance," or "kernel," on the one hand, and a changing, historically conditioned "expression," or "husk," on the other. Attractive as such a distinction might be to the apologete of this or that denominational tradition, it cannot be verified by an ecumenical historiography.

The Commission notes that "tradition" is a highly complex phenomenon, which includes the following elements:

(a) "That which is transmitted, the channels of transmission, and the effects of such transmission.

(b) The nuances and subleties of atmospheres involved in the process of traditioning: verbal and non-verbal, conscious and unconscious, emotional and rational, etc.

(c) The endeavor to orient and immerse persons and groups in persisting values and premises, and to provide them with proper experiences of initiation.

(d) The paradox that 'anti-traditionalists' also engage in the business of traditioning their cherished values and premises, thus creating a tradition of anti-traditionalism.

(e) The complication of the fact that the traditionary process may operate in either direction, toward entropy or renewal--and there are no infallible differentiae which tell when apparent continuities conceal an actual betrayal or a pseudo-morphosis of what was pretended to have been traditioned.

(f) The traditionary process includes the means aimed at perpetuating the old and familiar in the context of the novel and the strange, renovating the old by offering it as new, domesticating the strange by making it seem familiar--so that the conjunction of old and new turns out to be something actually distinctive.

(g) Thus, 'tradition' like its twin term 'communication,' embraces the various interchanges between persons and groups and cultures (Jew, Greek, Roman; European, American, Asiatic) in which there is mutual accommodation and indigenization whereby 'they' become 'we'."⁻⁴

This catalog makes clear that the notion of "tradition" is both generic and value-free. Which of these elements are to be found in any particular instance of the traditioning process can only be determined on the basis of a careful historical and theological investigation of the particular process in question. In the process as such, there are no absolute criteria for discriminating between faithful and unfaithful transmission.

(2) "traditions" (lower case, plural) denotes "the several, yet specific, patterns of traditioning by which the separated churches, and church families, have come to be distinct and distinguishable one from another" or, in a parallel definition, "the characteristic self-understandings embedded in the separate histories of the sep-

arated churches, or fragments of the church."[25] The difference between "tradition" and "traditions" can be understood as the difference between the traditionary process and context, on the one hand,
and on the other, the concrete forms which these take on over a
given historical span, e.g. the peculiar shape of a denominational
ethos as defined by its confessions, liturgy, polity, way of life,
etc. Here too, we have to do with a phenomenological notion, which
by itself implies no judgment about the fidelity or infidelity of
the traditionary pattern to the original. What is implied, however,
is that tradition as process and tradition as form, though really
distinct are only imperfectly separable: over a long enough span of
history the process and its content can assume various forms, but
they never exist without form, i.e. at any particular moment in history the traditionary process manifests itself as one or another
tradition pattern.

This form may be more or less adequate to the intended object--
this must be judged in the individual case--in any case, however, the
particular form is socio-culturally conditioned by the situation and
mentality of both transmitters and recipients. This last observation
introduces the possibility of isolating at least o n e r e l a -
t i v e c r i t e r i o n o f t h e a d e q u a c y o r
i n a d e q u a c y o f t h e t r a d i t i o n p a t -
t e r n . Where, namely, the traditionary process moves from one
culture to another, e.g. from Europe or America to Asia or Africa,
there must be a real translation from one pattern to a new one; the
content or traditum must become "acclimatized in its new soil and
situation, being woven into the fabric of that human society in the
midst of which it lives." This is what the Commission called the
process of "indigenization": "Each new church and each emergent
tradition requires a dual continuity: on the one hand, with the
Christian community in all ages and places; on the other, with the
human community in its own particular environment."[26] History shows,
however that this process of indigenization is often impeded because
the transmitters unwittingly identify the particular cultural forms
in which the Gospel has been indigenized in their own tradition with
the Gospel itself, thus they insist on imposing these forms on their
converts in the new culture. There the "traditions," which were adequate and useful in their original context, become disfunctional,
"alien elements which mark off Christianity (at least in this particular context) as 'foreign' or 'archaic.' The consequences are all
too often a painful de-culturalization of the new converts and a
spurious 'offense of the Gospel' to the unconverted."[27] Here again,
however, the Commission reminds us, there are no easy, fool-proof
tests of what constitutes proper and what improper indigenization.
What at the moment seemed right and proper may very well reveal itself at greater distance to have been a mistake and vice versa.

(3) Sharply distinguished against the two foregoing notions,
but also only imperfectly separable from them is the third term,
"the Tradition" (upper case, singular, with definite article). The
notion of "the Tradition" is the epistemological counterpart of the
theological notion of "the People of God": "if," the Commission
wrote, "we are able to speak with any clear meaning of 'the people
of God' and yet also acknowledge how diverse and different are the
several segments of that 'people,' have we not thereby presupposed
some sort of identity and continuity between this branch of the
household of faith and that? Even in their discord and disunity, the
major traditions in the Christian community point beyond themselves

to their common source and head. This divine origination, maintenance and prolepsis of the people of God in their historical exist-
ence--this is what we wish to denote by the term (the Tradition)."[58]

The Tradition, it must be emphasized, is not as such the content
handed down by the traditionary process. Rather it is the divine
agency which initiates, controls, corrects, and thus guarantees the
traditionary process. It is the divine factor which governs the historical life of the People of God. That is to say, the notion of
"the Tradition" is a specifically theological notion. In appealing
to it, the theologian makes an assertion that cannot be verified positively by critical historiography; the most such critical historical study can do, is to help the theologian to a deeper appreciation
of the external manifestations of this essential Tradition.[29] The
function of this notion, as noted above, is epistemological. It
represents the guarantee, so to speak, that the traditionary process
in the Church, despite all errors and detours, continues to transmit to all ages and peoples the message and reality of salvation
through Jesus Christ. In virtue of this divine reassurance, the
Church is encouraged to learn from and to correct the traditions
handed down from the past and to transform them as needed in handing
them on to future generations and cultures.

The relation between the essential Tradition and the many "accidental" traditions, as conceived by the TCTTNA, is a special instance of the relationship between the divine and the human as described in the preceding chapter. In entering into human history,
God has committed himself to the process of traditioning whereby his
message and work becomes acclimatized to each people, culture and
place. Without the traditioning process, the divine work would remain an empty abstraction, neither accessible to nor relevant for
the concrete individuals and communities to whom it is directed.[30]
Thus the divine paradosis employs the traditionary process to create,
reform, and regenerate the particular traditions in which it becomes
incarnate for each people, culture and community;[31] in doing so, however, it n e c e s s a r i l y s u b m i t s i t s e l f
to the limitations this tradition-
ing process imposes . In making use of human
agents, institutions, and cultural forms, the Spirit of God accepts
not only their particularity but also their fallibility. So necessary as the traditioning process is, if the message and reality of
salvation is to reach every member of divided sinful humanity and
lead them to the new People of God, which transcends all sinful divisions, there is always the risk that the divisions of fallen humanity will be reproduced in the Church or that the traditum will be
corrupted by addition, subtraction or qualification or that--through
a witting or unwitting identification of the traditum with the par-

ticular traditions or the traditores--the liberating gift of God may
be perverted into an instrument of imperialist oppression of one
people or community by another. In the words of the TCTTNA, "the
traditionary process is both precarious and treacherous. It is forever on the verge of corrupting either the substance or the spirit
of what is being traditioned. Traditio is therefore vulnerable to
the corruptions of both ill-meaning and well-meaning traditores."[32]

3. Recognizing the Tradition in the Manifold of traditions

The Tradition is nowhere present in a pristine pure form, un-
modified and uncorrupted by the traditions. Even in the Scripture
we do not have the Tradition apart from traditions; the Commission
wrote:

> "In the New Testament we see the beginnings of the traditionary
> process in the Christian community. We also see the first man-
> ifold of traditions. In the New Testament, the Tradition is
> traditioned with apostolic authority but it is everywhere mani-
> fested in a plurality of traditions (Pauline, Synoptic, etc.),
> with none entitled to a clear hegemony over all the others.
> Subsequently, when once the Church had bound itself to the Tra-
> dition in Scripture by closing the canon, all traditionary ap-
> peals had to include some sort of reference to the primacy of
> Scripture, yet every appeal to Scripture bears the cachet of
> its denominational hermeneutical style."[33]

For this reason the Commission accepted the Reformation slogan, sola
Scriptura, "insofar as it asserts and identifies the Tradition as
the prime datum of the New Testament," but they repudiated that polemical anti-traditional usage which "equates the New Testament and
the Tradition without qualification, or...rejects the evidence for
the living Tradition in the church through the ages."[34] For all its
special authority, Scripture has never stood and can never stand
alone; it is both preceded and accompanied by traditions; it itself
is embedded in and a part of the traditionary process. "The primitive Church created its Scriptures in the light of what had been
handed down by and about Jesus Christ. The primitive Church interpreted what had been handed down in the light of the Scriptures thus
created."[35] And even the Reformers' sola Scriptura was conditioned
by the traditions they had received and the new traditions they be-
queathed to their followers.[36] By the same token, however "there is
no notion of a tradition which is superior to Scripture, or which al-
ters the essential content of the apostolic message as it is depos-
ited in Scripture"; though the traditionary process is primordial

both to the Scriptures and the traditions underlying them, virtually all the post-biblical traditions of the churches acknowledge at least a relative primacy of the scriptural traditions.[37] Nevertheless, both the biblical and the post-biblical traditions look to the Tradition as their ultimate norm. In the words of the Commission, "all the manifold traditions are under the judgment of the Tradition, since the lordship of Christ over history is exercised through his participation in it."[38] This is the central axiom of the "catholic method" proposed by the American commissions.

The "catholic method" assumes that t h e   L o r d   h i m - s e l f   c o n t r o l s   t h e   t r a d i t i o n a r y   p r o - c e s s --not in the sense of eliminating the possibility of human error and sin corrupting the traditions, but rather in the sense that t h e   S p i r i t   o f   G o d   i s   c o n s t a n t l y   a t   w o r k   i n   t h e   C h u r c h   t o   r e n e w   a n d   r e - f o r m   t h e   t r a d i t i o n s . There are no easy or fool-proof tests for identifying the Tradition in the manifold of traditions, nevertheless, when he looks at the Church in its wholeness-- in time as well as in space--the theologian-historian "finds himself intuiting the Christian Tradition in, with, and under the manifold of church traditions. He does not," the Commission notes, "demand, or even expect, a single system of 'pure doctrine,' an exclusive liturgy, one perfect church order to supersede all others. As a historian, he has accepted the basic presuppositions of relativism, save the one false premise that relativism is an absolute. Thus, he sees the Church as the locus of God's revelation but not the pro-prietor thereof; she confesses the ultimate but always in proximate terms."[39]

Recognizing that his own judgments are always fallible, t h e   h i s t o r i a n - t h e o l o g i a n   n e v e r t h e l e s s   h a s   a n   i m p o r t a n t   r o l e   t o   p l a y   i n   t h e   p r o c e s s   by which the Spirit of God is constantly re-newing and reforming the traditions in which the Tradition is present among the many scattered flocks of the People of God. As historian, he can trace the mutations of tradition in each space-time context, identifying the various political, socio-economic, and cultural fac-tors which together with the overtly theological determined the par-ticular shape of the respective traditions. He can analyze the con-troversies over metamorphosis, pseudo-morphosis, schism, heresy,

apostasy and the like, revealing the defensive and compensatory me-
chanisms on the part of pathological traditionalisms and anti-tradi-
tionalisms. In this way the historian-theologian can help to clear
the air in many an ancient controversy which continues to exercise
a divisive influence in the contemporary Church. Beyond this, he
can, as theologian, help the Church at critical historic "moments"
of ecclesial decision to discern the freedom of the Tradition to
transcend and modify existing traditions.[40] As the Commission put
it:

> "The Christian Tradition may be discerned, but never defined
> exactly, in the Church's experience of pilgrimage in time and
> space, in her great seasons of reception and renewal, of re-
> vival and reformation. But it may also be 'foreseen' prolep-
> tically and eschatologically, as the traditum yet to be re-
> ceived by faith, yet to be handed on."[41]

Ultimately, of course, the question is, b y   w h a t   c r i -
t e r i a   s h a l l   t h e   i n d i v i d u a l   t h e o l o -
g i a n   (o r   t h e   C h u r c h   a s   a   w h o l e)
d i s c r i m i n a t e   between the abiding, though ever self-renew-
ing traditiones constitutivae and the transitory, though often all
too intransigent traditiones interpretativae.[42] The answer of the
TCTTNA is both disappointing and encouraging (one recalls the similar statement of the TCCCNA quoted on p. 172).

> "The criteria of authenticity which we is our Section have found
> ourselves considering seriously, turn out to be the commonplace
> ones: fidelity to the self-presentation of God in Scripture;
> loyalty to the central core of faith and order in the ancient
> Church; the continuity and legitimate development of the Chris-
> tian message in and through the great focussings of the Chris-
> tian mind; the experiences of the renewing power of the Holy
> Spirit, as resident Governor of the Church. But we are also
> agreed that these normative notions are not formally precise.
> We are not, therefore, surprised or disenchanted by the fact
> that these criteria, even when acknowledged, fail to produce
> practical consensus forthwith. Thus, we would stress yet again
> that our designation of criteria is a theologoumenon to the
> crisis of death and transfiguration which stands between our
> present state of division and the full reality of the unity we
> seek."[43]

The last sentence of this passage calls attention to the paradoxical
character of the "catholic method" conception of theological cri-
teriology. T h e   c r i t e r i a   t h e m s e l v e s   a r e
c a u g h t   u p   i n   t h e   p r o c e s s   t h e y   a r e
m e a n t   t o   d e t e r m i n e . Alone they provide no ready
answers to the theologians' questions; only in the process of trying
to achieve consensus do they reveal their power to evoke consensus;

only when the consensus has been achieved does their consensus-build-
ing potential become evident; only when church unity is effected will
the "catholic method" have attained full catholicity.

4. The "Catholic Method" for Roman Catholics?

Is the "catholic method" as practiced and defined by the American ecclesiological commissions a legitimate and desirable method for
the adherents of "high-church" ecclesiologies such as the Roman Catholic? To this question we must now turn. At the same time, however,
we must acknowledge that for the time being at least no definitive
answer to this question can be expected. At the moment Roman Catholic thinking finds itself in a state of flux. Classical dogmas and
theologoumena which would stand in the way of a Roman Catholic's
espousal of the "catholic method" are widely being reinterpreted and
in some cases openly called into question or outrightly denied. It
would be rash to attempt here to try to anticipate the eventual outcome of the contemporary debates; what we can do, however, is to
identify the issues involved.

a. The Boundaries of the Church Issue

It is clear that the traditional Roman Catholic definition of
the boundaries of the Church of Christ is diametrically opposed to
the fundamental postulate of the "catholic method" that the Tradition
cannot be equated with any singular denominational tradition. Even
in the theory of the vestigia ecclesiae, which serves as a justification for acknowledging a certain minimal ecclesial reality to the
ecclesiastical organizations of the separated brethren, there was
little place for the notion that the Roman Catholic Church could
learn anything from the experience of non-Roman Christians.

The constitutions, declarations and decrees of the Second Vatican Council opened up a number of new perspectives. The fundamental
step was taken by the Constitution on the Church as it declared:

> "This Church constituted and organized in the world as a society
> subsists in the Catholic Church, which is governed by the suc-
> cessor of Peter and by the Bishops in communion with him, al-
> though many elements of sanctification and of truth are found
> outside of its visible structure. These elements, as gifts
> belonging to the Church of Christ, are forces impelling toward
> catholic unity."[44]

In this passage the Council consciously abstained from identifying
the particular "Roman" tradition with "Catholic" tradition pure and
simple,[45] thus opening the way to a recognition of the legitimacy of

other traditions within the Catholic Church besides the Roman.[46]
Moreover, though the Council still identifies "Catholic Church" with
the communion of churches in union with the Roman Pontiff,[47] it refrained from absolutely identifying this "Catholic Church" with the
"one Church of Christ," preferring instead the more subtle expression "subsistit in" / "subsist in," i.e. to have existence in, to
continue, abide in, to be maintained in, to live in (N.B. the German
version translates "verwirklicht in," i.e. realized in).[48] Whatever
be the exact meaning of this term,[49] the intention is clearly to suggest that elements of the Church of Christ are also to be found outside the papal communion.[50]

In the Decree on Ecumenism the implications of this position
are spelled out in greater detail. In the ancient separated churches
of the East, the Council recognized sister churches (sorores), whose
diverse traditions, often reaching back to apostolic times, represent legitimate alternatives to those of the western church. Indeed,
in respect to these churches at least, the Council positively recommends an approach substantially in agreement with the "catholic method" proposed by the Americans. It declared:

> "...the heritage handed down by the apostles was received with
> differences of form and manner, so that from the earliest times
> of the Church it was explained variously in different places,
> owing to diversities of genius and conditions of life. All
> this, quite apart from external causes, prepared the way for
> divisions arising also from a lack of charity and mutual under-
> standing.
> For this reason the Holy Council urges all...to give due
> consideration to this special feature of the origin and growth
> of the Eastern Churches, and to the character of the relations
> which obtained between them and the Roman See before separation.
> They must take full account of all these factors and, where this
> is done, it will greatly contribute to the dialogue that is
> looked for."[51]

Not only was the Council prepared to admit the legitimate autonomy
of the eastern traditions for the peoples of the East,[52] it went on
to concede in principle the possibility that the eastern traditions
might be objectively superior to the western and that the western
church could learn from the 'eastern traditions.[53]

With regard to the non-Roman churches of the West, the Council
was much more reserved. Here the Council distinguished between
"churches" (ecclesiae) and "ecclesial communities" (communitates
ecclesiales.)[54] In part this distinction was prompted by respect
for the unwillingness of some Protestant denominations to designate

themselves as "churches,"[55] but at least in the mind of a very large
and influential group of Council fathers, the principal motive was
the unwillingness to accord full ecclesial status to Protestant
churches whose doctrine and church order they regarded as substantially deficient.[56]   Though the Decree takes pains to enumerate the
many ecclesial elements which despite division and heresy have been
retained in these denominations[57] and acknowledges that "historical,
sociological, psychological and cultural differences have contributed to their differentiation from the Roman tradition,"[58] the overall tenor of the Council's statement is that the traditions of these
churches are deficient. Thus one searches in vain for a positive
affirmation of their legitimacy, even in matters which are not of immediate dogmatic significance, e.g. liturgical forms,[59] and one finds
not the slightest hint of an acknowledgment of the ability of Protestant traditions to complement and enrich the life of the Catholic
Church in its wholeness.

It would be unfair to exaggerate the importance of this omission. The principle enunciated in the first chapter of the decree--
"All in the Church must preserve unity in essentials. But let all,
according to the gifts they have received enjoy a proper freedom,
in their various forms of spiritual life and discipline, in their
different liturgical rites, and even in their theological elaborations of revealed truth"[60]--this principle is evidently intended to
apply to relations with western non-Roman Christians as well as to
those with eastern Christians. Nevertheless the omission is symptomatic of a common attitude badly in need of correction.

Many Roman Catholic theologians are prepared to go well beyond
the positions taken by the Council regarding the ecclesial character
of the various churches of the Protestant traditions. The principal
grounds for the Council's reservation lay in the supposed deficiency
of Protestant belief concerning the sacraments--particularly the Eucharist and Orders--and the supposed invalidity of Protestant orders
due to the interruption of the apostolic succession. A two-pronged
attack since the Council has weakened the foundations of these sup-
positions. On the one hand, Roman Catholics are increasingly criticizing the traditional Roman-Catholic understanding and practice
of the sacraments and the hierarchy of ministry as neither scripturally nor historically tenable; on the other hand, encouraged by
Protestant efforts to reform their own understanding and practice
in the light of the fuller historical tradition, many Roman Catholics
are coming to a more positive judgment about the validity of Protestant sacraments and ministry. Significantly, these advances are not

only being put forward by individuals; increasingly they are being incorporated into the reports of Roman-Catholic/Protestant dialog groups, both official and unofficial.[61] On the other hand at least some of these contributions, especially the works of Hans Küng and the Memorandum of the German University Ecumenical Institutes, have evoked considerable opposition both on the part of individual Roman-Catholic theologians[62] and of official organs.[63] At the moment, therefore, the eventual fate of these probings remains in doubt.

Be that as it may, even the refusal to accord full ecclesial recognition to the Protestant denominations does not, of itself, prohibit Roman Catholics from making their own the "catholic method" proposed by the Americans. The method does not commit one to an uncritical inclusivism any more than it licenses an arbitrary eclecticism; on the contrary, it demands that each tradition be tested in terms of the whole constituted by the manifold of traditions. Hence it is thoroughly in keeping with the requirements of the method that an individual tradition should be judged defective in one or another point. Excluded is only the arbitrary, a priori prejudgment which makes one particular tradition the absolute standard by which all others are judged to be deficient, irrespective of the realities of Christian history. Excluded, therefore, is a unilinear conception of doctrinal development which sees the original traditum infallibly unfolding in a single direction represented by one particular denominational tradition, whereas all other traditions are seen as erroneous deviations from this single clear line. At the very least, the "catholic method" demands the willingness to recognize: (a) that one's own tradition, however faithful it may have been in holding fast to the substance of the traditum, has often expressed the traditum in ways which have made it difficult for other Christians to recognize, i.e. that one's own tradition is imperfect, that complimentary expressions of the traditum are conceivable. (b) Furthermore, it demands the willingness to learn from the experience of other traditions--if not with regard to the substance at least with regard to its historically conditioned expressions.

In this connection, it is necessary to take a critical look at an argument often raised in discussion of ministry. Against proposals to recognize presbyterial and congregational orders as legitimate alternatives to the episcopal order held by catholic-type churches, the objection is often raised that such proposals would

simply leap over fifteen hundred years of Christian experience. The
objection is a serious one and it demands a serious answer from the
proponents of such theories. However it implies a complimentary
question which the adherents of episcopal succession must be prepared to answer with equal seriousness. There is substantial evidence for the relatively late emergence (and even later exclusive
victory) of the catholic-type triple (quadruple, when the papacy is
considered) order out of an earlier, more flexible arrangement which
at least in certain regions was closer to what in the Reformation
came to be known as presbyterianism and congregationalism.[64] Furthermore, even after the establishment of the triple hierarchy, in the
course of the early second century, the empirical sociological form
of the episcopally organized communities more resembled the practice
of the post-Reformation Free-Church tradition than the pattern of
prelacy formed in the 4th to 15th centuries by the cultural and political influences of byzantine, frankish and germanic imperialism, of
feudalism and urban republicanism, and of late medieval nationalism
and statism.[65] In addition, the history of the medieval church reveals important undercurrents in both the theology and the practice
of church organization--e.g. the discussions of the validity of orders conferred by simple presbyters, the papal grants of ordaining
faculties to abbots in priestly orders, the numerous exemptions from
episcopal jurisdiction, etc.--currents recalling presbyterian and
congregational conceptions of church order and organization.[66] Finally there is the fact of the existence of presbyterian and congregational churches, which over five centuries have brought forth evident spiritual fruit and in some cases (at least in the practice of
their adherents) have apparently more faithfully reflected the priorities of the hierarchy of the Christians truths than their episcopal counterparts. Before the defender of episcopal orders demands
an answer to the question he puts to the proponents of non-episcopal orders, he must himself prepare an answer to the question: with
what right does episcopal ecclesiology ignore such elements of church
history. Is not the proponent of catholic-type ecclesiology equally
in danger of leaping over centuries of church tradition insofar as
these fail to support his conception? Anyone who would answer this
question negatively must be prepared to give both historical and
theological accounting for his answer.

In short, the boundaries of the Church issue does not present an insurmountable obstacle to the adoption of the "catholic method" by Roman Catholics. However, the de facto selective character of the catholic-type appeal to tradition calls attention to a more serious underlying issue complex, which for the sake of brevity we may call "the infallibility issue."

b. The Infallibility Issue

As the American commissions more than once observed, the representatives of high-church ecclesiologies of both the catholic and protestant types assert the existence of a divinely established, clearly definable norm for the doctrine, life, and organization of the Church. Whether they see this norm laid down in Scripture alone or in a hierarchically guaranteed post-biblical tradition, the adherents of this position concur—however much they differ on the specific content of such a norm—in the assertion that this norm binds the Church to specific dogmas and organizational forms. Moreover they concur in the assertion that this norm is infallibly recognized by the true Church, conceived either as the faithful as a whole or more narrowly as personified by the appointed teachers of the Church.

The particular dogmas and organizational forms alledged by this or that tradition as normative represent in every case formulae and institutions which found their normative expression in a particular socio-cultural constellation. Thus the history of the Church shows a variety of such responses and the proponents of dogmatic ecclesiologies are obliged to give an account of this variation. For those who locate the explicit norm in the remote past, all subsequent church history must appear as a process of corruption and degeneration insofar as a radical restoration-reformation does not intervene to break the chain of progressive degeneration. In the opposite view, where the explicit norm is seen in the most recent commitment of the Church's authority, past forms are reduced to vague and imperfect anticipations of the present and thus deprived of any corrective function over against prevailing norms.[68] Under these circumstances, dialog between the confessions becomes virtually impossible. Conflicting claims confront one another as impenetrable and immoveable blocks, with each partner awaiting the miraculous conversion of the other.

This was the impasse that the Americans sought to break with the leverage offered by their "catholic method". To achieve this

goal, however, it will be necessary to convince the adherents of
such dogmatic ecclesiologies, that they are not being asked to abandon their principles or convictions from the start. The "catholic
method" is a method, not a dogma, and as such, it is by no means
opposed to an infallibility postulate, though it may well at first
apprear repugnant to the infallibilist way of thinking. To illustrate
this thesis it will pay to look briefly at certain positions which
have emerged in the recent Roman Catholic debate over the infallibility issue as raised by the publication in 1971 of Hans Küng's
Unfehlbar? Eine Anfrage.[69] Without attempting to survey all the facets
of this controversy, much less to venture a solution or anticipate
the outcome, it is possible to call attention to certain issues
which have emerged in the debate with renewed clarity and which are
relevant for the matter at hand.

(1) One positive achievement has already emerged from the debate. Today even official instances in the Roman Catholic Church are
prepared to concede: (a) that the formulae which were fixed upon by
earlier church decisions do not necessarily represent the only possible adequate formulation of the intended content; (b) that in certain historical contexts, at least, they may prove misleading and
therefore require reformulation appropriate to the new situations;
and (c) that in most cases it is at least theoretically possible to
express the intended content with roughly the same degree of clarity
in alternative expressions formulated in other conceptual frames of
reference.[70] When this much, at least, is granted, the way stands
open to accept the fundamental postulate of the "catholic method,"
namely that there is no absolute one-to-one correspondence between
any particular traditional form and the essential traditum which it
expresses.

Thus the first point to note here is that the infallibility
dogma as currently interpreted even in official documents of the Holy
See does not of itself stand in the way of the adoption of the "catholic method" as worked out by the American Protestant ecumenists.
This method does not require the abandonment of any dogmatic position
in advance--not even the dogma of infallibility: it requires only
that every dogma be studied within the context of the whole experience of the whole Church and that no particular historical form be
absolutely equated with the essential traditum.

(2) The infallibility debate itself could benefit from a more intensive application of the "catholic method." Even the defenders of the dogma should see the advantages such a method offers. Precisely their own commitment to the progressive character of dogmatic clarification should encourage them to a more open, less apologetic handling of the history of this dogma. However much the roots of the definition of 1870 can be traced back through earlier centuries, the fact remains that the actual definition of 1870 is a novum in the history of the Catholic Church: never before had the matter been formulated with such precision or universal authority.[71] It is therefore a falsification of history to use this definition as a measure by which to sort the witnesses of earlier ages into supporters and opponents of the dogma. A more careful historiography has shown how much earlier formulations differ from the conception of 1870 and how much the 1870 conception has been modified in subsequent inquiry.[72] A truly "catholic" historiography of the infallibility dogma will have to give more attention than hitherto to the day-to-day practice of the Church: it is not enough to gather verbal testimonies; to be properly appreciated such testimonies must be seen against the background of party and institutional interests, communications techniques, etc. In short, a truly "catholic" study of the history of this dogma will have to pay far more attention to the sociological factors affecting the exercise of the Church's teaching authority in the different ages and cultures through which she has passed.[73] Furthermore, a truly "catholic" historiography requires the defenders of the dogma to pay closer attention to the effects of Roman Catholic claims outside the Roman Catholic Church. In the negative responses of the other churches to the dogma of 1870, important clues can be found indicating elements in prevailing theory and practice, which, at least for the outsider, evoke misleading or false conceptions and which therefore would benefit from reformulation.[74]

(3) At the heart of the infallibility debate is an epistemological issue concerning the nature of Christian truth, and the manner of its communication and reception. Traditional explanations of the infallibility dogma have been based on the neoscholastic assumption that there exist relatively sharp boundaries between individual truths of faith and that these boundaries can be conceptually articulated with relative precision. More recently, the discussions of the inspiration of Scripture and the development of dogma have led Catholic

theologians to see revelation not so much as the communication of
individual truths but rather as the communication of the Truth, a
global reality transcending conceptual-propositional articulation.
In this newer view, the theological and dogmatic articulation of
individual truths is more clearly seen to be imperfect and relative.
This position, for which K. Rahner and E. Schillebeeckx may be taken
as typical exponents, comes quite close to the position put forward
by the Americans on the tradition question. Although the exponents
of this newer Catholic position continue to hold fast to the verbal
definition of infallibility, they are prepared to admit: (a) that
one cannot always and with full certainty distinguish between fallible and infallible teachings of the Church;[75] (b) that the prevailing understanding and practical applications of even the infallible definitions can be "alloyed" with error;[76] and (c) that for
this and other reasons, reinterpretation or even a reformulation of
such definitions may be in order.[77] When this much has been conceded, the claim of infallibility loses most of its rigidity, and
the Catholic theologian is forced into relying on much the same "fallible" methods of historical and theological criticism as his non-
Catholic partner when it comes to determining what is authoritative
and what is not.

(4) Behind the classical Roman Catholic understanding of the
infallibility dogma stands a particular conception of the manner of
God's activity in the world and in the Church. This conception sees
God operating supernaturally in the Church by means of infused modifications of the natural human powers of the authoritative teachers
and their hearers. Like the neoscholastic notion of sharply defined
truths, this neoscholastic idea of a sharp division between supernatural and natural causality in the knowledge of faith has also increasingly come under criticism among Catholic theologians. The increasing awareness of the complex psychological and sociological influences on human action have forced theologians to a more subtle
understanding of the way God influences human responses. Till now,
this more subtle understanding has been applied primarily to the
action of God in the individual person or in the world as a whole;
it is necessary however, to inquire as well into its implications for
the life of the Church. Precisely in the debate over the infallibility and impeccability of the Church a dangerous tendency becomes
manifest, namely, to abstract the Church from the concrete men and

women who constitute it at any particular time and place in history. Expressions like "the mind of the Church" may be useful as attempts to express the transcendence of the Church in its historical wholeness over the particular, culturally conditioned incarnation of the Church in its concrete, erring and sinning members at any one moment. But such formulae can easily lead the theologian to forget that, at any given moment in its history, the Church on earth really has no other mind at its disposal than the individual minds of its living members. When one is prepared to admit this fact and to take serious account of it in ecclesiology, then it is difficult to see how one could propose an explanation of the presence of God in the Church which would differ significantly from that outlined by the Americans in the preceding chapter.

(5) Clearly the search for an ecumenically "catholic" ecclesiology would be made easier by a frank admission that the dogmatic definitions of the past are not infallible. Nevertheless the issue is not one to be decided on the basis of ecumenical expediency; the only way to resolve the infallibility issue is to test the dogma on its own merits. The same holds true, however, for the other dogmas which appear to stand in the way of ecumenical consensus in ecclesiology. Although the infallibility dogma offers a blanket guarantee for all the other dogmas of the Church, it does not by itself guarantee any particular doctrine for which the infallible guarantee is claimed. Confronted with any particular doctrine or practice inherited from the past as normative, the theologian is faced with the same questions whether or not he accepts the doctrine of infallibility. Whether he is an infallibilist or not, the theologian is forced to ask: (a) is the claim to normative character real or spurious; (b) what was the original intention; (c) how much of this original intention is retainable in the light of more refined scriptural and historical scholarship, more advanced natural and behavioral sciences, new cultural and philosophical perspectives, etc.; (d) how can the matter be translated into contemporary socio-cultural idioms. To none of these questions does the infallibility dogma offer a direct answer; at best it constrains him to "save" the tradition either by attempting to show that his new interpretation does not directly contradict the authoritative definition of the past or (where this is possible) to attempt to show that the presumed definition never really fell under the guarantee of infallibility. In

any case, the means by which the Roman Catholic theologian goes
about answering the above-mentioned questions are in fact the same
relative and "fallible" criteria that the "catholic"-thinking Protestant uses when he attempts to deal seriously with the traditions
of the past.

The plain fact of the matter is, that Catholic theologians--
encouraged by the theoretical concessions to historical criticism,
theological pluralism, and pastoral aggiornamento, in official docu-
ments--have taken for themselves a very broad liberty to criticize
or reinterpret hallowed traditions. A survey of recent Catholic
writings on Chalcedonian christology, original sin, church order,
etc., would reveal a spectrum of opinion hardly narrower than that
found in Protestant churches. At the same time, it must be frankly
admitted, that this de facto liberty is by no means accepted by the
papacy or by the majority of the hierarchy; it exists mainly because
no effective means have been found to restrict it. Herein lies the
weakness of every suggestion of a purely pragmatic skirting of the
infallibility issue. One must not underestimate the deleterious
effects of such an open split between theory and practice. Nothing
of what has been said here, therefore, is to be construed as an attempt to avoid the central issue in the infallibility debate, the
question, namely, whether or not some of the solemn definitions or
hallowed traditions of the past might not be wrong by the standards
of ordinary language. This issue can no more be settled by pragmatic
dexterity than it can by authoritative declaration; it is only to be
resolved by solid argument. The main point to be made in the present
context however, is that t h e   a d a p t a t i o n   o f   t h e
" c a t h o l i c   m e t h o d "   b y   h i g h - c h u r c h
t h e o l o g i a n s   n e e d   n o t   a w a i t   t h e
u l t i m a t e   r e s o l u t i o n   o f   t h e   i n f a l l i -
b i l i t y · i s s u e .   There is already enough room for it both
in official theory and in actual practice.

B. Functionalism

Next to "catholicity," the most distinctive feature of the American ecclesiology is an approach which seems best expressed by the
term "functionalism."[78] As the preceding pages testify, the word
"function" appears frequently in the American documents, and time

after time functionality is cited as the principal criterion for
judging the institutions and actions of the Church. The structure-
function relationship also makes its appearance in the American documents as a hermeneutical device for overcoming conceptual ambiguities and conflicts in the effort to understand and compare existing
denominations and historical traditions. Although observations relevant to functionalist methodology are found scattered throughout
the American documents, it is once again to a post-Lund F. & O. commission that we turn for the fullest explanation, in this case, the
Study Commission on Institutionalism (SCI). That this should be the
case is hardly surprising, for the primary postulate of the functional method is the assertion that the institutions of the Church
(indeed the Church itself in its temporal, empirical form) is not
an end in itself and that therefore it can only be defined in relation to the goal to which it is directed.[79] In essence, the functional method is a way of conceiving and evaluating the relationship
between the "constitutive and permanent" features of the Church and
those which are "derivative and historical."[80]

This, of course, was also the intention of the "catholic" method discussed in the preceding section. "Catholic" method and functional method are not alternatives; rather they are complementary
one to another.[81] Both derive their rationale from the fact that
"throughout its history, the Christian Church has expressed its common life, its worship and mission in a variety of forms, institutionalized both by different self-images and by diverse historical
and cultural circumstances."[82] However, whereas the "catholic" method defines the general framework or context of ecclesiological in-
vestigation--the Church as a whole rather than some particular tra-
dition--the functional method represents the specific way in which
the ecclesiologist goes about questioning the manifold of traditions
in which the Church as a whole finds expression. The key to the
functional method is a new distinction.

1. The Distinction between Order and Organization

We have seen that behind the proposal of the "catholic method"
lay the American's theologians' realization that none of the various
denominational attempts to establish its own particular historical
tradition as the Tradition pure and simple could stand the test of
critical historical verification. On the other hand, we have also

seen that the Americans claimed to be able to learn from a critical
investigation of the manifold of diverse traditions. Alone the distinction between the divine Tradition, the traditionary process, and
the traditional patterns, is unable to account for this paradox.
Only when a further distinction within the traditum itself is made--
a distinction between abiding principles and their transitory mani-
festations--can the "catholic" method be made to yield concrete results. The solution proposed by the SCI is the distinction between
"order" and "organization."[83]

In introducing this distinction, the SCI qualified it as "traditional." Obviously some such distinction of this sort is made in
practically every ecclesiology inasmuch as it admits to the existence of both permanent and transitory structures of the Church's
life.[84] How traditional the use of the terms "order" and "organization" is, however, is a question of a different order. It would appear to be a quite recent tradition, originating in the American
ecumenical conversations.[85] Already back in 1937, the CCULW had introduced the distinction between "order" and "polity," i.e. between
the ordering of the ministry (e.g. grades of ministerial office and
ordination procedures), on the one hand, and the organization of
church government (e.g. structures for the exercise of legislative,
administrative, and judicial powers).[86] The distinction between
"order" and "organization" is further anticipated by the ATC report,
where, in an effort to explain the position of those who deny the
existence of specific, unchanging patterns of church life, it distinguishes between recognizing "the need for church order," on the
one hand, and asserting that a "particular form of organization" be
necessary to the existence of the Church, on the other. The terms
"order" and "organization" here clearly have a broader meaning than
ministry and polity--issues of doctrinal standards and liturgical
discipline are also referred to--but there is no indication that the
ATC consciously reflected on the implications of such a distinction
for dealing with the question of continuity and discontinuity in the
Church.[87] The first explicit reflection on the distinction apparently occurred in a Toronto study group in preparation for the
Oberlin Conference of 1957. The Toronto group's exposition was incorporated into the report of Section 8, which was published in the
official report of the conference.[88] From here it was taken over by
the SCI,[89] which however introduced certain modifications and re-
finements of the original conception.[90] In the exposition which follows both versions are referred to since on some aspects the Toronto
paper is clearer than the SCI report. Discrepancies between the two
versions are noted where this seems appropriate.

The SCI offers the following nominal definitions of the two
terms "order" and "organization":

> "Order is in this context taken to denote the visible complex of
> institutions which is held to be essential to the contin-
> uous existence and identity of the Church as a community
> in history.
> Organization, on the other hand, refers to the broad range of
> institutional elements which, under varying historical

conditions, express some aspect or other of the community
which is structured and sustained by that 'order' [italics
added]."[91]

In defining both order and organization as "institutions," the Commission indicates that both involve a relationship between social
structures and social functions, whereby the distinction between
these two must be flexibly understood--what appears as a structure
in respect to one function or functional complex may itself be regarded as a function in respect to another.[92] By the same token, the
distinction between "order" and "organization" is a relative one.
Every "order," insofar as it is a structured relationship, is a form
of organization; in respect to more concrete and therefore more variable structures ("organization" simpliciter), however, "order" is
best viewed as a constant function capable of diversified organizational embodiment.[93]

To understand what the Americans intended with their distinction
it is necessary to break through the usual images which the words
"institution" and "structure" evoke when talking about the Church.
Ordinarily when we hear these terms we think of a priestly or bureaucratic hierarchy standing in the way of charismatic leadership
and grass-roots initiative. Sacerdotal hierarchies and denominational bureaucracies, however, represent only one type of organization; charismatic leadership, ad hoc initiative groups, etc. are
also forms of organization and structure, albeit less "visible" and
permanent.[94] Besides such leadership structures, there are also
other forms of organization which have nothing to do with offices and
officials or the absence thereof. Laws, public declarations, con-
tracts and agreements, rituals, ethical norms, social sanctions, etc.
also belong to the ambit of the sociological concepts intended by
the Commission.

The term "institution" designates a narrower concept than the
terms "organization" or "structure." An institution is a "definite
and established structure";[95] it supposes and provides for a certain degree of "stability and uniformity of social action around
some human need, basic or derived."[96] The distinction between the
two, however, is relative and flexible. What in one social context
appears to have sufficient stability and uniformity to be classed
as an institution, may in another context appear as disorder and
anarchy. It can also happen that a subgroup in a particular culture
institutionalizes within its own circle patterns of behavior which
represent the antithesis of the social norms prevailing in the
society as a whole; thus what appears to the "outsider" as chaotic
and without form has all the force of a stable and uniform social
norm for the "insider," although and because he sees his "anarchic"
behavior as an expression of his protest against prevailing norms
or even against the very principle of institutional norms as such.
"Anti-institutions" of this type have appeared repeatedly in the
history of the Church and have become the basis for many a denominational tradition. The refusal to admit their "institutional" character is one of the chief obstacles to ecumenical dialog on the part
of such churches.

Though the concepts "structure" and "function," "order" and organization," can be clearly distinguished, the boundary between them in practice is flexible, for they represent abstractions only virtually distinguishable in any particular example of human life. Where the boundary is to be drawn in any particular instance, depends on the level and angle of abstraction being considered. It is possible to arrange social functions and social structures in order of increasing or decreasing concreteness and specificity. On such a scale, the most generic functions appear at one end, the most particular structures at the other; in between, each level can be considered either as a structure, organizing the specific functions appropriate to the preceding stage of greater abstraction, or as a function to be organized by a more specific structure in the following stage of greater concretion. The reason for this ambivalence is that structure and function represent coordinate concepts: function specifies structure, structure concretizes function. Each function is realized with the aid of specific structures; these structures, however, modify the function itself inasmuch as they determine the means, manner, and conditions, under which the function is fulfilled. Corresponding to each structure is a specific set of functions which must be fulfilled if the original, generic function is to be fulfilled. Monogamy, simultaneous and successive polygamy, for instance, constitute three specifically distinct ways of structuring the institution of marriage; marriage and sexual promiscuity, in turn, represent more generic organizations of the basic functions of human sexuality. In the other direction, patriarchal, matriarchal and egalitarian relationships represent yet more specific organizations of monogamous or polygamous marriages. Each one of these levels of abstraction can be considered either under its aspect of organized function or under its aspect of functional organization.

These distinctions are necessary to understand what the Americans intend with their distinction between "order" and "organization." As the Toronto group explained, "unless order is to be thought of as abstract and invisible--in other words, in self-contradictory terms, since it is the visible form of a human community with which we have to do--it must itself be pictured as a kind of organization. The problem, then, is really one of distinguishing between a 'primary' organization (or 'Order') and a 'secondary' organization (or 'Organization' simpliciter)--i.e., between an ordered structure which at all times and in all places serves as the means by which God constitutes the Church as the Church and an organization which under particular circumstances gives effective expression to some aspect or other of the primary structure."[7] The primary organization or order will be a permanent and stable structure; hence it is always an "institution" in the sense described above. Furthermore it will be a constant, indeed necessary element in the social system to which it belongs, i.e. an "essential" institution. Secondary organizations or organizations simpliciter need not be either permanent nor uniform; they can be, but need not be institutions in the above sense. By the same token, they are "non-essential"; that is to say, the same function can be more or less fulfilled by a variety of organizations: they are interchangeable. "Secondary" organizations may be useful but not necessary--the function in question could be fulfilled without them, though not so easily perhaps. It can happen, however that, although no particular system of "secondary" organization is required to fulfill the function implicit in a primary or essential organization (order); this primary function

requires the mediation of some (though not any particular) "secondary" organization. The institution of marriage, for instance, can
exist without a formal contract regulating once and for all every
aspect of the distribution of labor and resources; it cannot, however, exist, i.e. fulfill its basic functions, unless there is some
sort of arrangement regarding the cohabitation of the partners;
nevertheless various arrangements (secondary organizations), e.g.
monogamy or polygamy, permanent or interrupted residence together,
etc., are available to achieve the intended function.[98]

It will immediately be clear that the distinction between "order" and "organization" is formal and relative rather than material
and absolute. Whether a particular institution is viewed as an
order or an organization depends very much on its place in the scale
of abstraction explained earlier. The more basic and generic the
function involved, the more essential and constant the immediately
corresponding structure; but in that case the structure itself is
also usually generic. Seldom does it happen that a generic social
need or function can be realized by only a single type of structure
fixed down to the very last detail. The rule is not absolute, but
generally the span of alternative structures is proportionate to the
degree of specificity of the functions involved. However, as we
have seen, the more generic a structure is, the more we are inclined
to view it as a "function" rather than as a "structure." Thus the
institution of marriage abstracted from its monogamous and polygamous organizational embodiment will be defined primarily as a functional relationship; in the definition of a specific type of marriage, on the contrary, e.g. the exclusive monogamous nuclear family
among American urban, working-class Catholics of third-generation
Irish ancestry, structural elements of highly specific type will
predominate. This means that a useful sign that one has to do with
an order rather than an organization is the discovery of a constant
function which is variously embodied in quite different organizing
structures.[99]

2. Apostolic Order and Catholic Organization

When dealing with such natural human institutions as the family
or the political community, it is relatively easy to distinguish between order and organization in terms of constant functions diverse-
ly embodied in a variety of structures.[100] With the Church, the matter is more complicated. The Church is not a human answer to intrinsic natural needs but rather a unique society of men, which has
been instituted at a particular moment of history and in a particular cultural setting by God; hence "it possesses and is partially
defined by a divinely given order, in which man is related to God on
the basis of God's action."[101] This introduces a historical element
into the notion of "order"-which is not present when the concept is
used with respect to a universal social reality like the family. To
speak of the "order" of the Church is like speaking of the "order"
of a particular family, distinguished from other families by its own

historical traditions and its structures of physical and cultural
continuity. "Apostolicity" is the term traditionally used to designate this historical element: "in the case of the Church, functional
order is grounded in the 'apostolic tradition,' which embodies the
particular historical revelation from which the Church's universal
mission springs."[102]

Two questions have divided the churches with regard to the apostolic tradition. One is the question where is it found: in the
Bible? in the Church as a whole? in a particular office or ecclesiastical institution? in particular extra-biblical traditions? The
other question asks what belongs to it: does it contain specific
norms or only general principles? does it dictate specific patterns
of organizational structure or simply give illustrations exemplifying
the essential considerations which the Church must take account of
in searching for new, more appropriate forms of organization? We
have seen the answer to these questions given in the course of the
American discussions. In short, their answer was that the apostolic
tradition (in the sense of the _traditum_) is to be found in a special
permanently normative way in the traditions canonized by the Church
as Scripture, but that for the discrimination between the apostolic
tradition and its conditioned expression in the scriptural traditions
it is also necessary to take account of the experience of the Church
as a whole embodied in the sum of all the historical traditions.
Furthermore they were unable to discover any fixed organizational
patterns as belonging to the apostolic tradition: even if such normative patterns do exist--as some individual theologians privately
believed--they are not yet ecumenically recognizable as such.

What then does belong to the apostolic tradition if not specific
organizational patterns? In view of their "catholic" view of the
manifold of traditions in the Church, the Americans concluded that
an essential _functional_ order could indeed be discerned under the
varied and transient _patterns of organization_.[103] This essential
order they set forth as follows: Granting (1) the divine institution
of the Church itself as a h i s t o r i c a l   v i s i b l e
c o m m u n i t y , the functions central to the apostolic tradition
would appear to revolve around (2) the three "essential and enduring
d o m i n i c a l   i n s t i t u t i o n s ,-" Gospel, Sacraments,
and Ministry, which are "God's appointed means of grace within the
visible fellowship of his Church."[104] Thus the Church must confess

and proclaim the Gospel. It must also administer the Sacraments as
the "visible...efficacious signs of the grace which sustains the
Church and the Christian in faith and love." Finally, "the Church
must necessarily be maintained as a visible fellowship, in and by
which the Gospel is preached and the Sacraments are administered,
and through which human communion with God is expressed and shared";
this is the function of the Ministry.[105] Besides these functions,
however, there are also others which though not of such direct dominical institution flow immediately from the nature of the Church as a
community in which men are united in loving service with God and with
each other. Here may be classed (3) the " r e s p o n s i v e
f u n c t i o n s " of the Church, e.g. worship, preaching and
teaching, pastoral care, service to the needy, and social action.
Furthermore there are (4) the functions inherent in maintaining a
c o m m o n   l i f e   a n d   a c t i v i t y   i n   t h e
c o n g r e g a t i o n and (5) in securing and expressing the
i n t e r d e p e n d e n c e   o f   t h e   i n d i v i d u a l
c o n g r e g a t i o n s   a n d   c h u r c h e s   w i t h
e a c h   o t h e r . Finally there is (6) the whole c o m p l e x
o f " o r g a n i z a t i o n a l ,   a d m i n i s t r a t i v e ,
l e g a l ,   f i n a n c i a l   a n d   o t h e r   a r r a n g e -
m e n t s   a n d   p r o c e d u r e s which are needed for the
continuous life and mission of the Christian community."[106]

Among these six "aspects of order and organization," the Institutionalism report notes "no sharp disjunction is permissible between
the realm of church order and the realm of organization."[107] The
reason, of course, is that none of the institutions and functions,
here recognized as more or less essential to the Church, ever exists
in naked purity. In reality they are always clothed in particular,
historically conditioned patterns of organization; this means that
at first at least, clarity in conceptual distinction can be purchased
only at the expense of greater abstraction. Provided one's "catholic" view of the manifold of traditions is sufficiently abstract, it
is possible to recognize in every one of these institutional dimensions of the Church "a clear distinction between the function which
remains constant through a variety of embodiments--requiring some
embodiment, but not bound to anyone in particular--and the particular organized expression of that function in any given time and place
[italics added]."[108]

Such abstract distinctions between apostolic order and catholic
organization are obviously insufficient to resolve all the disputed
issues which presently divide the churches. T h e y   d o ,
h o w e v e r ,   p r o v i d e   a   m e a n s   b y   w h i c h
a   p a t i e n t ,   e c u m e n i c a l   e c c l e s i o l o g y
c a n   p r o c e e d   s t e p   b y   s t e p   i n   t h e
d i r e c t i o n   o f   e v e r   i n c r e a s i n g   c o n -
c r e t e n e s s . Thus in surveying the whole manifold of traditions, as proposed by the "catholic" method, the ecclesiologist will
look primarily for regular, unique and typical functions rather than
for particular organizational patterns and structures. Having identified such functions, he can go on to evaluate the suitability of
the particular structures to its fulfilment. In this way he gains
a criterion, albeit a relative and fallible one, for judging the
value of each of the particular traditions with regard to the particular point at issue, and thus to select out the better traditions
as the basis for his next step, in which he looks for a yet more
concrete expression of the essential function. So described, of
course, this progression from the more abstract to the more concrete
is an idealization. In practice, the various functions are intercon-
nected, so that the effectiveness of a particular structure cannot
be judged by reference to one factor alone. Congregational election
and ordination of ministers might, for instance, be judged the most
effective structure for the selection and institution of qualified
men in the ministry; it is less effective, however, as an expression
of the apostolic character of the ministry and of the interdependence
of the individual congregations. Far from being an obstacle, however, such interference of criteria can serve positively the task
of an ecumenical ecclesiology by suggesting the outward boundaries
of what belongs to apostolic order as opposed to catholic organization.

By the same token, t h e   a p p l i c a t i o n   o f   t h e
f u n c t i o n a l   m e t h o d   c a n   b e   o f   i m p o r -
t a n t   s e r v i c e   i n   t h e   e f f o r t   t o   d e -
v e l o p   n e w ,   m o r e   e f f e c t i v e   f o r m s   o f
c h u r c h   o r g a n i z a t i o n in a particular socio-cultural
situation.[109] In the first place, the distinction between apostolic
order and catholic organization helps negatively by deliniating the
limits to the freedom of choice in the selection of new organiza-

tional models. Even more important, however, is the method's positive contribution. By defining ecclesiastical institutions by their
functions rather than their outward appearance and by distinguishing
various levels and priorities among these functions, the method proposed here provides a set of flexible tools for the search for and
refinement of new models of organization. In this way, it can provide a check on the passion for novelty, which traditionalists so
often accuse reformers of. At the same time, the functional method
prevents traditionalists from imposing or holding fast to outmoded
organizational details which under changed circumstances often become catastrophically disfunctional.

3. The Functional Method for Roman Catholics?

In principle, a Roman Catholic can have little difficulty with
the functional method in ecclesiology. The distinction between order
and organization is roughly equivalent to the classic distinction between de jure divino and de jure ecclesiastico in questions of church
structure, and the emphasis on function in the definition of social
structures is closely related to the teleological method of definition habitually employed in Roman Catholic social theory.

The objections raised by a Roman Catholic are less likely to be
directed against the principle itself as against particular applications.[110] Thus one is liable to object that the list of "essential
and enduring dominical institutions" is neither complete nor concrete enough. Of dominical institution, it might be contended, is
not a vague Gospel of Salvation but rather a definite set of divinely
revealed, propositionally articulated truths, which must be believed
on divine faith. Similarly it might be contended that the dominical
institution of the Sacraments includes all seven sacraments administered in the catholic-type churches, and that the essential signs and
conditions of validity have been definitively fixed as belonging to
apostolic tradition. The vague reference to a dominical institution
of "ministry" will hardly satisfy many Roman Catholic theologians,
who would contend that the threefold hierarchy of orders and the twofold hierarchy of jurisdiction are specific organizational patterns
of divine institution, that ordination through bishops in apostolic
succession is the divinely fixed method of the transmission of ministry, etc. Further they will call for a recognition of the infal-

lible teaching magisterium of the church as a distinct element of
dominical institution, etc.

This is not the place to treat objections of this sort as to
their material content. In fact, an inner-catholic discussion of
these matters is in progress, and a wide variety of qualifications
and corrections are being proposed in relation to the traditional
Roman Catholic conception of the de jure divino elements of the
Church's constitution. The fact is that even when one follows only
the increasingly narrow stream of traditions which flows into the
traditional Roman Catholic conception, it is often difficult to ver-
ify an apostolic tradition for many of the distinctive elements of
the Catholic conception,[111] hence the explanations offered by their
defenders do not always find general acceptance even among the adherents of these positions. In any case a discussion of these matters is now in progress, and each issue must be decided on its own
merits--a task far beyond the scope of the present study.

What is here to the point, is a formal answer to this type of
objection as a class. It would be quite unfair to expect non-Catholic theologians, engaged in an ecumenical dialog from which Catholics by their own choice had absented themselves, to come to agreement of their own accord on the basis of the Roman Catholic teaching.
The fact that their methodology did not bring them to such conclusions as long as non-Catholics were forced to work only among themselves says little or nothing about the conclusions to which the
same methodology would lead were it practiced in the context of a
dialog with Roman Catholics. There is nothing in the functional
method outlined here which a priori forbids the recognition of specific institutions (i.e. organizational patterns as well as characteristic functions) as belonging to apostolic tradition;[112] on the
contrary, the Americans themselves pointed to the existence of the
three "dominical institutions." The Catholic theologian, however,
cannot expect his non-Catholic partner simply to take the work of the
Catholic Church for the apostolic character of this or that element
of the particular Roman Catholic tradition; he has the task of offering solid historical and theological arguments to make this claim
plausible. This means, above all, that he find a way of defining the
apostolic element which has perdured under the various forms manifested by a critical study of the Church's history. Precisely because the essential order of the Church never appears in naked purity,

the theologian is confronted with the difficult task of determining what belongs only to the changeable outward appearance and what belongs to the substance--which is precisely the intention of the functional method.

At the heart of many, indeed most Roman Catholic objections to the "minimalist" results of ecumenical dialog is in reality an epistemological issue. Despite vehement protestations of the inability of the human mind to comprehend the mysteries of faith, Catholic theology at least since the Reformation has tended to operate on the assumption that, under the influence of the Spirit working through the Magisterium, we are able to achieve more or less clear and distinct ideas about particular aspects at least of these mysteries. Under this assumption, the historical dogmatic definitions constitute permanent fences, so to speak, fixing once and for all, the conceptual boundaries within which further clarification can be sought.[113] Hence the return to earlier, less precise formulations or the drafting of new consensus formulae which do not include the details contained in traditional definitions appears to thinkers of this type as a betrayal of historical progress.

An image can perhaps make this type of thinking more intelligible (provided, of course, it be remembered that an image is intended, not a caricature). The development of dogma and theology, for this way of thinking, is rather like a set of chinese boxes, each of which when opened reveals another of yet smaller dimensions. To expand the image somewhat into an allegory, one might think of revealed truth as collection of individual truths each packed in its own tiny box. These boxes in turn are packed together as sets into larger packages, these packages in turn being likewise arranged in sets which are packed in yet larger packages, and so forth. Accordingly the development of theology and dogma would be comparable to the process of step by step opening these packages and cataloging their contents. One begins with the large package; once it has been opened, the original packing can be discarded, at best an historical record might be kept of its appearance. The contents i.e. the next smaller packages are taken out, their relationships one to another are noted for future reference and then put in order on the appropriate shelf of the mind. Then one takes one of the packages and proceeds to open it as before; here too the contents, again a series of packages, will be taken out, cataloged and filed in the place on the

shelf where the original package belonged; the original packaging,
on the contrary, has served its purpose and can be disposed of. In
this way the theological process proceeds to solve one question after
the other, even though at each step new mysteries come to light.
Nevertheless, the process so conceived is clearly irreversible. Once
a package has been opened, it serves no point to put it back together
again. At best, one can make an effort to recall the original order
of the pieces in the package and to try to discover the relationships they bear to the elements of other packages belonging to the
whole.

When the process of theological cognition is conceived in this
way, the temptation is very great to fasten onto individual words or
details of appearance and practice and to make of them touchstones
of orthodoxy. Right belief about the Eucharist, for instance, will
be judged by whether or not one accepts the words "transubstantia-
tion" or "conversio," whether or not the Sacrament is reserved, etc.
Because concepts are virtually identified with the words expressing
them, individual propositions take on a significance which they may
not have when seen in larger context. The assertion "Bread remains
bread, wine wine" may indeed be an absolute negation of every sort of
eucharistic presence; it need not be, however; in context it may mean
no more and no less than what traditional catholic theology meant
when it insisted against the ultra-realists, that the properties of
bread and wine remain unchanged in the Eucharist.[114]

Too easily such a conception of the theological process forgets
that, in our ordinary knowledge of things (as even scholastic philosophy admits), we are almost never in a position to isolate the single
formal specific difference which distinguishes one nature from another; instead we have to rely on a congeries of more or less typical
properties, which we have come to recognize through practical experience with the object under study.[115] A different observer, observing
the same object under other circumstances and with a different point
of view, is liable to set different accents in his definition, to
give greater priority to this or that property, and to contest the
appropriateness of one element or the other of our definition. In
theological matters this is all the more the case, since we are dealing not with natural phenomena but with human relationships and institutions in which the mysterious working of God finds historical
expression; how much more difficult is it therefore to isolate the

specificum from its incidental socio-cultural embodiment.[116]
Might it not be that in such cir-
cumstances an agreement on the
basic functions and relationships
to be served would suffice at least for the
acknowledgment that, however deficient our conceptualization, we indeed intend the same theological reality in our different denominational and academic traditions. Further might it not be asked whether such acknowledgment doesn't in fact suffice as a foundation for
mutual recognition, relying upon God's merciful power to fill up what
may be lacking in our conceptions and practice and to lead us together to a deeper and richer appreciation of his gifts.[117]

There is no room here to pursue these questions further. To
raise them by no means implies that they must without further ado be
answered in the affirmative. On the other hand, anyone who would immediately offer a negative response must be prepared to give a plausible account of his motives. It will not do simply to appeal to the
authority of the Magisterium, where such a conception of the development of theology and dogma has found expression in the declarations
of Popes Pius X, Pius XII, and Paul VI as well as in numerous episcopal declarations. Nor does it suffice to decry the spread of nom-
inalism, relativism, historicism, etc. in our day. Those who object
to methods of ecumenical theology in the name of such a conception of
dogmatic truth have a clear obligation to provide their opponents
with a coherent, plausible account of how such a cognition process
is possible in the Church, given the facts which have been revealed
about the human manner of knowing by psychological, sociological and
epistemological investigation. At the moment we still wait for such
an account.

C. Provisionalism
1. Provisional Ecclesiology in Practice

From the beginning, as we have seen, the Americans were concerned with the practical implications of their ecclesiological theory. In their critique of prevailing methods in the ecumenical dialog, the Americans time and again insisted that theological research and discussion remain
sterile unless accompanied by a

step by step process of institutionalizing in practice of the
unity discovered in theory . They repu-
diated as theologically erroneous and sociologically suspect the
claim of those who would defer serious ecumenical practice until
unity had been fully achieved in theory.[118] In committing themselves
to maintaining a close interaction between theory and practice, the
Americans realized that they would be leaving themselves open to making mistakes, that the institutionalization of church unity at one
level might eventually become an obstacle to the achievement of unity
on a deeper level. At the same time, however, they were acutely
aware that the continued maintenance of existing institutionalized
division would only give free rein to those "non-theological" forces
arising from socio-cultural division which so easily slip into the
mantle of unrelinquishable theological confession. Threatened by
this twin danger, the Americans found comfort in the theological
principle that the Church, essential though it be in the divine plan
of salvation, is also in its innermost nature provisional.[119] Precisely as a human instrument in the power of God for the salvation
of the world, it is subject to all those limitations which are inherent in human activity and organization.

This conviction cannot be dismissed as radical humanism, as a
denial of the divine transcendence and a repudiation of the Incarnation; it cannot be defamed as a repudiation of the historicity of the
Church. On the contrary, however much anyone might wish to dispute
the correctness of the American ecclesiologists' theological analysis,
there is no disputing its profoundly theological intention and character. It is precisely from their intensive study of the history of
God's work in its fulness that the Americans arrived at the conclusions they did, concerning the provisional character of the Church.

2. Provisionalism for Roman Catholics?

Slowly but surely an awareness of the Church's provisional character is also growing within the Roman Catholic Church. The travails
of the Council and the post-counciliar reform, the rise of a vocifer-
ous traditionalist-fundamentalist movement more "Catholic" than even
the pope and the hierarchy, has made clear even to more conservative
Roman Catholic theologians and churchmen the danger of all too narrowly identifying specific, time-conditioned expressions of the

Church's life with the unchangeable essentials.[120] Gradually we are becoming more modest in our claims to have clearly defined once and for all the boundaries between the de jure divino and the de jure humano elements of the Church's faith and constitution. Gradually we are learning to put aside the narrow legalistic tutiorism which led to such ecumenical scandals as the habitual conditional rebaptism of converts from Protestantism and even from some of the ancient churches of the East. We are learning to take risks both in inner-Catholic reform of teaching, discipline, and organization, and also in the ecumenical field. The once rigid adherence to the principle, no sacramental communion without full ecclesiastical communion --exception being made only in case of danger of death--has now been loosened at least with respect to the Orthodox Churches,[121] and various initiatives are under way to extend this also to Protestant churches.[122] In principle, therefore, we have already come to acknowledge the methodological axiom of the American ecclesiologists, namely that the institutionalization of partial forms of church unity can be an important step in the pursuit of full unity, and that the institutionalization of such partial forms does not of itself imply either the abandonment of one's own ecclesiological standpoint nor the recognition of the full equality of that held by ones partner.

Admittedly, in practice we remain hesitant; particularly when it comes to Catholic-Protestant relations, we are often inclined to make demands which we do not make in respect to the Orthodox and which even within our own ranks are virtually uninforceable, e.g. in regard to de facto adherence of the church membership to the official standards of belief. In part such hesitancy is justifiable by serious theological issues; in large measure it is understandable as sociopsychological residue of centuries of rivalry and mutual oppression. Here a greater willingness to examine the "non-theological" motives in our behavior and attitudes would well become us. Nevertheless in principle, there is no reason for a Roman Catholic not being able to subscribe to the American demand for a progressive provisional institutionalization of our koinonia with the separated churches. As to the individual forms this might take, each case must be considered on its own merits, and there is no place to go into that here. We can

here, however, call attention to some of the practical principles
recommended by the Americans for dealing with such questions.

3. Practical Principles of Provisional Ecclesiology

(a) Every church must be prepared for s e l f - c r i t i -
q u e .   In particular it must constantly be on guard against the
innate tendency of its bureaucratic organization and its social function as custodian of traditional values to fall into a rigid, juridical traditionalism, which stifles legitimate initiatives and op-
poses necessary innovations. To admit this is not to reduce the
Church to the level of an ordinary human society; it is simply to insist that the Church, inasmuch as it is human as well as divine, is
as much subject to the Gospel demand for radical metanoia as the individual believer.[123]

(b) The basis for judging the appropriateness of both old and
new formal structures is the degree to which they c o n c r e t e -
l y   s e r v e   o r   d i s s e r v e   t h e   h i e r a r c h y
o f   f u n c t i o n s   inherent in the Church.[124] This is not to
say that the Church is free to structure itself ad libitum. Naturally the Church is obliged to respect the dominical and apostolic
order of the Church, but it will do this best when it concentrates
on the universal factors embodied in such offices rather than holding fast to outmoded externals. The essential office of the episcopacy would be much more visible as a sign of communion were it
stripped of so many of the trappings of prelacy which have clung to
it since the Middle Ages.

(c) Ecumenical institutionalization must respect the need for
b o t h   c o n t i n u i t y   a n d   f l e x i b i l i t y ,   a
need which is both theological and sociological.[125] Even aside from
the strictly theological duty of maintaining the continuity of the
apostolic order, there is a sociological need (not without its theological dimensions) for the members of a church to be able to recognize their own heritage in the new ecumenical institution. This need
must not be misunderstood as an invitation to an arbitrary denominational horse-trading; the governing principle must always be the
ability of the forms in question to best fulfil their intended functions (including those belonging to the apostolic order), and not
simply a principle of proportional parity of the borrowings from the
respective traditions. Nevertheless, precisely in judging the func-

220

tionality of a particular organizational form for a particular segment of the Church, account must be taken of those forms which have
contributed to the particular ethos of this group.[126] Where such
diversity is taken into account, however, there is also a need for
the different groups entering into an ecumenical organization to be
able to recognize in the varient forms a real "catholic" identity,
i.e. a respect for the insights contributed by the different heri-
tages entering into union. Thus whatever may be decided with respect
to the sacramental validity of congregational and presbyterian ministries, it is hardly conceivable that a union of such churches with
the Roman Catholic Church would be possible without some degree of
introduction of congregaticnal and presbyterian organizational principles into the churches of Roman observance, and the admission of
an even greater place for such organizational principles among the
churches having their origins in these backgrounds.

(d) Special care must be taken t h a t   t h e   n e w
e c u m e n i c a l   i n s t i t u t i o n s   d o   n o t in their
turn h a r d e n   i n t o   n e w   o b s t a c l e s to further
ecumenical progress.[127] That such a danger lurks in the institutions
of joint church boards, councils and inter-communion is undeniable.
This however is no reason to reject such organizational forms in
principle. The responsibility for keeping the dialog on more fundamental issues going, falls squarely on the theological and ecclesiastical leadership, but it is also important for institutionalizing
appropriate provisions for such ongoing effort. The Faith and Order
Department of the WCC offers an important example of what can be
done in this direction.[128]

(e) Special care must also be taken to maintain o p e n
c o m m u n i c a t i o n   a t   a l l   l e v e l s   o f   t h e
c h u r c h in the course of ecumenical dialog and negotiation.[129]
One of the saddest experiences of the ecumenical movement is the
gradual isolation of its participants from their respective churches.
In part, this is perhaps the inevitable result of the dialog itself,
participation in which evokes an experience of consensus and unanim-
ity which can only imperfectly be communicated to those not directly
involved in the conversing or negotiating group. The fault cannot be
sought only here however. Ecumenical union represents a threat to
comfortable habits on the part of denominational leadership and
grass-roots membership. Sometimes the denominations more or less

consciously make use of their ecumenical commissions as a way of conveniently side-tracking the ecumenically-minded gadflies in their
ranks. The work of the commissions is then ignored until one day a
concrete result emerges which appears to threaten denominational
identity or convention, then suddenly the denomination explodes in
a burst of protest, which upon closer analysis reveals that the pro-
testors have made little serious effort to understand the motives
which led the ecumenists to their recommendation. Another factor
leading to the breakdown of ecumenical dialog and negotiation is the
attempt to keep the ecumenical discussion behind closed doors until
the denominational leadership has made its decision on the finished
product of the negotiations. Not only does this prevent the kind
of interchange with the grass-roots so necessary for the development
of a really workable plan; more seriously it has the effect of leaving the grass-roots fully unprepared for the plan which suddenly
bursts upon them like a thunderstorm. Inevitably this generates re-
sentments and misunderstandings, which in churches with representative polity can lead to the plan being voted down, or in churches
with more authoritarian structure lead to its being frustrated in day
to day local practice. Clearly there is no foolproof way of avoiding
such dangers; in any case, however, the work done by the COCU offers
some interesting models and object lessons.

III. THE VISION OF A CHURCH CATHOLIC, EVANGELICAL AND REFORMED

At the end of thirty years of intensive ecumenical theological
research, the American ecclesiological renaissance found its capstone
in the drafting of the first theologically founded plan for a "united
and uniting," "catholic, evangelical and reformed" Church of Christ
in the United States. Since 1970 a thoroughly revised version of
this draft lies before the churches for consideration and amendment.
At the 1973 conference, the COCU delegates were forced to acknowledge that the time was not yet ripe for a plan of union, that the
sociological presuppositions for union must first be erected before
further progress could be made on a concrete plan of union. Thus
for the time being, the work on the plan of union as such has been
tabled, though work continues on the generation of an ecclesiological
consensus and the elaboration of ecumenical liturgical life, as well
as on the integration of congregational life and administrative organization. Thus, although the ultimate fate of the COCU endeavor
and its draft plan for the time being hangs in abeyance, it nevertheless deserves serious consideration by ecclesiologists without as
well as within the Consultation.

In the 1970 Plan of Union, all the various streams and currents
which we have examined in the course of this study come together and
in one way or another find expression. What was this vision of a
uniting Church "catholic, evangelical and reformed"?

The first point to note--the COCU vision is an open, not a
closed, once-and-for-all fixed vision: self-consciously it proclaims
its own provisional character.[130] A work of Protestant theologians
and churchmen, it represents the ultimate "catholic" achievement of
an ecumenism which, in view of the non-participation by Catholic
churches other than the Protestant Episcopal, was perforce required
to operate within a Protestant milieu. Admittedly the Catholic and
Orthodox churches participated in the COCU discussions as observers,
but observer status is too distant to allow the sort of existential
commitment required by the search for full unity. Probably it is
historically necessary that "catholic" unity first be achieved by the
churches of the Protestant tradition before the Catholic Churches
will take them seriously as full partners in the quest for a full
unity. Be that as it may, it is undeniable that the realization by
Protestant churches of a "catholic" unity along the lines of the COCU

vision would represent a serious challenge to the Catholic and Orthodox Churches, each with its own particularist ecclesiology.

Admittedly, the COCU Plan is in the first place a plan for the
formation of a united national church. Some have criticized this as
a defective grasp of the full meaning of catholicity. Anticipating
this objection, the Plan itself declares:

> "The Church of Christ Uniting intends to be in fact a uniting as
> well as a united church. This means emphasizing the united
> church's incomplete and provisional character and our desire to
> press steadily forward toward a wider unity both within this
> nation and beyond its borders. We recognize the dangers in a
> church organized solely on a national basis, as nationalistic
> attitudes may pervert or silence the prophetic voice of the
> church so that God's judgment on the nation's domestic and for-
> eign policies may not be articulated clearly. Yet there must
> be meaningful identification with the nation if the church is
> to serve as a voice of conscience. The dangers are matched
> with opportunities. The uniting churches desire to form more
> than a new and more inclusive denomination. We seek full re-
> conciliation with earlier and still separated Christian churches
> as we do with those of more recent divisions. The specific pur-
> pose of this union is not the merger of denominations, but the
> formation through union of a dynamic united and uniting church.
> This pilgrimage has as its ultimate goal the unity of the whole
> church." [original italics].[131]

Nor does the plan leave it at pious confession; in the last chapter,
under the title, "Reaching beyond this community," it lays down concrete organizational measures to insure that the united church continue steadfastly and selflessly to pursue its vocation to be a
uniting church as well, making explicit declaration to continue to
seek unity with the churches of the Catholic and Orthodox traditions.[132]

What will come of all this, remains to be seen. Roman Catholic
reactions so far have been mixed.[133] Although individual theologians
have expressed high praise for the catholicity of the COCU venture,
the tone of the official pamphlet published by the American bishops
conference is considerably more reserved. Despite generous acknowledgment of the COCU achievements, there is a strong undertone of
warning to Catholics not to mistake the Protestant catholicity of the
COCU for true catholicity. It is true, of course, that specific
Roman Catholic themes, e.g. the Papacy, the Councils, Mariology,
Priesthood, the Saints, etc., are missing from the Plan. This is not
surprising, for a consensus on these matters supposes a level of
Roman Catholic commitment to and participation in the project which
hitherto from the Catholic side has not been forthcoming; neverthe-

less it should be noted that the Plan leaves room for these matters, which would be the object of future negotiations. Moreover it must be noted that within the Catholic Church a movement for revision of traditional notions and practices is gaining increasing momentum, so that one can legitimately hope for a convergence on such issues instead of demanding Protestant conversion. All this of course is matter for the future; for the present we must look at the existing plan as it lays before us. What vision of the Church does it express? How does this vision compare with our own?

One of the first things that strikes the Catholic-minded observer is the emphasis in the COCU materials on a strong liturgical life. The "sacrament of the Lord's Supper" is unequivocally declared to be at the heart of the church's life,[134] and is to be celebrated with appropriate liturgical forms based on Catholic traditions.[135] The passages of the Plan dealing with the Lord's Supper include a frank confession of its sacramental character as effective sign of the real presence of Christ with his people through participation in his body and blood; it is acknowledged to be "an act of sacrifice in which we are united with Christ in his self-offering to the Father; with him we offer ourselves in praise, thanksgiving, and service."[136] It is seen as a concelebration by all Christ's people; but it shall be presided over by a bishop or presbyter with deacons and lay persons assisting.[137] Besides the Lord's Supper, the sacrament of Baptism-Confirmation also finds extensive treatment in the Plan. Both infant baptism and baptism of consenting believers are recognized as legitimate alternative traditions,[138] but provision is made for a solemn act of confirming baptismal vows—in the case of consent baptism as a part of the baptismal service. The plan declares: "confirmation is a response to and fulfillment of baptism with the gift of the Holy Spirit as a preparation and strengthening of every Christian for ministry and mission to the world."[139] In keeping with an older Catholic tradition, the Plan

"recognizes the sacramental character of other acts from the records of the Gospel and from the Tradition of the Church. These include the Word of God heard, preached, or expressed in the visual arts, marriage, ordination, declaration of the forgiveness of sin, anointing of the sick, foot washing, feeding of the hungry, the giving of drink to the thirsty, the welcoming of the stranger, the clothing of the naked, the visiting of the sick and the imprisoned."[140]

Likewise in its organizational structure the church envisaged
by the Plan reveals its affinity with the churches of the Catholic
tradition. The Plan declares that "all ministry in the church is a
gift from Jesus Christ," and that its normative standard is his own
"exemplary life and servanthood," it recognizes distinct ministries
of the ordained and the unordained as aspects of the one ministry.[141]
Although the mission of the laity is defined primarily in terms of
the presence of the church in the world; the Plan also acknowledges
the theological dignity of the diverse offices and ministries exercised by laymen within the church itself.[142] By the same token, although the ministry of the ordained is defined primarily in terms of
their function within the church, it explicitly calls attention to
their role in the ministry to the world as well. As to the ordained,
the Plan declares that:

> "within the ministry of the whole people of God there is and has
> been from the beginning a particular ministry representative of
> God who calls and of the church which ordains. This ministry
> is derived from Christ's action through his apostles and, under
> the guidance of the Holy Spirit, continues to derive its au-
> thority from the living Christ. ... The ordained ministers
> of the church bear particular responsibility as guardians of
> the Gospel, Scripture and Tradition. It is their task to help
> equip God's people to share in the total service of the church,
> to proclaim and teach God's word responsibly and articulately,
> and to celebrate the sacraments with God's people. The or-
> dained minister of the Word and sacraments thus expresses,
> represents, and serves the redemptive work of Christ through
> his church in a particular, but not exclusive way."[143]

The Plan acknowledges the traditional threefold ministry, though this
is understood in keeping with oldest Catholic tradition as a col-
legiate ministry of functionally distinct offices rather than as a
hierarchical cursus honorum: for this reason the text adopts the
order presbyter, bishop, deacon, thus emphasizing the privotal role
of the bishop as "symbol and agent of unity and continuity" in a
church endowed with a manifold of parallel ministries each with its
own specific authority in respect to the holders of other offices
in the Church.[144] Ordination in the church will be by laying on of
hands in the presence of the congregation, this being performed by a
bishop together with representatives of all offices and orders of the
ordained and unordained ministry, i.e. laymen as well as clergy.[145]
Through a carefully planned series of unification services the Plan
proposed to guarantee the historical succession of the ordained
episcopate.[146]

This conception of ministry finds expression in the parochial and synodal organization of the church. The basic unit of the church is the parish, the local community integrating diverse congregations and developing task groups for the more intense expression of particular aspects of the church's life and mission[147] under the leadership of one or more ordained ministers assisted by a mixed lay-clergy parish council.[148] These units, in turn, will be organized into a structure of district, regional, national (and ultimately, it is hoped, international) jurisdictions to secure the communication and coordination of the local churches with each other. At each of these levels there is provision for a representatively elected and temporally limited presiding bishop assisted by a council composed of clerical and lay representatives, further provision being made for church courts, and other curial offices, boards, and commissions.[149] The similarity of this structure to the proposals for structural reform of the Roman Catholic Church is self-evident.

An important concern of Catholic ecclesiology is the place accorded the magisterium in any vision of the Church. Though the COCU Plan does not use the term or devote a special section to a systematic exposition of the matter, it would be a serious mistake to accuse it of having ignored the reality. Speaking of the special authority of the Apostles' and Nicene Creeds, the Plan declares:

> "The united church will use these creeds as acts of praise and allegiance that bind it to the apostolic faith of the one church in all centuries and continents. In its duties as guardian of the truth of the Gospel, the united church will teach the faith of the creeds, recognizing their historically conditioned character, their corporate nature, and the principle that they are for the guidance of the members of the church and are to be used persuasively and not coercively."[150]

As to other historical confessions, the Plan agrees to their continued use "as enrichments of its [the church's] own understanding of the Gospel, it will not however, use any of these confessions as an exclusive requirement for all, nor permit them to become a basis for divisions in the new community."[151] By the same token it makes provision for the ongoing need to "confess and communicate its faith in contemporary language and in new forms under the authority of Scripture and with the guidance of the Holy Spirit" by new confessions and declarations,[152] as well as its responsibility to speak out on moral issues within and without the church. In all of this, how-

ever, the Plan sees the role of the living magisterium as persuasive
rather than coercive:

> "Only by costly, individual choice and obedience can a person
> trust in Jesus Christ and be fully committed to him. It is
> only by his grace that a person is enabled to do this and to
> become a member of his body. Corporate confessions are in-
> tended to guard, encourage, elicit, guide, and direct this
> personal commitment, not to substitute a corporate act for
> it."[153]

As already noted, the Plan affirms that the "responsibility as
guardians of the Gospel, Scripture and Tradition" lies in a particular way with the ordained ministers,[154] and elsewhere it declares
that "the bishops together with other office bearers in the church
have a corporate responsibility for safeguarding the faith, order,
and worship of the united church."[155] That there is no direct provision for the papacy in this vision is self-evident, but the principles set down in the document reveal, upon closer look, interesting possibilities for the eventual institutionalization of the sort
of pastoral primacy embodied by Pope John XXIII.[156] Obviously this
is a matter for the future dialog between COCU and the Roman Catholic
Church; that a good number of highly sensitive issues remain to be
solved is a fact that cannot be denied. Nevertheless, the room for
further development of both sides must not be ignored.

This, in brief, is an outward picture of the future "catholic,
evangelical and reformed" Church envisaged by the American theologians at the end of their thirty years endeavor. In terms of its
own self-understanding, the following passage from the plan gives
perhaps the best brief survey of the direction taken by the American
ecclesiologists. Here, in abbreviated form, are all the elements of
an ecclesiological approach, whose details we have followed in the
previous chapters. The Plan declares:

> "This venture toward a united and uniting church must be rooted
> in an understanding of the nature and mission of the church.
> The church must be seen in historical perspective as a continua-
> tion of the apostolic church of the New Testament and as a con-
> temporary body of believers that is also open to the future.
> But while the church lives in history, it cannot be seen simply
> in historical terms. There is in addition a theological di-
> mension that grows out of the mystery of God's presence in the
> life of his church and the continuing empowering action of his
> Spirit. We can deal with the church adequately only as we ac-
> knowledge the limitations of the languages of men to express
> the mystery of God's action in history except in symbols and
> images and at the same time recognize the appropriateness of
> quite concrete and even sociological language to describe the

humanness of the church as a community of believing men. The two approaches to the church must be held in constant tension."[157]

This expressed will to keep the two approaches together, the theological and the empirical, is what ultimately stands out as the distinguishing mark of the American venture into ecclesiology. How well their ultimate vision of the Church has succeeded in living up to this ideal is a question which cannot be answered here. Nor is it a question which can ever be adequately answered in the abstract. The COCU Plan is but one step in an ongoing process having a united church as its goal. Only practice can fill the imagined projections of that vision with real life, and only then will it be possible to pass judgment on the degree to which full catholicity can be attained by this approach. A judgment passed now on the basis of prevailing Roman Catholic opinion cannot be the final one. What the Americans saw so clearly was the way in which the outcome of ecumenical dialog is influenced by the degree of ecumenical practice that accompanies it: unity in plurity must be experienced vitally before it can be fully grasped conceptually.

The Roman Catholic Church together with the other catholic-type are being invited today to enter into such experience. Important beginnings have been made, though on the theological level a considerable body of Roman Catholic churchmen and theologians are unprepared to go beyond the comparative methods, whose inadequacy became so evident in the course of Protestant ecumenism. Perhaps some of the ideas worked out in the course of thirty years of American Protestant ecumenical ecclesiology could be of help in overcoming the new impass which threatens the future of Catholic ecumenism. That is the hope in which this study was undertaken.

APPENDIX I

PAPERS OF THE AMERICAN THEOLOGICAL COMMITTEE ON THE CHURCH

The following list has been compiled on the basis of an annotated list found in the files of F.W. Tomkins, supplemented and
modified in the light of Tomkin's annotated minutes of the ATC
meetings. These files are found in the World Council of Churches
Archives in Geneva.

1st Meeting, June 2-3, 1939

no papers presented

2nd Meeting, Oct. 20-21, 1939

no papers presented

3rd Meeting, May 31-June 1, 1940

B.S. Easton, "The Church in the New Testament," 16pp.
C.T. Craig, "The Kingdom of God and the Church," 10pp.
H.J. Cadbury, The Informality of the Early Church, 5pp.
W.M. Horton, "The Kingdom of God and the Church," 13pp.
E.H. Wahlstrom, "The Sense in which the New Testament is Norma-
tive for the Doctrine of the Church, 5pp.
F.S. Mackenzie, "The Sense in which the New Testament is Norma-
tive for the Doctrine of the Church, 6pp.

4th Meeting, Nov. 15-16, 1940

B.H. Branscomb, "By Way of Review," 4pp.
R. Davidson, "Notes on the Doctrine of the Church in the
Old Testament and the New, 8pp.
L.C. Lewis, "The Sense in which the New Testament is Normative
for the Doctrine of the Church, 9pp.
H.F. Rall, "The Concept of the Church as affected by the Under-
lying Theological Viewpoint," 10pp.
F.W. Loetscher, "The Significance of Dissent in the Life of
the Church and for the Doctrine of the Church," 10pp.

5th Meeting, June 5-6, 1941

E.H. Wahlstrom, "To the Question of the Normativeness of the
New Testament," 4pp.
K.S. Latourette, "The Relation of the Church and the Environ-
ment:..." 6pp.
W.O. Carver, "The Importance of a Functional Study of the Church,"
9pp. plus 3pp. Supplement
G.W. Richards, "The Significance of Dissent in the Life of the
Church," 14pp.

6th Meeting, Nov. 21-22, 1941

Special Committee, "Report of the Special Committee on the Work
of the American Theological Committee, 1939-1941"
(written by C.T. Craig as chairman), 10pp.
W.E. Garrison, "Authority in the Early Church," 10pp.

W.W. Slabaugh, "The Concept of the Church held by the Church
of the Brethren"(paper written by Prof. Mallicott),
2pp.
H.J. Cadbury, "The Society of Friends and the Idea of a Chris-
tian Society," 2pp.
L.C. Lewis, "The Protestant Episcopal Church in the United
States of America," 2pp.
D. Horton, "The Distinctive Features of the Congregational
Christian Church," 2pp.
T.G. Tappert, "The Lutheran Doctrine of the Church," 2pp.

7th Meeting, May 21-23, 1942

W.O. Carver, The Doctrine of the Church as held by Baptists
and Disciples," 2pp.
G.W. Richards, "The Nature and Function of the Church according
to the Reformed and Presbyterian Communions in the
United States and Canada...," 11pp.
W.W. Slabaugh, "Is the New Testament Normative for the Doctrine
of the Church," 5pp.
E.T. Clark, "The Conception of the Church as held by the Pentecostal Bodies" (written at the request of the Com-
mittee), 4pp.
W.M. Horton, "Significant Areas of Agreement amid the Diversity
of Historical Christianity," 10pp.
H.F. Rall, "Authority in the Early Church: A summary of discus-
sion and a constructive statement," 8pp.
B.H. Branscomb, "Conservation and Innovation in Christian Begin-
nings," 9pp.
T.S. Boyle, "The Apostles and the Early Church," 8pp.
H.P. Van Dusen, "The Ethical Reality and Function of the Church"
--papers of the Chicago Ecumenical Discussion Group.
W. Horton, et al., "Questionnaire on the Church," 1p.

8th Meeting, Nov. 19-20, 1942

K.S. Latourette, "Divisive and Unifying Tendencies in Revival
Movements with Special Reference to American Chris-
tianity," 9pp.
G.W. Richards, "A Distinctive Conception of the Church in the
Mid-Nineteenth Century," 10pp.
H.F. Rall, "The Methodist Conception of the Church," not printed.
T.G. Tappert, "The Functions of the Church in Relation to its
Members," 6pp.
T.S. Boyle, "A Response to the Questionnaire on the Church,"
  "   "   "The Doctrine of the Church" issued by the General
Synod of the Church of England in Canada, 1942.
L.S. Mudge, "A Response to the Questionnaire on the Church," 4pp.
Faculty of Western Theological Seminary, "A Response to the Ques-
tionnaire on the Church," 3pp.
A.J. Hays, "A Response to the Questionnaire on the Church," 2pp.
J. Haroutunian, "A Response to the Questionnaire on the Church,
2pp.
W.W. Slabaugh, "A Response to the Questionnaire on the Church,"
rev. ed. 2pp.
W.O Carver, "A Response to the Questionnaire on the Church," 6pp.
E.H. Wahlstrom, "A Response to the Questionnaire on the Church,"
4pp.
T.G. Tappert, "A Response to the Questionnaire on the Church,"
2pp.
W.E. Garrison, "A Response to the Questionnaire on the Church,"
4pp.

9th Meeting, July 15-16, 1943

G.W. Richards, "Historical Preface" to the Preliminary Report,
6pp.
C.T. Craig, "Preliminary Report on the Study of the Church,"
written for the sub-committee appointed Nov. 1942,
by its chairman, 16pp.
B.H. Branscomb, "The Relation between the Concepts of continuity, authority, and uniformity, on the one hand,
and innovation, freedom and variety on the other,"
not printed.
H.F. Rall, "Concerning the Concept of Authority," 2pp.
W.C. Robinson, "The Authority of Holy Scripture," not printed.

10th Meeting, Nov. 18-20, 1943

G.W. Richards, "Historical Preface"
C.T. Craig, Revised Draft of the Report on the Study of the
Church, 30pp.
W.O. Carver, "The Baptist Conception of the Church," 6pp.
R. Davidson, "The Reformed Conception of the Church," 3pp.
"   "   "Response to the Questionnaire on the Church,"
W.E. Garrison, "Response to the Questionnaire on the Church
representing the Disciples of Christ," rev. state-
ment, 4pp.
W.M. Horton, "Digest of Answers by Three Congregationalists to
the Questionnaire on the Church," 3pp.
D. Horton, "Response to the Questionnaire on the Church," 1p.
W.M. Horton, "Resoonse to the Questionnaire on the Church," 1p.
M. Spinka, "Response to the Questionnaire on the Church," 1p.
L.C. Lewis, "The Protestant Episcopal Church in the United
States of America," approved and read by R.K.
Yerkes, 5pp.
H.F. Rall, "The Methodist Conception of the Church," 9pp.
B.H. Branscomb, "Response to the Questionnaire on the Church,"
2pp.
A.C. Knudson, "The Methodist View of the Church,"1p.
I.E. Holt, "Response to the Questionnaire on the Church," 3pp.
P. Quillian, "Response to the Questionnaire on the Church," 3pp.
G.T. Rowe, "Response to the Questionnaire on the Church," 2pp.
R.W. Goodloe, "Response to the Questionnaire on the Church," 3pp.
J.T. Carlyon, "Response to the Questionnaire on the Church," 2pp.
W.V. Sweet, "Response to the Questionnaire on the Church," 2pp.
F.W. Loetscher, "The Presbyterian Conception," 7pp.
F. Caldwell , "Response to the Questionnaire on the Church," 2pp.
W.C. Robinson, "Response to the Questionnaire on the Church,"
2pp.
G.W. Richards, "The Church View of the Evangelical and Reformed
Church," 9pp.
Faculty of Eden Theological Seminary, "Response to the Question-
naire on the Church," 3pp.
Theol. Mission House of the E.& R. Church, "Response to the
Questionnaire on the Church," 2pp.
T.F. Herman, "Response to the Questionnaire on the Church," 2pp.
D. Dunn, "Response to the Questionnaire on the Church," 2pp.
I.H. De Long, "In What Sense did Christ Found the Church?" 5pp
O.S. Frantz, "Response to the Questionnaire on the Church," 1p.
N.C. Harner, "Response to the Questionnaire on the Church," 2pp.
L.E. Bair, "Response to the Questionnaire on the Church," 1p.

E. Martin, "A Response to the Questionnaire on the Church, the
Church of God, Andersonville, Ind. (rev. ed.), 3pp.
C.E. Brown, "Response to the Questionnaire on the Church," 1p.

11th Meeting, July 27-28, 1944

L.C. Lewis, "The Anglican Conception of the Church," 8pp.
W.D. Barclay, "Christina Unity and Church Unity," not printed.
W.O. Carver, "The Church Extension of the Incarnation," 13pp.
W.C. Robinson, "Ecumenicity," 21pp.

12th Meeting, Dec. 9-11, 1944

H.J. Cadbury, "A Quaker View of the Church," 6pp.
F.W. Tomkins, "The Nature of the Church's Continuity," 5pp.
F.W. Loetscher, "The Status of Children in the Church prior to
their Personal Confession of Faith, according to
the Presbyterian Church in the U.S.A., 2pp.
T.G. Tappert, "The Status of Children in the Church prior to
their Personal Confession of Faith," 2pp.
R.K. Yerkes, "The Attitude of the Episcopal Church to Children,"
3pp.
B.H. Branscomb, "What is the Status in the Methodist Church of
Baptized Children not yet ready for Admission," 1p.
K.S. Latourette, "The Status in Baptist Churches of Children
prior to their Personal Confession of Faith," 1p.
C.T. Craig, "The Church and the Sphere of Salvation," 9pp.
E.H. Wahlstrom, "The Lutheran Statement," 7pp.

13th Meeting, June 28-29, 1945

G.W. Richards, "Is Church Union Possible and Desirable?" 10pp.
K.S. Latourette, "What Kind of Church Union is Desirable?" 7pp.
C.T. Craig, "The Christological Foundation of the World Council
of Churches," 12pp.
W.M. Horton, "The Nature of the Church's Continuity,"
W.O. Carver, "The Nature of the Distinction between Clergy and
Laity," 8pp.
L.C. Lewis, "What is meant by 'divinely authorized'?" 5pp.
T.S. Boyle, "Unifying and Divisive Elements in Christian Worship,"
8pp.

14th Meeting, June 27-28, 1946

C.T. Craig, Review of "Church, Continuity and Unity" by H. Burn-
Murdoch, 5pp.
L.C. Lewis, "Notes on Dr. Craig's Review of Burn-Murdoch's
'Church, Continuity and Unity'," 4pp.
E.H. Wahlstrom, "What is meant by 'divinely authorized'?" 9pp.
W.E. Garrison, "Creeds and Unity," 10pp.
W.C. Robinson, "Unitive and Divisive Elements in Christian Wor-
ship," 7pp.
G.C. Pidgeon, "The Christological Basis of the World Council
of Churches," 12pp.

15th Meeting, Jan. 30-31, 1947

G.W. Richards, "Shall We Continue our Emphasis on Orthodoxy and
Conformity rather than on Purposes and Objectives?"
9pp.
T.G. Tappert, "The Function of Creeds and Confessions in the
Church," 7pp.

W.W. Slabaugh, "The Nature of the Church's Continuity," 5pp.
H.F. Rall, "The Doctrine of Salvation in Ecumenical Thought".

16th Meeting, Oct. 9-11, 1947

N. Flew "Report on Plans for the Theological Committee on the
              Church," not printed.
W.O. Carver, Report on Meeting of World Baptist Alliance, n.p.
W.E. Garrison, "   "   "   " World Conv. of Disciples, "
Rall & Craig, "   "   "   " Ecum. Methodist Conf.," "
Wahlstrom,   "   "   "   " Lutheran World Federation, "
E. Hardy, "Attitudes of the Orthodox Bodies toward the WCC," "
C.T. Craig, "Foreign Monographs on the Church".
E.H. Wahlstrom, Review of "A Book about the Church by Swedish
              Theologians".
W.D. Barclay, "The Distinction between Clergy and Laity".
W.O. Carver, "The Nature of the Distinction between Clergy and
              Laity," [same paper as at the June, 1945 meeting].

17th Meeting, Oct. 20-22, 1949

W.E. Garrison, "A Comparison between the Report of Section I
              at Amsterdam on 'The Universal Church in God's
              Design,' and the American Theological Committee's
              Report on 'The Nature of the Church," not printed.
W.O. Carver, "The Attitude of the Southern Baptists to the World
              Council of Churches and the Ecumenical Movement,"
              not printed.
W.M. Horton, "A Comparison between the Conferences in Edinburgh
              and Amsterdam".

Special Meeting of the American Theological Committee, April 13-14, 1951

G.W. Kelsey, "The Effect of Racial Patterns on American Church
              Life," 8pp.
G. Cragg, "Disunities Created by Differing Patterns of Church
              Life," 5pp.
W.D. Barclay, "A Study in Self Examination," 5pp.
A.O. Miller, "Approach toward Ecumenicity in Christian Theology,"
              6pp.
W.E. Garrison, "The Effects of New Community on Frontier Situa-
              tions," 6pp.
K.S. Latourette, "Factors in the American Situation which make
              the Desire for Unity urgent and the Search for
              Unity difficult," 4pp.
W.E. Garrison, "Two Turning Points in Church History," 6pp.
T.G. Tappert, "A Brief Bibliograohy which may contribute to the
              Illumination of Non-theological Factors in the
              Making of Church Union in North America," 1p.

APPENDIX II

INTERSEMINARY STUDY COMMITTEES

I.A. "The Challenge of our Culture"

James Luther Adams	Walter M. Horton
Elmer J.F. Arndt	James H. Nichols
John K. Benton	Victor Obenhaus
Conrad Bergendoff	Wilhelm Pauck
Clarence T. Craig, chm.	Roland W. Schloerb
Buell G. Gallagher	Edmund D. Soper
H.C. Goerner	Ernest F. Tittle
Georgia Harkness	Amos N. Wilder
Joseph Haroutunian	Daniel D. Williams

I.B. "The Church and Organized Movements"

James C. Baker	Morgan Odell
Eugene Blake	Pierson Parker
Karl Morgan Block	Clarence Reidenbach
John Wick Bowman	John Skoglund
Elliot Van N. Diller	Dwight Smith
Galen Fisher	Frederic Spiegelberg
Robert M. Fitch	Everett Thomson
Buell G. Gallagher	Elton Trueblood
Cyril Cloyn	Aaron Ungersma
George Hedley	Hugh Vernon White
John Krumm	Lynn T. White
Randolf Crump Miller, chm.	George Williams

II. "The Gospel, the Church and the World"

Earl Ballou	William Stuart Nelson
John C. Bennett	H. Richard Niebuhr
Nels F.S. Ferré	Justin Nixon
Joseph Fletcher	Norman Pittenger
Herbert Gezourk	James McD. Richards
Robert R. Hardy, Jr.	Luman J. Shafer
Elmer Homrigshausen	Paul Scherer
Stanley Hopper	Wyatt A. Smart
John Knox	George F. Thomas
Kenneth S. Latourette,chm.	Frank Wilson
Benjamin Mays	

III. "Toward World-wide Christianity"

Edwin R. Aubrey	Henry Smith Leiper
Roswell P. Barnes	John A. Mackay
John C. Bennett	Elmore N. KcKee
Arlo A. Brown	O. Frederick Nolde, chm.
E. Fay Campbell	Lawrence Ross
J.W. Decker	Stanley Rycroft
H. Paul Douglass	Matthew Spinka
Charles Iglehart	A.L. Warnhuis
E.F. Johnson	A.R. Wentz
Charles T. Leber	Alexander C. Zabriskie

APPENDIX III

COCU STUDY COMMISSIONS

1963 Commissions (DIGEST, I-II, p.43)

1. "Scripture, Tradition and the Guardians of Tradition"
   Elmer F.J. Arndt, chm.   Floyd V. Filson
   Richard S. Emerich   Harold Heininger
   Gerald Ensley   Ronald E. Osborn

2. "Analysis of the Participating Communions"
   George Beazley   Alden D. Kelley, chm.
   Truman B. Douglass   Edwin Kimbrough
   L.L. Huffman   Kenneth G. Neigh

3. "The Worship and Witness of the Church"
   Matthew W. Clair, Jr.   Charles K. Dean
   Gerhard W. Grauer   Paul Washburn
   William J. Jarman, chm.   James M. Tunnell

1964 Commissions (DIGEST, III, p. 143)

1. "One Ministry"
   George G. Beazley, alt.   Floyd V. Filson
   John Booty, alt.   Ronald E. Osborn
   David G. Colwell   Paul A. Washburn, chm.
   Powell M. Dawley

2. "One Baptism"
   Richard S. Emrich   William J. Jarman
   Jolly B. Harper   K. James Stein, alt.
   Roger Hazelton   Cary N. Weisiger, III, chm.
   J. Gordon Howard

3. "One Table"
   Elmer J. Arndt, chm.   Dale Fiers
   Francis Burrill   Reginald Fuller, alt.
   Wayne K. Clymen   Janet Harbison
   Gerald Ensley   Harold Heininger

1965 Commissions (DIGEST, V, p.284)

1. "The Ordained Ministry in a United Church"
   Richard S Emrich   Paul Stauffer
   E. Harris Harbison   Paul Washburn
   Roger Hazelton, chm.   John Park Winkler
   Robert Huston

2. "Ordination in a Church Catholic, Evangelical and Reformed"
   Truman B. Douglass   Albert C. Outler, chm.
   William J Jarman   W. Maynard Sparks
   Albert T. Mollegen   Cary N. Weisiger, III

1966 Commission to draw up a Plan of Union (DIGEST, V, p.25)
   Stephan F. Bayne   Paul S. Minear
   George G. Beazley, Jr.   Richard Hildebrand
   Eugene Carson Blake, chm. Paul Washburn
   F. Gerald Ensley

<u>1967</u> "Commission on Structure" (DIGEST, VI, p.83)

Elmer J.F. Arndt, chm.
Stephen F. Bayne, Jr.
George G. Beazley
Truman B. Douglass
A. Dale Fiers
C.R. Findley
Rachel Henderlite
Richard Hildebrand
Robert Huston

Frederick D. Jordan
R.L. Jones
James K. Matthews
Eugene E. Morgan
Kenneth Neigh
T. Watson Street
William P. Thompson
Paul A. Washburn
William J. Wolf

Alternates

John Butler
Priscilla Chaplin
Robert F. Gibson, Jr.
J.A. Ross Mackenzie

J. Robert Nelson
J.L. Pierson
William C. Schram
George Shipman

Participating Observers and Consultants

Yoshio Fukuyama
Herman Harmelink, III

David W. Jenks
Colin Williams

<u>1968</u> Commissions (DIGEST, VII, pp.55, 72, 77, & 83)

1. Commission on "Unification of Members

G. Wayman Blakely
E. Waren Brice
C.R. Findley
James O. Gilliom
E. Harris Harbison
Rachel Henderlite

George L. Hunt, secy.
William J. Jarman, chm.
J. Robert Nelson
Isiah Scipio
William J. Wolf

2. Commission on "The Unification of Ministries"

Bertram W. Doyle
Roger Hazelton
George L. Hunt, secy.
Frederick D. Jordan
John R. Knecht
James I. McCord, chm.

Albert T. Mollegen
Ronald Osborn
Albert Outler
H.B. Shaw
T. Watson Street

3. Commission on "Provisional Structure of the United Church"

Elmer J.F. Arndt
Stephen F. Bayne, Jr.
William A. Benfield, Jr.,alt.
A. Dale Fiers
Richard Hildebrand
Raymond V. Kearns, secy.
James A. Millard, Jr.

John H. Sallerwhite
George Shipman
B. Julian Smith
Norman L. Trott
James M. Tunnell, Jr., chm.
W.J. Walls
Paul Washburn

4. Commission on "Response to Principles"

Helen Baker
Peter Day
Richard Hildebrand
J.C. Hoggard
Robert W. Huston

Raymond V. Kearns, Jr., chm.
J.A. Ross Mackenzie
E.P. Murchison
Paul S. Stauffer
Paul Washburn

<u>1969</u> Commission for the "Plan of Union" (DIGEST, VIII, p. 44-45)

William A. Benfield, Jr.,chm.
George G. Beazley, Jr.
G. Wayman Blakely
Richard W. Cain
James O. Gilliom

E.P. Murchison
John H. Sallerwhite
William P. Thompson
Paul Washburn
William J. Wolf

Alternates

E. Warner Brice
Bertram W. Doyle
Robert W. Huston
William J. Jarman
Joseph A. Johnson

Raymond V. Kearns, Jr.
James I. McCord
Cecil Murray
Lawrence I. Stell

APPENDIX IV

NORTH AMERICAN WORKING GROUP OF THE DEPARTMENT OF STUDIES
"MISSIONARY STRUCTURE OF THE CONGREGATION"

1962 Membership [Concept (blue), 1 (Sept.1962), 16-17]

J.C. Michael Allen	L.D. Johnson
Leila Anderson	Walter Kloetzli
Francis Ayres	John R. Lee
Donald Benedict	Eoin S. Mackay
Peter Berger	Martin E. Marty
Lawrence Burkholder	Carl Michaelson
Stanrod Carmichael	Howard Moody
Paul Chapman	Jitsuo Morikawa, chm.
William A. Clebsch	Robert Raines
Arnold B. Come	Letty Russell
John H. Cooley	Robert W. Spike
Rufus Cornelsen	C.J. Stewart
Gordon Cosby	Bruce Weaver
Harvey Cox	George W. Webber
A.E. Dimmock	Charles West
Gabriel Fackre	Gibson Winter
Archie Hargraves	Andrew J Young
Ralph M. Holdeman	Thomas Weiser, secy.
Ruel Howe	Jesse H. Ziegler
Elisabeth Johns	

1962 Additions [Concept (blue), 2 (July, 1963), 32-33]

Evelyn L. Green	Gerald M. Hutchinson
William H. Hollister	Theodore O. Wedel

1964 Additions [Concept (blue), 5 (1964), 19-20]

James Alter	Reynold W. Johnson
Edgar J. Bailey	Tracey K. Jones
Roswell P. Barnes	Gerald Jud
Markus Barth	Francis Maeda
James S. Clarke	M.C. Patterson
Robert C. Dodds	A.M. Pennypacker
Hans Frei	Jon L. Regier
Walter Harrelson	Lee C. Silver
W.T. Holland	Walter Sikes
J. Ray Hord	Arthur Thomas
Leslie Hunt	Colin Williams

FOOTNOTES TO CHAPTER I

[1] As late as 1932, Harry Emerson Fosdick, one of the most influential spokesmen for theological liberalism and the Social Gospel, could speak of the Church only in such negative terms [See his As I see Religion (New York: Harper, 1932); chapter I, "What is Religion" reprinted in Contemporary Religious Thought: An Anthology (New York: Abingdon-Cokesbury, 1949, p. 19)]. An extreme, but not untypical expression of this attitude is found in John Dewey's A Common Faith: the Terry Lectures (New Haven: Yale Univ. Press, 1934) which sharply rejects any form of ecclesiastical institutionalization of religion. Needless to say, there were exceptions to this attitude. The "Fathers" of liberal and Social Gospel theology, men like Charles A. Briggs, William Adams Brown, and Walter Rauschenbusch, show a deep theological interest in the Church despite their criticism of some of its particular manifestations. Indeed a detailed historical study of ecclesiology in America during the liberal period would reveal a much stronger interest in and serious reflection on the Church than contemporary witnesses themselves perceived.

[2] The decisive contribution to that opinion was the work of Burnett H. Streeter, The Primitive Church studied with special reference to the origins of the Christian ministry (New York: Macmillan, 1929).

[3] This was the dominant motivation of the Federal Council of Churches movement. See the works of its first President and chronicler, Charles S. Macfarland, esp. his Christian Unity in the Making; the first twenty-five years of the Federal Council of Churches of Christ in America, 1905-1930 (New York: FCC, 1948).

[4] See Walter M. Horton, "Systematic Theology: Liberalism chastened by tragedy," in Protestant Thought in the Twentieth Century, ed. A. S. Nash (New York: Macmillan, 1951), pp. 114-5. For a contemporary witness, see William Adams Brown, The Church Catholic and Protestant (New York: Chas. Scribner's Sons, 1935), pp. x and 4.

[5] The coupling of a rediscovery of the reality of sin and the rediscovery of the importance of the Church is to be found in almost every contribution to the series "How My Mind has Changed in this Decade," The Christian Century, 56 (1939).

[6] Characteristic of this trend is the provocative work of H. Richard Niebuhr, William Pauck and Francis P. Miller, The Church against the World (Chicago--New York: Willett, Clark, 1935).

[7] See John A. Mackay, "The Adequacy of the Church Today," in Corpus unum: Report of the North American Ecumenical Conference, Toronto, 3-5 June, 1941 (Toronto: n. publ., 1941), pp. 30-1. Dr. Mackay was the creator of the phrase "Let the Church be the Church," which became the slogan of the Oxford meeting. On the background of the rediscovery of the Church in the ecumenical movement, see Ruth Rouse and Stephen Neill, A History of the Ecumenical Movement, 1517-1948, 2nd ed. (Philadelphia: Westminster, 1967), pp. 574-7.

[8] The North American commission issued its report in five separate volumes:
1. The Meanings of Unity, report no. 1 prepared by the Commission on the Church's Unity in Life and Worship: Commission IV for the

World Conference on Faith and Order, Edinburgh, 1937, ...drafted
for the Commission by Angus Dun (Faith and Order Papers, O.S.
No. 82; New York--London: Harper & Bros., 1937).
2. The Communion of Saints, report no. 2 ...drafted by Gaius Jackson Slosser (F. & O. Papers, O.S. No. 83; ...);
3. The Non-Theological Factors in the Making and Unmaking of Church
Union, report no. 3 ...drafted by William L. Sperry (F. & O. Papers, O.S. No. 84; ...);
4. A Decade of Objective Progress in Church Unity 1927-1936, report
no. 4 ...drafted by H. Paul Douglass (New York--London: Harper
& Bros., 1937).
5. Next Steps on the Road to a United Church, report no. 5 ...
drafted by William Adams Brown (F. & O. Papers, O.S. No. 85; ...).
For the purposes of the present study, these reports will be cited
as MEANINGS, COMMUNION, NON-THEOL., DECADE, NEXT STEPS, respectively.

[9]The report of the American Theological Committee is entitled: The
Nature of the Church: A report of the American Theological Commit-
tee of the Continuation Committee, World Conference on Faith and
Order, George W. Richards, Chairman, and Frederick W. Loetscher,
Secretary, (Chicago--New York: Willett, Clark, 1945).[Hereafter
cited NATURE.]

[10]No final report of the Chicago Group was ever drawn up or published,
two of its working papers, however, were published in mimeographed
form and circulated by the Life and Work study department secretar-
iat in Geneva. They are:
1. The Ethical Reality and Function of the Church, A Memorandum by
the Chicago Ecumenical Discussion Group, Study Department of the
Universal Christian Council for Life and Work, No. 3 E/41 (Geneva, May, 1941), 17pp. mimeo. (Hereafter cited as ETHICAL.)
2. Preaching as an Expression of the Ethical Reality of the Church,
a Memorandum of ... No. 13 E/42 (Geneva, Oct., 1942), 18pp.
mimeo. (Hereafter cited as PREACHING.)

[11]The Interseminary Series, 5 vols. (New York--London: Harper & Bros.,
1946-7)
I. The Challenge of our Culture, ed. Clarence T. Craig;
II. The Church and Organized Movements, ed. Randolph C. Miller;
III. The Gospel, the Church and the World, ed. Kenneth S. Latour-
ette;
IV. Toward World-Wide Christianity, ed. O. Frederick Nolde;
V. What Must the Church Do?, by Robert S. Bilheimer.
(Hereafter cited as INTERSEMINARY I, II, III, IV, V, respectively.)

[12]The Biblical Doctrine of Man in Society, by G. Ernest Wright and an
Ecumenical Committee in Chicago ("Ecumenical Biblical Studies," 2;
London: SCM, 1954). (Hereafter cited as MAN.)

[13]The publications of the study are:
1. The Purpose of the Church and its Ministry, by H. Richard
Niebuhr in collaboration with Daniel D. Williams and James M.
Gustafson (New York: Harper & Bros., 1956) (Hereafter cited as
PURPOSE);
2. The Ministry in Historical Perspective, ed. by H. Richard
Niebuhr and Daniel D. Williams (New York: Harper & Brow., 1956);
3. The Advancement of Theological Education, by H. Richard Niebuhr

and Daniel D. Williams (New York: Harper & Bros., 1957).

[14] The Nature of the Unity We Seek: Official Report of the North American Conference on Faith and Order, Sept. 3-10, 1957, Oberlin, Ohio, ed. by Paul S. Minear (St. Louis: Bethany, 1958). (Hereafter cited as OBERLIN.)

[15] The four North American reports are contained in:
1. Report of the Theological Commission on Christ and the Church (F. & O. Papers, N.S. No. 38; Geneva: WCC Commission on Faith and Order, 1963);
2. Report of the Theological Commission on Tradition and Traditions (F. & O. Papers, N.S. No. 40; ...
3. Report of the Theological Commission on Worship (F. & O. Papers, N.S. No. 39; ...
4. The Report of the Study Commission on Institutionalism (F. & O. Papers, N.S. No. 37; ...
All four booklets, separately paged, were published also in a one volume edition under the title Faith and Order Findings (New York: Harper, 1963). The individual booklets are cited here as CHRIST, TRADITION, WORSHIP, and INSTIT., respectively.

[16] Eugene Carson Blake, "A Proposal toward the Reunion of Christ's Church," A sermon preached at Grace Episcopal Cathedral, San Francisco, on Sunday, Dec. 4, 1960, in Christian Century, 77, 51 (Dec. 21, 1960), 1508 - 1511b.

[17] The acts of the Consultation on Church Union have been published yearly beginning in 1963 in the Digest of the Proceedings ...(Fanwood, later Princeton, N.J.: COCU, 1963ff) [hereafter cited as DIGEST with the volume no.]. In addition its official statements have been reproduced in a series of small books commonly designated by their jacket covers
1. COCU, The official Reports of the Four Meetings of the Consultation--Red Book (Cincinnati: Forward Movement, 1966);
2. Principles of Church Union, adopted by the Consultation at its meeting 1966--Blue Book (Cincinnati: Forward Movement, 1966);
3. Consultation on Church Union, Principles of Church Union: Guidelines for Structure: A Study Guide--Green Book (Cincinnati: Forward Movement, 1967).
[Hereafter cited as COCU red, blue, or green, respectively.]
In 1970 the Consultation published the proposed Plan of Union for the Church of Christ Uniting, commended to the Churches for study and response by the Consultation on Church Union, March 9-13, 1970, at St. Louis, Mo. (Princeton: COCU, 1970) [hereafter cited as PLAN].

[18] The report of the North American Working Group entitled "The Church for the World," was published together with that of the Western European group in the book The Church for Others and the Church for the World: A Quest for structures for missionary congregations... (Geneva: WCC, 1968), pp. 55-133 [hereafter cited as MISSIONARY].

[19] Because this epoch is so near to the present, a detailed history of American theology between the Social and the Secular Gospels has yet to be written. The following works however help to communicate at least a general impression of the moods and tendencies. Unfortunately their treatment of ecclesiology is generally very brief and most generic:

Charles S. Macfarland, Current Religious Thought (New York: Revell, 1941).

Paul S. Minear, "Wanted a Biblical Theology," Theology Today, 1, 1 (April 1944), 47-58.

John C. Bennett, "American Churches in the Ecumenical Situation," Ecumenical Review, 1, 1 (Autumn, 1948) 57-64.

Carl F. Henry, Fifty Years of Protestant Theology (Boston: Wilde, 1950).

Protestant Thought in the Twentieth Century, ed. A. S. Nash (New York: Macmillan, 1951).

David W. Soper, Major Voices in American Theology, 2 vols. (Philadelphia: Westminster, 1952-5).

Otto W. Heich, Amerikanische Theologie in Geschichte und Gegenwart (Breklun: Jensen, 1954).

L[otan] Harold De Wolf, Trends and Frontiers of Religious Thought (Nashville: Nat. Meth. Stud. Movement, 1955).

James R. Branton, Millar Burrows, James D. Smart, Robert McAfee Brown, "Our Present Situation in Biblical Theology," Religion in Life, 26, 1 (Winter, 1956-7), 5-39.

Wilhelm Pauck, "Theology in the Life of Contemporary American Protestantism," in Religion and Culture: Essays in honor of Paul Tillich, ed. by W. Leibrecht (New York: Harper, 1959), 270-83.

Daniel D. Williams, What Present Day Theologians are Thinking, rev. ed. (New York: Harper, 1959).

Roger Hazelton, New Accents in Contemporary Theology (New York: Harper & Row, 1960).

Sidney E. Ahlstrom, "Theology in America: A Historical Survey," in Religion in American Life, Vol. I: The Shaping of American Religion, ed. J. W. Smith and A. L. Jamison (Princeton: University Press, 1961), pp. 232-321.

Nels F. S. Ferré, Searchlights on Contemporary Theology (New York: Harper & Row, 1961).

Robert T. Handy, "The American Scene," in Twentieth Century Christianity, ed. St. Neill, rev. ed. (Garden City: Doubleday, 1963), pp. 179-216.

Walter M. Horton, "The Development of Theological Thought," in Twentieth Century Christianity ..., pp. 253-84.

William Hordern, Introduction, Vol. I of New Directions in Theology, ed. W. Hordern (Philadelphia: Westminster, 1966).

Lloyd J. Averell, American Theology in the Liberal Tradition (Philadelphia: Westminster, 1967).

John C. Cooper, The Roots of the Radical Theology (Philadelphia: Westminster, 1967).

Martin E. Marty, "Introduction [American Protestant Theology Today]," in Frontline Theology, ed. D. Pearman (London: SCM, 1967), pp. 13-28.

Fritz Buri, Gott in Amerika: amerikanische Theologie seit 1960 (Bern: P. Haupt, Tübingen: Katzmann, 1970).

[20] See Walter M. Horton, "Systematic Theology," in Protestant Thought in the Twentieth Century, ed. cit., pp. 114-9; also George Hammar, Christian Realism in Contemporary American Theology: A Study of Reinhold Niebuhr, W. M. Horton, and H. P. Van Dusen (Uppsala: Lundqvist/New York: Stechert, 1940).

[21] See William Hordern, The Case for the New Reformation Theology (Philadelphia: Westminster, 1959).

[22] See the symposium by James R. Branton et al. cited in note 19; also Connoly Gamble, Jr., "The Literature of Biblical Theology: A bibliographical study," _Interpretation_, 7 (1953), 466-80.

[23] One of the first major statements of this position was the 1947 Reuschenbusch lectures by Daniel Day Williams, _God's Grace and Man's Hope_ (New York: Harper, 1949), in which Williams sharply criticizes the existentialist-individualism of much neo-orthodox ecclesiology.

[24] Tillich articulated his method of correlation in his _Systematic Theology_ (Chicago: Univ. of Chicago Press, 1951), I: 59-67.

[25] Carl Henry's lectures "Dare We revive the Modernist--Fundamentalist Controversy," published in the first volume of the new conservative biweekly he edited, _Christianity Today_, 1, 18 (June 10, 1957), 3-6 & 25; 19 (June 24) 23-26; 20 (July 8) 15-18; 21 (July 22) 23-6 & 38, announced the new conservative program, with a sharp critique of earlier fundamentalist neglect of ecclesiology.

[26] Edward J. Carnell was perhaps the most important systematic theologian of the evangelical movement in the fifties. His untimely death in 1967 prevented him from ever developing a systematic conservative ecclesiology out of the rich material scattered throughout his writings. Carnell's _The Case for Orthodox Theology_ (Philadelphia: Westminster, 1959) represents a classic statement of the conservative position.

[27] Two series of articles published in conjunction with the Oberlin Conference give a cross-section of evangelical ecclesiology: (1) the scholarly series "The Nature of the Unity We Seek," with articles by Edward J. Carnell (Bapt.), Theron D. Price (So. Bapt.), Martin H. Franzmann (Mo. Synod Luth.), and John Yoder (Menn.), published in _Religion in Life_, 26, 2 (1957), 191-222; and (2) the more popular series "The Body Christ Heads," with articles by Richard C. Halverson (Presby. Ch. U.S.A.), William Boyd Hunt (So. Bapt.), J. Theodore Mueller (Mo. Synod Luth.), Harold J. Ockenga (Congr.), W. Stanford Ried (Ch. of Canada), Samuel M. Shoemaker (Prot. Ep. Ch.), which appeared in _Christianity Today_ 1, 22 (Aug. 19, 1957), 3-13. Conservative evangelical theologians were also consulted in the preparations for the 1963 Faith and Order Conference in Montreal, but their contributions have never been published.

[28] Of very high quality and interest is the Southern Baptist symposium on the Church published in the late fifties: _What is the Church_, ed. Duke McCall (Nashville: Broadmann, 1958).

[29] One of the main reasons for the neglect of ecclesiology among fundamentalists is the strong influence of Dispensationalism--the notion propagated by the Plymouth Brethren movement in the 19th century, that the churches and their ministries have all fallen hopelessly into apostasy; human reform and renewal efforts, even when biblicistically inspired, are of no avail; all the congregation of true believers can do is to separate itself as far as possible from the apostate churches and await the millenium. This teaching had profound influence in the conservative wings of such major denominations as the Lutheran Missouri Synod, the Presbyterians, the Southern Baptists. See Ernst R. Sandeen, "Toward a historical interpretation of the origins of Fundamentalism," _Church_

History, 36 (1967), 66-83; also C. Norman Krauss, Dispensationalism in America (Richmond: John Knox, 1958).

[30] Harry Nelson Wiemann's The Source of Human Good (Chicago: Univ. of Chicago Pr., 1946) gave the first explicit articulation of the neo-naturalist position. A valuable survey of the development of naturalist religious philosophy in America, taking note of its ecclesiology, is offered by George F. Thomas' article "The Philosophy of Religion," in Protestant Thought in the Twentieth Century, ed. cit., pp. 71-101.

[31] See William Horden, Introduction, 23-54.

[32] Will Herberg's analysis Protestant, Catholic, Jew: An essay in American religious sociology (Garden City: Doubleday, 1956) initiated this critique. Among the most important works which appeared before 1962 are:

A. Roy Eckhardt, The Surge of Piety in America: An Appraisal (New York: Association, 1958).

Gabriel and Dorothy Fackre, Under the Steeple (Nashville: Abingdon, 1958).

Martin Marty, The New Shape of American Religion (New York: Harper, 1959).

Peter L. Berger, The Noise of Solemn Assemblies (Garden City: Doubleday, 1961).

James M. Gustafson, Treasure in Earthen Vessels: The Church as a human community (New York: Harper, 1961).

Gibson Winter, The Suburban Captivity of the Churches (Garden City: Doubleday, 1961).

David O. Moberg, The Church as a Social Institution (Englewood Cliffs: Prentice Hall, 1962).

Gayraud Wilmore, The Secular Relevance of the Church (Philadelphia: Westminster, 1962).

One of the first critiques of the Church-centered theology of the previous decades was Henry P. Van Dusen's The Vindication of the Liberal Theology: A Tract for the Times (New York: Scribners, 1963), pp. 123ff. The years 1963-9 saw a flood of literature criticizing the American church-establishment and the ecclesiology that supported it.

[33] A pioneering study of the influence of the freedom movement on the American churches and their ecclesiology is the book by Robert W. Spike, The Freedom Revolution and the Churches (New York: Association, 1965).

[34] The "New Theology" collection edited by Martin Marty and Dean Pearman (New York: Macmillan, 1964) is a convenient documentation of this development. See Colin W. Williams, The Church, Vol. IV of New Directions in Theology Today (Philadelphia: Westminster, 1968), pp. 1-26, for an interpretation of this world-wide phenomenon.

[35] Robert Bilheimer writes: "Most of the leading thinkers in the churches are not identifiable first by their denominational affiliation, and in part this is due to the interchange of opinion and fellowship which is constantly in process through informal meetings as well as through individual contact. The prevalence of inter-denominational worship, and the use by persons of one church of worship booklets issued by another church are powerful contributors to

this informal but real unity. Increasingly the development of theology and the vitality of worship cross denominaticnal lines"
(INTERSEMINARY V, pp. 82-3).

[36] See the standard histories and historical studies of the American
Church by Jerald C. Brauer, William A. Clebsch, Winfred E. Garrison,
Robert T. Handy, Winthrop S. Hudson, Franklin H. Littell, Sidney E.
Mead, H. Richard Niebuhr, J. Willard Sperry, William W. Sweet, as
well as the histories of the individual denominations and traditions. The four volumes of collected studies, Religion in American
Life, ed. J. W. Smith and A. L. Jamison (Princeton Studies in American Civilization; Princeton: Univ. Press, 1961), offers a convenient orientation.

[37] H. Richard Niebuhr, The Social Sources of Denominationalism (New
York: H. Holt, 1929), seems to have been the first to recognize the
distinctiveness of the American denomination from the Troeltschian
categories. Subsequently the notion has been corrected and refined
by religious sociology. A valuable recent discussion of the problem can be found in Brian Wilson's Religion in Secular Society: A
sociological comment (London: C. A. Watts, 1966), paperback ed.
(Harmsworth, Middlesex/Baltimore, Md.: Penguin, 1969), pp. 227-49.
Milton Yinger, The Scientific Study of Religion (New York: Macmillan,
1970), pp. 251-81 develops a much more complex three dimensional
classification scheme; likewise Günther Kehrer, Religionssoziologie,
(Sammlung "Göschen," 1228; Berlin: W. De Gruyter, 1968), 58-68. For
our purposes here, however, the generic notion of denomination suf-
fices.

[38] See Yinger, op. cit., pp. 260-1.

[39] A classic study of this phenomenon is Paul M. Harrison's Authority
and Power in the Free Church Tradition (Princeton: Univ. Press,
1959).

[40] See Sidney Mead, "Denominationalism, the Shape of Protestantism in
America," Church History, 23 (1954), 291-330.

[41] Among the numerous good histories of ecumenical cooperation in
America, the works of Samuel McCrea Cavert, H. Paul Douglass,
Robert T. Handy, Robert Lee, Charles S. Macfarland, and Ross W.
Sanderson, deserve special mention.

[42] See J[ohn] Webster Grant, The Canadian Experience of Church Union
(Ecumenical Studies in History 8; London: Lutterworth, 1967).

[43] See Douglas Horton, The United Church of Christ, Its origins, organization and role in the world today (New York: Nelson, 1962).

[44] This theme has been studied by both church and secular historians.
Especially valuable is H. Richard Niebuhr's The Kingdom of God in
America (Chicago--New York: Willett, Clark, 1937) and Robert T.
Handy, A Christian America: Protestant Hopes and historical reali-
ties (New York: Oxford Univ. Press, 1971).

[45] Sidney E. Mead, "The Nation with the Soul of a Church," Church
History, 36 (1967), 262-83.

[1] Already in 1933, an attempt had been made to constitute an "American Committee of Theologians" to study the nature of the Church, with William Adams Brown, Frank Gavin, Wesley Soper, and Willard Sperry as initial members. Due to financial difficulties, however, nothing came of the project (See F. W. Tomkins, "Chronological Checklist of Commissions and Committees," typewritten memo, May, 1960, p. 9a [Archives of the WCC, Geneva]. On the foundation of the American Edinburgh commission see The 1934 Meeting of the Continuation Committee held at Hertenstein... Sept. 3-6 (F. & O. Papers, O.S. No. 71; Winchester--New York: The Committee, 1934), pp. 11-2, also William Adams Brown, Toward a United Church (New York: Scribner's, 1946), p. 112.

[2] MEANINGS, p. v. European members of the commission were Hamilcar S. Alivisatos, Charles Merle d'Aubigné, Albert S. Monahan, Otto Piper, Friedrick Siegmund-Schultze. (ibid., p. vi).

[3] Angus Dun, "Report of the Commission on the Empirical Approach to Unity," March 12-3, 1935, mimeographed minutes, pp. 1-2 [WCC Archives, Geneva]. (Hereafter referred to as Dun, MINUTES.)

[4] The lists of these can be found in the introductory sections of each of the published volumes.

[5] See MEANINGS, p. vi.

[6] Dun, MINUTES, p. 3, note 2.

[7] MEANINGS, p. viii.

[8] COMMUNION, p. vii.

[9] NON-THEOL., p. vii.

[10] Douglass conducted the survey alone. The sources from which he obtained his information are listed in DECADE, p. xiii.

[11] A brief sketch of some developments of this sort is found in DECADE, pp. xvi-xx.

[12] NEXT STEPS, p. 2.

[13] The most important published sources for the origins of the American Theological Committee are: The 1938 Meeting of the Continuation Committee held at Clarens, Switzerland, Aug. 29-Sept. 1 (F. & O. Papers, O.S. No. 91; Oxford--New York: Continuation Committee, 1938) esp. p. 37 and The 1939 Meeting of the Continuation Committee, held at Clarens, Switzerland, Aug. 21-3, 1939 (F. & O. Papers, O.S. No. 92; Oxford--New York: Continuation Committee, 1939), pp. 23-9. Its progress up to 1943 is summarized in George W. Richards' "Historical Statement" in NATURE, pp. 115-22. A complete set of the minutes of the Committee meetings as well as an almost complete set of its working papers is to be found in the WCC Archives in Geneva.

[14] See G. W. Richards' report to the 1939 Continuation Committee Meeting (loc. cit.), pp. 26-7, concerning the criteria of selection.

[15] NATURE, pp. 117-8.

[16] C. H. Dodd's letter to the World Council's Commission on Faith and Order published under the title "Unavowed Motives in Ecumenical Discussions," in Ecumenical Review, II (1949-50), 52-6.

[17] The session was held on April 13-4 at Drew University. A series of individual papers on the topic--particular attention being given to the peculiarities of the American experience--were discussed and then forwarded after revision to the International Conference held at Bossey, Switzerland, Nov. 6-12, 1951. The report of this meeting appeared under the title "Non-theological Factors that may hinder or accelerate the Church's Unity," in Ecumenical Review, IV (1951-2), 174-80.

[18] See Richards' "Historical Statement" in NATURE, pp. 113-22.

[19] Ibid., p. 119.

[20] Ibid., p. 122; for details see "Report of the Special Committee on the Work of the American Theological Committee, 1939-1941" prepared by Clarence T. Craig, Richard Davidson, Eric H. Wahlstrom, George W. Richards, 10 pp. mimeo. [WCC Archives, Geneva].

[21] NATURE, pp. 7-8.

[22] Ibid., p. 8.

[23] Ibid., p. 11.

[24] Ibid., pp. 11-3.

[25] Ibid., p. 13.

[26] Ibid., p. 15.

[27] Ibid., pp. 16-7.

[28] Ibid., p. 28.

[29] Richards' list of papers read and discussed in the Committee (pp. 119-21) is incomplete. For the complete list, based on the F. W. Tomkins minutes and archives, see Appendix I.

[30] W. A. Visser't Hooft, "Report of the Work of the Provisional Committee," WCC (in process of formation), mimeo., pp. 5-6 [WCC Archives, Geneva].

[31] The early history of the group is summarized in the memorandum "Formation and Procedure of the Chicago Group in conjunction with the Program of the Study of the Universal Christian Council for Life and Work (based on a report by Prof. Edwin E. Aubrey, convener of the group)," mimeo., 1940 [WCC Archives, Geneva]. Its subsequent history can be traced in the "Reports of the Work of the Provisional Committee," WCC (in process of formation) by W. A. Visser't Hooft. An incomplete set of the minutes of the Chicago Group's meetings is likewise available in the WCC Archives in Geneva. Regrettably the study remained largely unreported because of the war situations.

[32] "The Ethical Reality and Function of the Church," a synopsis prepared by John Knox and submitted to the Chicago Ecumenical Study Group as a possible basis for discussion, mimeo., 5 pp. [WCC Archives, Geneva].

[33] The paper was issued by the Study Department in mimeographed form in May, 1941 and was circulated widely. Copies of this and the other relevant papers are found in the WCC Archives, Geneva.

[34] See the European comments contained in the Genevan archives, also the article by George F. Thomas, "Corpus Christi and Corpus Christianorum," in Christendom, VII, 1 (Winter, 1942), 24-34.

[35] See Corpus Unum, the report of the North American Ecumenical Conference... Toronto, Canada, June 3-5, 1941 (New York--Toronto: Conference Committee, n.d.), pp. 22-3.

[36] Thomas, art. cit.

[37] "Preaching as an Expression of the Ethical Reality of the Church," a memorandum by the Chicago Ecumenical Discussion Group, Oct. 1942. Study Department of the Universal Christian Council for Life and Work, No. 13 E/42; mimeo., Geneva.

[38] ETH. REALITY, p. 5.

[39] Ibid., esp. p. 7.

[40] See ibid., p. 11.

[41] See "Minutes of American Committee for the World Council of Churches" Oct. 17, mimeo. p. 9 [WCC Archives, Geneva].

[42] INTERSEMINARY V, pp. ix-x.

[43] Ibid., pp. 121-3. For a list of the members of these comissions, see Appendix II.

[44] Ibid., pp. vii-viii.

[45] Ibid., p. 80, see Paul Scherer's article "The Nature of the Church," in INTERSEMINARY III, esp. pp. 38-43.

[46] John A. Mackay, "The Biblical and Theological Basis for the Ecumenical Goal," in INTERSEMINARY IV, pp. 47-8.

[47] BIBL. DOCT., pp. 13-5.

[48] Ibid., p. 8.

[49] Ibid., pp. 66-7; see also p. 77, 83 and 106ff.

[50] Ibid., p. 12.

[51] Ibid., p. 97.

[52] Ibid., p. 101.

[53] See The Advancement of Theological Education, ed. J. M. Gustafson (New York: Harper & Bros., 1957), pp. ix-x.

[54] "Forward" in PURPOSE, p. ix. Niebuhr, Williams and Gustafson were aided by an eight man advisory committee, the list of whose members is found in PURPOSE, p. xiv. This advisory body was not however directly responsible for the theological work.

[55] The membership of this section included: Roland Bainton, Edward Hardy, Winthrop Hudson, John Knox, Sidney Mead, Robert Michaelsen, Wilhelm Pauck and George Williams (ibid., p. xiv).

[56] The Ministry in Historical Perspective, ed. by H. R. Niebuhr and D. D. Williams, (New York: Harper & Bros., 1956).

[57] "The data, insights and ideas gained from these sources and from the studies of many special documents have been worked through by the members of the staff, individually and in many seminar sessions. Now they venture to report on what they believe to have learned in the course of their study and attempt to state what they think is the main content and meaning of the long discussion that is going on among theological educators. On many matters of fact the statements can be relatively precise and objective. But when it deals with principles and aims it must undertake to set forth what has been variously expressed by many or has been only implicit in what others have communicated. In this respect the report cannot be 'objective' but must remain a somewhat personal effort to clarify and organize ideas about Church, ministry and theological education that seem to be 'in the air' or that seem to be developing in 'the climate of opinion.' This first volume, in particular, is necessarily an essay of this sort" (PURPOSE, pp. xii-xiii). Niebuhr acknowledges his particular indebtedness to the contributions of Williams and Gustafson, his two collaborators.

[58] Ibid., p. 1.

[59] Ibid., p. 95.

[60] Ibid., p. 19.

[61] Ibid., pp. 57-8.

[62] Ibid., p. 19.

[63] Ibid., p. 31.

[64] By "Christism" Niebuhr means the attempt to center Christian faith, worship, and activity around Jesus Christ rather than around the one God, with whom we are reconciled by Jesus' ministry. This point is developed in Niebuhr's Radical Monotheism and Western Culture (New York: Harper, 1960).

[65] PURPOSE, p. 57.

[66] Ibid., pp. 107-8.

[67] The basic history of the Oberlin Conference and its preparation is sketched by Paul Minear in the chapter, "The Conference in Context," in OBERLIN, pp. 11-27. Archival material, including a collection of the mimeographed working papers, "Study Grist and Gist," and orientation papers for each of the twelve conference sections, can be found in the Faith and Order archives of the WCC in Geneva. The published report contains, in addition to the major addresses, the schedule of the conference (OBERLIN, pp. 42-3) and an account of the proceedings (ibid., pp. 144-8). Despite the participation of Eastern Orthodox delegates and Roman Catholic observers, the theology of the Church developed in the Oberlin reports remained so thoroughly in the tradition of ecumenical American Protestantism, that the Orthodox felt obliged to issue a separate statement signaling their distance from it; see OBERLIN, pp. 159-63.

[68] Minear, "The Conference in Context," OBERLIN, pp. 15-9. A list of the regional study groups and their members is printed as the third appendix in OBERLIN, pp. 302-4. Their assignments regarding the orientation papers were as follows:

Austin, Tex.	"Report on the Table of the Lord," 5 pp. mimeo. (Sect. 4);
Boston	"Report on Forces at Work on the College Campus," 37 pp. mimeo. (Sect. 11);
Chicago	"An Ecumenical Commentary on the Greenwich Plan," 23 pp. mimeo. (Sect. 8);
Durham, N.C.	"Racial and Economic Stratification," 37 pp. mimeo. (Sect. 12);
Honolulu	"Local Church Unity and its Ecumenical Implications," 15 pp. mimeo. (Sect. 5);
Minneapolis	"Report on Doctrinal Consensus and Conflict," 10 pp. mimeo. (Sect. 2);
Nashville	"Report on Imperatives and Motivations," 21 pp. mimeo. (Sect. 1);
Newark	"Report on Baptism into Christ," 7 pp. mimeo. (Sect. 3);
New York	"Report on Authority and Freedom in Church Government," 13 pp. mimeo. (Sect. 7);
Pittsburgh	"Report on Racial and Economic Stratification," 15 pp. mimeo. (Sect. 12);
Saint Louis	"Councils of Churches and Federated Churches," 4 pp. mimeo. (Sect. 6);
Seattle	"Report on Baptism into Christ," 10 pp. mimeo. (Sect. 3);
Washington	"Report on Governmental Policies and Programs," 16 pp. mimeo. (Sect. 10);
Saskatoon	"Report on Doctrinal Consensus and Conflict," 9 pp. mimeo. (Sect. 2);
Toronto	"Report on Order and Organization," 15 pp. mimeo. (Sect. 8);
Vancouver	"Report on Doctrinal Consensus and Conflict," 5 pp. mimeo. (Sect. 2).

[69] OBERLIN, p. 20.

[70] Ibid., p. 214.

[71] Ibid., p. 231.

[72] Particularly significant here were the preliminary reports of the four American Faith and Order Commissions which will be discussed in the next section.

[73] A summary of these discussions will be found in "The Proceedings of the Conference," OBERLIN, 148ff. The procedure used in drafting the section reports was as follows. On Saturday, Sept. 7, the chairmen of the divisions, Gerald R. Cragg (Div. I), Robert Tobias (Div. II) and Merrimen Cunningham (Div. III), gave an oral report on the progress of discussions in their sections. In the light of the comments and criticisms aired in the following discussion, these chairmen, together with other division members drew up a draft statement which was distributed to all the delegates by Monday, Sept. 9. These drafts were discussed, amended and approved in the course of the plenary sessions on Monday and Tuesday, with provision being made for the editorial committee to incorporate the amendments and suggestions into the final text before publication.

[74] OBERLIN, p. 167.

[75] These discussions and the subsequent votes are recorded in "Proceedings," ibid., pp. 151-3, 155-6.

[76] OBERLIN, p. 29.

[77] "The Universal Church in God's Design," Report of Sect. I, First Assembly of the WCC, Amsterdam, Aug. 22-Sept. 4, 1948, as reproduced in A Documentary History of the Faith and Order Movement, ed. L. Vischer (Abbott Books; St. Louis: Bethany, 1963), pp. 76-7, nn. 5-8. See John E. Skoglund and J. Robert Nelson, Fifty Years of Faith and Order (New York: Committee for the Interseminary Movement, 1963), pp. 69-78.

[78] "Final Report of the Third World Conference on Faith and Order, held at Lund, Aug. 15-28, 1952," in A Documentary History..., ed. Vischer, p. 92, n. 23.

[79] Ibid., p. 96, n. 39; pp. 101-2, n. 58; p. 104, n. 69; pp. 111ff, n. 119.

[80] Primary sources for the history of this and the other three commissions are the published reports, both final and interim, plus the annual reports to the F. & O. Working committee meetings, printed in the Minutes of the Working Committee Meetings (Geneva: WCC, 1954ff.). Finally there are the working papers, meeting minutes and correspondence of the commissions to be found in the Genevan Faith and Order archives.

[81] CHRIST, p. 34.

[82] "Christ and the Church, Report of the Theological Commission on the Church and the Churches," ibid., pp. 7-34.

[83] Ibid., p. 9.

[84] Among the more important papers are the following:
W. Norman Pittenger, "The Doctrine of Christ and the Doctrine of the Church," prepared for the American Section of the TCCC

Meeting, Aug. 8-12, 1955, rev. with an appended note (FOC/TCCC /NA, Sept., 1955), 18 pp. plus 1 p. mimeo.

Floyd V. Filson, "The Old Testament and Jesus Christ," prep. for the TCCC Meeting, July, 1955, and rev. after discussion (FOC /TCCC/NA, July, 1955), 12 pp., mimeo.

Nels S. F. Ferré, "The humanity of Jesus," ... prepared for the Am. Sect. of the TCCC Meeting, Aug. 8-12, 1955, and revised ... (FOC/TCCC/NA, April, 1956), 21 pp., mimeo.

Paul S. Minear, "The Conception of the Church as the Body of Christ within the context of the different ways in which the New Testament speaks of Christ, the Spirit, and the Church: A Prospective Survey and some Sample Borings," outline of a study prepared for the Am. Sect. of the TCCC Meeting, Aug. 8-12, 1955 (FOC/TCCC/NA, April, 1956), 6 pp., mimeo.

Walter Harrelson, "Spirit in the Old Testament," revision of a paper presented to the No. Am. Sect. of the TCCC (FOC/TCCC/NA, Aug., 1956), 24 pp., mimeo.

Edward R. Hardie, "Word and Sacrament in the Early Church," prep. for the TCCC Meeting, Aug., 1956, and edited after discussion (FOC/TCCC/NA, Aug., 1956), 15 pp., mimeo.

Claude Welch, "The Church as Being and Coming to Be," ...prep. for the TCCC Meeting, July 15-9, 1957), 16 pp., mimeo.

H. Richard Niebuhr, "The Church Defines Itself in the World," draft paper prep. for the TCCC, June, 1958 (FOC/TCCC/NA, June, 1958), 8 pp., mimeo.

Floyd V. Filson, "The Holy Spirit in the New Testament," (FOC/TCCC /NA, 1960), 17 pp., mimeo.

In addition to these papers, very extensive minutes were kept of the discussions and afterwards mimeographed and distributed. A useful guide to this material is provided by the paper prepared by C. Welch, "Extracts from papers and discussion of the American Section of the Commission on Christ and the Church, 1955-1958" (FOC /TCCC/NA, May, 1959), 15 pp., mimeo. A similar extract of the European contributions had been prepared by P. S. Minear. All of these materials are to be found in the F. & O. Archives in Geneva.

[85] Directly or indirectly, the commission discussions inspired or influenced a large number of publications. Three of these are of particular importance for the present study. They are:

John Knox, The Early Church and the Coming Great Church (Nashville: Abingdon, 1955), 160 pp.

Paul S. Minear, The Images of the Church (Philadelphia: Westminster, 1960), 294 pp.

Claude Welch, The Reality of the Church (New York: Scribner's, 1958), 254 pp.

All three were discussed in whole or in part in the course of the Commission's work.

[86] Robert L. Calhoun, "Christ and the Church," in OBERLIN, pp. 52-78. Calhoun's paper was prepared on the basis of the discussions of the first draft in the course of the 1957 Commission meeting.

[87] "The Divine Trinity and the Unity of the Church," in One Lord--One Baptism, Report...presented to the Comm. on F. & O. of the WCC, 1960 (Studies in Ministry and Worship; Minneapolis: Augsburg, 1960), pp. 7-42. C. Welch was responsible for the initial outline of this report as well as for the final editing; the drafting of the individual sections was divided among the participants in the Tutzing

meeting (See "Joint Meeting of the Theological Commission on Christ and the Church," Tutzing, July 20-31, 1959 (TCCC, May, 1960) mimeo., pp. 1-4.

[88] J. Robert Nelson, "Report of the American Section of the Theological Commission on Christ and the Church," in Commission on Faith and Order, Minutes of the Commission Meeting held at St. Andrews, Scotland, Aug. 3rd to 8th, 1960 (WCC, Comm. on F. & O. Geneva: WCC, 1960) [hereafter abbreviated ST. ANDREWS], pp. 19-24.

[89] See NOTES (1960), pp. 31-5.

[90] CHRIST, p. 11.

[91] Ibid., p. 18.

[92] Ibid., pp. 18-9.

[93] Ibid., p. 19.

[94] Ibid., p. 20.

[95] Ibid., p. 32.

[96] Ibid., p. 33.

[97] TRADITION, pp. 10-1.

[98] Ibid., p. 11.

[99] Ibid., p. 28.

[100] Ibid., pp. 5-29. Besides the final report, the TCCCNA issued two papers as its interim report; these are: Javoslav Pelikan, "Overcoming History by History," and Albert C. Outler, "Traditions in Transit," published together with the interim reports of the European Section of the Tradition Commission and of the Institutionalism Commission in The Old and the New in the Church (Studies in Ministry and Worship, 18; Minneapolis: Augsburg, 1961), pp. 36-42 and 43-51 respectively. G. Florovsky and W. D. Hay presented a brief report at the St. Andrews meeting of the F. & O. Comm. (ST. ANDREWS, pp. 44-6).

[101] WORSHIP, p. 49. Alexander Schmemann and Daniel D. Williams were also members of the commission, but they were unable to participate in its work.

[102] INSTIT., p. 5.

[103] Ibid. This problem came out into the open at the 1959 meeting in Tutzing, Germany, where a methodological split opened up between the theological-juridical approach embodied in the paper of Dr. Hans Dombois of Heidelberg, and the more sociological approach represented by the paper of Dr. James Gustafson of Yale. The ensuing discussion led to the formulation of a consensus statement, "The Church as Koinonia and Institution," published in "Institutionalism," a special issue of The Division of Studies Bulletin [WCC], 6, 1 (Spring, 1960), 30-1.

[104] INSTIT., p. 30.

[105] As a supplement to its report, the commission published a collection of its working papers under the title Institutionalism and Church Unity: A Symposium prepared by the Study Commission on Institutionalism..., ed. by N. Ehrenström and W. G. Muelder (New York: Association, 1963).

[106] The SCI's interim report (OLD & NEW, pp. 52-91) is virtually identical with the final report. Nils Ehrenström and Walter Muelder reported for the Commission at St. Andrews (ST. ANDREWS, pp. 71-7).

[107] INSTIT., p. 23.

[108] Eugene Carson Blake, A Proposal toward the Reunion of Christ's Church (Philadelphia: Office of the General Assembly of the U.P.C. U.S.A., 1961). Blake's sermon was a publicity sensation that received wide coverage in the secular and religious press. Among others, The Christian Century [77, 51 (Dec. 21, 1960), 1508-11] carried the text in full. Blake's original proposal calling for a union both catholic and reformed was later amended to "truly catholic, truly evangelical, and truly reformed," (see DIGEST IV, pp. 22-7).

[109] Minutes of the General Assembly of the United Presbyterian Church in the U.S.A. Pt. I, Journal, 173rd Gen. Ass., Buffalo, N. Y., May 17-24, 1961 (U.P.C.U.S.A. Gen. Ass. Ser. 6, vol. 14, Philadelphia: Office of the Gen. Assembly, 1961), 454-7.

[110] COCUred, p. 7.

[111] Ibid., pp. 7-8. Since the work of the Consultation is still proceeding, the definitive history remains to be written. Numerous, more or less popular sketches have appeared in the official publications of the Consultation as well as in the various books, symposia, and articles, published in connection with it. The best sketch of its history through 1968 is the article by its Executive Secretary, Prof. Paul A. Crow, "Ecumenism and the Consultation on Church Union," Journal of Ecumenical Studies, 4, 4 (1967-8), 581-602; Crow's article, "The Church--a New Beginning," in Church Unity at Midpoint, ed. P. A. Crow and W. J. Boney (New York: Association, 1972), pp. 20-37, carries the account through 1971.

[112] See DIGEST I-II, p. 43 (=COCUred, p. 9). A membership list for the various commissions is appended to this study, Appendix III. The reports are found in DIGEST I-II, pp. 44-9 (=COCUred, pp. 23-30).

[113] The statements as finally approved by the plenary assembly appear in DIGEST III, pp. 20-32 (=COCUred, pp. 36-53).

[114] DIGEST IV, pp. 19-29 (=COCUred, pp. 60-74).

[115] DIGEST I-II, p. 45 (=COCUred, p. 24).

[116] DIGEST III, pp. 23-4 (=COCUred, p. 41).

117 Outline of a Possible Plan of Union, prepared by a special commission of the COCU for discussion at the 5th meeting of the Consultation, Dallas, May 2-5, 1966 (Fanwood, N. J.: Office of the Exec. Secretary, April 1, 1966), 105 pp., mimeo. The text as amended and approved (i.e. Preamble and Chapters 1-4) or accepted (sections on Structure and on Stages and Steps) was published in DIGEST V, pp. 38-65, 74-87 (=COCUblue, pp. 11-53 and 67-90). The preamble and first four chapters which the Dallas Assembly had approved under the title "Principles of Church Union" were reproduced in COCUgreen, pp. 19-60, which was issued to replace COCUblue after the 1967 Cambridge meeting.

118 See DIGEST VI, pp. 22ff.

119 DIGEST V, pp. 67-73 (=COCUblue, pp. 57-66, and COCUgreen, pp. 9-17). In general the ecclesiology of all these documents is in the classical tradition; nevertheless here and there the influence of the radical ecclesiology of the Missionary Structures of the Congregation study makes its appearance, as, for example, the decision to recognize "task groups for mission, education and service" as ecclesiastical units ["A Paper on the Structure of the Church," DIGEST V, p. 75 (=CCCUblue, p. 680)], and in some of the "Guidelines for the Structure of the Church," DIGEST VI, pp. 88ff. (COCUgreen, pp. 65ff).

120 Published as received, under the title "The Work of the Commission on Structure," DIGEST VI, pp. 37-40.

121 Published as received, under the title "Presuppositions of Church Structure," DIGEST VI, pp. 75-84.

122 Published as amended and officially approved for transmission to the churches, under the title "Guidelines for the Structure of the Church," DIGEST VI, pp. 87-93 (=COCUgreen, pp. 63-73).

123 Referred back to committee and left unpublished.

124 See note 114 above.

125 DIGEST V, pp. 94-100 (=COCUgreen, pp. 79-89).

126 "A Resolution on developing a plan of union," resolution no. 6 adopted by the Consultation, May 3, 1967, in DIGEST V, pp. 12-3 (=COCUgreen, pp. 74-5).

127 DIGEST IX, pp. 87-190; also published separately as A Plan of Union for the Church of Christ Uniting (Princeton: COCU, 1970), 104 pp. The plan is both an ecclesiological confession and a fundamental constitution for the uniting church. Appended to it are a ceremonial for "The Service of Inauguration of the Church of Christ Uniting"—the service by which congregations and their ministries, denominational organizations and their bishops or executives are merged—and an ordinal for future ordinations to the three ministerial offices in the church. The plan is an entirely new text, though it re-echos many of the ideas and formulations of the earlier COCU documents. Its structure is also new; in brief:

Chapt. I. "To begin anew"--a brief ceremonial preamble stating the
intention of the participating churches to "covenant together
in this Plan of Union for the Church of Christ Uniting (CCU)."

Chapt. II. From Unity to Union--a confession of faith in the unity
to which God brings his divided people, followed by a statement of the principles which shall govern the pursuit of this
unity in the Church of Christ Uniting.

Chapt. III. What it Means to be God's People--a definition of fundamental ecclesiological doctrine: in human perspective, in
biblical perspective, and in theological perspective.

Chapt. IV. To be Members of this Community--a theological and juridical determination of the nature and conditions of membership
in the Church at large and in this united church.

Chapt. V. The Living Faith--a confession of the uniting church's
faith; followed by a statement of the church's teaching on and
attitude toward Scripture, Tradition and the traditions, the
Creeds, the historic confessions of the particular churches,
and such affirmations of faith which the uniting church may
adopt in the future; next a statement of the church's moral responsibility toward victims and practitioners of racism, and
injustice; and finally a statement concerning the witness of
faith in liturgy and action.

Chapt. VI. The People at Worship--a definition of the nature of worship generally and of the specific principles governing the
forms of worship to be practiced in the uniting church. There
follow statements on Scripture, preaching and the sacraments.

Chapt. VII. To be Ministers of Christ--a comprehensive declaration
of the uniting church's teaching on the ministry of Christ, of
the Whole People of God, of the laity, of the ordained presbyters, bishops and deacons.

Chapt. VIII. Organizing for Mission--a theological and juridical
formulation of the uniting church's polity, distinguishing
parish, district, regional and national levels.

Chapt. IX. Reaching beyond this Community--a statement of principles
governing relations with other churches, with conciliar organizations, with world communions and confessional associations,
with jewish communities, and with other groups, communities and
associations of a social, religious, or political character.

[128] Perhaps the best indicator of the suddenness of this climatic shift
is the fact that in 1964, only four years after its 1960 decennial
survey "How My Mind has Changed," the Christian Century felt the
need to publish a series "How I am making up my mind." On the implications of this shift of mood for the COCU see especially:

Peter L. Berger, "A Call for Authority in the Christian Community,"
[Address to the 10th Plenary Meeting] DIGEST X (1971), pp. 113-
29;

Martin E. Marty, "The New Generation and COCU," in Church Unity at
Midpoint, pp. 178-89;.

George Peck, "Church Unity and the Future: Some Theological Tensions in the COCU Plan of Union," Andover Newton Quarterly 12,
1 (Sept. 1971), 12-23;

Preston N. Williams, "COCU and the Cultural Revolution," [Address to
the 10th Plenary Meeting], DIGEST X (1971), pp. 131-43, repro.
in Church Unity at Midpoint, pp. 118-27.

129At the Eleventh Plenary session of the COCU in Memphis, April 2-6,
1973, it was decided to put aside for the time being the work on a
concrete plan of union, since the responses of the churches had
revealed "general agreement among the churches on matters of faith,
worship and the basic nature of the church's ministry, but a general unreadiness to accept the organizational structures proposed
for a united church" ("The Way Ahead," DIGEST XI (1973), p. 53; see
"The Significance of the Response to a Plan of Union for the COCU,"
[report of the Implications Team], ibid., pp. 157-90); Convinced
that the development of a concrete plan cannot precede the process
the churches growing together on the local and middle-judicatory
levels, the plenary session determined five priority areas in which
action would be undertaken to promote such growing together: (1)
strategies to deal with institutional racism in existing and future
church structures; (2) revision of the sections on faith, worship,
and ministry, of the original plan as "a theological basis for
working toward mutual recognition of members and ministries and
further development of a plan of union" ("The Way Ahead," ibid.,
p. 54); (3) promotion of experimental communities committed to a
shared life based on the "marks of wholeness" of the Church of
Christ Uniting (ibid., p. 54; see "A Proposal for Generating Communities," ibid., pp. 191-9); (4) further theological and sociological study of the forms of the church at the local level; and
finally (5) the development of a "regular but occasional" "interim
eucharistic fellowship." (See "Guidelines for Interim Eucharistic
Fellowship," ibid., pp. 218-30.) The summer of 1973 also saw the
return of the United Presbyterian Church to full COCU membership.
The 1972 General Assembly of that denomination had voted to with-
draw from membership, but this decision was reversed by an overwhelming majority vote at the 1973 assembly. (See W. J. Boney,
"COCU: Memphis and After," in Journal of Ecum. Studies, 10, 3
(Summer, 1973), 654-7.)

130Title of a book by Mark Gibbs and Thomas R. Morton, God's Frozen
People: A book for and about Christian Laymen (Philadelphia:
Westminster, 1965). For an example of the new attitude see John P.
Brown, "The Taste and Smell of Our Salvation and COCU," in Church
Unity at Midpoint, pp. 190-200.

131The phrase originated with Archie Hargraves ["Go where the action
is," Social Action 20, 6 (Feb., 1964), 15-35], who compares God's
work in the world to a floating crap game, to which the Church,
like a confirmed gambler, whose "major compulsion upon rising each
day is to know where the action is," so he can get in there to "dig
it." (ibid., p. 17). Harvey Cox took up the image in Secular City:
Secularization and urbanization in theological perspective (New
York: Macmillan, 1964), pp. 125ff. Both Hargraves and Cox were
active in the North American Working Group for the study of the
"Missionary Structures of the Congregation." As originally conceived, the notion was a directive to the existing churches to go
where the action is; many people, however, frustrated by the stog-
giness of the existing churches, turned it into an indicative
statement to the effect that the real church is already there where
the action is, namely in the non-ecclesiastical groups actively
working at reform, renewal, or revolution.

[132] A brief account of the origins of the Missionary structures of the Congregation study is offered by Colin W. Williams' "Preface" in WHERE, pp. v-vii. As sources for the work of the Study, especially the contributions of the North American Working Group, the following should be mentioned:

1. "The Church for the World": Report of the North American Working Group of the department of Studies in Evangelism, published in MISSIONARY, pp. 55-129.

2. "The Quest for Structures of Missionary Congregations," Interim report of the Study "Missionary Structures of the Congregation" to the Central Committee of the WCC meeting at Enugu, Nigeria, 1965, published in Planning for Mission: Working Papers on the New Quest for Missionary Communities, ed. T. Wieser (New York: The U. S. Conf. for the WCC, 1966), pp. 220-8.

3. The working papers and meeting minutes of the different working groups appeared in the mimeographed bulletin issued by the WCC Study Dept., Concept. This bulletin was issued in two sections distinguished according to the color of the cover page: Concept (red), Papers from the Dept. on Studies in evangelism, issued quarterly and publicly; then Concept (blue), occasionally published special issues for members of the working groups. The papers, together with a complete bibliography of the Concept issues, were gathered together for publication by T. Wieser in PLANNING.

4. Colin Williams, Chairman of the Department of Studies of the WCC, incorporated large amounts of the groups' discussion materials and oral contributions into the two popular presentations of the study which he authored, namely Where in the World? Changing forms of the Church's witness (New York: NCCC, 1963), and What in the World? (New York: NCCC, 1964) [These two books are referred to by the abbreviations WHERE and WHAT].

[133] MISSIONARY, p. 61.

[134] Ibid., pp. 60-1.

[135] Ibid., p. 63. See "Minutes, North American Working Group, Consultation, Seabury House, Greenwich, Conn., Feb. 4-6, Concept (blue) 8 (1964), 6-8.

[136] Williams offers a stirring account of this discussion in WHAT, pp. 82-92.

[137] MISSIONARY, p. 63.

[138] The history of these groups and a presentation of their ecclesiological reflections constitute the appendix to the North American Working Group's report, ibid., pp. 95-126.

[139] Ibid., p. 98.

[140] Ibid., pp. 63-4; for a list of participants in the North American Working Group, see Appendix IV.

[141] Ibid., p. 67.

[142] Ibid., p. 56.

[143] Ibid., p. 67.

[144] MISSIONARY, p. 70.

[145] Ibid., p. 72.

[146] Ibid., p. 75.

[147] Ibid., p. 78.

[148] Ibid., p. 81.

[149] Ibid., p. 83.

[1] Paul Scherer, "On the Nature of the Church," INTERSEMINARY III, pp. 29-30.

[2] NATURE, p. 8.

[3] Ibid., pp. 29-30.

[4] Ibid., pp. 35-6.

[5] Ibid., pp. 40, 41-2.

[6] Ibid., pp. 51-2.

[7] Ibid., p. 64.

[8] Ibid., pp. 63-4.

[9] Ibid., p. 66.

[10] Ibid., pp. 66-7.

[11] Ibid., p. 56.

[12] Ibid., pp. 84-93 passim.

[13] Ibid., pp. 94-101 passim.

[14] Ibid., pp. 102-12 passim.

[15] Ibid., p. 59.

[16] Ibid., pp. 73-6.

[17] Ibid., p. 77.

[18] WORSHIP, p. 57.

[19] Ibid., p. 55.

[20] See INSTIT., p. 21.

[21] The classic example is a conference of an Evangelical Academy (CHURCH, p. 84).

[22] The discussion of the Freedom Movement at the Feb. 1964 meeting of the NAWG brought out clearly the ecclesial character of the organization, its leadership, and its assemblies, as the following passages from William's summary of that discussion reveal: "In the midst of this mixed community 'the marks of the church' would seem to be present--even though their fullness may not be manifest. Thus in the Monday night meetings, preparing for action, there is often powerful preaching: the Word brought in touch with the concrete issues before them. The Biblical drama is heavily used: here is a call for total commitment, a readiness to give one's life in the cause of true community. Here too there are prayers: and prayers in which the living needs of the situation of action are brought within the circle of God's redeeming work in Christ. Word

and worship are brought into living contact with the day to day
questions arising in battle to change the structures of the world
toward the Goal of true community. The problems of life are taken
up into the gospel, and orders are given for the direction of their
action in the world. ... It is noticeable that in the Monday
night meetings the forms that are used are the forms of the old
revival meeting with which the Negro has long been familiar. The
preaching, with audience participation and personal testimony; the
symbolic commitment through prayers and songs which draw forth the
total response of self within the group; the stress on the free
movement of the Spirit--all these are old. But what has happened
here is the turning of these out into the world, so that the emo-
tion is not directed inward. The direction of attention is to
what ought to be happening in the world and the way it should happen. God is calling us to obedience at the place of his action.
He is calling us for active witness by word and deed to his Lordship as it is being made known in the events of the world."
(WHAT, pp. 86-8).

[23] See CHURCH, pp. 70, 72-3.

[24] See CHRIST, p. 28. The report explains: "By 'event' we mean here
the dynamic energizing by Christ and the Spirit in the Church, the
spontaneous quality of the human response, and the 'processive'
character of the community's life in grace."

[25] CHURCH, pp. 72-3.

[26] See DIGEST V, p. 75 (=COCUblue, pp. 68-9); also OBERLIN, pp. 214-5
and the various statements of the NAWG, e.g. PLANNING, pp. 223-4;
CHURCH, p. 70; WHAT, pp. 5-10; and WHERE, pp. 4-8. As used here,
the term "congregation" is taken in the traditional sense of the
parish-congregation. In the Missionary Structures of the Congregation study the tendency was rather to use the word "congregation" in a broader sense to include all localized forms of church
work (See Concept (blue) 2 (Feb. 1963), 29; and PLANNING, p. 220
note). The distinction between "congregation" and "task force"
as two distinct types of localized ecclesial reality was first
made in the original COCU draft outline of a plan of union.

[27] DIGEST V, p. 75 (=COCUblue, pp. 68-9). In the 1970 Plan, the proposal has been made to unite congregations and task-forces in an
over-arching local unit called the "parish." "The community called
the parish redefines the front-line expression of church life where
people live and work. Consisting normally of several congregations
and developing task groups, it is the local governmental unit of
the church for expressing the most complete and efficient ministry
possible. The competitive drive at present for every existing congregation, no matter how limited its resources, to attempt a full
program of worship, education at every level, fellowship and action
will be minimized in this new framework" (PLAN, p. 57).

[28] The term "task-force" originated simply as a designation for the
regional sub-committees which resulted from the 1964 reorganization
of the NAWG; there was no initial thought of creating a new ecclesiological expression; nevertheless it soon became apparent that
the term filled a semantic vacuum. For this reason it was adopted
by the COCU drafters (See note 26). Already back in the forties

the CEDG had called attention to the ecclesial reality of such groups, though it found no convenient catch-all term for them (See ETH. REALITY, p. 2 and Benne·;, RESULTS, p. 152).

[29] See the Enugu report of the North American and European sections (PLANNING, pp. 223-6).

[30] CHURCH, pp. 84-5.

[31] The CEDG report, speaking of the visible Church, states: "...the church, when thought of as a concrete social entity usually refers to a corporate body of believers who recognize Jesus Christ as their head. They acknowledge him to be the source of a socio-historical institution possessing a definite reality and function, and to be the author and perfector of their faith. This corporate body provides those forms of fellowship that arise out of the common concern for Word and sacrament, and that are needed for the practice of the Christian way of life. Thus the church as a concrete social entity includes all those forms of organization that provide patterns of experience and behavior for men and women who are committed to a common loyalty to Jesus Christ. These types of organization include those forms of fellowship that are given expression through local congregations and through the organic or corporate groupings of the church referred to as denominations, national and provincial churches and sects" (ETH. REALITY, p. 2). The report goes on to add that federations of Churches both regional and world-wide also constitute churches in this sense.

[32] See MEANINGS, pp. 34-9.

[33] Both the Outline Plan and the 1970 Plan envisage a superstructure of district, regional, and national units under the supervision of bishops with mixed lay-clerical councils at their sides. In addition each unit is to have its electoral and legislative convention and a church court for judiciary matters. [DIGEST V, pp. 76-9 (=COCUblue, pp. 67-75); PLAN, pp. 56-72]. Especially noteworthy is the emphatic commitment of both versions to the open, union-minded character of the proposed united church; every effort is to be made to avoid the creation of a self-satisfied super-denomination, which could be a new barrier to further ecumenical progress [see the "Letter to the Churches" (1966) in DIGEST V, pp. 69-70 (=COCUgreen, p. 13); also PLAN, pp. 73-5]. The 1973 decision to shelve for the time being the work on the organizational sections of the plan of union represents not a retreat from but rather an intensified commitment to the study of these matters (see DIGEST XI, pp. 54, 170-6, 183-7).

[34] PURPOSE, pp. 8-9.

[35] See MEANINGS, pp. 17-34; also OBERLIN, pp. 217-22. Of councils, the Oberlin report says: "The councils are instruments through which denominations, congregations, and individual Christians are brought into a closer relationship to the whole Church and the wholeness of the Church. While councils of churches are not the unity we seek, we believe that either they have a place in that unity or help in its discovery. In some sense, through their councils churches remind themselves that they are in a larger unity of 'the Church,' therefore, while councils and federations are not a

church nor the Church, they have something of the nature of the
Church about them. They are a continual reminder of a unity in
Christ which is wider than that of the congregation, the denomina-
tion or a national or regional church." (OBERLIN, p. 219).

[36] NATURE, pp. 19-23.

[37] This problem was extensively discussed in both the ATC and the
TCCCNA.

[38] CHURCH, p. 70.

[39] Similar tendencies are noted by the CCULW's study of The Communion
of Saints in a number of particular traditions, e.g. Lutheran
(COMMUNION, p. 28); Reformed (ibid., pp. 30-3); Methodist (ibid.,
p. 38); Free Church (ibid., pp. 39-40); and Quaker (ibid., pp. 40-
1).

[40] See ibid., pp. 42-3.

[41] The Ethical Reality paper puts the matter so: "The church as an
historical, empirical reality involves much more than the various
formal and informal types of association that may obtain among
Christians. The religious experience of the members of any group-
ing of Christians is also a part of the empirical reality of the
church" (ETH. REALITY, p. 2).

[42] MEANINGS, p. 1; see Dun, MINUTES, p. 3.

[43] MEANINGS, p. 1.

[44] Ibid., pp. 2-3.

[45] Ibid., p. 5.

[46] Ibid., p. 17.

[47] Ibid., pp. 6-9.

[48] Ibid., pp. 9-11.

[49] Ibid., pp. 11-4.

[50] Ibid., pp. 16-6.

[51] Ibid., pp. 17-8.

[52] Ibid., pp. 18-25.

[53] Ibid., pp. 26-7.

[54] Ibid., pp. 27-9.

[55] Ibid., pp. 30-1.

[56] Ibid., pp. 32-4.

[57] Ibid., pp. 31-2.

[58]MEANINGS, p. 36.

[59]Ibid., pp. 35, 37.

[60]Ibid., p. 36.

[61]Ibid., p. 39.

[62]Ibid., p. 38.

[63]Ibid., pp. 37-8.

[64]The church sociologist H. Paul Douglass distinguishes between ecclesia, designating the institutional phase of the Church's organized life, and koinonia, designating those "aspects of the life of
any society which are more fundamental than the institutional"
(INTERSEMINARY IV, p. 170); he goes on: "The better part of the
Church is not fully ecclesiasticized. It exists as a habit of
cooperation based on the 'we-feeling'. It has a unity sustained
by common symbols. It possesses a recognizable Christian mores.
It has functional if not legal authority. It creates a variety of
agencies on a voluntary basis, for example the World Council of
Churches. All these are objective social phenomena. They manifest the koinonia. They constitute an imperfect but still considerable degree of working unity. They are not mere incidents but
rather the marks of the Church at its deepest levels. Institutions
are inevitable, but they are inherently superficial. This includes
the Church as ecclesia. Normally institutions register the results
of more basic processes" (INTERSEMINARY IV, p. 172; see also
MEANINGS, p. 37 and ETH. REALITY, p. 3).

[65]See COMMUNION, pp. 43-6.

[66]ETH. REALITY, p. 3.

[67]Ibid.

[68]Ibid.

[69]INTERSEMINARY III, p. 31.

[70]PURPOSE, p. 19.

[71]Ibid., p. 21. The Wright Commission calls attention to the role of
worship in mediating this experience in the New Testament community
(MAN, p. 68).

[72]OBERLIN, p. 54.

[73]Ibid., p. 55.

[74]Lest there be any misunderstanding, it is well to note here the
definition of "institution" given in the SCI report: "...sociology
defines an institution as a definite and established structure
(goals, means, value orientations, sanctions) built around and sustaining one or more specific functions (sex control, sustenance,
education, total social control). These two conceptual elements
of structure and function illuminate many problems in institution-

alism. A social function may be fruitfully understood as a whole activity which accomplishes a desired end or fulfills a basic need for society and for the individuals which make up that society. The desired end may be normatively interpreted, for example, by theological belief." (INSTIT., p. 6). Thus not only organizational structures but also creeds, dogmas, worship orders, etc. fall under the general category of institutions. What distinguishes institutions from more informal structures is their "definite and established" character. Any expression of faith, worship or service in the Church necessarily has some structure; only when this structure takes on definite, established character, however, does one properly speak of an institution. Where this character becomes rigid and disfunctional, where such institutions become ends in themselves, absorbing the social energies for their own self-aggrandizment instead of channeling them to fulfill the necessary functions of the society as a whole, one has to do with the phenomenon of "institutionalism" in the pejorative sense of the term (INSTIT., p. 5). The distinctions made here have generally been observed by all the American commissions, though their terminology varies somewhat from that proposed by the SCI.

[75] See PURPOSE, p. 21; also ETH. REALITY, p. 3. The Episcopalian Theodore Wedel accused the Roman Catholic Church of having no doctrine of the Church as community but only of the ecclesiastical institution [The Coming Great Church (New York: Macmillan, 1945), p. 95.]

[76] See Peter Berger and Thomas Luckmann, The Social Construction of Reality. A Treatise on the Sociology of Knowledge (Anchor Books; Garden City: Doubleday, 1967).

[77] NEXT STEPS, p. 10.

[78] NATURE, p. 23.

[79] Ibid.

[80] Ibid., p. 24.

[81] ETH. REALITY, p. 2.

[82] Ibid.

[83] INTERSEMINARY III, p. 32.

[84] Ibid., p. 41.

[85] Ibid., pp. 41-4.

[86] PURPOSE, p. 19.

[87] Ibid., p. 21.

[88] Ibid., p. 22.

[89] CHRIST, p. 28; for the sociological justification of this theological assertion see INSTIT., pp. 5-6.

266

[90] INSTIT., p. 20; see also CHRIST, pp. 28-9.

[91] DIGEST V, p. 67 (=COCUgreen, p. 9).

[92] Ibid., p. 39 (=COCUgreen, p. 22).

[93] DIGEST VI, p. 87 (=COCUgreen, p. 63).

[94] See CHURCH, pp. 65-6.

[95] Ibid., p. 68.

[96] The theological faith of the Church serves as the normative interpretation of the believer's experience of the empirical reality of the Church (see INSTIT., p. 6). The sociologist investigating the empirical phenomenon need not personally share this belief, but he must at least intellectually work with it if he would understand how the empirical reality is experienced by its members. See ETH. REALITY, p. 2 and INSTIT., p. 7.

[97] The CCULW called attention to this at the beginning of its discussions. (See Dun, MINUTES, p. 3): "Each type of existing church tends to picture unity as an extension of its own form of unity. The Anglican thinks of unity in terms of a common standard of Faith and Order, with allowance for variations in the forms of worship and of government with the national sister-churches. The Congregationalist thinks of unity as a working federation of local churches with wide freedom of local usage and standards of allegiance." This diversity extends to the interpretation of the New Testament texts dealing with the Church. See NON-THEOL., p. 11. For a theoretical analysis of this phenomenon see TRADITION, pp. 11-3.

[98] In 1937 the CCULW had insisted on the need of the Faith and Order Movement to take greater cognizance of this phenomenon and offered a brief but pregnant reflection on the influence of "the non-theological factors in Christian theology" (NON-THEOL., pp. 9-12). The theme recurs in virtually all the American studies here under consideration.

[99] C. H. Dodd, "Unavowed Motives in Ecumenical Discussions," Ecumenical Review, II (1949-50), 54-5.

[100] Berger and Luckmann, Social Construction, p. 95. It will be recalled that Berger was one of the religious sociologists who participated in the NAWG.

[101] Ibid., p. 96.

[102] The analogy is suggested by Paul Minear's use of the word "constellation" to describe the major complexes of New Testament images referring to the Church (Minear, IMAGES, pp. 67, 82, 90).

[103] See Minear, PROSPECTIVE SURVEY, p. 1; in the final version of his study Minear listed 96 separate images.

[104] See Minear's distinction between major and minor images, IMAGES, pp. 66-7.

[105] Minear, PROSPECTIVE SURVEY, pp. 3-5.

[106] See TCCC Interim report ONE LORD, pp. 27-8.

[107] Thus the ecclesiological publications of the exegetes C. T. Craig, Theodore Wedel, John Knox, and Paul Minear, to name but a few typical examples, are essentially systematic works.

[108] See MAN, p. 12; and NOTES (1960), pp. 13-4.

[109] See NOTES (1958), pp. 36, 38.

[110] See for instance COMMUNION, p. 1; MAN, p. 10, and NOTES (1960), pp. 13-4.

[111] See Connolly Gamble Jr., "The Literature of Biblical Theology: A bibliographical study," Interpretation, 7 (1953), 466-80. Gamble notes the following six characteristics of Biblical Theology: (1) "Biblical theology builds upon sound historical and critical investigation of the Bible"; (2) "Biblical theology insists that historical and critical study must advance to an adequately theological interpretation which recognizes and sets forth the unity of the Bible. Building upon historical and literary analysis the biblical theologian goes on to synthesize the resultant data in a unitary pattern derived from the Scripture itself." (3) "A third characteristic of biblical theology is its understanding of history as organic... The Bible is history, but of a peculiar kind. It is sacred history—not a record of human convictions and their evolution, but an account of the mighty deeds of God. These deeds are unified and cohesive, guiding a chosen people into God's supreme purpose—into Christ." (4) "Biblical theology tries to enter into the biblical viewpoint. ... Modern biblical interpreters adopt the categories of the biblical authors, rather than employing a dogmatic or philosophical framework." (Nevertheless, Gamble insists, biblical theology remains distinct from systematic or dogmatic theology.) (5) "It recognizes the limitations of 'objective' study and the necessity for subjective commitment as prerequisite for understanding of the Bible. Interpretation of Scripture demands that the interpreter must put himself at the service of its central proclamation of Jesus, the crucified and risen Christ." (6) "It emphasizes that the ultimate outcome of biblical study is personal encounter with the living God, whose Word is spoken through the human words of Scripture." (pp. 471-5).

[112] MAN, p. 10. See also the very important methodological explanation of the TCCCNA in CHRIST, pp. 11-5.

[113] See also NOTES (1954), pp. 3-4; (1957), pp. 11, 36, 38; (1960), pp. 9. 13-4, 19-20, 26-7.

[114] This distinction is brought out most clearly in the difference between the North American and the European sections' approaches to the tradition problem (see TRADITION, pp. 11-3).

[115] The Communion of Saints report represents a classic example of this technique, see especially the hermeneutical observations at the outset (COMMUNION, pp. 1-10 passim).

[116] To these we will return in chapter V.

[117] This is more or less the approach adopted by the TCCCNA in its attempt to elaborate a theology of the Church in the perspective of a trinitarian history of salvation.

[118] COMMUNION, pp. 1, 8-9.

[119] Ibid., p. 7.

[120] Ibid., p. 1.

[121] Ibid., pp. 2-4.

[122] Ibid., p. 2.

[123] Ibid., pp. 1-2. The Wright Committee stresses the fact that in the New Testament the most evident characteristic of the community is that its individual members perceived themselves to be "drawn into an intimate, personal and affectional relationship with the Lord who loved them" (MAN, pp. 65, also 97-9).

[124] COMMUNION, pp. 4-5. In the citation the biblical references have been inserted in place of the cross-references given in the actual text.

[125] Ibid., pp. 5-6.

[126] Ibid., pp. 7-8.

[127] Ibid., pp. 8-9.

[128] Ibid., p. 9.

[129] Ibid., p. 12.

[130] Minear, IMAGES, pp. 138-43.

[131] Ibid., pp. 161-2.

[132] Ibid., p. 161.

[133] Calhoun, OBERLIN, p. 67; see also MAN, pp. 81-8.

[134] COMMUNION, p. 44.

[135] Ibid., pp. 44-5. The Wright Committee describes the New Testament view in terms which come closest to the second of these interpretations; their report lays stress on "the intimate, personal and affectional relationship" between the believer and his Lord in the Church (MAN, pp. 65-6).

[136] NATURE, p. 12; Cadbury and Richards took this position in the papers they presented at the 1940 and 1941 meetings; Rall appears to have taken a similar, though more moderate position in the course of the discussion. See SPECIAL COMMITTEE, p. 3.

[137] INTERSEMINARY IV, p. 170.

[138] INTERSEMINARY IV, p. 172.

[139] Ibid., pp. 173-4.

[140] Ibid., p. 173.

[141] INSTIT., p. 5.

[142] INTERSEMINARY IV, p. 173. The Wright study takes a rather similar position in describing the organization of the New Testament community. It notes how the charismatic character of the institutions of the New Testament church preserved it from the institutionalist tendency towards rigidity and self-centeredness. "The kingship of Christ in the New Testament and of God himself over Israel was exercised from the heavenly throne. Yet it was known to be nonetheless effective because God ruled by chosen human media and by direct communication through his heavenly messengers (angels), his word (and wisdom), and his Spirit. This meant that all organization and government were conceived to be of divine institution and sanction, or else they were useless, unprofitable, even sinful. This also meant that any institution which apparently had received a permanent blessing could find itself in condemnation and deprived of blessing when it failed to fulfill its God-given task. The conception of a direct heavenly rule meant the subjection of all human organization to it, and every promise and blessing given by God was contingent on obedient loyalty" (MAN, pp. 84-5; see also p. 87).

[143] CHRIST, pp. 13-4. This consensus was achieved at the 1956 meeting of the Commission [NOTES (1956), p. 14; also Calhoun, OBERLIN, pp. 56-7, and NOTES (1960), pp. 9, 10, 12]. The report of the Commission contains very full expositions of the relationship between Christ and the Church, but because the general perspective is that of a systematic elaboration of the question within the larger theological framework of the People of God theme, it seems better to reserve the treatment of this matter till the next chapter. It is significant that in the 1960 discussion of the jointly issued interim report the American section criticized this paper's overly christocentric character. [NOTES (1960), p. 17].

[144] Brown's report for the CCULW, for instance, interprets the Body-of-Christ idea in such a way as to bring it into the orbit of the People-of-God notion (NEXT STEPS, p. 10). The ATC report recommends the People-of-God motif as the most comprehensive basis for an ecumenical ecclesiology (NATURE, pp. 22-3). Among the contributions to the Interseminary symposium, Scherer concentrates on the koinonia and People-of-God motifs, subordinating the Body idea to these notions (INTERSEMINARY III, pp. 32ff). Mackay, on the other hand, treats the Body theme separately, but the overall effect of his treatment is to situate it in the larger perspective provided by the "People" motif (INTERSEMINARY IV, pp. 48-54). In his summary volume, Bilheimer follows Mackay's line of thinking (INTERSEMINARY V, p. 31). Likewise the Wright report (MAN, pp. 65ff, 81ff). As might be expected, PURPOSE (p. 21) reflects the same clear preference for a theocentric over christocentric ecclesiology which he promoted in the discussions of the TCCCNA. The Oberlin Conference (at which Minear, and Calhoun, another strong proponent of the theocentric approach, played a leading role) moves along similar lines in its stress on the heilsgeschichtliche character of of the Church's as God's people. (OBERLIN, pp. 176-9).

[145]Welch, (REALITY, pp. 187-9) notes that interest in the Body-of-Christ theme is characteristic of catholic-minded theologies. One must add, as he himself elsewhere suggests, that it also finds favor in radical congregationalist or denominationalist ecclesiologies.

[146]Of primary importance here is Minear's initial unpublished outline PROSPECTIVE SURVEY together with the published volume, IMAGES, which resulted from his investigations for the TCCCNA. Other sources, e.g. Mackay INTERSEMINARY IV and Welch REALITY are more valuable for the systematic elaboration of the Body theme.

[147]To these may be added, according to Minear, certain implicit allusions in non-pauline sources, e.g. Mk. 14:22par; Jn. 2:19-21; Heb. 10:5, 10; 13:3, 11-2; I Pet. 2:24 (PROSPECTIVE SURVEY, p. 3; also IMAGES, p. 173).

[148]Minear, PROSPECTIVE SURVEY, p. 3; also Mackay, INTERSEMINARY IV, pp. 51-2; MAN, pp. 81-2; Calhoun, OBERLIN, pp. 67-8.

[149]Minear, PROSPECTIVE SURVEY, p. 3; see also NOTES (1960), p. 30.

[150]Welch, REALITY, pp. 165-9; Welch sharply criticizes this tendency, noting that the stress on organism interpreted as corporate personality is seriously misleading. (See also ibid., pp. 180-8, where he undertakes a detailed critique of catholic attempts to build an ecclesiology on the basis of the Body-of-Christ idea.)

[151]MAN, p. 81.

[152]Ibid., p. 32. Elsewhere the report declares [citing G. Johnson, The Doctrine of the Church in the New Testament (Cambridge, 1943), p. 111]: "...the primitive Church was almost exclusively a charismatic community, and 'for Paul the Ecclesia was essentially an almost world-wide fellowship of the Spirit, taking form and name in local congregations, cells in the one Body of the exalted Christ'." (MAN, p. 87). In the 1960 TCCCNA meeting the same point was made [NOTES (1960), p. 30]; Harrelson states: "The body is knit together by agape (I Cor. 12 & 13)."

[153]Mackay, INTERSEMINARY IV, p. 54; a parallel development of the Body-of-Christ theme from the conservative side is found among the Southern Baptist contributions to two conservative evangelical symposia on the Church published as a reaction to the Oberlin Conference, i.e. W. Boyd Hunt's article in "The Body Christ Heads," Christianity Today, 1, 22 (Aug. 19, 1957), 7-8; and Theron D. Price's contribution in "The Nature of the Unity We Seek," Religion in Life, 26, 2 (Spring, 1957), esp. 201-3.

[154]OBERLIN, p. 178. Not all the members of the section, however, concurred in deduction of an imperative to organizational union (ibid., p. 184). The danger of separating the theological reality of the Church as Body of Christ from the empirical reality as organized community was discussed at the joint meeting of the TCCC in 1957. Sensitive to this danger, the American members generally criticized a concentration on the Body image to the neglect of the correctives offered by the other images. [NOTES (1957), pp. 3ff.]

[155] Mackay, INTERSEMINARY IV, p. 52.

[156] ETH. REALITY, p. 7.

[157] NATURE, p. 26.

[158] CHRIST, pp. 1, 32; see Calhoun, OBERLIN, p. 68 and Welch, REALITY, pp. 179-80.

[159] This expression was discussed in Nelson's report of the TCCCNA's work to the 1960 meeting of the F. & O. Cent. Com. in 1960 (ST. ANDREWS, pp. 21-2, 25).

[160] CHRIST, p. 19; see also Pittenger, DOCTRINE, pp. 16-7; and Welch, REALITY, pp. 81, 179. On the other hand the commission was seriously interested in the epistemological possibilities of an analogous application of the christological categories governing the relation of the divine and the human in Christ to the relation of divine and human factors in the life of the Church. More of this in the next chapter.

[161] See Minear, IMAGES, pp. 228-44, for an exposition of the complementary relationships between these themes.

[162] Welch, REALITY, pp. 176-7.

[163] Mackay, INTERSEMINARY IV, pp. 52-3; also OBERLIN, pp. 178-9; Minear, IMAGES, pp. 190-5, 210-3; Hardie, WORD, pp. 20-1.

[164] CHRIST, p. 20; more clearly still in COCU PLAN, p. 18.

[165] See CHRIST, pp. 21-6; Minear, IMAGES, p. 223, and 233-4, 243-4.

[166] Welch, REALITY, pp. 186-7; he accuses catholic-type ecclesiology of falling into this error.

[167] See CHRIST, p. 19. Welch calls special attention to this problem in chapter IV of his book which was discussed at the Commission's 1957 meeting and revised accordingly. He notes how the bridal image can offer a useful corrective to such tendencies.

[168] "As the Incarnate Son was truly man, so is the Church wrought out of the stuff of human existence. The Church is shaped out of the realities of human historicity and sociality. Therefore the Church is not some 'ideal' community, existing in airy abstraction from the affairs of men. Neither is it 'spiritual' in the sense that it is to be contrasted with the hard and inevitable materialities of that world of history and sociality. To call the Church ideal or spiritual in those senses is to fall into ecclesiological docetism akin to the ancient heresy which denied to our Lord his physical body, his historical actuality, his immersion in the stuff of common life. We protest against every view of the Church which in a mistaken effort to exalt its nature as the body of Christ, succeeds only in making it purer than its Lord" (CHRIST, p. 24).

[169] See CHRIST, pp. 13, 20, 24. The individual papers contributed to the commission are all but unanimous on this point.

[170] The term "cognitional interest" (Erkenntnisinteresse) is borrowed, of course, from the work of Jürgen Habermas [Erkenntnis und Interesse, Frankfurter Antrittsvorlesung vom 28.6.1965, publ. in his Technik und Wissenschaft als "Ideologie" (Editions Surkamp; Frankfurt: Surkamp Verlag, 1968), pp. 146-68 and systematically elaborated in his Erkenntnis und Interesse (Theorie 2; Frankfurt: Surkamp Verlag, 1968). The basic idea, however, had already been elaborated by H. Richard Niebuhr in his paper on defining the Church in the world. He wrote: "A definition always involves the activity of both practical and theoretical reasoning in the subject. ... A definition is descriptive but also normative; it implies decision as well as perception and conception. This is probably true of the simplest word-definitions...[but] the involvement of both practical and theoretical reasoning is more significant and more apparent when men define themselves or one of their institutions. Definitions of Democracy as government of, for and by the people, or as respect for minority rights are both descriptive and decisive or imperative. Decision is present in such cases not as resolution to use a word in a certain way but as choice of an essence which is to be conserved or realized. The theoretic statement is formulated as part of a logic in which imperative or decision-sentences will follow description, but decision has also preceded the theoretic formulation." (CHURCH, p. 2). He goes on to distinguish the various types of practical decisions which precede definition, namely: decisions about purpose--the practical goal underlying the theoretic investigation; about distinction--the phenomena which the normative definition will accept as relevant or reject as irrelevant or antithetical; about context--the positive relationships which the definition will illuminate (ibid., p. 3). He notes, however, that these decisions are normally made implicitly and can be brought to light--albeit only imperfectly--only "critical self-examination in community." (ibid., p. 4). For this reason Habermas' term "interest" seems more appropriate than Niebuhr's "decision" to designate what is involved here.

[171] I Pet. 2:9-10; Rom. 9:25-6; see Minear, IMAGES, pp. 67-72.

[172] Minear lists:
a) political and national analogies: Israel, a Chosen Race, a Holy Nation, the Twelve Tribes, the Twelve Patriarchs, Circumcision, Abraham's Sons, Exodus, His House or Kingdom, Remnant, the Elect (IMAGE, pp. 71-84);
b) pastoral analogies: the Flock, the Lambs who rule (IMAGE, pp. 84-6);
c) metaphors drawn from cultic tradition: the Holy City, Mt. Zion, the Holy Temple, Priesthood, Sacrifice, Aroma, Festivals--esp. Passover, and Sabbath (ibid., pp. 89-103).

[173] Minear, IMAGES, p. 70.

[174] Principally the New-Creation theme itself (see also MAN, pp. 64-5), and the themes Kingdom of God, company of soldiers fighting against Satan, the Coming Age. The other sub-themes which Minear associates with the New-Creation constellation tend rather to the organic Body-of-Christ notion (see IMAGES, pp. 105-11; 124-5, 135). The union of the two, People-of-God and New-Creation, is already expounded in Calhoun's report to Oberlin (OBERLIN, pp. 64-9).

[175] On the connection between the People-of-God and the Body-of-Christ thematics see Minear, IMAGES, pp. 228-44; also Calhoun, OBERLIN, pp. 67-8.

[176] See Minear, IMAGES, pp. 135, 172, 244-9.

[177] NATURE, p. 22.

[178] Ibid., p. 23.

[179] Niebuhr, CHURCH, p. 4.

[180] Ibid., p. 5.

[181] See CHRIST, p. 30; also Minear, IMAGES, pp. 255-67, where an attempt is made to draw the implications of the New Testament image ecclesiology for the controverted questions concerning the four classic marks of the Church, the place of the laity, the nature of ministerial orders and ordination.

[182] DIGEST V, pp. 67-8 (=COCUgreen, pp. 9-10).

[183] NATURE, pp. 23-4. This is not to say that they totally neglected the pneumatic element in the Church; see, for example pp. 13-6. Nevertheless this element is not prominant in the explicit treatment of the People-of-God motif.

[184] MAN, pp. 66-8, 78-9. Here too the pneumatological aspect of the Church is explicitly treated in another context (see pp. 84-8), though this may perhaps best be regarded as a continuation of the earlier exposition.

[185] Mackay, INTERSEMINARY IV, pp. 50-1.

[186] OBERLIN, p. 179. This statement is the conclusion of a long, detailed exposition of the trinitarian economy of salvation.

[187] This and the following quotation from the "Open Letter" follow immediately the text quoted above [DIGEST V, p. 68 (=COCUgreen, p. 10)].

[188] DIGEST V, p. 68 (=COCUgreen, p. 11).

[189] See NATURE, pp. 23-4; MAN, pp. 79-88.

[190] This represents the consensus achieved at the 1963 meeting in the paper "Scripture Tradition and the Guardians of Tradition,": "By Tradition [capital "T" to distinguish it from the particular "traditions" of the churches] we understand the whole life of the Church, ever guided and nourished by the Holy Spirit, and expressed in its worship, witness, way of life, and its order" [DIGEST I-II, pp. 44-5 (=COCUred, p. 24)].

[191] See Outler's report of the TCTTNA to Oberlin: "Our Common History as Christians" OBERLIN, pp. 79-89.

[192] See NATURE, pp. 22-3.

[193]Minear, IMAGES, pp. 67, 70-1; cf. 253-4.

[194]The ATC, for instance, devoted a substantial reflection to the relationship of the Church to Israel and the Kingdom, but in its report, these considerations come at the beginning, whereas the development of the People-of-God motif as a systematic ecclesiological category comes only at the end. Similarly the TCCCNA separates the two themes in its final report, though not in Nelson's interim report (ST. ANDREWS, p. 21). In the joint Interim Report of 1960, the two themes are also separated (ONE LORD, pp. 13-4); but this way of handling the matter met sharp criticism in the 1960 American discussion of this report [NOTES (1960), pp. 22-3.].

[195]NATURE, pp. 9-10.

[196]Thus in the passage quoted above from the ATC report; see also Mackay, INTERSEMINARY IV, pp. 48-51; OBERLIN, p. 177; CHRIST, pp. 21-2. The point is also made in many of the preparatory papers of this last commission. Elsewhere the topic is not treated explicitly enough to merit a judgment.

[197]CHRIST, p. 21.

[198]Mackay, INTERSEMINARY IV, p. 49.

[199]CHRIST, pp. 21-3 (the other quotations in this paragraph are from the same pages). See Nelson, ST. ANDREWS, p. 21. This matter was the object of considerable discussion in the Commission; see NOTES (1954), p. 5; (1956), pp. 7, 28-30; (1957), pp. 34, 45, 48; (1960), pp. 12-5, 23-4, 25-8.

[200]ETH. REALITY, p. 4; the expressions of the Oberlin papers are similar (OBERLIN, p. 177).

[201]CHRIST, pp. 21-6. Interestingly enough, the 1960 joint Interim Report included a section of "The Church and the Kingdom" (ONE LORD, pp. 39-40). The question of the Kingdom arose then in the context of the American discussion of this report at the 1960 section meeting. The tendency to equate the Kingdom with the rule of God already begun in the present age though not yet realized in all its fullness--this tendency is evident in this discussion and is perhaps the clue to the omission of a separate consideration of the matter in the North American Section's final report [see NOTES (1960), pp. 25-6].

[202]Thus ETH. REALITY, p. 4: "No achievement of Christian unity can be a substitute for the kingdom of God, even though all increase in Christian unity is a part of the coming of the kingdom. ...in neither the consecrated individual nor the community of the faithful is the kingdom of God fully realized, though we have an earnest of its coming." (See also pp. 6-9 of the same.) The ATC calls attention to the fact that some interpreters hold that in calling the Twelve Jesus was launching the Messianic kingdom as a divine society on earth, which would develop from their work of preaching the Gospel (NATURE, p. 10); the Commission itself, however, opts for the eschatological view (NATURE, p. 26). The TCCCNA declares that "the Church knows the Spirit as earnest of things to come;" "the Church looks to his [Jesus'] coming again in glory"

(CHRIST, p. 4), and "the Church indeed participates in the fullness
of victory and life which is in Christ; it is indeed given the
'first-fruits' of the Spirit; it has indeed already begun to live
in the new age. But the final 'end' is not yet. The struggle for
its right acknowledgment of the sovereignty of Christ is still
waged within the Church itself. There is sin within the Church.
...the Church lives in hope. Together with the whole creation it
awaits and longs for the final word of God's judgment in Christ"
(CHRIST, p. 25). An even stronger statement of the eschatological
dimension is found in Nelson, ST. ANDREWS, p. 22.

[203] CHRIST, p. 23.

[204] ETH. REALITY, p. 4; CHRIST, pp. 22-6.

[205] ETH. REALITY, p. 4; CHRIST, p. 23.

[206] ETH. REALITY, p. 4; CHRIST, pp. 23, 25. The sinfulness of the
Church was of course treated by the other commissions as well. Here
we are concerned only with its mention in conjunction with the
Israel-Kingdom theme.

[207] Already suggested in NEXT STEPS, p. 16, the role of worship is also
mentioned in NATURE, p. 11; ETH. REALITY, pp. 6-7; Mackay, INTER-
SEMINARY IV, pp. 48-51, MAN, pp. 67-8; PURPOSE, p. 23; WORSHIP,
pp. 57-8 (see also Welch, REALITY, pp. 71-2); COCUred, pp. 24,
38-9.

[208] MAN, pp. 67-8.

[209] See MAN, pp. 68-88. Particular attention is called to the Wright
paper's presentation of the charismatic character of New Testament
church organization and COCU's treatment of the common ministry of
the whole people of God. (MAN, pp. 84-8; and DIGEST III, pp. 21-2
-COCUred, pp. 38-9).

[210] MAN, pp. 79-81.

[211] COMMUNION, pp. 44-5.

[212] Thus it distinguishes between the medieval conceptualists, who
questioned only the ability of man to formulate an essential concept, while acknowledging the existence of intrinsic natures, and
the modern conceptualists ecclesiologists, who would admit no reality behind the human ideas of the Church except the empirically
perceivable relationships among the believers composing it (COM-
MUNION, p. 45).

[213] The ontological question is put more clearly by Scherer, INTER-
SEMINARY III, pp. 30-1; Calhoun, OBERLIN, p. 76; Welch, REALITY,
passim; Minear, IMAGES, pp. 20-1, 254-5; Nelson, ST. ANDREWS, p. 22.

[214] Niebuhr (PURPOSE, pp. 12-3, 16) speaks of "the Church in its wholeness" as the context in which all the more specific manifestations
of the Church participate.

[215] Minear, IMAGES, pp. 254-5.

[216] CHRIST, p. 19; Calhoun, (OBERLIN, p. 21) uses the term "sacramental."

[217] Nelson, ST. ANDREWS, p. 21.

[218] See Minear, IMAGES, pp. 18-9, also 222.

[219] DIGEST VI, p. 87 (=COCUgreen, p. 63).

[220] Minear, IMAGES, pp. 228-32.

[221] Speaking of the New Testament, Minear writes: "...we have not found in any writer the inclination to reduce the profusion [of images] to order, to weave the various strands into a single tapestry, or to arrange the kinds of figurative language into a neat pattern. At times it may seem that the writers did their best to prevent later systematizations from succeeding. One consequence of this profusion is surely this: no one figure can be selected as the dominating base line of all thought about the church. The writers start their thinking not from one image, building upon its foundation a complex set of figurative constructions, but they seem to start from a reality that lies beneath and behind all the images. No writer makes a single image serve in a passage of any length as the only or the sufficient analogy for the community of faith. There is, however, an equally significant corollary. If no figure dominates the stage, all figures gain in import by sharing that stage. Only after we have surrendered the futile effort to choose one image as the key to the others do we grasp the overwhelming synoptic impact of all the images" (Minear, IMAGES, p. 222).

[222] Again Minear: "Image after image points beyond itself to a realm in which God and Jesus Christ and the Spirit are at work. It was of that work and of that realm that the New Testament writer was thinking as he spoke of Kingdom or temple or body. ... No important image retains its full range of reference unless the activity of God within the Church is understood as an activity that operates in and through the Messiah and the Spirit. This is surely why the New Testament offers no definition of the church per se as a separate or autonomous entity. Contemporary modern thought, by contrast, demands definitions that are church-centered in a way foreign to the New Testament" (IMAGES, p. 223). See also Welch, REALITY, pp. 20-1; and PURPOSE, p. 19.

[223] Niebuhr, CHURCH, pp. 2-4; see note 169.

[224] CHRIST, p. 24.

[225] Nelson, ST. ANDREWS, p. 23.

[226] This was already evident in the CCULW's interpretation of the empirical approach, see Chapt. II, pp. 29f.

[227] Welch gives an extended critique of the traditional answers to the question of the "paradox" of the Church; in the end he rejects even the "both-and" solution, not because it is wrong, but because it begs the question by failing to give an account of the "how." "Not denying that the mysteries of faith are finally beyond our comprehension, we can and must explore them to the fullest possible beyond

extent. Otherwise we risk falling into the trap of making paradox
itself a theological principle, adopting this as the appropriate
test of Christian affirmation. Or we reduce theology to a simple
recitation of biblical terms. Or we find ourselves using such
utterly vague expressions as 'in some way'..., which really reveal
only that we do not know exactly what we want to say. The task of
theology is precisely to try to avoid such ambiguities, to say so
far as possible in what ways we refer to the church as sinful society and as people of God, to Christ as man and as God" (Welch,
REALITY, pp. 39-40).

[228] See CHRIST, pp. 11, 13, 20, where this is described as "catholicity
in method." As we have seen, however, this principle is found
throughout the American materials; see esp. note 143 for further
references.

[229] See PURPOSE, p. 19.

[230] See NATURE, pp. 24-6.

[231] Ibid., p. 26.

[232] Welch, REALITY, p. 31.

[233] Ibid., pp. 31-2.

[234] Ibid., p. 32. Such a notion of the theological Church as "pattern"
for the empirical Church was discussed and rejected by the TCCCNA
at its 1960 meeting [NOTES (1960), p. 14].

[235] CHURCH, pp. 65-6. The following quotations are from the same passage.

[236] Welch, REALITY, pp. 33-4, see also CHRIST, p. 24.

[237] CHURCH, p. 64.

[238] Ibid.

[239] Ibid., p. 66.

[240] Welch, REALITY, pp. 35-6.

[241] Ibid., p. 37.

[242] Ibid., pp. 37-8.

[243] Ibid., p. 38.

[244] Ibid., pp. 39-40.

[245] NEXT STEPS, p. 10.

[246] See ibid., pp. 10-4.

[247] NATURE, p. 24.

[248] ETH. REALITY, p. 3.

[249] Scherer, INTERSEMINARY III, p. 40. Scherer acknowledges his indebtedness for this idea to H. R. Niebuhr ["The Hidden Church and the Churches in Sight," Religion in Life, 15, 1 (Winter, 1945/6), 114].

[250] CHRIST, pp. 19-20. See the highly significant exchange in NOTES (1957), pp. 41-3; and (1960), pp. 16, 25-7. The notion of participation was never very clearly defined by the Commission. In his book, Welch gives the following explanation: "Participation, we may say, means having ones being fundamentally in another--though without, of course, loss of selfhood or absorption into one another. And in the ways we have been describing, we are able to see how the life of the Christian in relation to Jesus Christ means participation in his humanity. The relation to him designated as faith, obedience, acceptance, love, hope, etc., is not an 'external' relation, an 'accident' in contrast to 'substantial' selfhood, but a relation which enters into the fabric of personal existence in such a way as to determine its nature as personal existence. As the being of the self is constituted indissolubly in relation to other selves and to God, the new humanity in the Church is found and constituted by being drawn into the event of the life of Jesus Christ. Participation in Christ may be described after the analogy of our participation in one another in the complex interrelation of life in community, both in space (i.e. in relation to other contemporary selves) and in time (i.e. in relation to past selves). It may be designated as sharing, with Christ and with others, in covenant responsibility. It may be spoken of in terms of action, as the pattern of the life of Christ is embodied in the life of his followers. It may be referred to under the rubric of hope, of life lived together toward and determined by its completion and perfection in union with Christ in the kingdom. And in all these ways, the humanity of the Christian man depends upon and is drawn into the being of Christ... This is an 'adoptive' sonship, because it derives from his incorporation of our humanity into himself and our life in him through faith. It is really sonship, however, because this means not merely a likeness between the humanity of the Christian and the humanity of Christ but a real sharing (albeit incomplete and imperfect) by the new humanity in the church in the crucified and risen manhood of Christ" (Welch, REALITY, pp. 163-4). See also Knox, EARLY CHURCH, pp. 50-62.

[1] See esp. NATURE, pp. 14-5.

[2] MEANINGS, pp. 49-50.

[3] Final Report of the Third World Conference on Faith and Order in Lund, Aug. 15-28, 1952, in DOC. HIST., p. 88.

[4] Welch, REALITY, pp. 187-8.

[5] See the critique of the Interim Report in NOTES (1960), p. 17.

[6] See MEANINGS, p. 50.

[7] NATURE, p. 26.

[8] Nelson, ST. ANDREWS, p. 20.

[9] Ibid.

[10] Ibid.

[11] Ibid., p. 21.

[12] Ibid., pp. 21-2. The quotation within the quotation is from a remark by Florovsky in the course of the 1958 meeting. The whole passage deserves quoting, because it makes clear just how intimate the connection between christology and soteriology was intended to be understood. "Christology is introduced in the New Testament in a definitely if not exclusively soteriological context. The person of Christ...is the message of salvation, and the whole emphasis is on the purpose of Jesus Christ. His presence is presented and interpreted in the context of his redemptive work and his redemptive purpose. At the same time, everything we find in the Scripture seems to have a definite emphasis, that salvation is an act and a grant of God and in no sense a human achievement. Also God works to save with human means, and divine purpose is accomplished in the life which is perfectly human, the historical life, death transcended by the mystery of the resurrection and the glorification of Jesus Christ." (cited from Welch, EXTRACTS, Am. Sect., p. 4). Statements of similar intent by other commission members can be found throughout the section meeting minutes.

[13] Ferré, HUMANITY, p. 1. See also Welch, REALITY, pp. 112-6. As authorization for his statement, Ferré (HUMANITY, p. 1) cites Ignatius of Antioch: "When I heard some people saying, 'If I don't find it in the original documents, I don't believe it in the gospel,' I answered them, 'But it is written there.' They retorted, 'That's just the question.' To my mind it is Jesus Christ who is the original documents. The inviolable archives are his cross and death and his resurrection and the faith that came by him. It is these things and through your prayers that I want to be justified ('Letter of Ignatius to the Philadelphians,' in Richardson, Early Christian Fathers, p. 110)."

[14] CHRIST, p. 18. Regrettably there seems no way of avoiding an equivocation in the use of the word "nature" to refer to Christ and to the Church. In christology the term "nature" has traditionally been

used in a very restricted technical sense to designate the two
(abstract) operative principles in the incarnate Word as opposed
to the single (concrete) subject. This usage has been followed by
the TCCCNA in its christological discussion, though the difficulties raised about traditional christology in the course of these
discussions indicates that the members did not feel altogether at
ease with such a way of thinking. In ecclesiology, on the contrary, no distinction between person and nature is traditionally
made. Here therefore the American theology could operate with a
more concrete notion of "nature," as when they describe the nature
of the Church as a divine-human reality--a use of the term "nature"
more akin to the pre-Chalcedonian, Cyrillic usage, as the TCCCNA
itself suggests; see CHRIST, pp. 17-8. See Welch, REALITY, p. 89,
note 1.

[15]CHRIST, p. 18. See the critical discussions of this notion in
Ferré, HUMANITY, pp. 7-14, and Welch, REALITY, pp. 99-112.

[16]Welch (REALITY, p. 85, note 4) suggests that the communicatio idi-
omatum must be thought together with "the more active and soteriological concept of communicatio operationem."

[17]CHRIST, p. 18. See Ferré, HUMANITY, pp. 3-7, and Welch, REALITY,
pp. 78-89.

[18]CHRIST, p. 18, see also p. 19; and ST. ANDREWS, pp. 22-3.

[19]CHRIST, p. 18. See Welch, REALITY, pp. 220-5.

[20]CHRIST, pp. 18-9.

[21]ST. ANDREWS, p. 22.

[22]Ibid.

[23]See Pittenger, DOCTRINE, p. 6.

[24]See chapt. III, pp. 130ff.

[25]Pittenger, DOCTRINE, p. 11; the text is included in Welch
EXTRACTS, p. 3. See also Welch, REALITY, pp. 89-98.

[26]CHRIST, pp. 17-8.

[27]Ibid., p. 18.

[28]Ibid.

[29]Ibid.

[30]Ibid. Welch goes so far as to suggest, "the lordship of Christ is
exhibited in his identification with sinful man, particularly with
the disobedient Son Israel. Herein is revealed the heart of God's
grace and love, which is his being God. And as his self-humilia-
tion is an act of God's love, it is a possibility of his being, and
not a contradiction but the true disclosure of his omniscience and
glory" (Welch, REALITY, p. 85).

[31] CHRIST, p. 18.

[32] See Florovsky's comment at the 1958 Meeting (Welch, EXTRACTS, p. 4) cited above in note 12.

[33] CHRIST, p. 16.

[34] ST. ANDREWS, pp. 21-2.

[35] See again the Florovsky comment, loc. cit.

[36] ST. ANDREWS, p. 21.

[37] Ibid.

[38] Ibid., p. 22.

[39] Ibid.

[40] Ibid.

[41] See ibid., pp. 21, 23-4, and CHRIST, pp. 19-20.

[42] ST. ANDREWS, p. 21.

[43] CHRIST, p. 19.

[44] ST. ANDREWS, p. 25.

[45] See CHRIST, pp. 19-20.

[46] See the paper by E. R. Hardie, "Word and Sacrament in the Early Church," (FOC/TCCC/NA, Aug. 1956) mimeo.

[47] ST. ANDREWS, p. 23.

[48] Ibid., p. 24.

[49] See CHRIST, pp. 19-20.

[50] Welch, REALITY, pp. 152-64. See note 250 of Chapt. III for a brief summary of Welch's explanation.

[51] ONE LORD, pp. 21, 23-5.

[52] ST. ANDREWS, pp. 23-5.

[53] CHRIST, p. 19, see also pp. 20, 22, and 23. See Welch, REALITY, pp. 91-3.

[54] CHRIST, p. 19.

[55] Ibid.

[56] Ibid., pp. 19-20.

[57] Ibid., p. 20. See Welch, REALITY, pp. 29-30, 38-41.

[58] CHRIST, p. 24.

[59] ST. ANDREWS, p. 21.

[60] CHRIST, p. 19.

[61] ST. ANDREWS, p. 21.

[62] Harrelson, SPIRIT, pp. 29f.

[63] Ibid.

[64] ST. ANDREWS, p. 22.

[65] Ibid., p. 23.

[66] Ibid.

[67] NOTES (1956), p. 9; the text is cited in Welch, EXTRACTS, p. 9.

[68] ST. ANDREWS, p. 23.

[69] Ibid.

[70] NOTES (1956), p. 11; cited also in Welch, EXTRACTS, p. 11.

[71] Ibid.

[72] See ONE LORD, pp. 15-6.

[73] CHRIST, p. 21.

[74] Ibid., p. 22.

[75] Ibid., pp. 25-6.

[76] Ibid., pp. 22-3.

[77] NOTES (1956), p. 17.

[78] CHRIST, p. 23; see also pp. 20-1.

[79] Ibid., p. 21.

[80] ETH. REALITY, p. 3.

[81] Ibid.

[82] Ibid., p. 4.

[83] MAN, pp. 66-7.

[84] Ibid., p. 84.

[85] Ibid., p. 88.

[86] Ibid., p. 77.

[87] MAN, p. 108.

[88] See NATURE, p. 25, and PURPOSE, pp. 19-21.

[89] Thomas, CORPUS, pp. 6-8.

[90] CHRIST, p. 23, also p. 31; see NOTES (1956), p. 20 and Niebuhr, CHURCH.

[91] CHRIST, p. 23. The TCCCNA itself invites comparison of its statements with those of the joint European and American Study Commission report on "The Lordship of Christ over the World and the Church," Arnoldshain, March 31 - April 5, 1959, which appeared in The Ecumenical Review, XI (1958-9), 437-49. Although in substance the two reports are similar, there are important differences of expression suggesting subtle differences between European and American attitudes. The "Lordship of Christ" report also calls attention to the ambiguity of the New Testament attitude toward the world and to the reality of the rule of God in the world as well as in the Church. Nevertheless, it never sharply distinguishes between world in the sense of the whole creation and 'world' in the sense of the opposition of fallen creation to the divine activity. Indeed though the fourth proposition of the "Lordship" report suggests that through the Church the world comes to recognize itself as the new creation (loc. cit., 443), the overall impression given is that world is at best understood as a synonym for the secular society, to which the Church is sent (see Prop. 5, loc. cit., 443)--something a good deal less than the totality of creation turned to God, which is intended in the TCCCNA report (see CHRIST, p. 31). True the "Lordship" report insists that world and Church compenetrate, that the Church too is only provisional, and that in the Church as in the world the Lordship of Christ can be obscured (see Prop. 2, loc. cit., 442); yet even here, the world appears more as the inferior, unenlightened partner who receives from the Church rather than gives as well as receiving.

[92] CHRIST, pp. 23-4, also p. 31.

[93] Ibid., p. 23.

[94] Ibid.

[95] Ibid., p. 24.

[96] The NAWG was to formulate this with even greater clarity than the TCCCNA; see MISSIONARY, pp. 69-70.

[97] CHRIST, p. 24, also pp. 31-2, and ST. ANDREWS, p. 23.

[98] CHRIST, p. 25, see ST. ANDREWS, p. 23.

[99] CHRIST, p. 25. Niebuhr (CHURCH, p. 6) speaks of "the churchly character of the societies of the world." They too, he suggests, are elected to being, summoned to be covenant communities and to fulfil missions in the realm of God.

[100] CHRIST, p. 25.

[101]CHRIST, p. 25; see ST. ANDREWS, p. 23. Niebuhr (CHURCH, pp. 7-8) suggests: "Though it sounds paradoxical it seems nevertheless to be true that the important difference between the Church and the world is that the church knows itself to be world before God while the world does not know this but thinks that it can be like God. Perhaps it would be better to say that the Church consists of that portion of humanity which, knowing God, knows that man is not God and has made the decision before God that it will never play God but let God be Lord."

[102]See the exchange between Welch, Calhoun, Ferré and Florovsky at the 1960 Meeting [NOTES (1960), pp. 16-7]. Perhaps Florovsky's remarks come closest to expressing what the Commission intended in its explanation of proposition four. (Note that the text given in the minutes is a summary paraphrase not a verbal stenograph): "In one sense Gregory of Nyssa and Cyril of Alexandria could speak this way and we ought not to be misled by their Platonic language. The logos or second Person of the Trinity did not assume a man but humanity, historic humanity, in a sense the whole of humanity. This is more than a Platonic idea. It is a mysterious solidarity of humanity and not an aggregate. Morally it is a single multi-personal reality. The idea of the solidarity of mankind is a biblical notion. This view of the Incarnation is one reason we find so little in the Fathers about the Church. At every point a doctrine of the Church is present in the doctrine of the impersonal humanity of Christ, beginning with Irenaeus and his doctrine of 'recapitulation.' This does not mean that we share in hypostatic union, but we do share in a 'new creation' made explicit in the Incarnation of the Word. The Church is not an extension of the Incarnation, but an implication of the Incarnation," [NOTES (1960), p. 16]. See also Welch, REALITY, pp. 91-4 and pp. 152-80.

[103]NOTES (1960), p. 8.

[104]CHRIST, p. 24, also p. 32.

[105]This comes out in the passage in which the TCCCNA report goes on to explain the way in which the Church is both absorbed in and yet separated from the 'sinful world' with which Christ brings her into conflict. "The Church does not preserve its self-identity by arrogant assertion of itself as over against the world, or by protective isolation from the world. It is most surely separate from the sinful world when it most fully embodies and most humbly expresses the Servant-form of the incarnate Lord, and becomes the Servant suffering for the world, bearing in its body the dying of Christ for man, and thus demonstrating in action its willingness to make the world's suffering its own. Conversely, the Church is most surely absorbed in the sinful world when it is afraid to spend its life and seeks rather to save itself, when it becomes self-defensive and trusts its own wisdom or strength, and when in spiritual pride it holds aloof from the world or in pride of power it seeks to control the world for its own ends" (CHRIST, p. 24).

[106]See CHRIST, p. 19.

[107]Ibid., p. 23.

[108]CHURCH, p. 67.

[109] CHURCH, p. 63.

[110] MEANINGS, p. 49.

[111] CHRIST, p. 26.

[112] Ibid.

[113] Ibid., p. 27.

[114] "The basic and originating conviction of Christian faith is that God has acted in Jesus Christ. And the basic reality of the Church is constituted by the event thus asserted: God in Christ acting through the Spirit, with the human response to that action. This means that the event, or Christ's action with the Holy Spirit's empowering response, is the prius of the Church." (CHRIST, p. 28).

[115] The text gives manifold reasons for this necessity: "the structured expression of Christ's activity in the Church is not only required by man's historical and social condition. Above all, it is required by the definiteness of the Incarnation, by the enduring identity of the Spirit, and by the fact that in the response men make to Christ in the Spirit they are not extricated from their proper manhood but act in a truly embodied way. Furthermore, the continuity of the event, establishing the consistency of the fellowship of Christian faith, worship and life can be maintained and has been maintained, only in definite patterns. Similarly, the mission of the Church—its apostolicity or 'sentness'—necessitates now as always a structure of mission, a genuine apostolicity, which will guarantee and symbolize the abiding sentness which is integral to its nature" (CHRIST, p. 28).

[116] CHRIST, p. 28.

[117] NATURE, pp. 16-7; see also NEXT STEPS, pp. 11-3, and OBERLIN, pp. 207, 224-9.

[118] The treatment of the work of the Spirit in the Church is found in the section entitled "The Church as Event and Institution," CHRIST, pp. 27-30. That this agreement was not reached lightly can be seen by comparing the position taken in the final report with the disagreements expressed in the 1956 discussions; see NOTES (1956), esp. pp. 15-20.

[119] CHRIST, p. 27.

[120] Ibid.

[121] Ibid., p. 28.

[122] Ibid., p. 27.

[123] Ibid., p. 28.

[124] Ibid., p. 27.

[125] Ibid.

[126] Floyd V. Filson, "The Holy Spirit in the New Testament" (FOC/TCCC/ NA, n.p., 1960) mimeo. 17 pp. The discussion is summarized in NOTES (1960), pp. 25-30.

[127] Filson, HOLY SPIRIT, p. 14.

[128] Ibid.

[129] Ibid., p. 15.

[130] Ibid., pp. 15-6.

[131] Ibid., p. 16. This is not to say that the function does not re- quire that its form have "official" character. There is no opposi- tion between function and office. By the same token, however, there is not opposition between the notion of office as such and the idea of changing structural forms of that office.

[132] Ibid., pp. 16-7.

[133] Ibid., p. 15.

[134] NOTES (1960), p. 30.

[135] CHRIST, p. 28.

[136] See CHRIST, p. 27 and also p. 11 (where reference is made to Cal- houn's explanation of "catholicity" in his Oberlin adress; see OBERLIN, pp. 74-5) and p. 15.

[137] CHRIST, p. 14.

[138] Ibid., p. 15.

[139] Ibid., pp. 12-3.

[140] Ibid., pp. 14-5.

[141] Ibid., p. 28.

[142] Ibid., p. 27.

[143] Filson, HOLY SPIRIT, p. 17.

[144] CHRIST, p. 29; the same conclusion was expressed in INSTIT., p. 21.

[145] Filson, HOLY SPIRIT, p. 17, gives a partial list of tests of the Spirit contained in the New Testament. Scattered throughout the texts of the post-Lund commissions, the Oberlin reports, the COCU documents and the NAWG reports can be found numerous examples of such relative criteria.

[146] CHRIST, p. 10.

[147] Ibid., p. 15.

[148] "We do not claim that by examining the nature of the Church in the light of its relation to its Lord we have succeeded in solving all

the problems which have perplexed and divided Christendom, But we
have found that our approach has made the formidable controversies
of the past seem less intractable, and we have been led further
into the understanding of God's self-revelation which is the foundation of all Christian unity." (CHRIST, p. 9).

[149] See CHRIST, pp. 29-30.

[150] COCU, "An Open Letter to the Churches," DIGEST V, pp. 69-70 and 73
(=COCUgreen, pp. 12-3 and 17).

[1] For a general exposition of the theory-practice relationship from an American theological perspective, see PURPOSE, pp. 126-31.

[2] See TRADITION, pp. 7-14.

[3] Ibid., p. 12.

[4] Ibid., p. 7.

[5] This is well documented in the paper prepared by the CCULW after the first meeting in 1935; see Dun, MINUTES, 1ff.

[6] This point was made repeatedly in the American documents; see esp. NEXT STEPS, pp. 10-3, 26-9; NATURE, pp. 16-7; TRADITION, pp. 12-3, 18-21; INSTIT., p. 19.

[7] C. H. Dodd, "Unavowed Motives in Ecumenical Discussion," The Ecumenical Review, 2 (1949/50), 54-5. The passage quoted here was cited by the TCTTNA in its report, TRADITION, p. 8.

[8] Ibid., p. 12.

[9] CHRIST, p. 11.

[10] TRADITION, p. 15.

[11] Ibid., p. 12.

[12] CHRIST, p. 11.

[13] TRADITION, p. 12.

[14] Ibid., p. 13. See also J. Pelikan's exposition of the Commission's thinking on "theological historicism" in his report, "Overcoming History by History," OLD & NEW, pp. 40-2. That the "relativism" espoused by the Commission is an a posteriori induction rather than an a priori postulate or deduction is evidenced by the explicit repudiation of an absolute relativism on p. 19 of the Commission's final report.

[15] TRADITION, p. 19.

[16] Ibid., pp. 21-3.

[17] Ibid., p. 13.

[18] Ibid.

[19] Ibid. Elsewhere the Commission writes: "Pluralism is a plain fact of all Christian history. The diversity of the traditions must be acknowledged even as the integrity of the Tradition is confessed. This diversity cannot be overcome by a simplicist appeal to New Testament Christianity, the consensus quinquaesaecularis, the vincentian canon, or any other primitivistic paradigm (such as the idealization of the 13th or the 16th centuries). None of the plural traditions has the intrinsic authority to disinherit the other. All have a basic

right to be considered and appraised in the light of their professed intention to be obedient to the Tradition." (TRADITION, p. 19.)

[20] Ibid.

[21] See A. Outler's report "Traditions in Transit" in OLD & NEW, p. 44.

[22] TRADITION, p. 18.

[23] Ibid., p. 16.

[24] Ibid., pp. 16-7.

[25] Ibid., p. 17.

[26] Ibid., p. 22.

[27] Ibid., pp. 22-3.

[28] Ibid., pp. 17-8. By contrast the European section defined "the Tradition" in such a way as to virtually identify it with the Church as the "continuation...throughout all ages" of "the History of God himself on earth, centered in the history of the Incarnation" (K. E. Skydsgaard, "Tradition as an Issue in Contemporary Theology," OLD & NEW, pp. 29-30; see also ST. ANDREWS, pp. 42-3). For the American section, on the contrary, "the Tradition" is in the Church but not identical with it; rather it is understood as the originating, controlling and anticipating action of the Spirit of God in the Church (see TRADITION, p. 19; also Outler, OLD & NEW, p. 46).
The 1963 consensus of the COCU follows the European rather than the American definition: "By Tradition we understand the whole life of the Church, ever guided and nourished by the Holy Spirit, and expressed in its worship, witness, way of life and its order" [DIGEST I-II, pp. 44-5 (=COCUred, p. 24)]. Whatever advantages such a definition might have, it has the decisive disadvantage of conflating precisely what the TCTTNA was so careful to distinguish, namely: (a) the divine-human traditionary process; (b) the divine source and guidance of this process; (c) the substance of what is handed down, i.e. the traditum; and (d) the pattern or form in which this substance has been clothed in apostolic times. The COCU text declares: "As such, Tradition includes both the act of delivering by which the good news is made known and transmitted from one generation to another" [DIGEST I-II, p. 45 (=COCUred, p. 24)]; as a result "traditions" (with a small "t") are written off as "teachings and practices which obscure or corrupt rather than express the revelation to which the Scriptures witness" [DIGEST I-II, p. 44 (=COCUred, p. 24)]. Such a statement would be inconceivable for the TCTTNA; elsewhere, in fact, the same COCU consensus document follows a value-free definition of "traditions" which is not unlike that formulated by the TCTTNA [see DIGEST I-II, p. 45 (=COCUred, p. 25)].

[29] TRADITION, pp. 18-20.

[30] See ibid., p. 8 and 22-3, also CHRIST, p. 24.

[31] TRADITION, p. 19.

[32] TRADITION, p. 22; see Outler's explanation of the inherent pull of the traditionary process towards reactionary traditionalism and anarchic anti-traditionalism (Outler, NEW & OLD, pp. 45-6).

[33] TRADITION, p. 19.

[34] Ibid., p. 18; see Pelikan, OLD & NEW, pp. 36-42.

[35] TRADITION, p. 21.

[36] Ibid.

[37] Ibid.; see Pelikan, OLD & NEW, pp. 38-9.

[38] TRADITION, p. 18.

[39] Ibid., p. 19, also p. 27.

[40] See ibid., pp. 20, 23-4, 27, and Outler, OLD & NEW, pp. 44-6.

[41] TRADITION, p. 27.

[42] See ibid., pp. 20 and 27, also Outler, OLD & NEW, p. 44.

[43] TRADITION, p. 20.

[44] "Haec Ecclesia, in hoc mundo ut societas constituta et ordinata, subsistit in Ecclesia catholica, a successore Petri et Episcopis in eius communione gubernata, licet extra eius compaginem elementa plura sanctificationis et veritates inveniantur, quae ut dona Ecclesia Christi propria, ad unitatem catholicam impellunt" [Const. de Eccl. c.I, art. 8 (Citta del Vaticano: Typis polygl. Vat., 1964) 9-10; NCWC translation, p. 8].

[45] The footnote to the official text cites the Professio fidei tridentina (Denz Schön. 1868), which has "Sancti catholica, apostolica Romana Ecclesia"; it also refers to Vat. I., Const. dogm. "Dei Filius," c. 1 (Denz.-Schön. 3001), which uses the same expression.

[46] See Const. de Eccl., c. 2, art. 13.

[47] See ibid., c. 2, art. 14.

[48] See Kleines Konzilskompendium, hrsg. K. Rahner and H. Vorgrimler, 2. erg. Aufl. (Herder Bücherei, Bd. 270-3; Freiburg, Basel, Wien: Herder, 1967), p. 8. On the other hand this concession is weakened by the intervention of Paul VI which forced the introduction of the term "catholica" in Decr. de. Oecum. (Citta del Vaticano: Typis polygl. Vat., n.d.), c. 1, art. 17.

[49] See A. Grillmeier, "Kommentar zum I. Kapitel der Dogm. Konst. über die Kirche, Art. 8, 2, in Das Zweite Vatikanische Konzil, Dokumente et Kommentare, 1 Teil (LThK, Ergänzungsband I; Freiburg-Basel-Wien: Herder, 1966), pp. 174-5.

[50] See Kleines Konzilskompendium, p. 107.

[51] "Tradita autem ab Apostolis haereditas diversis formis et modis acceptata est et inde ab ipsis Ecclesiae primordiis hic et illic varie explicata ob diversitatem quoque ingenii et vitae condicionum. Quae omnia, praeter causas externas, propter defectum etiam mutuae comprehensionis et caritatis separationibus ansam praebuerunt.

Quamobrem Sacrosancta Synodus omnes quidem, sed praesertim eos exhortatur qui in instaurationem plenae communionis optatae inter Ecclesias orientales et Ecclesiam catholicam incumbere intendent, ut debitam considerationem habeant de hac peculiari condicione nascentium crescentiumque Ecclesiarum Orientis et de indole relationum, quae inter eas et Sedem Romanam ante separationem sibi efforment, Haec accurate servata ad dialogum intentum summopere conferent" (Decr. de Oecum. c. 3, art. 14; NCWC trans. p. 15).

[52] Decr. de Oecum. c. 3, art. 16.

[53] "Quae supra de legitima diversitate dicta sunt, eadem placet etiam de diversa theologica doctrinarum enuntiatione declarare. Etenim in veritatis revelatae exploratione methodi gressusque diversi ad divina cognoscenda et confitenda in Oriente et in Occidente adhibiti sunt. Unde mirum non est quosdam aspectus mysterii revelati quandoque magis congrue percipi et in meliorem lucem poni ab uno quam ab altero, ita ut tunc variae illae theologicae formulae non raro potius inter se complere dicendae sint quam opponi" (Decr. de Oecum. c. 3, art. 17).

[54] Ibid., c. 3, tit., and art. 19ff.

[55] See DOCUMENTS, p. 355, note 45.

[56] This is especially evident in Decr. de Oecum., c. 3, art. 22.

[57] Ibid., c. 3, art. 20-3.

[58] Ibid., c. 3, art. 19.

[59] In the section on the prayer life of the dissident western Christians, the text passes over in silence the creative enrichment of the Christian worship tradition through Protestant hymnody, prayer forms, etc; yet it makes a point of calling attention to the "notable features of the liturgy which they shared with us of old" [Ceteroquin cultus oerum nonnumquam elementa conspicue communis antiquae liturgiae prae se fert" (Decr. de Oecum., c. 3, art. 23; NCWC trans.)].

[60] "In necessariis unitatem custodientes, omnes in Ecclesia, secundum munus unicuique datum, cum in variis formis vitae spiritualis et disciplinae, tum in diversitate liturgicorum rituum, immo et in theologica veritatis revelatae elaboratione, debitam libertatem servent; ..." (Decr. de Oecum., c. 1, art. 4; NCWC Translation, p. 8).

[61] See especially "The Ordained Ministry in Ecumenical Perspective," Statement of the international F. & O. Consultation held at Marseilles, Sept., 1972, published in Study Encounter 8, 4 (1972), 1-22, also the statement by the Groupe des Dombes, "Accord doctrinal entre catholiques et protestants sur l'Eucharistie," in Documenta-

tion catholique, Nr. 1606 (April 2, 1972), 334-8; and the Memorandum der Arbeitsgemeinschaft ökumenischer Universitäts-institute, Reform und Anerkennung kirchlicher Ämter (Munchen: Chr. Kaiser/ Mainz: M. Grünewald, 1973). Further international or european documents of this type can be found in Um Amt und Herrenwahl: Dokumente zum evangelisch/romisch-katholischen Gespräch, hrsg. G. Gassmann et al. (Ökumenische Dokumentation 1; Frankfurt am Main: O. Lembeck/J. Knecht, 1974).

[62] See, for example, the generally negative reviews of the Memorandum originally published in KNA-Kol. in early 1972 and reproduced in Amt im Widerstreit, hrsg. K. Schuh (Berlin: Morus, 1973)--hereafter cited as AMT. The same volume reprints the more positive review by K. Rahner which originally appeared in the Frankfurter Allgemeine Zeitung (14 Feb. 1973).

[63] Most recently, the declaration of the Congregation for the Faith, Erklärung zur katholischen Lehre über die Kirche, die gegen einige heutige Irrtümer zu verteidigen ist, vom 24 Juni, 1973 (Citta del Vaticano: Typis polygl. Vat., 1973), 21 pp.

[64] The diversity of New Testament church order and the gradual emergence and spread of mono-episcopacy in the latter part of the first and the beginning of the second centuries is generally conceded by Roman Catholic exegetes and historians today. Increasingly the discussion has concentrated on the factors which led to the gradual displacement of alternative organizational structures, and on the question whether or not this relatively late option for mono-episcopacy is reformable. A similar trend can be traced in the discussion of the gradual development of the person primacy of the Roman bishop.

[65] Only recently have Roman Catholic theologians become sensitive to this problem. Today the consideration of the sociological aspects of the development of Church order and organization is widely accepted, and the mass of literature dealing with both general trends and specific phases of development has assumed enormous proportions.

[66] Hitherto Roman Catholic theologians have tended to treat these matters all too apologetically, their concern being to show how they pose no threat to prevailing dogmas and theological opinion. Such studies also have their place in the dialectic of theological advance; indeed they serve a very important role in helping to uncover false antinomies postulated by similarly biased historiography rooted in other ecclesiological traditions. Nevertheless, an exclusively apologetic treatment tends often to underestimate the seriousness of the practical departure from positions maintained only theoretically. Only recently, for instance, are Catholic historians coming to admit the contribution of the late medieval exemption practice and the grants of habitual exercise of quasi-episcopal jurisdiction by simple priests or even laymen (e.g. abbesses, bishops-elect, or the territorial prince and his jurists) to the development of the Reformation concepts of church office. What value does the theoretical maintenance of a principle have when in practice the exceptions, at least over wide regions of the church, have become the rule? This question can no longer be ignored by our ecclesiology.

[67] See the exposition and critique of both the progressive and regressive theories of doctrinal development by J. Ratzinger, Das Problem der Dogmengeschichte in der Sicht der katholischen Theologie (Arbeitsgemeinschaft für Forschung des Landes Nordrhein-Westfalen, Geisteswiss. H. 139; Köln-Opladen: Westdeutscher Verlag, 1966).

[68] Hans Küng, Unfehlbar? Eine Anfrage (Einsiedeln: Benziger, 1970); American trans. Infallible? An Inquiry, trans. E. Quinn (New York: Doubleday, 1970); English trans. Infallible? An Enquiry, trans. E. Mosbacher (London: Collins, 1971).

[69] The more important contributions to the controversy have been collected in the two compendia Zum Problem der Unfehlbarkeit: Eine Antwort auf die Anfrage von Hans Küng, hrsg. K. Rahner (Quaestiones disputatae, 54; Freiburg, Basel, Wien: Herder, 1971), and Fehlbar? Eine Bilanz, hrsg. H. Küng (Einsiedeln: Benziger, 1973). Further bibliography can be found in this volume. P. J. FitzGerald has recently published a very valuable analysis of the debate using the methods of linguistic analysis, "Infallibility--A Secular Assessment" Irish Theol. Quarterly, 61 (1974), 3-21. The present state of the controversy is reflected in the conciliatory correspondence between Professors Küng Rahner, which was published as "Versöhnliches Schlusswort unter eine Debatte," Publik-Forum 2, 11 (1. June, 1973), 12-5.

[70] In addition to the affirmations of the Council in the decree on Ecumenism quoted above, one may cite here the recent declaration of the Congregation on Faith, where it treats of the historical conditioning of the formularies of faith:
"Hinsichtlich der geschichtlichen Bedingtheit ist vor allem zu beachten, dass der Sinn, den die Glaubensaussagen enthalten, zum Teil von der Aussagekraft der angewandten Sprache in einer bestimmten Zeitepoche und unter bestimmten Lebensverhältnissen abhängt. Es kann unter anderem geschehen, dass eine dogmatische Wahrheit zunächst in einer unvollkommenen, jedoch nicht falschen Weise ausgedrückt wird und dann später, wenn man sie im grösseren Zusammenhang mit den übrigen Glaubenswahrheiten oder menschlichen Erkenntnissen betrachtet, vollständiger und vollkommener ausgesagt wird. Ferner beabsichtigt die Kirche durch ihre neuen lehrmässigen Verlautbarungen, das, was in der Hl. Schrift oder in früheren Aussagen der Tradition schon in irgeneiner Weise enthalten ist, zu bekräftigen oder deutlicher herauszustellen: gleichzeitig aber bemüht sie sich gewöhnlich auch darum, bestimmte Fragen zu lösen oder Irrtümer zurückzuweisen. All diesen Umständen muss Rechnung getragen werden, damit jene Aussagen richtig verstanden werden. Wenn auch die Wahrheiten, die die Kirche durch ihre dogmatischen Formeln in der Tat zu lehren beabsichtigt, sich von den wandelbaren Begriffen einer gewissen Epoche unterscheiden und auch ohne diese ausgedrückt werden können, kann es andererseits mitunter geschehen, dass jene Wahrheiten ebenso vom kirchlichen Lehramt in Worten vorgetragen werden, die selbst Anzeichen einer solchen begrifflichen Bedingtheit an sich tragen.
Nach diesen Überlegungen muss gesagt werden, dass die dogmatischen Formeln des kirchlichen Lehramtes von Anfang an dazu geeignet waren, die geoffenbarte Wahrheit an andere weiterzugeben, und für immer geeignet bleiben, sie denen zu vermitteln, die diese richtig verstehen. Daraus folgt jedoch nicht, dass jede einzelne von ihnen dieses in gleichem Mass gewesen ist oder bleiben wird. Aus diesem Grunde bemühen sich die Theologen, genau aufzuzeigen, welches die

Lehrabsicht ist, die jene verschiedenen Formeln wirklich enthalten, und bieten mit dieser ihrer Arbeit dem lebendigen Lehramt der Kirche, dem sie unterstehen, eine wertvolle Hilfe. Aus demselben Grunde kann es ferner geschehen, dass alte dogmatische Formeln und andere, die diesen eng verbunden sind, im alltäglichen Gebrauch der Kirche lebendig und fruchtbar bleiben, indem ihnen jedoch in geeigneter Weise neue Erklärungen und Aussagen hinzugefugt werden, die ihren ursprunglichen Sinn bewahren und erläutern. Andererseits ist mitunter schon der Fall eingetreten, dass in diesem alltäglichen Gebrauch der Kirche einige Formeln durch neue Ausdrucksweisen ersetzt worden sind, die vom kirchlichen Lehramt eingeführt oder approbiert wurden und denselben lehrmässigen Inhalt deutlicher und vollständiger zum Ausdruck bringen.

Der Aussagegehalt der dogmatischen formeln aber bleibt in der Kirche stets wahr und koharent, auch wenn er mehr verdeutlicht und besser verstanden wird" (Erklärung, pp. 13-4).

Needless to say, this passage is full of difficulties; nevertheless it represents the most sweeping concession to date by an official instance on the historical relativity of the Church's formularies of faith. Only time will tell whether or not the Magisterium of the Roman Catholic Church will eventually move to an even more open position. The experience of the change in attitude toward biblical inerrancy suggests that the Erklärung will not be the final decision on the issue.

[71] Siehe K. Rahner, "Zum Begriff der Unfehlbarkeit in der katholischen Theologie," in Zum Problem Unfehlbarkeit, pp. 11-4.

[72] For a brief summary see Y. Congar, "Die Normen für die Ursprungstreue und Identität der Kirche im Verlauf ihrer Geschichte," Concilium 9. Jg. H. 3 (März, 1973), 156-63. Further bibliography can be found in the other articles of this Concilium number as well as in the Rahner and Küng collections.

[73] Considerable work has been done along these lines for the 19th century development, see for example R. Aubert, "Motivations theologiques et extra-theologiques des partisans et des adversaires de la definition de l'infaillibilité," in L'Infaillibilité. Son aspect philosophique et théologique. Actes du Colloque..., Rome, 5-12 janvier 1970, ed. E. Castelli (Paris: Aubier, 1970), pp. 91-112; C. Langlois, "Die Unfehlbarkeit--eine neue Idee des 19. Jahrhunderts," in Fehlbar? pp. 146-60; and R. Lill, "Historische Voraussetzungen des Dogmas vom Universalepiscopat und von der Unfehlbarkeit des Papstes," Stimmen der Zeit 95, 11 (Nov. 1970), 289-303. Lill in particular calls attention to the contribution of new communications possibilities to the inflation of the popular appreciation of the papal office. This is a line of investigation which must be pursued in regard to the earlier centuries as well.

[74] As an example of what must be done here, see P. McGrath's evaluation of Salmon's argument in his contribution to the above mentioned Concilium number (McGrath, "Der Begriff der Unfehlbarkeit," loc. cit., 185-91). Even among vigorous opponents of Küng's position there is widespread agreement that the term "infallible" is unfortunate because of the misleading associations it evokes.

[75] The expression appears in K. Rahner, "Kritik an Hans Küng," in Zum Problem Unfehlbarkeit, pp. 35-7. See also E. Schillebeeckx, "Das Problem der Amtsunfehlbarkeit," in Concilium, 9, 3 (März, 1973), 206.

[76] Rahner, loc. cit., p. 46; Schillebeeckx, loc. cit., 206-7.

[77] Rahner, "Replik," in Zum Problem Unfehlbarkeit, pp. 55-6; Schillebeeckx, loc. cit., 208. A different, but none the less urgent question, is whether the sort of revision proposed by these authors really can pass as a simple reinterpretation and reformulation. When, for instance the monogenistic postulate of an original sin by Adam and Eve living in the Garden of Paradise and endowed with preternatural gifts is abandoned, it is difficult to see how this can be regarded as merely an "interpretation" of the explicit teaching of the Council of Trent on the subject. Admittedly both theories are attempts to explain one and the same reality, but the modern interpretations literally contradict what is emphatically taught by the first three canons of the Tridentine decree on original sin (see Denz.-Schön., 1511-13). If the modern position on "original sin" be true, then by any ordinary standard of speaking, the tridentine canons are erroneous, however much they may envisage--like every indeliberately false statement--the true object of discourse.

[78] The term "functional method" is not used by any of the official reports (the reference to a "functional approach to religion" in INSTIT., p. 6, refers to a sociological, not a theological approach). W. O. Carver, however, presented a paper to the ATC in 1941 entitled "The Importance of a Functional Study of the Church" 9 pp. mimeo.; and the need for special considerations of ecclesiological structures in terms of their functions is found already in the documents of the CCULW.

[79] See Carver, op. cit.; but note also the reservations expressed by the ATC in NATURE, p. 24. The functional approach is primarily concerned with the organizational, i.e. institutional aspects of the Church in her this-worldly, empirical state.

[80] INSTIT., p. 20.

[81] See TRADITION, pp. 8-9 and INSTIT., p. 19.

[82] Ibid., p. 20.

[83] Ibid.

[84] See Ehrenström, ST. ANDREWS, p. 74.

[85] The only source referred to in the papers of the commission is the report of section 8 of the Oberlin Conference in OBERLIN, pp. 229ff; see INSTIT., p. 18, note 1; also Ehrenström, INSTITUTIONALISM, p. 29, note 9. Even as late as the New Delhi Conference in 1961, the distinction is nowhere referred to in international F. & O. statements.

[86] See MEANINGS, pp. 11-2. The suggestion is made as a critique of the Lausanne Conference's conflation of the two issues. Such confusion,

the CCULW explains, is understandable because over large stretches of the Church's history the ministerial order and the constitutional organization of the churches appeared inseparable from each other. Only in more recent history has the constitutional development of many denominations led to a division of the two issues. Increasingly, for instance, churches with episcopal orders have adopted the structures of democratic representative government, especially in respect to the legislative power; whereas other churches without episcopal orders have introduced episcopal-type administrative organizations.

[87] NATURE, p. 17. The very choice of the words "order" and "organization" seems more a coincidence than a result of conscious reflection. Otherwise the distinction is never mentioned in the papers of the Commission.

[88] The group was in fact the Commission on Faith and Order of the Canadian Council of Churches. The proposal evidently came from the arrangements committee for the Oberlin Conference; where it ultimately originated can no longer be traced. To judge from the context, in which the distinction was intended to be discussed at Oberlin, i.e. section 8, "The Variations in Denominational Polities" (OBERLIN, pp. 229-38), the original intention appears to have been the distinction between ministerial order and ecclesiastical polity, more or less as proposed by the CCULW two decades earlier. In fact, however, the Toronto Group developed its explanation along the more general lines anticipated by the ATC report. See Toronto Study Group, "Report on Order and Organization" (North American Conference on F. & O., Orientation Paper, Section 8; n.p., [1956]), mimeo., 15 pp.--abbrev. Toronto, ORDER. The portion of the section report dealing with the distinction (OBERLIN, pp. 231-6) is for the most part an abridged version of the Toronto paper.

[89] See Muelder, OBERLIN, p. 99.

[90] The most notable modification was to distinguish "a graded rank system of levels of institutions, all of which possess theological dignity in varying degrees." (Ehrenström, ST. ANDREWS, p. 74).

[91] INSTIT., p. 21.

[92] The Commission defines "institution" as "a definite and established structure (goal, means value orientation, sanction) built around and sustaining one or more specific functions"; a social function, in turn, is explained as "a whole activity which accomplishes a desired end or fulfills a basic need for society and for the individuals which make up that society" (INSTIT., p. 6.)

[93] Toronto, ORDER, pp. 3-4 and 5.

[94] See INSTIT., pp. 10-1. The point is constantly forgotten in Catholic polemic against the conception of a charismatic structure of the Church. In pleading for greater flexibility in the conception of church office no serious theologian is advocating total anarchy. The office of an elected chief-of-state with a limited term of office is as much an office as that of an hereditary, life-long monarch. The ability of the collective, through appointed organs

and procedures, to elect, correct, and if necessary impeach the
executive officer does not denude such officers of official status
and real authority.

[95] INSTIT., p. 6.

[96] Ibid., p. 7.

[97] Toronto, ORDER, pp. 3-4.

[98] The development of this particular example is based on Toronto,
ORDER, pp. 4-5.

[99] Ibid., p. 5.

[100] Ibid.

[101] Ibid., p. 6.

[102] Ibid., p. 8.

[103] Ibid., pp. 6-7.

[104] INSTIT., pp. 21 & 23; and Toronto, ORDER, p. 6.

[105] Toronto, ORDER, p. 6. It is precisely with regard to the ministry
that the greatest disputes occur regarding the content of the apostolic tradition. Thus, as the Toronto paper observes, despite all
disagreements about the manner of divine institution of the ministry
and the patterns of its organization, "we should presumably agree
that apart from the divine call to certain persons to perform these
kerygmatic and sacramental functions in the congregation, the Church
would no exist as an ordered community, so that the entrusting of the
ministerial function to particular persons within the fellowship is
an element of Church Order distinct from the Gospel which is proclaimed and the Sacraments which are administered" (ibid.).

[106] INSTIT., p. 21.

[107] Ibid.

[108] Toronto, ORDER, p. 7; also pp. 11-2.

[109] See the general reflections of the NAWG in MISSIONARY, pp. 66, 68,
91-2, and the "clues for understanding structures" worked out in the
Commission report. Likewise of interest is the COCU document "Guidelines for the Structure of the Church" [DIGEST VI, pp. 87-94 (=COCU-
green, pp. 63-73)].

[110] See for instance the objections raised in AMT to the Memorandum,
Reform und Anerkennung, where a functional method similar to that
proposed by the Americans was adopted by a european Catholic-Protestant dialog project.

[111] One example is the different Catholic attempts to explain the rise
of the threefold hierarchy as an expression of apostolic tradition.
H. Bacht ("Kritische Fragen zur Verkündigungauftrag und Struktur der

Ämter," AMT, p. 63) is prepared to admit that given the existence of an office with episcopal character, the later development of the subordinated presbyter and deacon orders and the concommitant focusing of the apostolic office in the monoepiscopate is a "Frage der innerkirchlichen Praktabilität."

[112] L. Scheffczyk grants as much in his critique of the use of the functional method by the Memorandum (Scheffczyk, "Das kirchliche Amt im Verständnis der katholischen Theologie," AMT, pp. 17-8). As we have seen, the Americans' formulation of the functional method by no means substantiates Scheffczyk's charge that this method supposes "das die Kirche im Wesen ein rein natürlich-soziologisches Gebilde sei" (ibid., p. 18). On the contrary, every ecclesiology is obliged to take due account of the sociological factors in the Church if it is to escape the counter-charge of ecclesiological docetism.

[113] This conception is repeatedly expressed in the statements of recent popes and of the Roman curia, see for instance, prop. 4 of the Oath against Modernism (Denz.-Schön. 3541), Pius XII, "Humani generis," nn. 565-7 and 569 (Denz.-Schön. 3881-4 and 3886-8); Paul VI, "Ecclesiam suam," AAS 56 (1964), 614-6, 626-7; "Mysterium Fidei," AAS 57 (1965), 757-8; "Siamo particolarmente liete," AAS 58 (1966), 652-4. In the last case it is interesting to note what passage Paul VI quotes from the address by John XXII at the opening of the Council, namely "...oportet ut haec doctrina certa et immutabilis, cui fideli obsequium est praestandum, ea ratione pervestigetur et exponatur quam tempora postulant nostra. Est enim aliud ipsum depositum fidei, seu veritates, quae veneranda doctrina nostra continentur, aliud modus quo eaedem enuntiantur, eodem sensu eademque sententia" [italics added] (loc. cit.). See also Paul VI, "Ogni volta," AAS 57 (1965), 723.

[114] See for instance, K. Schuh, "Vorwort," in AMT, pp. 12-4.

[115] This point cannot be pursued here. For the thomistic school, see L. Regis, Epistemology, trans. I. C. Byrne (New York: Macmillan, 1959), pp. 290-7, also T. Guzie, The Analogy of Learning (New York: Sheed & Ward, 1960), pp. 82-3.

[116] The Schreiben der Bischöfe des deutschsprachigen Raumes über das priesterliche Amt. Eine biblisch-dogmatische Handreichung (Trier: Paulusverlag, 1970), pp. 40-1, contains what is perhaps the first open acknowledgment of this fact in an official statement.

[117] See H. Fries' explanation of the meaning of "recognition" ("Anerkennung"), Fries, "Was heisst Anerkennung," AMT, pp. 110-21.

[118] Theologically such progressive institutionalization is necessary, because it expresses the unity of Christ's Church which already exists; sociologically, because it helps create that experience of unity which alone can envigorate the theoretical discussion. See NON-THEOL., p. 3; NEXT STEPS, p. 8, and INSTIT., p. 22.

[119] See CHRIST, pp. 25-6.

[120] See, for instance, the Schreiben der deutschen Bischöfe an alle, die von der Kirche mit der Glaubensverkündigung beauftragt sind. Sonderdruck, hrsg. Sekretariat der Deutschen Bischofskonferenz (n.p. [1967]), pp. 6-7.

[121] See "Instructio de particularibus cusibus admittendi alios christianos ad communionem eucharisticam in Ecclesia catholica," No. 5, AAS 64 (1972), 523-4.

[122] The first official step towards allowing Catholics to participate in the Protestant Lord's Supper appears to be the directives issued on Nov. 30, 1972, by Bishop L.-A. Elchinger of Strasbourg; see "L'Hospitalité eucharistique pour les foyers mixtes," Documentation catholique, no. 1626 (18 Fev., 1973), 161-5. A critical study of this instruction will be found in Avery Dulles, "Ministry and Intercommunion: Recent Ecumenical Statements and Debates," Theol. Studies, 34 (1973), 655-61.

[123] INSTIT., p. 23.

[124] Ibid., also the report of Section 8, OBERLIN, pp. 233-8.

[125] INSTIT., pp. 23-4, and again OBERLIN, pp. 236-8.

[126] See INSTIT., pp. 25-6.

[127] See Ibid., pp. 26-8; also the report of Section 6, OBERLIN, pp. 219-22.

[128] See OBERLIN, p. 220.

[129] See INSTIT., pp. 26-8.

[130] PLAN, pp. 13-4.

[131] Ibid., p. 13.

[132] Ibid., pp. 73-4.

[133] See the official publication Consultation on Church Union: A Catholic Perspective (Washington: USCC Publications Office, 1970) with its contributions by Bishop William W. Baum and Father George H. Tavard, [hereafter cited as CATH. PERSP.] also Richard P. McBrien, "The COCU Plan of Union," in Andover Newton Quarterly, 12, 1 (Sept. 1971), 24-33. Considerably more positive in their estimation of the Plan are John T. Ford, "The Vision of the Church in A Plan of Union," The Christian Century, 88 42 (Oct. 20, 1971), 1229-32, reproduced in Church Union at Midpoint, ed. P. A. Crow, Jr. and W. J. Boney (New York: Association, 1972), 99-112; and John F. Hotchkin, "COCU and the wider Reality of Ecumenism," in Church Union at Midpoint, loc. cit., 215-21.

[134] PLAN, p. 35.

[135] See An Order of Worship for the Proclamation of the Word of God and the Celebration of the Lord's Supper with Community (Cincinnati: Forward Movement, 1968), also the ordinal printed at the end of PLAN, pp. 90-102.

[136] PLAN, p. 36.

[137] Ibid., p. 37.

[138] PLAN, p. 34.

[139] Ibid., p. 35.

[140] Ibid., p. 37. This is one of the points singled out for Roman Catholic criticism, e.g. Baum in CATH. PERSP.', p. 24. Such criticism easily forgets that the concept of seven sacraments is a relatively late medieval restriction of an earlier more inclusive notion and is fraught with problems when viewed in full historical context.

[141] PLAN, p. 38.

[142] Ibid., pp. 39 and 41.

[143] Ibid., p. 44.

[144] Ibid., pp. 44 and 46-55; also COCUred, p. 42. The order adopted by the COCU list has also been the subject of Roman Catholic Criticism, e.g. Baum, CATH. PERSP., p. 25 and Tavard, loc. cit., 40-1. Such criticism is apt to forget that the COCU order represents a return to an older tradition which sees the college of presbyters and the college of deacons as two distinct orders differentially related to the bishop's office, the former as his advisors and ceremonial accompaniment, the latter as his agents and representatives.

[145] PLAN, pp. 44-5. For the ordination rites themselves, see PLAN, pp. 90-102. The participation by laymen in the laying on of hands really should not cause the Roman Catholic theologian insurmountable difficulties. The participation by simple priests in the traditional Roman Catholic rite was equally hard to accommodate to an atomizing scholastic theology which insisted on analyzing the significance of individual elements of sacramental action in isolation one from another. The significance of the COCU proposal lies in the expression it gives to the concelebration of all members and ranks of the church in the ordination; this, however, by no means needs to be understood in opposition to the specifically distinct roles of the bishop and the other ordained participants in the ceremony.

[146] This service is given in PLAN, pp. 83-9.

[147] "The community called the parish redefines the front-line expression of church life where people live and work. Consisting normally of several congregations and developing task groups, it is the local governmental unit of the church for expressing the most complete and efficient ministry possible" (PLAN, p. 57). Under the notion "task group" would fall such Roman Catholic institutions as sodalities and confraternities, religious communities, etc.

[148] PLAN, p. 61. Here as elsewhere, the Plan proposes the principle, two laymen to each ordained minister. No provision is made for a clerical or episcopal veto power; on the other hand, it is by no means certain that such a power must be juridically institutionalized in the church. The ancient ideal of a council was unanimous consensus rather than one group voting down the other, be it on the basis of greater number or superior authority. (See H. Küng, Strukturen der Kirche (Quaestiones disputatae, 17; Freiburg-Basal-Wien: Herder, 1962), 38-46.

[149] See PLAN, chapt. 8, pp. 56-72.

[150] PLAN, p. 27.

[151] Ibid.

[152] Ibid., pp. 27-8.

[153] Ibid., p. 27.

[154] Ibid., p. 44.

[155] Ibid., p. 51; see also p. 49.

[156] The Plan calls for the election every four years of a national presiding bishop, with the possibility of a single re-election. The electing body is the national assembly, a representative body composed of the presiding bishop of each region, plus representatives of the district bishops, ordained ministers and laymen of each region according to the proportion six laymen and two ministers to each bishop (PLAN, pp. 68-71).

[157] PLAN, p. 15.

BIBLIOGRAPHY

(All entries are alphabetical, irrespective of their character
as book, article, or mimeographed document. Abbreviated titles
are listed in alphabetical sequence with other entries.)

AAS - Acta Apostolica Sedis.

"Accord doctrinal entre catholiques et protestants sur l'Eucharistie" (Groupe de Dombes) in Documentation catholique,
Nr. 1606 (Avril 2, 1972), 334-38.

The Advancement of Theological Education, by H.R.Niebuhr and
D.D.Williams (New York:Harper, 1957).

Ahlstrom, Sidney E. "Theology in America: A historical Survey"
in Religion in American Life, Vol. I, The Shaping of American Religion, ed. J.W.Smith and A.L.Jamison (Princeton:
Univ. Press, 1961), pp.232-321.

AMT - Amt im Widerstreit, hrsg. K.H Schuh (Berlin: Morus,1973).

Aubert, R., "Motivations théologiques et extra-théologiques des
partisans et des adversaires de la définition de l'infaillibilité," in L'Infaillibilité. Son aspect philosophique et théologique. Actes du Colloquo III Rome,
5-12 janvier, 1970, ed. E. Castelli (Paris: Aubier 1970),
pp. 91-112.

Averell, Lloyd J., American Theology in the Liberal Tradition,
(Philadelphia: Westminster, 1967).

Bacht, H, "Kritische Fragen zur Verkündigungsauftrag und Struktur der Ämter" in Amt im Widerstreit, hrsg. K.H Schuh
(Berlin: Morus, 1973), pp. 59-66.

Baum, Bishop William W., "A Catholic Perspective", in Consultation on Church Union. A Catholic Perspective
(Washington, D.C.: USCC, 1970), pp. 21-27

Bennett, John C. "American Churches in the Ecumenical Situation",
Ecumenical Review 1,1(Autumn, 1948), pp 57-64.

Bennett RESULTS - _____, "Results of an Ecumenical Study",
Christendom 9,2 (Spring 1944), 142-151.

Berger, Peter, and Thomas Luckmann, The Social Construction
of Reality. A Treatise on the Sociology of Knowledge
(Anchor Books; Garden City: Doubleday, 1967).

_____, "A Call for Authority in the Christian Community
" Address to the 10th Plenary Meeting
DIGEST, X(1971), 113-29.

_____, The Noise of Solemn Assemblies (Garden City:
Doubleday, 1961).

Blake, Eugene Carson, "A Proposal toward the Reunion of
    Christ's Church, "A sermon preached at Grace Episcopal
    Cathedral, San Francisco, on Sunday Dec.4, 1960, in
    The Christian Century 77,51 (Dec.21,1960), 1508a-1511b;
    reprint (Philadelphia: Office of the General Assembly of
    the U.P.C.U.S.A., 1961).

"The Body Christ Heads: A Symposium", G.C. Berkouwer, et al.
    Christianity Today, 1,22 (Aug.19, 1957), 3-13.

Boney, W.J., "COCU :Memphis and After", Journal of Ecumenical
    Studies, 10.3 (Summer, 1973), 654-657.

Branton, James R. et al., "Our Present Situation in Biblical
    Theology", Religion in Life 26,1 (Winter, 1956-57), 5-39.

Brown, William Adams, The Church Catholic and Protestant
    (New York: Scribner's, 1935).

_____, Toward a United Church (New York: Scribner's, 1946).

Buri, Fritz, Gott in Amerika: amerikanische Theologie seit 1960
    (Bern: Haupt/Tübingen:Katzmann, 1970).

Calhoun, OBERLIN - Calhoun, Robert L. "Christ and the Church"
    in The Nature of the Unity We Seek:... Oberlin, ed.
    P.S. Minear (St. Louis: Bethany, 1958), 52-78.

Carnell, Edward J., The Case for Orthodox Theology (Philadel-
    phia: Westminster, 1959).

_____, "The Nature of the Unity We Seek; 2. An Orthodox
    Protestant View", Religion in Life, 26,2 (Spring 1957),
    191-199.

Carver, W.O., "The Importance of a Functional Study of the
    Church," (American Theol. Common Faith and Order; n.p.,
    June 1942); mimeo. [WCC Archives].

CATH. PERSP. - Consultation on Church Union: A Catholic Per-
    spective (Washington: VSCC Publ. Office, 1970).

Cavert, Samuel McCrea, Church Cooperation and Unity in
    America: A historical review, 1900-1970 (New York:
    Association, 1970).

"The Church as Koironia and Institution" in "Institutionalism",
    special issue of The Division of Studies Bulletin WCC ,
    6,1 (Spring 1960), 30-31.

COCU, An Order of Worship for the Proclamation of the Word of
    God and the Celebration of the Lord's Supper with the
    Community (Cincinnati: Forward Movement, 1968).

COCUblue - Principles of Church Union, adopted by the Consultation at its Meeting 1966 - - blue book (Cincinnati: Forward Movement 1966).

COCUgreen - COCU, Principles of Church Union: Guidelines for Structure: A Study Guide - - green book (Cincinnati: Forward Movement, 1967).

COCUred - COCU, The Official Reports of the Four Meetings of the Consultation - - Red Book (Cincinnati: Forward Movement, 1966).

Commission on Faith and Order, Minutes of the Working Committee Meeting ...(WCC, Comm. on F.+O.; Geneva: WCC, 1954-1963).

COMMUNION - The Communion of Saints, Report 2 prepared by the Commission or the Church's Unity in Life and Worship: Commission IV for the World Conference on Faith and Order, Edinburgh, 1937, drafted by G.J.Schlosser (F+O Papers, O.S. No.83; New York - London: Harper 1937).

Concept (blue). Papers from the Department on Studies in Evangelism, Special Issues of the Missionary Structures of the Congregation Study (Geneva: WCC, 1962-1967).

Concept (red). Papers from the Department on Studies in Evangelism, 12 Numbers, (Geneva WCC 1962-1967).

Congar, Yves, "Die Normen für die Ursprungstreue und Identität der Kirche im Verlauf ihrer Geschichte", Concilium 9.Jg. H.3 (März 1973), 156-163.

Const. de Eccl. - Constitutio dogmatica de Ecclesia, Sacros. Oecum. Conc. Vat.II (Citta del Vaticano: Typis polygl. Vat., 1964); Engl. Trans.: Constitution on the Church Second Vatican Council, Nov. 21, 1964 (Washington, D.C.: NCWC,1964).

Corpus Unum, the report of the North American Ecumenical Conference, Toronto, Canada, June 3-5, 1941 (New York - Toronto: Conference Comm., n.d).

Cox, Harvey, Secular City; Secularization and urbanization in theological perspective (New York: Macmillan, 1964).

Craig, Clarence T., et. al. "Report of the Special Committee on the Work of the American Theological Committee, 1939-1941" (n.p., n.d.), mimeo. [WCC Archives].

CHRIST - Report of the Theological Commission on Christ and the Church (F+O. Paper N.S. 38; Geneva: WCC, 1963).

Crow, Paul A. "The Church - - A New Beginning" in Church
Unity at Midpoint, ed. P.A. Crow and W.J. Boney (New York:
Association, 1972), pp. 20-37.

_____, "Ecumenism and the Consultation on Church Union",
Journal of Ecumenical Studies 4,4 (1967-8), 581-602.

DECADE - A Decade of Objective Progress in Church Unity,
1927-1936, Report 4 prepared by the Commission on the
Church's Unity in Life and Worship: Commission IV for the
World Conference on Faith and Order, Edinburgh, 1937, ...
drafted by H.P. Douglass (New York - London: Harper, 1937).

Decr. de Oecum. - Decretum de Oecumenismo, Sacros. Oecum. Conc.
Vaticano: Typus polygl. Vat., n.d.); Engl Trans.: Decree
on Ecumenism, Second Vatican Council, Nov. 21, 1964
(Washington, D.C.: NCWC, 1964).

Denz. - Schön - Denzinger-Schönmetzer, Enchiridion symbolorum
... 32 ed. (Barcellona - Freiburg i. Brg. - Rome - New York:
Herder, 1963).

Dewey, John, A Common Faith: The Terry Lectures (New Haven:
Yale Univ. Press 1934).

De Wolf, L. Harold, Trends and Frontiers of Religions Thought
(Nashville: Nat. Meth. Stud. Movement. 1955).

DIGEST Iff - COCU, Digest of the Proceedings ... Vol I -
(Fanwood,N.V. Princeton,N.J.: COCU, 1963-   ).

DOC. HIST. - A Documentary History of the Faith and Order
Movement ed. L. Vischer (Abbott Books; St Louis:
Bethany, 1963).

DOCUMENTS - The Documents of Vatican II, W.M. Abbott, gen. ed.,
(New York: Guild/America/Association 1966).

Dodd,C.H., "Unavowed Motives in Ecumenical Discussions" in
Ecum. Rev. 2 (1949-50), 52-56.

Douglass INTERSEMINARY IV - Douglass, H.Paul, "Ecumenicity in
America" in Towards World-Wide Christianity, ed. O.F.
Nolde Vol. IV of The Interseminary Series (New York -
London: Harper, 1946), pp. 169-199).

Dulles, Avery, "Ministry and Intercommunion: Recent Ecumenical
Statements and Debates", Theological Studies 34(1973),
655-661.

Dun MINUTES - Dunn, Angus, "Report of the Commission on the
Empirical Approach to Unity" March 12-13, 1935 mimeo.
[WCC Archives].

Eckhardt, A.Roy, The Surge of Piety in America: An Appraisal (New York: Association, 1958).

Ehrenstrom, INSTITUTIONALISM - Ehrenstrom, Nils, "The Quest for Ecumenical Institutionalization" in Institutionalism and Church Unity, ed. by N. Ehrenstrom and W.G Muelder (New York: Association 1963), pp.23-36.

Ehrenstrom, ST. ANDREWS - _____, Report of the Study Commission on Institutionalism in Commission on Faith and Order, Minutes of the Commission Meeting held at St. Andrews, Scotland, Aug. 3rd to 8th, 1960 (WCC, Comm. on F.+O.; Geneva: WCC, 1960), pp. 71-75.

Erklärung zur katholischen Lehre über die Kirche, die gegen einige heutige Irrtümer zu verteidigen ist, vom 24. Juni, 1973 (Citta del Vaticano: Typis polygl. Vat., 1973).

ETHICAL - The Ethical Reality and Function of the Church, A Memorandum by the Chicago Ecumenical Discussion Group, Study Department of the Universal Christian Council for Life and Work, no. 3, E/41 (Geneva, May 1941), mimeo.

Fackre, Gabriel and Dorothy, Under the Steeple (Nashville: Abingdon, 1958).

Fehlbar? Eine Bilanz, hrsg. v. H. Küng (Einsiedeln:Benzinger, 1973).

Ferré, HUMANITY - Ferré, Nels S.F., "The Humanity of Jesus", ...prep. for the Am. Sect. of the TCCC Meeting, Aug. 8-12, 1955, and rev. ... (FOC/TCCC/NA, April,1956),mimeo. [WCC Archives].

_____, Searchlights on Contemporary Theology (New York: Harper & Row, 1961).

Filson, HOLY SPIRIT - Filson, Floyd V. "The Holy Spirit in the Testament", (FOC/TCCC/NA,1960, mimeo. WCC Archives .

_____, "The Old Testament and Jesus Christ", prep. for the TCCC Meeting, July, 1955, and rev. after discussion (FOC/TCCC/NA, July, 1955), mimeo. [WCC Archives].

Fitzgerald, P.J., Infallibility - -"A Secular Assessment", Irish Theological Quarterly 61 (1974), 3-21.

Fries, Heinrich, "Was heißt Anerkennung", in Amt im Widerstreit, hrsg v. K.H. Schuh (Berlin:Morus,1973) pp.110-121.

Ford, John T., "The Vision of the Church in A Plan of Union", The Christian Century 88,42 (Oct.20,1971), 1229-1232,repr. in Church Union at Midpoint, ed. P.A. Crow Jr. & W.J. Boney (New York: Association 1972), pp. 99-112.

"Formation and Procedure of the Chicago Group in conjunction
with the Program of the Study of the Universal Christian
Council for Life and Work (based on a report by E.F.
Aubrey, convenor of the group)," (n.p., 1940) mimeo.
[WCC Archives].

Fosdick, Harry E, Chapter "What is Religion", from As I See
Religion (New York: Harper 1932), repr. in Contemporary
Religious Thought: An anthology (New York: Abingdon -
Cokesbury 1949), pp. 13-20.

Franzmann, Martin H., "The Nature of the Unity We Seek, 4.
A Missouri Synod Lutheran View", Religion in Life, 26,2
(Spring, 1957), 207-214.

Gamble, Connoly, Jr., "The Literature of Biblical Theology:
A bibliogrphical study", Interpretation, 7(1953),
466-480.

Gibbs, Mark, and Thomas R. Morton, God's Frozen People: A
book for and about Christian Laymen (Philadelphia:
Westminster, 1965).

Grant, J[ohn] Webster, The Canadian Experience of Church Union
(Ecumenical Studies in History 8; London: Lutterworth,
1967).

Grillmeier,A, "Kommentar zum I. Kapitel der Dogm. Konst. über
die Kirche" in Das Zweite Vatikanische Konzil, Dokumente
et Kommentare, 1. Teil (LThK, Ergänzungsband I; Freiburg -
Basel - Wien: Herder, 1966).

Gustafson, James M., Treasure in Earthen Vessels:The Church as
as a human community (New York: Harper, 1961).

Guzie, Tad, The Analogy of Learning (New York: Sheed & Ward,
1960).

Habermas, Jürgen, "Erkenntnis und Interesse" Frankfurter An-
trittsvorlesung vom 28.6.1965, publ. in his Technik und
Wissenschaft als "Ideologie" (Editions Surkamp; Frankfurt:
Surkamp Verlag 1968), pp. 146-168.

_____, Erkenntnis und Interesse (Theorie 2; Frankfurt: Sur-
kamp, 1968).

Halverson, Richard C., "The empire-changing face that rocked
the world" in "The Body Christ Heads: A Symposium",
Christianity Today, 1,22 (Aug.19, 1957), 5-7.

Hammar, George, Christian Realism in Contemporary American
    Theology: A study of Reinhold Niebuhr, W.M Horton, and
    H.P. Van Dusen (Uppsala: Lundgvist/New York: Steckert,
    1940).

Handy, Robert T. "The American Scene" in Twentieth Century
    Christianity, ed. St. Neill, rev. ed. (Garden City:
    Doubleday, 1963), pp. 179-216.

_____, A Christian America: Protestant hopes and historical
    realities (New York: Oxford Univ. Press, 1971).

Hardie,WORD - Hardie, Edward R., "Word and Sacrament in the
    Early Church", prep. for the TCCC Meeting, Aug., 1956
    edited after discussion (FOC/TCCC/NA, Aug., 1956), mimeo.
    [WCC Archives].

Hargraves, Archie, "Go where the action is", Social Action,
    20,6 (Feb., 1964), 15-25.

Harrelson,SPIRIT - Harrelson, Walter, "Spirit in the Old
    Testament", revision of a paper presented to the No.Am.
    Sect. of the TCCC (FOC/TCCC/NA, Aug. 1956), mimeo.
    [WCC Archives].

Harrison, Paul, Authority and Power in the Free Church
    Tradition (Princeton: Univ. Pr., 1959).

Hazelton, Roger, New Accents in Contemporary Theology
    (New York: Harper, 1960).

Heick, Otto W., Amerikanische Theologie in Geschichte und
    Gegenwart (Breklun: Jensen, 1954).

Henry, Carl, "Dare We Revive the Modernist - Fundamentalist
    Controversy", Christianity Today, 1,18 (June 10,1957),
    3-6+25; 19(June 24,1957) 23-26; 20(July 8,1957), 15-18;
    21 (July 22,1957), 23-6 +38.

_____, Fifty Years of Protestant Theology (Boston:Wilde,1950).

Herberg, Will, Protestant, Catholic, Jew: An Essay in American
    religious sociology (Garden City: Doubleday, 1956).

Hordern, William, The Case for the New Reformation Theology
    (Philadelphia: Westminster, 1959).

_____, Introduction, Vol I of New Directions in Theology,
    ed. W. Hordern (Philadelphia: Westminster, 1966).

Horton, Douglas, The United Church of Christ, Its origins,
    organization and role in the world today (New York:
    Nelson, 1962).

Horton, Walter M., "The Development of Theological Thought"
in Twentieth Century Christianity ed. St. Neill, rev. ed
(Garden City: Doubleday, 1963), pp. 253-284.

_____, "Systematic Theology: Liberalism chstened by tragedy",
in Protestant Thought in the Twentieth Century, ed.
A.S. Nash (New York: Macmillan 1951), pp. 105-124.

"L'Hospitalité eucharistique pour les foyers mixtes", Documentation catholique, no. 1626 (18 fév. 1973), 161-165.

Hotchkin, John F., "COCU and the Wider Reality of Ecumenism",
in Church Union at Midpoint ed. P.A.Crow, Jr. and
W.J. Boney (New York: Association, 1972),pp. 99-111.

"How I am Making up my Mind" Series, The Christian Century,
81 (1964), repr. as Frontline Theology ed. Dean Pearman
Richmond: John Knox/London: SCM 1967).

"How My Mind has Changed in this Decade", 1st Series in The
Christian Century, 56 (1939).

"How My Mind Has Changed", 3rd Series, The Christian Century,
Vol. 76-77 (1959-1960).

Hunt, W[illiam] Boyd, "Voluntary and not regimented, spiritual
and not mechanical" in "The Body Christ Heads: A Syposium",
Christianity Today, 1,22(Aug. 19, 1957), 7-8.

"Instructio de particularibus casibus admittendi alios christianos ad communionem eucharisticam in Ecclesia catholica",
AAS 64(1972), 518-525.

INTERSEMINARY I - The Challenge of our Culture ed. C.T. Craig,
Vol. I of The Interseminary Series (New York - London:
Harper, 1946).

INTERSEMINARY II - The Church and Organized Movements, ed.
R.C. Miller, Vol. II of The Interseminary Series (New York
- London: Harper, 1946).

INTERSEMINARY III - The Gospel, the Church and the World, ed.
K.S. Latourette, Vol. III of The Interseminary Series
(New York - London: Harper, 1946).

INTERSEMINARY IV - Toward World-Wide Christianity, ed. O.F. Nolde, Vol. IV of The Interseminary Series (New York - London:
Harper, 1946).

INTERSEMINARY V - What Must the Church Do? by R.S. Bilheimer
Vol. V of The Interseminary Series (New York- London:
Harper, 1947).

INSTIT. - The Report of the Study Commission on Institutionalism (F+O. Paper, N.S. 37; Geneva: WCC, 1963).

Institutionalism and Church Unity: A Symposium prep. by the
Study Comm. on Institutionalism ..., ed by N. Ehrenstom
and W.G. Muelder (New York: Association, 1963).

Joint Meeting of the Theological Commission on Christ and the
Church," Tutzing, July 20-31, 1959 (TCCC, May, 1960),
mimeo. WCC Archives .

Kehrer, Günther, Religionssoziologie (Sammlung Göschen, 1228;
Berlin: De Gruyter, 1968).

Kleines Konzilskompendium, hrsg. v. K. Rahner u. H. Vorgrimler,
2. erg. Aufl. (Herder Bücherei, 270-73; Freiburg - Wien:
Herder, 1967).

Knox, EARLY CHURCH - Knox, John, The Early Church and the Coming
Great Church (Nashville: Abingdon 1955).

_____, "The Ethical Reality and Function of the Church", a
synopsis prepared by ... and submitted to the Chicago
Ecumenical Study Group (n.p., n.d.), mimeo. [WCC Archives].

Krauss, C.Norman, Dispensationalism in America (Richmond:
John Knox, 1958).

Küng, Hans, Strukturen der Kirche (Quaestiones dispatatae 17;
Freiburg - Basel - Wien: Herder, 1962).

_____, Unfehlbar? Eine Anfrage (Zürich-Einsiedeln-Köln:
Benziger, 1970), Am. Trans.: Infallible? An Inquiry,
trans. by E. Quinn (New York: Doubleday, 1971); Engl.
Trans.: Infallible? An Enquiry, trans. by E. Mosbacher
(London: Collins, 1971).

_____ und Karl Rahner, "Versöhnliches Schlußwort unter eine
Debatte" Publik-Forum 2, II (1.Juni 1973), 12-15.

Langlois,C. "Die Unfehlbarkeit - - eine neue Idee des 19. Jahrhunderts", in Fehlbar? Eine Bilanz, hrsg. v. H. Küng
(Einsiedeln: Benziger, 1973), pp. 146-160.

Lill, R., "Historische Voraussetzungen des Dogmas vom Universal-
episkopat und von der Unfehlbarkeit des Papstes", Stimmen
der Zeit 95, II (Nov. 1970), 289-303.

"The Lordship of Christ over the World and the Church", Report of the Joint European and American Study Commission, Arnoldshein, March 31- April 5, 1959, in The Ecumenical Review II (1958/9), 437-449.

Macfarland, Charles S., Christian Unity in the Making; the twenty-five years of the Federal Council of Churches of Christ in America, 1905-1930 (New York: FCC, 1948).

_____, Current Religious Thought (New York:Revell, 1941).

Mackay, John A., "The Adequacy of the Church Today" in Corpus unum: Report of the North American Ecumenical Conference, Toronto, 3-5 June, 1941 (Toronto: n.p., 1941), repr. in Christendom 6.4 (Autumn 1941), 483-494

Mackay, INTERSEMINARY IV - _____, "The Biblical and Theological Bases for the Ecumenical Goal", in Toward World-Wide Christianity, ed. O.F. Nolde, Vol. IV of The Interseminary Series (New York-London: Harper, 1946), pp. 40-58.

McBrien, Richard P., "The COCU Plan of Union" Andover Newton Quarterly 12,1 (Sept., 1971), 24-33.

MAN - The Biblical Doctrine of Man in Society, by G.E. Wright and an Ecumenical Committee in Chicago (Ecumenical Biblical Studies 2; London: SCM, 1954).

Marty, Martin E., "Introduction" American Protestant Theology Today in Frontline Theology ed. D. Pearman (London: SCM, 1967), pp. 13-28.

_____, "The New Generation and COCU?" in Church Unity at Midpoint, ed. P.A. Crow, Jr and W.J. Boney (New York: Association, 1972), pp. 179-189.

_____, The New Shape of American Religion (New York: Harper, 1959).

Mead, Sidney, "Denominationalism, the Shape of Protestantism in America", Church History, 23 (1954), 291-330.

_____, "The Nation with the Soul of a Church", Church History, 36 (1967), 262-283.

MEANINGS - The Meanings of Unity, Report no. 1 prepared by the
    Commission on the Church's Unity in Life and Worship:
    Commission IV for the World Conference on Faith and Order,
    Edinburgh, 1937, ... drafted for the Commission by A. Dun
    (F+0 Papers, O.S. No. 82; New York - London: Harper, 1937).

The 1934 Meeting of the Continuation Committee held at Herten-
    stein in Sept. 3-6 (F+O. Papers, O.S. No. 71; Winchester -
    New York: The Committe, 1934).

The 1938 Meeting of the Continuation Committee held at Clarens,
    Switzerland, Aug. 29-Sept.1 (F.+O. Papers, O.S. No. 91;
    Oxford - New York: Continuation Committee, 1938).

The 1939 Meeting of the Continuation Committee held at Clarens,
    Switzerland, Aug. 21-23 (F.+O. Papers, O.S. No. 92; Oxford
    - New York: Continuation Committee, 1939).

Minear, IMAGES - Minear, Paul S., The Images of the Church
    (Philadelphia: Westminster, 1960).

Minear, PROSPECTIVE SURVEY - _____, "The Conception of the
    Church as the Body of Christ within the Context of the
    Different Ways in which the New Testament speaks of Christ,
    the Spirit, and the Church: A prospective survey and some
    sample borings", outline of a study prepared for the Am.
    Sect. of the TCCC Meeting, Aug. 8-12, 1955 (FOC/TCCC/NA,
    April, 1956), mimeo. [WCC Archives].

_____, "Wanted a Biblical Theology", Theology Today 1.1
    (April, 1944), 45-58.

The Ministry in Historical Perspective, ed. by H.R. Niebuhr
    and D.D. Williams (New York: Harper, 1956).

Minutes, North American Working Group, Consultation Seaburg
    Honse, Greenwich, Conn., Feb. 4-6, Concept (blue),
    (1964), 3-5.

Minutes of the American Committee for the World Council of
    Churches, Oct 17, 1944, mimeo. [WCC Archives].

Minutes of the General Assembly of the United Presbyterian
    Church in the U.S.A. Pt.I, Journal 173rd Gen. Ass.,
    Buffalo, N.Y. May 17-24, 1961 (UPCUSA Gen. Ass. Ser. 6,
    vol. 14; Philadelphia: Office of the Gen. Assembly, 1961),
    454-457.

MISSIONARY - North American Working Group, "The Church for the World", The Report of the ..., in The Church for Others and the Church for the World: A Quest for structures for missionary congregations ... (Geneva: WCC, 1968), pp. 55 - 133.

Moberg, David O., The Church as a Social Institution (Englewood Cliffs: Prentice Hall, 1962).

Mueller, J. Theodore, "The apostolic emphasis ... is unity of doctrine", in "The Body Christ Heads: A Symposium", Christianity Today, 1,22 (Aug. 19, 1957), 8-10.

NATURE - The Nature of the Church: A Report of the American Theological Committee of the Continuation Committee, World Conference on Faith and Order, (Chicago - New York: Willett, Clark, 1945).

"The Nature of the Unity We Seek", Leslie Newbegin et al. Religion in Life, 26,2 (Spring, 1957), 181-222.

Nelson, ST. ANDREWS - Nelson, J. Robert, Report of the American Section of the Theological Commission on Christ and the Church, in Commission on Faith and Order Minutes of the Commission Meeting held at St. Adrews, Scotland, Aug. 3rd to 8th, 1960 (WCC, Comm. on F.+O.; Geneva: WCC, 1960).

New Theology, ed. by M. Marty and D. Pearman (New York: Macmillan, 1964).

NEXT STEPS - Next Steps on the Road to a United Church, Report 5 prepared by the Commission on the Church's Unity in Life and Worship: Commission IV for the World Conference on Faith and Order, Edinburgh, 1937, ... drafted by W.A. Brown (F.+O. Papers, O.S. No. 85: New York - London: Harper, 1937).

Niebuhr, H. Richard, William Pauck and Francis P. Miller, The Church against the World (Chicago - New York: Willett, Clark, 1935).

Niebuhr, CHURCH - _____, "The Church Defines Itself in the Worls", Draft paper prep. for the TCCC, June 1958 (FOC/TCCC/NA, June 1958) mimeo. [WCC Archives].

_____, "The Hidden Church and the Churches in Sight", Religion in Life 15,1 (Winter, 1945/6), 106-118.

_____, The Kingdom of God in America (Chicago - New York: Willett, Clark, 1937).

Niebuhr, H.R., in collaboration with D.D. Williams and
    J.M. Gustafson, The Purpose of the Church and its Ministry
    (New York: Harper, 1956).

_____, Radical Monotheism and Western Culture (New York:
    Harper, 1960).

_____, The Social Source of Denominationalism (New York:
    Holt, 1929).

NON-THEOL. - The Non-Theological Factors in the Making and
    Unmaking of Church Union, Report 3 prepared by the Commission
    on the Church's Unity in Life and Worship: Commission IV for
    the World Conference on Faith and Order, Edinburgh, 1937,...
    drafted by W.L.Sperry (F.+O. Papers, O.S. No. 84; New York -
    London: Harper, 1937).

Non-theological Factors that may hinder or accelerate the
    Church's Unity", in Ecum. Rev. 4 (1951-52), 174-180.

NOTES (1954) - Notes on a Meeting of the Theological Commission
    on Christ and the Church held in Scott Hall, Evanston, USA,
    6-11 August 1954, WCC, Div. of Studies Comm. on Faith and
    Order (FOC/TCCC, Jan. 1955) mimeo. [WCC Archives].

NOTES (1956) - Notes on discussion at a Meeting of the Theologic-
    al Commission on Christ and the Church, held at Greenwich,
    Conn. Aug. 6-10, 1956, World Council of Churches, Comm. on
    Faith and Order (FOC/TCCC/NA, Nov. 1956) mimeo. [WCC Ar-
    chives].

NOTES (1957) - Minutes of the Joint Meeting of the American and
    European Sections, Yale Divinity School, July 15-19, 1957,
    WCC, Div. of Studies, Comm. on Faith and Order (TCCC,
    April 1958), mimeo. [WCC Archives].

NOTES (1960) - Meeting of the North American Section, Yale
    Divinity School, 17-21 June, 1960, Theological Commission
    on Christ and the Church, WCC, Div. of Studies, Comm. on
    Faith and Order (TCCC/NA July Oct. 1960) mimeo [WCC Ar-
    chives].

OBERLIN - The Nature of the Unity We Seek: Official Report of
    the North American Conference on Faith and Order, Sept.
    3-10, 1957, Oberlin, Ohio, ed. by Paul S. Minear (St Louis:
    Bethany, 1958).

Ockenga, Harold John, "The Bible ... is anthoritative for
the evangelical" in "The Body Christ Heads: A Symposium",
Christianity Today, 1,22 (Aug. 19, 1957), 10-11.

OLD & NEW - The Old and the New in the Church (Studies in
Ministry and Worship, 18; Minneapolis: Augsburg, 1961).

ONE LORD - One Lord - - One Baptism, Report of the Theological
Commission on Christ and the Church pres. to the Comm.
on F.+ O. of the WCC, 1960 (Studies in Ministry and Worship;
Minneapolis: Augsburg, 1960).

"The Ordained Ministry in Ecumenical Perspective", Statement of
the International F. + O. Consultation held at Marseilles,
Sept., 1972, in Study Encounter 8,4 (1972), 1-22.

Outler OBERLIN - Outler, Albert C., "Our Common History as
Christians", in The Nature of the Unity We Seek: ...
Oberlin ed. P.S. Minear (St. Luois: Bethany, 1958),79-89.

_____, "Traditions in Transit" in The Old and the New in the
Church (Studies in Ministry and Worship, 18; Minneapolis:
Augsburg, 1961), pp. 43-51.

"Outline of a Possible Plan of Union", prep. by a special commission of the COCU for discussion at the 5th meeting of
the Consultation, Dallas, May 2-5, 1966 (Fanwood, N.J.:
Office of the Exec. Secretary, April 1, 1966), 105pp.

Pauck, Wilhelm, "Theology in the Life of Contemporary American
Protestantism" in Religion and Culture: Essays in honor of
Paul Tillich, ed. by W. Leibrecht (New York: Harper, 1959),
pp. 270-283.

Paul VI "Ecclesiam suam" AAS, 56 (1964), 609-659.

_____, "Mysterium fidei" AAS, 57 (1965), 753-774.

_____, "Ogni volta", AAS, 57 (1965), 721-724.

_____, "Siamo particolarmente lieti", AAS, 58 (1966), 649-655.

Peck, George, "Church Unity and the Future", Andover Newton
Quarterly 12,1 (Sept., 1971), 12-23.

Pelican, Jaroslav, "Overcoming History by History" in The Old
and the New in the Church (Studies in Ministry and
Worship, 18; Minneapolis: Augsburg, 1961), pp. 36-42.

Pittenger, DOCTRINE - Pittenger, W.N., "The Doctrine of Christ
and the Doctrine of the Church", prep. for the Am. Sect.
of the TCCC Meeting, Aug. 8-12, 1955, rev. with appended
note (FOC/TCCC/NA,Sept.,1955).mimeo. WCC Archives .

PLAN - COCU, Plan of Union for the Church of Christ Uniting,
    commended to the Churches for study and response ...
    March 9-13, 1970, at St. Louis, Mo. (Princeton: COCU,
    1970), [=DIGEST IX, pp. 87-190].

PLANNING - Planning for Mission: Working Papers on the New
    Quest for Missionary Communities, ed. T. Wieser (New
    York: The U.S. Conf. of the WCC, 1966).

PREACHING - Preaching as an Expression of the Ethical Reality
    of the Church, A Memorandum by the Chicago Ecumenical
    Discussion Group, Study Department of the Universal
    Christian Council for Life and Work, No. 13, E/42
    (Geneva, Oct. 1942), 18pp., mimeo. [WCC Archives].

Price, Theron D., "The Nature of the Unity We Seek, 3.
    A Southern Baptist View" Religion in Life, 26,2 (Spring,
    1957), 200-206.

Protestant Thought in the Twentieth Century ed. A.S. Nash
    (New York: Macmillan 1951).

PURPOSE - The Purpose of the Church and its Ministry by
    H.R. Niebuhr in collaboration with D.D. Williams and
    J.M. Gustafson (New York: Harper, 1956).

"The Quest for Structures of Missionary Congregations" Interim
    report of the Study "Missionary Structures of the Congre-
    gation" to the Central Committee of the WCC meeting at
    Enuga, Nigeria, 1965, in Planning for Mission ... ed.
    T. Wieser (New York: U.S. Conf. for the WCC, 1966),
    pp. 220-228.

Rahner, Karl, "Kritik an Hans Küng", in Zum Problem Unfehlbar-
    keit ..., hrsg. v. K. Rahner (Quaestiones disputatae, 54;
    Freiburg - Basel - Wien: Herder 1971), pp. 27-48.

_____, "Replik. Bemerkungen zu: Hans Küng, Im Interesse der
    Sache", in Zum Problem Unfehlbarkeit ... hrsg. v. K. Rah-
    ner (Quaestiones disputatae, 54; Freiburg - Basel - Wien:
    Herder, 1971), pp. 49-70.

_____, "Zum Begriff der Unfehlbarkeit in der katholischen
    Theologie", in Zum Problem Unfehlbarkeit ... hrsg. v.
    K. Rahner (Quaestiones disputatae, 54; Freiburg - Basel -
    Wien: Herder 1971), pp. 9-26.

Ratzinger, Joseph, Das Problem der Dogmengeschichte in der Sicht
    der katholischen Theologie (Arbeitsgemeinschaft für For-
    schung des Landes Nordrhein-Westfalen, Geisteswiss., H. 139;
    Köln-Opladen: Westdeutscher Verlag, 1966).
Reform und Anerkennung kirchlicher Ämter, Memorandum der Arbeits-
    gemeinschaft ökumenischer Universitätsinstitute (München:
    Chr. Kaiser/Mainz: M. Grünewald, 1973).
Regis, Louis, Epistemology, trans. I.C. Byrne (New York:
    Macmillan, 1959).
Reid, W. Stanford, "Outward conformity common ... in a totalita-
    rian age" in "The Body Christ Heads: A Symposium",
    Christianity Today, 1,22 (Aug. 19, 1957), 11-12.
Religion in American Life, ed. J.W. Smith and A.L. Jamison,
    4 vols (Princeton: Studies in American Civilization;
    Princeton: Univ. Press, 1961).
Richards, George W., "Historical Introduction" in The Nature
    of the Church : A Report of the American Theological
    Committee ... (Chicago-New York: Willett, Clark, 1945),
    pp. 115-122.
Rouse, Ruth and Stephen Neill, A History of the Ecumenical
    Movement, 1517-1948, 2nd ed. (Philadelphia: Westminster,
    1967).
Sandeen, Ernst, "Toward a Historical Interpretation of the
    Origins of Fundamentalism", Church History, 36 (1967),
    66-83.
Scheffezyk, Leo, "Das kirchliche Amt im Verständnis der katho-
    lischen Theologie" in Amt im Widerstreit hrsg. K.H. Schuh
    (Berlin: Morus, 1973), pp. 17-25.
Scherer, INTERSEMINARY III - Scherer Paul, "The Nature of the
    Church" in The Gospel, the Church and the World, ed.
    K.S. Latourette, Vol. III of The Interseminary Series
    (New York - London: Harper, 1946), pp. 27-58.
Schillebeeck, Eduard, "Das Problem der Amtsunfehlbarkeit",
    Concilium 9,3 (März 1973)
Schoemaker, Samuel M. "...organic rather than organizational".
    in "The Body Christ Heads: A Symposium", Christianity
    Today, 1,22 (Aug. 19, 1957), 12-13.

Schreiben der Bischöfe des deutschsprachigen Raumes über das
priesterliche Amt. (Trier: Paulusverlag, 1970).

Schreiben der deutschen Bischöfe an alle, die von der Kirche
mit dem Glaubensverkündigung beauftragt sind, Sonderdr.
hrsg. v. Sekretariat der Deutschen Bischofskonferenz
(n.p. 1967).

Schuh, K.H. "Vorwort" in Amt im Widerstreit hrsg. K.H. Schuh
(Berlin: Morus, 1973), pp. 9-16.

Skoglund, John E. and J. Robert Nelson. Fifty Years of Faith
and Order (New York: Commettee for the Interseminary
Movement, 1963).

Skydsgaard, K.E., "Tradition as an Issue in Contemporary
Theology", in The Old and the New in the Church (Studies
in Ministry and Worship, 18; Minneapolis: Augsburg, 1961),
pp. 20-35.

Sontag, Frederick and John K. Roth, The American Religious
Experience: The Roots, Trends, and Future of American
Theology (New York: Harper, 1972).

Soper, David W., Major Voices in American Theology, 2 vols.
(Philadelphia: Westminster 1952-55).

Spike, Robert W. The Freedom Revolution and their Churches
(New York: Association, 1965).

SPECIAL COMMITTEE - Report of the Special Committee on the
Work of the American Theological Committee, 1939-1941
(n.p., Nov. 1941), mimeo. WCC Archives .

ST. ANDREWS - Commission on Faith and Order, Minutes of the
Commission Meeting held at St. Andrews, Scotland, Aug. 3rd
to 8th, 1960 (WCC, Comm. on F. + O.; Geneva: WCC, 1960).

Streeter, Burnett H. The Primitve Church (New York: Macmillan
1929).

Tavard, George H., "A Catholic Perspective" in Consultation
on Church Union: A Catholic Perspective (Washington, D.C.:
1970), pp. 28-45.

TCCC Interim report ONE LORD - "The Divine Trinity and the
Unity of the Church" in One Lord - - One Baptism, Report
of the Theological Commission on Christ and the Church
pres. to the Comm. on F.+O. of the WCC, 1960 (Studies in
Ministry and Worship; Minneapolis; Augsburg, 1960),
pp. 7-42.

Toronto,ORDER - Toronto Study Group, "Report on Order and
     Organization", North American Conference on Faith and
     Order, Orientation Paper: Section 8 (n.p., n.d.),
     mimeo. [WCC Archives].

TRADITION - Report of the Theological Commission on Tradition
     and Traditions (F.+O.Paper, N.S. 40; Geneva: WCC, 1963).

Thomas,CORPUS - Thomas, George F., "Corpus Christi and Corpus
     Christianorum" Christendom 7,1 (Winter 1942), 24-34.

_____, "The Philosophy of Religion" in Protestant Thought
     in the Twentieth Century, ed. A.S. Nash (New York:
     Macmillan, 1951), pp. 71-101.

Tillich, Paul, Systematic Theology 3 vols (Chicago: University
     of Chicago Press 1951-1963).

Twentieth Century Christianity, ed. St. Neill, rev. ed.
     (Garden City: Doubleday, 1963).

Um Amt und Herrenwahl: Dokumente zum evangelisch/römisch-katho-
     lischen Gespräch, hrsg. v. C. Gassmann u.a. (Ökumenische
     Dokumentation 1; Frankfurt a.M: O Lembeck/ J. Knecht, 1974).

Van Dusen, Henry P., The Vindication of the Liberal Theology:
     A Tract for the Times (New York: Scribners, 1963).

Visser't Hooft, W.A. "Report on the Work of the Provisional
     Committee, WCC (in process of formation), (1940-1945)
     mimeo. [WCC Archives].

Wedel. Theodore, The Coming Great Church (New York: Macmillan
     1945).

Welch,EXTRACTS - Welch, Claude, "Extracts from Papers and
     Discussion of the American Section of the Commission on
     Christ and the Church, 1955-1958" (FOC/TCCC/NA, May 1959),
     mimeo. [WCC Archives].

Welch,REALITY - _____, The Reality of the Church (New York:
     Scribners, 1958).

WHAT - Williams, Colin, What in the World? (New York: NCCC, 1964)

What is the Church, ed. D. McCall (Nashville: Broadman, 1958).

WHERE - Williams Colin, Where in the World? Changing forms of
     the Church's witness (New York: NCCC, 1963).

Wiemann, Harry Nelson, The Source of Human Good (Chicago:
     Univ. of Chicago Pr., 1946).

Williams, Colin W. The Church, Vol IV of New Directions in
    Theology Today (Philadelphia: Westminster, 1968).

Williams, Daniel D., God's Grace and Man's Hope (New York:
    Harper, 1949).

_____, What Present Day Theologians are Thinking, rev. ed.
    (New York: Harper, 1959).

Williams Preston, "COCU and the Cultural Revolution", Address
    to the 10th Plenary Meeting , DIGEST X(1971), 131-143.

Wilmore, Gayraud, The Secular Relevance of the Church
    (Philadelphia: Westminster, 1962).

Wilson, Brian, Religion in Secular Society: A sociological
    comment (Harmsworth, Middlesex/Baltimore, Md: Penguin,
    1969).

Winter, Gibson, The Suburban Captivity of the Churches
    (Garden City: Doubleday, 1961).

WORSHIP - Report of the Theological Commission on Worship
    (F.+O. Paper, N.S. 39; Geneva: WCC, 1963).

Yinger, Milton, The Scientific Study of Religion (New York:
    Macmillan, 1970).

Yoder, John, "The Nature of the Unity We Seek, 5. A Historic
    Free Church View". Religion in Life, 26,2 (Spring, 1957),
    215-222.

Zum Problem der Unfehlbarkeit: Eine Antwort auf die Anfrage von
    Hans Küng, hrsg. v. K. Rahner (Quaestiones disputatae, 54;
    Freiburg - Basel - Wien: Herder, 1971).

DATE DUE

GAYLORD			PRINTED IN U S.A